A-LEVEL

Leisure &
Recreation

■ SARAH MCQUADE (EDITOR) ■ PAUL BUTLER ■ JIM JOHNSON
■ STEWART LEES ■ MARK SMITH

Hodder & Stoughton
A MEMBER OF THE HODDER HEADLINE GROUP

Orders: please contact Bookpoint Ltd, 78 Milton Park, Abingdon, Oxon OX14 4TD. Telephone: (44) 01235 827720, Fax: (44) 01235 400454. Lines are open from 9.00–6.00, Monday to Saturday, with a 24 hour message answering service. Email address: orders@bookpoint.co.uk

British Library Cataloguing in Publication Data
A catalogue record for this title is available from The British Library

ISBN 0 340 782 196
First published 2000
Impression number   10 9 8 7 6 5 4 3 2 1
Year   2005 2004 2003 2002 2001 2000

Typeset by Fakenham Photosetting Ltd, Fakenham, Norfolk.
Printed in Great Britain for Hodder & Stoughton Educational, a division of Hodder Headline Plc, 338 Euston Road, London NW1 3BH by J W Arrowsmith, Bristol.

CONTENTS

THE AUTHORS

The authors are all Edexcel unit writers and consultants, and have been closely connected to the development of the new Leisure and Recreation Vocational A Level for 2000.

Sarah McQuade (editor) is a Lecturer at York College and has been heavily involved in the planning, design and delivery of GNVQ and Vocational A Level since the awards were first conceived.

Paul Butler is Programme Coordinator for Leisure and Tourism at Tower Hamlets College. He was previously Area Manager of two leisure centres, and has a wealth of experience in the leisure industry.

Jim Johnson is Education and Training Development Officer for the Assocation of London Government Sports Partnership, a Running Sport tutor for Sport England, and a Senior Tutor for the National Coaching Foundation.

Stewart Lees is a Higher Education Programme Manager in Cornwall and a highly experienced teacher of Leisure and Recreation awards. He is also an Edexcel External Verifier and has a leisure industry background.

Mark Smith is Programme Leader for Leisure, Tourism and Sport at Chelmsford College. He coordinates a range of courses, spanning GCSE, A Level, GNVQ, National Diploma and HND.

ACKNOWLEDGEMENTS

Thanks to the author team for all their hard work, energy and effort, in compiling the text. Thanks also to Gil Lester and Richard Twigg for their support, help and advice.

The authors and publisher would like to acknowledge the following for use of copyright text and illustrative material:

© Crown Copyright (from Office for National Statistics), pp. 21, 22, 23, 24, 25, 28, 156; action**plus**, pp. 89, 93, 105, 132, 133, 138, 141, 153, 154, 185, 187, 190; Corbis, pp. 8, 46, 47, 71, 109, 140; Dave Thompson/Life File, p.113; PA Photos Ltd., p.111; Paul Doyle/Photofusion, p.100.

Every effort has been made to trace copyright holders but this has not always been possible in all cases; any omissions brought to our attention will be corrected in future printings.

CHAPTER 1

Investigating Leisure and Recreation

Aims and Objectives

Through the study of this Unit you will have the opportunity to:

- **research the structure and scale of today's UK leisure and recreation industry**
- **investigate the key factors that have contributed to the rapid growth of the leisure and recreation industry since the 1960s**
- **learn that it is made up of many public, private and voluntary organisations that interact to supply an enormous range of products and services to consumers**
- **investigate the wide-ranging career opportunities available in leisure and recreation so that you can identify possible employment opportunities to match your aspirations, skills and abilities**

Introduction

Consider for a minute, before continuing with this text, what your hobbies are. What do you like to do for fun? What sort of activities do you participate in? Where do you go during your leisure or free time? Do you tend to participate alone or with others, if so who are they? What sort of costs are associated with your leisure time?

More specifically what was the last leisure activity you took part in? Where was it? Who was it with? How much did it cost you? The next leisure activity you participate in, might well be this evening or at the weekend, but what will it be?

By thinking about the answers to these questions, you should have started to think about the extent of your involvement in the recreation and leisure industry.

In order to understand and analyse the impact the industry has on our lives, the lives of those around us, on society and on the economy, we need to consider the industry as a whole. That is, we need to think about more than just our own participation to understand leisure and recreation provision.

Defining Leisure and Recreation
What is leisure?

Leisure is a concept often referred to in conjunction with 'recreation'. Both terms are in fact 'umbrella' terms designed to encompass the massive range of activities undertaken outside of the 'working day'. The traditional working day is from 9.00a.m.–5.00p.m., Monday to Friday. This will vary according to the type of industry you work in and the organisation you work for.

The scope of the leisure and recreation industry and the provision within it is vast.

Before we consider the structure of provision within the industry let us define what we mean by the terms leisure and recreation.

The *Oxford English Dictionary* (1985) defines leisure as:

❝Freedom or opportunity to do something ... Opportunity afforded by unoccupied time ... Time allowed before it is too late ... The state of having time at one's own disposal, free time ... A spell of free time ... Leisureliness, deliberation.❞

It defines recreation as:

❝The action of recreating (oneself or another), or fact of being recreated, by some pleasant occupation, pastime or amusement.❞

To consider this definition further we must clarify the word 'recreate'. What does recreate mean?

❝To refresh or enliven (the mind, the spirits, a person) by some pastime, amusement or occupation ...❞

The Institute of Leisure and Amenity Management (ILAM) (1999, www.ilam.co.uk) offer an industry-led definition of the term. While the industry itself is constantly evolving and adapting to reflect current social and economic conditions in response to consumer demand and expectations, ILAM states that leisure is:

❝The identification and satisfaction of a community's needs for the purposeful use of leisure time, irrespective of whether the service is delivered directly or facilitated through a range of partnerships. It consists of services utilised during the time not required for paid employment, parenting, domestic life or public duties and is for the purpose of recreation and an improved quality of life.❞

 **DID YOU KNOW?**

Nationally, the leisure industry generates £10 billion per year (1997).

Source: CIPFA Estimates England and Wales

ACTIVITY

Leisure activities

Spend ten minutes brainstorming a range of activities that would 'refresh or enliven' an individual outside of their work or study commitments.

Defining leisure

Our lives often revolve around the commitments we have to:

- our work or study
- the time we spend travelling to and from work and home
- completing chores, household or otherwise
- other essential activities, such as sleeping.

The rest of the time could be said to be our own free time in which we can choose to do what we want, when we want and with whom we want – given the ideal circumstances of course! Our choice of activities may starkly contrast with the choice of others, but that free time presents us with the opportunity to pursue our own interests, activities, ambitions and goals.

This free time has traditionally been referred to as 'leisure time'. You will need to understand that leisure time is specific to the individual and therefore a unique philosophy and difficult to quantify.

DISCUSSION

Physical activity is said to positively influence health and fitness. Do you do enough 'active' activity?

In an attempt to categorise the activities pursued during an individual's leisure time, distinctions can be made on the basis of whether the activity requires some degree of energy expenditure, that is, whether the activity is active or passive.

ACTIVITY

Active and passive activity

Leisure activities can be referred to as either active or passive.

Make a list of the leisure activities that you have participated in over the last ten days or refer to the list that you have already created.

How many of those can be classed as active? What about others in your student group, are they active?

Public participation in, and demands for, leisure and recreation services are made possible by the provision of a range of resources and facilities through which services, products and activities can be 'bought'.

Leisure and recreation industry provision caters for the individual who may wish to participate alone, as part of a family, or part of a larger group or club. This provision should also cater for needs based both indoor and outdoor, in and around the home and in both the town and the countryside.

A further distinction makes reference to the location of the activity, that is, whether the activity is home based or away from the home.

Many demands are met through resources and equipment in the home. Provision within the home by organisations therefore occupies essentially a secondary role, that is, the products and equipment (such as, TV, video, CD player, Playstation and now significantly PCs and access to the Internet) are themselves the source of the recreational activity, as opposed to the organisation or provider.

Some demands are met through outdoor facilities, such as gardens and allotments, through the provision of parks, play areas and open spaces, or through sports grounds.

Other demands are met through the provision of a range of indoor facilities for the purposes of entertainment and socialising, such as music, art, drama, literary activities, sport and physical recreation and education. Isn't it ironic that what we as students perceive to be 'commitments' and therefore part of our working day, others see as forming an integral part of their leisure time!

Leisure industry provision

The demands of the individual are very diverse and it should be acknowledged at this stage that it would be virtually impossible for one organisation to cater for such diversity of interest, that is, to provide and cater for all interests right across the leisure and recreation spectrum. It would mean that the organisation would have to encompass a vast and contrasting range of service and activity provision into their portfolio and this, in terms of the cost implications and the effectiveness of the organisation, is prohibitive.

Some organisations, particularly multinationals like Whitbread plc are involved in the provision of a contrasting range of services, from eating and drinking to fitness and activity. Yet they cannot physically cater for all people, all interests and all needs. This is why there are literally thousands of organisations involved in the provision of leisure and recreation.

Provision refers to either a product, service or activity. In order to fully understand the range of provision, you will need to be able to distinguish between these three concepts.

The *Oxford English Dictionary* (1985) offers the following definitions:

Product

❝ That which is produced by any action, operation, or work; a production; the result. ❞

This definition implies that it is a tangible product, meaning you can touch and feel it, and indicates that there is some element of ownership or possession. Examples might include a home computer, cross-training shoes, a Big Bertha golf club or a 4 × 4 vehicle.

Service

❝The action of serving, helping or benefiting; conduct tending to the welfare of another … Friendly or professional assistance. Supply of needs.❞

This definition states that the consumer is receiving some sort of help, instruction or guidance in order that they may take part in the activity. It may result in a temporary state of ownership, for example, a table in a restaurant, a seat at a theatre, a seat on Centre Court on Ladies' semi-final day, or a piece of aerobic fitness equipment in a gym.

Activity

❝The state of being active; the exertion of energy … Energy, diligence, liveliness.❞

This definition suggests that some sort of energy expenditure is required in order to participate, whether it is for the purposes of competition (sport), physical recreation (rambling) or just for fun (Tenpin bowling).

 ACTIVITY

Provision: a product, service or activity?

Identify a range of activities that you like to participate in, or use the list that you have already created. Think of activities that your parents or family enjoy and add these to the list.

Now, using the definitions and explanations given, type each activity in the list as either a product, service or activity. What do these lists tell you about provision?

A popular misconception is that the leisure and recreation industry is restricted to the provision of activities within leisure centres and sports stadiums. It is not.

In order to improve your understanding of the industry and to appreciate the breadth of activities, services and products comprised and offered within it, it can be divided into a number of component areas or contexts:

- arts and entertainment
- sports and physical recreation
- heritage
- catering and accommodation
- countryside recreation (including outdoor activities)
- home-based leisure.

The boundaries between contexts are not always distinct and you will find that there may be some overlap in the type of provision within different contexts.

For example, The Swallow Hotel, which is a national chain of hotels, has a four-star hotel near York's city centre. On face value, this facility would be ideally placed within the context of catering and accommodation. However, The Swallow Hotel boasts a range of complementary facilities for both its guests and non-members. These facilities include a fitness suite with sauna rooms and swimming pool, a health and beauty salon and a restaurant and conference and banqueting facilities. If these facilities were to be viewed as separate entities and as such, distinct from the hotel, each would fall into a different context of provision.

ACTIVITY

Contrasting provision on a single site

Can you think of another example of a single site which, due to the different types of facilities available and the activities offered, means that it falls into more than one sector of provision.

Name your example, write down the different facilities and activities, and state which component area of the industry each falls into.

The leisure and recreation industry – component areas

In order to understand the nature of provision we must define more specifically the component areas.

The following definitions and examples of different types of facilities or venues and their locations, aim to highlight the range of provision within each component area.

Arts and entertainments
The arts and entertainment sector is a key contributor to culture and creative expression in the UK. It contributes to providing rich opportunities for life-long learning through job diversity, tourism, the night time economy and through community arts groups and the education functions of larger organisations, such as the Millenium Dome.

It has been suggested that the arts and entertainment sector helps to improve an individual's mental health through personal achievement, self-expression and relaxation. Table 1.1 lists examples of arts and entertainment venues.

TYPE OF FACILITY/ VENUE	EXAMPLES
Art galleries	The National Gallery, London The Tate, London and sister Gallery in Liverpool
Ballet and opera	Covent Garden Opera House
Concert halls/ music venues (classical/rock/ contemporary)	Royal Albert Hall, London Symphony Hall, Birmingham GMEX Centre, Manchester Roundhay Park, Leeds Don Valley Stadium, Sheffield
Cinemas	Warner Bros Showcase Odeon
Theatres	Theatre Royal, York The Alhambra, Bradford London's West End District
Libraries	National Library, London Central Library, Birmingham
Pubs and nightclubs	The Firkin Brewery chain of pubs Yates Wine Lodge Tom Cobleigh's (and Playbarn) Tall Trees, Yarm Gatecrasher, Sheffield Heaven, London The Temple Nightclub, Bolton
Amusement and theme parks	Alton Towers, Staffs Blackpool Pleasure Beach Millennium Dome

TABLE 1.1 *Examples of arts and entertainment venues*

DID YOU KNOW?

The Temple Nightclub in Bolton has just had a £5 million pound facelift where there are now three dance floors, four bars, a swimming pool and a mini-cinema.

Source: *Leisure Opportunities*, Issue No. 248

Sports and physical recreation

Sport England (formerly The Sports Council) in its third edition of the *Digest of Sports Statistics for the UK* (1989), in distinguishing sport from other types of activity stated that sports were considered to be those recreational activities that require a measure of physical effort and skill. Sport includes varying degrees of organisation, elements of competition and the emphasis on the outcome tends to influence the quality of that competition.

FIGURE 1.1 *The Millennium Dome*   Source: *Corbis*

Recreation, when referred to in context with sports and physical activity, suggests that some degree of energy expenditure is involved. It differs from sport participation *per se* in that the competitive element, in terms of trials, games, matches and races, has been removed from the equation.

Table 1.2 identifies contrasting examples of provision within the sports industry.

TYPE OF FACILITY/VENUE	EXAMPLES
In terms of sports participation at a local/regional/territorial level of competition, much of the provision is via sports clubs which tend to incorporate a range of sports (both summer and winter) and cater for a range of abilities:	
Sports clubs	Slazenger Sports Club, Wakefield
In terms of elite participation, although this is to a certain extent developed through the club system, most sports tend to have Centres of Excellence:	
National Centres of Excellence	Lilleshall, Shropshire – football, cricket, gymnastics Bisham Abbey, Bucks – tennis, hockey, rugby Crystal Palace – swimming, athletics
Under the banner of sport and recreation a significant majority spend their leisure time in a secondary capacity, that is, spectating. When events are hosted by the facilities/venues listed below the majority of participants are spectators. These facilities, however, are also used by clubs and groups for training purposes:	
Athletics tracks	National Indoor Arena, Birmingham Gateshead Stadium
Cricket	Lords New Road, Worcester

TYPE OF FACILITY/VENUE	EXAMPLES
Cycle tracks	Manchester Velodrome
Football and rugby football grounds/stadiums	Riverside Stadium, Middlesborough Pittodrie, Aberdeen Millennium Stadium, Cardiff
Golf courses	St Andrews, Scotland The Belfry, Sutton Coldfield Wentworth, Surrey
Greyhound racing	Hall Green, Birmingham
Ice Hockey	Sheffield Arena
Hockey	National Stadium, Milton Keynes
Horse Racing	Wetherby Epsom
Motor racing circuits	Donnington Park, Leicestershire Silverstone
Tennis	Queens Club, London Edgbaston Priory, Birmingham

More attention to people's own individual levels of fitness has resulted in a sharp rise in individual and group or class training. The growth of the hi-tech individual exercise facilities in the 1990s has been prolific.

Leisure centres/clubs	David Lloyd Leisure, Nationwide Next Generation, Edinburgh Doncaster Dome
Fitness clubs	Fitness First, London Virgin Active's Life Centre, Leeds – both 24-hour clubs
Gyms	Golds Gym, London Emporers, York
Health Club and Spas	The Academy, Harrogate Forest Mere Health Farm, Hampshire Celtic Manor Resort, Wales
Swimming/leisure pools	Ponds Forge, Sheffield Hydro, Harrogate

TABLE 1.2 *Contrasting provision within the sports industry*

FIGURE 1.2 *Health suites*

📷 **DID YOU KNOW?**

York has 3.84 million visitors per year, spending £247 million. It has 2,600 listed buildings, 12 scheduled ancient monuments and the City Walls.

Source: York Council, *Towards a Leisure Plan for York*, March 1999

📷 **DID YOU KNOW?**

The number of visits to museums dropped by 4% during 1997–8.

Source: Museum and Galleries Commission

In terms of facilities, usage and activities, it is worth noting that some of the larger venues are used not only to house elite sporting competitions but also other events, such as music concerts, charity events and exhibitions.

For example, Wembley Stadium was home to Net Aid in 1999 and Live Aid in 1984 and Gateshead Stadium has been used by the likes of Tina Turner and Rod Stewart. Obviously, this type of leisure activity would fall within the context of arts and entertainment as opposed to sports and physical recreation.

Heritage

Sites of heritage in the UK not only provide an essential part of the infrastructure for tourism, but have allowed us to preserve and celebrate buildings and collections for posterity and education.

There are a number of cities throughout the UK which occupy a unique place in terms of the country's heritage. The continued prosperity of these sites (Table 1.3) serves to ensure a sense of place and belonging in terms of charting the nation's history.

Such venues and facilities are often used for purposes other than heritage. Examples of the use of sites for the purposes of television productions (home-based leisure) include Castle Howard in Yorkshire, which was the site for the filming of *Brideshead Revisited* and an episode of *Dangerfield* which was filmed at Kenilworth Castle.

The use of heritage sites for other remits include Leeds Castle in Kent which hosted an open-air ballet production of *Swan Lake*. The grounds of Castle Howard were also the site of a concert hosted by Shirley Bassey for her 60th birthday which culminated in a fireworks extravaganza (arts and entertainments). Simply Red have performed at Warwick Castle; Elton John at Chatsworth.

In terms of participation rates, Tables 1.4 and 1.5 highlight the fact that heritage is one of the most important sectors in the leisure and recreation industry. The Office of National Statistics has compared the growing attendance statistics at some of the most popular tourist attractions charging for admission and these data suggest that the rate of growth has been steady.

However, in terms of museum attendances and visits, predictions suggest that the overall trend of slow growth may well be reaching a plateau, as supply is slowly exceeding demand.

TYPE OF FACILITY/VENUE	EXAMPLES OF FACILITIES/VENUES
Ancient monuments	Stonehenge, Wiltshire Callanish Standing Stones, Scotland Hadrian's Wall Roman Baths and Pump Rooms, Bath
Ruins	Bolton Abbey, Yorkshire Dales Fountains Abbey, Ripon, Yorkshire
Stately homes	Aston Hall, Birmingham Blenheim Palace, London Castle Howard, Yorkshire
Castles	Kenilworth Castle, Warwickshire Leeds Castle, Kent Taymouth Castle, Perthshire, Scotland
Religious buildings	York Minster Coventry Cathedral
Transport museums	The National Railway Museum, York
Industrial heritage and museums	Ironbridge Gorge, Shropshire Natural History Museum, London Museum of Science and Industry, Manchester
Military relics/sites	Imperial War Museum, London HMS Victory, Portsmouth

TABLE 1.3 *Examples of heritage sites*

The venues highlighted in bold are listed as sites within the context of heritage:

VENUE (IN RANK ORDER)	1991	1993	1994	1995	1996	1997
Madame Tussaud's	2.2	2.4	2.6	2.7	2.7	2.8
Alton Towers	2.0	2.6	3.0	2.7	2.7	2.7
Tower of London	1.9	2.3	2.4	2.5	2.5	2.6
Natural History Museum[1]	1.6	1.7	1.6	1.4	1.6	1.8
Chessington World of Adventures	1.4	1.5	1.6	1.7	1.7	1.7
Science Museum[2]	1.3	1.3	1.3	1.5	1.5	1.5
London Zoo	1.1	0.9	1.0	1.0	1.0	1.1

TABLE 1.4 *Attendance rates (millions)*

[1] *Admission charges introduced in April 1987*

[2] *Admission charges introduced in 1989*

Other heritage attractions ranked within the top 20 include:

ATTRACTION	NUMBER OF VISITORS (1995)
Windsor Castle	1,212,305
Edinburgh Castle	1,037,788
Roman Baths and Pump Rooms in Bath	872,915
Warwick Castle	803,000

TABLE 1.5 *Top four heritage attractions*

 DID YOU KNOW?

Eating out, as an industry is worth £20.6 million. The number of adults who now visit a restaurant for one evening at least once a week is 16% compared with only 3% in 1989.

Source: *Eating Out – Ten-Year Trends*, **Mintel**

Catering and accommodation

The concept of eating out has changed drastically in the last decade and this has been reflected in the sector's massive growth. The forces deemed responsible for its expansion include increased wealth, more women at work, more tourists and the 'cash-rich, time-poor factor'.

This area covers a wide range of facilities and Table 1.6 highlights the scope of provision.

TYPE OF FACILITY/VENUE	EXAMPLES
Some of these venues have complimentary facilities, that is, other than for sleeping and eating. Some facilities will even hire aspects of their accommodation for conferences, exhibitions and banquets.	
Hotels (international standard)	The Ritz, Savoy, Dorchester – London
Hotels – 4-star and below	The Swallow Hotel, York The Marriot, Leeds The Hilton, Watford
Castles	Durham Castle
Motor lodges	Travel Inn Travelodge
Inns/Bed and breakfast	The Tennants Arms, N. Yorkshire
Self-catering	Rental cottages let for holiday purposes
Hostels	YHA, Ambleside YMCA
Camping and caravanning	Pontins Hawkswick Cote Caravan and Camping Park, Yorkshire Dales

Since the mid-1980s there has been a rapid growth in the provision of a 'home away from home'. This provision gives individuals/groups the opportunity not only to participate in a multitude of activities (both active and passive) but also allows them to either self-cater (from on-site supermarkets) or dine out at a range of contrasting eateries.

Leisure and holiday villages	Oasis Forest Holiday Villages, Lakes Centre Parks, Nottingham Butlins, Minehead

Thanks to the influence of many different cultures and regional cuisines, British food is now an eclectic mix of fast food and lively, interesting, mouth-watering tastes and as such there is a multitude of choice when it comes to eating out.

Fast food outlets	McDonalds and Burger King Harry Ramsden's
Sandwich Shops	Subway
Pubs and Inns	The Firkin Brewery Chain TGI Fridays
Ethnic	Italian, Chinese, French, Indian, Mexican and more
Gourmet restaurants	Langans Brasserie La Garolle – Albert Roux Quatre Saisons – Raymond Blanc

Some eateries are housed within other contexts, for example, most health and fitness clubs have restaurants or some sort of food provision. Most retail outlets also have provision for dining, such as Harvey Nicholls and The Trafford Centre in Manchester.

TABLE 1.6 *Examples of facilities and venues in the catering and accommodation sector*

DID YOU KNOW?

There are ten national parks, six forest parks, 36 designated areas of outstanding natural beauty, 22 environmentally sensitive areas, almost 200 country parks approved by the Countryside Commission, 800 km (500 miles) of designated heritage coastline and about 2,000 historic buildings and some 3,600 gardens open to the public.

Source: British Tourist Authority 1999, from web site http://www. visitbritain.com

Countryside recreation (including outdoor activities)

Countryside recreation is associated with participation in outdoor activities.

The issue of the placement of **outdoor activities** within a context or component area is a contentious one. There is a suggestion that because outdoor activities inevitably involve some degree of energy expenditure that they should be placed within the context of Sport and Physical Recreation. However, because they take place outside it is argued that they should be placed within the realm of countryside recreation. For the purposes of this text outdoor activities have been deemed to be an integral aspect of Countryside Recreation, even though there is some provision in urban areas (Sheffield Ski Village) and at indoor facilities (Link Centre climbing wall, Swindon).

Outdoor activities do tend to take place in the natural environment (natural venues) although some areas are contrived, that is, they are purpose-built to cater for specific activities and can be labelled as man-made or artificial venues. Table 1.7 identifies a range of activities and these have been grouped according to type.

TYPE OF ACTIVITY	EXAMPLES OF FACILITIES/VENUES	
	ARTIFICIAL VENUES	NATURAL VENUES
Land-based activities:		
Skiing	Sheffield Ski Village Tamworth Snow Dome	Aviemore Glenshie
Climbing	Keswick Climbing Wall	Cow and Calf Crags, Ilkley Llanberris Pass, Snowdonia
Walking/hiking/ orienteering		Lake District, Yorkshire Dales Dartmoor
Pony trekking	The Indoor School at Newport Riding Academy	East Riding Equestrian Centre
Air-based activities:		
Gliding	White Horse Gliding Club, Ripon	
Ballooning	Virgin Balloon Flights	
Parachuting	Target Skysports	
Hang gliding		
Water-based activities:		
Fishing	Kilnsey Trout Farm, Yorks	Taymouth Castle Estate, Scotland
Water skiing	Holme Pierrepoint Nottingham	Lake Windermere
Canoeing	Tees Barrage	River Trent
Rowing	River Avon, Stratford upon Avon	Henley upon Thames Stratford upon Avon
White water rafting	Tees Barrage	
Wind surfing	Graham Water, Lincs	Menai Straits, Anglesey
Sailing	Edgbaston Reservoir	Cowes, Isle of Wight

TYPE OF ACTIVITY	EXAMPLES OF FACILITIES/VENUES	
	ARTIFICIAL VENUES	NATURAL VENUES
Much like organised sporting activity, there are nationally recognised Centres of Excellence for outdoor activities:		
Mountain activities		Plas-Y-Brenin, Gwynedd
Water sports	Holme Pierrepoint, Nottingham	

TABLE 1.7 *Activities and venues grouped by type*

Home-based leisure

The *General Household Survey* (1996) shows that most leisure participation, in terms of both active and passive pursuits, is undertaken in the home.

 **DID YOU KNOW?**

85% of all households have access to a garden. Domestic gardening is now a £2 billion industry.

Source: *Towards a Leisure Plan for York*, City Of York Council, March 1999

The type of home-based leisure activities engaged in will be influenced by a number of variables including location, the availability of a garden and the standard of living enjoyed at that home.

Most important, home-based leisure is relatively cheap. For example, money that is already invested in a computer (either owned or rented) allows for varied and additional use by all members of the household (for example, computer games and the Internet). It does not therefore involve significant additional expenditure (just the price of the games and phone call costs when on-line).

Sport England (1987) *Leisure and the Home* survey found that different types of homes offered contrasting potential as centres for leisure. They suggested that people's satisfaction with their home related to some extent to what they were able to do there and to how well the home accommodated their equipment and activities.

The amount of leisure time available to the occupants will vary according to a number of factors, including:

- work/study/travel commitments
- family commitments and therefore chores
- ownership and or tenancy arrangements
- the amount of labour saving appliances which could also include 'hired help' such as a cleaner, gardener or nanny. This may release members of the household from monotonous tasks and so create greater leisure time
- material possessions of the household which may be leisure instruments themselves, for example, television, video, radio and home computers.

Table 1.8 shows the three key areas to acknowledge within the context of home-based leisure.

HOME-BASED LEISURE	ACTIVITY	MEDIUM
The media in the home	Television viewing	Video, DVD and laser discs Sky and its interactive channels Cable
	Music listening	Radio CDs Tapes and or records
	Reading	Newspapers, magazines, books Ceefax Internet
	Computing	PCs Internet and World Wide Web
The home as an object of leisure	Home improvement DIY	House itself
	Cultivation	Garden
The home for leisure and social activity	Physical recreation and fitness activity	Keep-fit videos Fitness equipment (for example, step machine and Nordic Track)
	Indoor games and hobbies	Trivial Pursuit and other board games Sewing/knitting
	Social gatherings and parties	Dinner parties Murder Mystery evenings Tupperware parties

TABLE 1.8 *Home-based leisure activities*

CASE STUDY *Oasis Forest Holiday Villages (www. oasishols.co.uk)*

Oasis Forest Holiday Villages is part of the Rank Group plc, a multinational commercial organisation and one of the leading leisure and entertainment companies.

Oasis is more than just the stereotypical holiday village of the 1970s and has been described by many as 'a home, away from home'.

Oasis is set in 400 acres of pine forest on the edge of the Lake District National Park. It is the perfect location for tranquil holidays or short activity breaks. The setting is completely natural, on the doorstep of self-contained luxurious lodges.

Within the 400 acres are a number of facilities or venues designed to cater for all leisure interests. Oasis has been constructed so as to give every individual the opportunity to pursue their leisure time as they see fit.

These leisure interests are provided for within a range of facilities, which are identified on the village map (Figure 1.3). Use the information given to complete the activity on page 20.

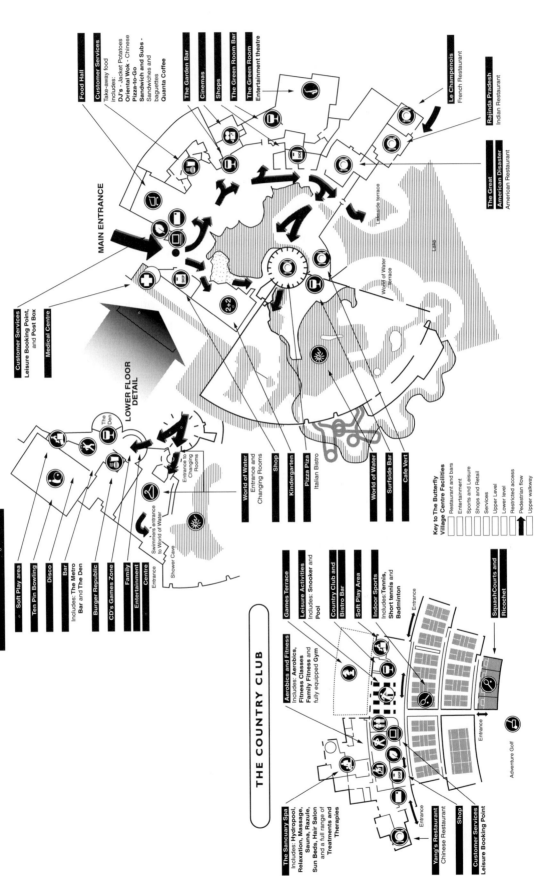

FIGURE 1.3 *Oasis Village map showing the layout of facilities*

Oasis have categorised their provision using the following directory:

Sports and other activities

- the Country Club, catering for any indoor sport
- World of Water
- cycle trails
- astro-turf
- fitness suite and gymnasium
- adventure playground

Children's activities

- forest
- soft play areas
- climbing castle
- crazy golf

Health and beauty and the world of water

- sanctuary spa
- exercise swimming pool
- children's pool area
- slides, flumes, rides, wave machine
- sun deck and lounge area

Adult entertainment

- cinema
- The Green Room
- restaurants and wine bars

Shops/restaurants and bars

- The Supermarket
- Broughams (crafts and gifts)
- Playtime (toys and games)
- The Wet Look (swimwear)
- Le Sport (sporting goods)
- Tom Cobleigh's
- Hard Rock Café
- Italian, Chinese, Indian and Asian cuisine.

ACTIVITY

Analysing on-site provision at Oasis Forest Holiday Villages

Oasis want to analyse their existing on-site provision. That is, they want to analyse the range of activities in terms of participation rates to assess whether they are cost effective. That is, are the activities attended in sufficient numbers to warrant them being advertised for the forthcoming season?

There are too many activities to analyse at random, therefore you have been employed to structure their existing range of activities into a number of logical components or a directory of provision.

You will need to obtain a comprehenisve list of all the on-site activities. Contact Oasis either directly or indirectly (web site, brochure).

You could structure their provision into a number of different category types:
- by facility, venue, or activity type
- as products, services or activities
- by degree of energy expenditure (active or passive), or whether it is home based or away from the home
- or use an original order.

Additional tasks

Compare Oasis' provision with current provision at competitor organisations, for example Centre Parcs.

Highlight the differences between the two in terms of on-site activities? Is there anything that Centre Parcs offers or does differently that Oasis should be aware of?

The development of the leisure and recreation industry

From the work completed at the beginning of this Chapter, you should have a good understanding of the range of provision made available by different sectors of the industry.

Today, the consumer demand for leisure and recreation provision right across the sector is both varied and immense. This was not always the case. Growth patterns in the industry can be best illustrated from 1960 onwards. Relative prosperity, evident in the UK during the 1960s, was best represented by:

- increasing car ownership
- shorter working week
- longer holidays
- the active promotion of leisure pursuits.

These factors conspired to encourage wider participation in sport and other recreational activities. The massive growth of the industry can be attributed to the socio-economic and technological developments since the 1960s coupled with changing customer needs. We should consider these factors in more detail.

Socio-economic factors

There are a number of what might be termed socio-economic factors, that is, lifestyle factors that have resulted in the growth of the industry. Let's look at these in greater detail.

Changing demographics

It is important to understand that demographic profiles provide necessary insight into changing markets, that is, both real (current and existing markets) and potential markets.

Table 1.9, taken from the Office for National Statistics (ONS), highlights both the geographical and population trend changes that have taken place since 1981. The ONS has stipulated that some of these figures are provisional.

KEY TERMS

Demographics refers to the statistical study of births and deaths in a given population.

RESIDENT POPULATION ALL PERSONS (MILLIONS)			
	1981	**1991**	**1996**
United Kingdom	56,352.20	57,807.90	58,801.50
North East	2,636.20	2,602.50	2,600.50
North West and Merseyside	6,940.30	6,885.40	6,891.30
Yorkshire and the Humber	4,918.40	4,982.80	5,035.50
East Midlands	3,852.80	4,035.40	4,141.50
West Midlands	5,186.60	5,265.50	5,316.60
Eastern	4,854.10	5,149.80	5,292.60
London	6,805.60	6,889.90	7,074.30
South East	7,245.40	7,678.90	7,895.30
South West	4,381.40	4,717.80	4,841.50
England	46,820.80	48,208.10	49,089.10
Wales	2,813.50	2,891.50	2,921.10
Scotland	5,108.20	5,107.00	5,128.00
Northern Ireland	1,537.70	1,601.40	1,663.30

TABLE 1.9 *UK geographical population trends, 1981–96* © *Crown Copyright (ONS)*

Table 1.10 identifies population trends since 1984 by gender and age.

UNITED KINGDOM POPULATION	1984	1994	1995	1996	1997
Number of males (millions)	27.5	28.6	28.7	28.9	29.0
Number of females (millions)	29.0	29.8	29.9	29.9	30.0
Percentage of population aged under 16	21.0	20.7	20.7	20.6	20.5
Percentage of population between 16 and retirement age 59–64	61.0	61.1	61.2	61.3	61.4
Percentage of population over retirement age 60–65+	17.9	18.2	18.2	18.1	18.1
Percentage of population aged 75 years+	6.3	6.8	7.0	7.1	7.2

TABLE 1.10 *UK population trends by age and gender, 1984–7*   © *Crown Copyright (ONS)*

DISCUSSION

Look closely at the figures in the tables and the changing patterns over the last two decades?

What do the figures in terms of statistical trends tell you about the population?

What do you think are the implications of these trends on the workforce, on leisure time and on the industry?

It can be seen that the trend is towards a decline in the under 16 age group while the population percentage between 16 and retirement age has remained relatively constant.

The most significant statistic for the industry is the demographic downturn in the 'active' populations, that is, there is an increase in the population above retirement age, most noticeably in the 75+ group. Significantly, the 65+ (or retired) age group, like the unemployed and mums and toddlers, are a user or target group in their own right.

Work commitments/arrangements

In the last 30 years the nature of working arrangements and commitments has changed.

The context of employment is still constructed on the varied basis that it always has been. Most individuals' working habits are dictated by necessity, that is, they are compelled to work because of the nature of their commitments, which are primarily linked to their finances and family, or dependants. Individuals can undertake full-time employment, work shifts on a rotating basis, take on paid overtime, or work part-time. Some employees may even prefer to work seasonally, perhaps overseas.

The ONS has produced statistics that provide a comprehensive overview of the status of those in employment over a 14-year period in the UK (Table 1.11).

	1984	1990	1994	1995	1996	1997	1998
All persons (millions)							
In Employment	24	26.9	25.7	26	26.2	26.7	26.9
ILO Unemployed[1]	3.2	2	2.7	2.5	2.3	2	1.8
All Aged 16 and Over	43.8	45.1	45.5	45.6	45.7	45.9	46.1
Men							
In Employment	14.1	15.3	14.2	14.4	14.4	14.7	14.9
ILO Unemployed[1]	1.9	1.2	1.8	1.6	1.5	1.3	1.1
All Aged 16 and Over	21.1	21.8	22.1	22.1	22.2	22.3	22.4
Women							
In Employment	9.9	11.6	11.5	11.6	11.8	12	12
ILO Unemployed[1]	1.3	0.8	0.9	0.8	0.8	0.7	0.7
All Aged 16 and Over	22.8	23.3	23.4	23.4	23.5	23.6	23.6
Average usual hours worked per person per week							
All	38.3	39	38.2	38.3	38.1	38.1	38
Men	44.3	45.1	44.4	44.4	44.2	44.1	44
Women	30	31	30.6	30.7	30.6	30.8	30.8

TABLE 1.11 *Status of people in employment in the UK 1984–98*

[1] The International Labour Office's (ILO) measure of unemployment refers to people without a job who were available to start work in the two weeks following their interview and had either looked for work in the four weeks prior to the interview or were waiting to start a job they had already obtained

© Crown Copyright (ONS)

The statistics suggest that the number of unemployed has reduced over the time period and that more people, most noticeably women, are now in employment.

There is now less emphasis on taking up full-time employment; many people enjoy a job share or split of a single position, many individuals undertake part-time work to suit their own commitments and schedules and some take up casual work as and when they see fit. For example, there is an infinite number of teachers on the books of supply agencies across the country. This is not necessarily because they cannot find full-time paid employment, but rather because they enjoy the luxury of working at their convenience.

Early retirement

The retirement age has been reduced in the last 30 years from 70 for a man and 65 for a woman to 65 and 60 years respectively. More and more people are now taking up the opportunity of early retirement, some even as early as 50 years of age.

The retired population has now been acknowledged by the industry as a target or user group in its own right. For some years Sport England have had a campaign which specifically targets the 50+ age group in order to improve participation in active pursuits and so promote a healthy lifestyle.

Standard of living

The data published by the Office for National Statistics from the Family Expenditure Survey 1998–9 show some significant changes in the standard of living enjoyed by people in the UK.

Table 1.12 shows the rise in average and weekly wage earnings since 1981. The increase might on the surface appear to be considerable. However, you must remember that the rise in inflation (around 2.5% annually) has also been significant.

DISCUSSION

How much money would you expect to earn each week when you start full-time employment?

	1981	1994	1995	1996	1997
Average earnings (GB only) (£ per week)	124.9	325.7	336.3	351.5	384.5

TABLE 1.12 *UK average weekly earnings, 1981–97*   © *Crown copyright (ONS)*

Table 1.13 (page 25) highlights a range of material possessions, some of which are labour saving devices which free up what used to be time committed to chores. The other possessions are an integral part of home-based leisure. Material possessions deemed to be items of leisure are listed in bold.

Availability of leisure time

Martin and Mason (from *Leisure Forecasts* 1999–2003) in their retrospective analysis of leisure trends over the last three decades, noted that up until the mid-1970s, the availability of leisure time had been declining throughout the twentieth century, most notably so over the post war period (after 1945).

Between 1975 and 1984 working hours for full-time employees fell by around one hour per day. By 1985, full-time male workers were working an average of 40.3 hours per week. 1985 marked the end of the post war trend of declining working hours.

By 1989, the average week for full-time male workers had increased to 44.1 hours. This upward trend continued and in 1995 the number of

DISCUSSION

Ask your parents and grandparents, or friends and neighbours about their leisure time. What do they do? How does their leisure time differ from yours?

More specifically ask them what has been the single most important factor in either freeing up or taking away their leisure time?

YEAR	1981	1994	1995	1996	1997–98
MATERIAL POSSESSIONS	HOUSEHOLDS (%)				
Car	61.8	69.0	69.7	69.0	70.0
Television	96.6	N/A	N/A	N/A	N/A
Telephone	75.8	91.1	92.4	93.1	94.0
Refrigerator				49.4	51.0
Fridge-freezer or Deep freezer	N/A	85.7	86.8	90.7	90.0
Dishwasher	N/A	18.4	19.9	19.8	22.0
Tumble dryer	N/A	50.4	50.6	51.5	51.0
Microwave oven	N/A	67.2	70.1	75.1	77.0
Washing machine	80.7	89.0	90.9	91.0	91.0
Video	N/A	76.4	79.2	81.8	84.0
Home computers	N/A			26.7	29.0
Second dwelling in the United Kingdom	N/A	3.3	3.3	3.7	4.0
Compact disc player	N/A	45.8	50.9	59.3	63.0

© *Crown Copyright (ONS)*

TABLE 1.13 *Material possessions and the percentage of UK households that have them, 1981–98*

working hours reached 46.8 per week for full-time employees. It should be acknowledged at this stage that some of this increase was due to opportunity to take advantage of paid overtime, made available by some employers, notably the manufacturing industries.

Full-time female employees' hours also reached a low point in 1985 at 38.5 hours per week. Their commitment to full-time work in terms of the number of weekly hours also increased slightly to 39.7 hours in 1995.

Martin and Mason, when reflecting upon the current trends in leisure time available noted that, in addition to longer working hours there had also been sharp increases in time spent on:

- household duties such as shopping
- domestic travel (commuting time to and from work as a major factor)
- childcare.

All of these have contributed to a reduction in leisure time available.

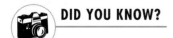

DID YOU KNOW?

The 48-hour week rule, originating from the 1993 European Community Directives, the Working Time Regulations came into force on 1 October 1998.

This pattern, however, is likely to change with the advent of new technology and time-saving equipment which have traditionally included labour-saving devices such as the washing machine, dishwasher and the automated car wash. Most significantly, with the introduction of the Internet, people are slowly but surely starting to complete laborious household chores such as the shopping from home. With an increase in disposable income more and more people are taking advantage of child care services (baby sitting and a 'nanny') which allows the parents more leisure time or certainly make available to the parents 'quality time' away from the children.

Some employees, particularly members of sales teams such as those within the pharmaceutical industry, are encouraged to work from home. They have made comprehensive use of the lap-top computer, mobile phone and e-mail and have, therefore, negated the need to work from an office base.

Paid holiday entitlement

The majority of working individuals, most significantly those in full-time employment, are rewarded with paid holiday entitlement, the average is 20 days annually plus bank holidays.

Some organisations will reward continued long service (15 years plus) with an annual increase in paid holiday entitlement of say one extra day each year.

Car ownership and the public transport systems

There are currently 22 million cars on the road, of which almost 17 million households have access to and the regular use of a car. Table 1.14 shows the increase in car ownership in the UK over a 12-year period.

	1985	1994	1995	1996	1997
Licensed road vehicles (all types) (millions)	21.2	25.2	25.4	26.3	27.0
Private motoring: households with regular use of car (millions)	13.0	15.7	16.2	16.4	16.7
Motor vehicles registered for the first time (all vehicles)(thousands)	2,309	2,249	2,307	2,410	2,598

TABLE 1.14 *Increase in UK car ownership, 1985–97*

DISCUSSION

Some people have even gone as far as to suggest that it is possible to exist from within the confines of your own home as long as you have a PC, modem and telephone line, credit card and presumably some sort of exercise equipment!

Could you?

The growth in the number of two-car families is a result of Britain's increasing prosperity and is a reflection of the diversity of interests and increasing independence within a single family. This increasing diversity may be dictated by work commitments, the maturity of the children or now more significantly leisure interests.

As a result more families and individuals are mobile and access to and from facilities and venues is therefore easier as there is limited reliance on public transport.

In your student group, find out how many people are driving. How many own their own car?

How many have access to the vehicles of their parents/guardians? How many people always get a lift from parents?

How many are forced to rely on public transport?

 DISCUSSION

Can you think of financial commitments other than loans, mortgages, rents, bills, transport costs and food?

Write these down now.

More and more young people now have almost full access to a car which has reduced their dependence on parents and guardians to be transported to and from various places.

The increase in the sheer volume of traffic of Britain's roads, not only private vehicles but also public transport and goods vehicles, has led to traffic congestion and delays in journey time, particularly on public and bank holidays.

The public transport system has undergone some key developments over the last 30 years. This system which includes road, rail, sea and air (buses, planes and trains) has increased significantly in size over this period. The combined transport systems now 'ferry' more people to and from places of residence to work and other bases, particularly leisure organisations.

One of the most significant changes within the transport system has been that of the privatisation of aspects of the industry most notably the railways, who since privatisation have been beset by problems, accidents and considerable time delays.

Disposable income

Disposable income is defined as the amount of money remaining for spending at the earner's discretion after all financial commitments have been met. Such commitments may include financial loans, mortgages, rents, bills, transport costs and food, among others.

In order to consider disposable income we need to identify wage earnings – the amount of money earned will tend to dictate how much money can be earmarked as disposable.

Table 1.15 represents statistics published by the ONS and highlights not only the average gross weekly earnings but identifies any regional or geographical discrepancies in earnings.

You must realise that some individuals have a tendency to live outside of their means. That is, in order to fund their leisure time, they may tend to rely on the use of the 'plastic fantastic' credit cards and may take advantage of 'interest free' and 'buy now – pay later' deals.

DISCUSSION

Do you work? How much money do you earn each week?

What do you spend your money on? How much money do you have left once you have met your financial commitments?

Do you have any store or credit cards? Have you purchased anything on a 'buy-now pay later' scheme or used an 'interest free credit for the first three months' incentive? If not, would you contemplate it?

	APRIL 1997 £	
	MALE	**FEMALE**
United Kingdom	407.3	296.2
North East	360.1	269.0
North West and Merseyside	386.4	277.4
Merseyside	381.7	284.4
Yorkshire and the Humber	363.9	268.9
East Midlands	369.2	260.3
West Midlands	375.4	268.5
Eastern	399.5	295.9
London	541.3	386.3
South East	428.3	306.5
South West	382.4	274.8
England	414.0	301.3
Wales	363.5	269.0
Scotland	378.0	272.4
Northern Ireland	355.9	265.2

TABLE 1.15 *UK average weekly gross earnings, April 1997*

Source: © *Crown copyright (ONS)*

Technological developments

Two major technical innovations that have had a profound effect on people's leisure time in the second half of the twentieth century have been the car and the television. A third major development is also becoming evident, the Internet.

Car
Car ownership is reputed to be the single most important determinant of out-of-home leisure activities. In terms of facilitating participation it does provide a formidable means of travel and access in terms of door-to-door transport. Although not necessarily the cheapest mode of travel, it is often the most convenient.

Television
By 1975, television viewing was the most popular leisure activity with

DID YOU KNOW?

Currently (1999) satellite and cable television is in 30% of UK homes.

Source: *Leisure Forecasts, 1999–2003*

DISCUSSION

Ask your student group how many have cable, satellite or digital television in their homes?

Work out the percentage. What does it tell you?

over 98% of British people involved at some stage. By 1999, the number of households in Britain without access to at least one set was nil.

The last few years of the twentieth century have witnessed a major push towards digital television viewing. The government has confirmed that analogue broadcasts will end in 2013, thus bringing an end to the nature of the current viewing era.

Sky television has been one of the major players in the digital revolution. One of Sky's most unique features allows the consumer a far more pro-active role in their viewing, that is through its interactive channels, particularly live sport.

Through cable, satellite and now digital television, the number of channels available for the consumer has increased significantly. There were four channels in 1982 and it is anticipated that as many as 400 channels will be available in the year 2002.

The impact of modern television has been significant in that the ability of channels to fund themselves through advertising has diminished and, as a result, there has been a significant move towards 'pay-per-view' television. Current examples of this include Sky's 'Fight Night', where the price of the viewing is considerably cheaper if it is ordered well in advance as opposed to just hours or minutes before the bout. Sky's Box Office movie channels have also proved to be very popular, with a price (currently £3, at the beginning of the year 2000) which is not quite as competitive as most video rentals, but does negate the time spent commuting to the outlet.

The video industry is currently undergoing a transitional period as there is some uncertainty as to whether the future is with Digital Versatile Disc –Video (DVD–V), you may have seen these discs for rent in your local video store, or with Electronic Digital Delivery (EDD).

EDD could seemingly replace the physical distribution of videos. You would order by telephone, a computer or even a television remote control. Videos would then be transferred to decoders in VCRs and played in the same manner as conventional videos.

Internet

The last five years have seen the newest and possibly the most significant technological development – the computer and Internet. Currently, however, it is underused. That is, of those private homes with access to the Internet their usage is limited primarily to e-mail and information seeking. Most private users have still to make use of the on-line shopping facilities that exist with organisations like Tesco. It is expected that this trend will change as more households go on-line and as more individuals become computer and Internet literate.

Often when confronted with new technology people are loath to be adventurous and identify the capacities that this technology holds for them. Once people become familiar with the abilities of their PC and modem and trusting of the services promised, the current reluctance should change.

In 1975 micro-electronic equipment like the Walkman, the video, the PC, the camcorder, the Gameboy and Playstation were not available on the market, they were products that nobody had or wanted simply because they did not exist. Imagine what the future may hold!

DISCUSSION

Consider the technological developments that await us in the future. What will they enable us to do, that we cannot do now?

Changing consumer needs

When an organisation is considering the range of products, activities and services it may provide, it should take into account the many personal factors which determine whether or not individuals are able to participate.

Personal and social constraints are beyond the control of providers but they should be aware of personal factors which can influence participation rates and levels. These include an individual's age, gender, marital status, time commitments, state and level of employment and income.

These factors directly affect:

- disposable income
- car ownership
- employment characteristics (including the number of days holiday and the proportion which is paid)
- time available for recreation
- the influence of significant others (parents, spouses, friends)
- education
- social and cultural factors.

When considering their provision in terms of the type and range of products, services and activities offered organisations should certainly take into account other variables such as attitudes, interest, skills, physique and fitness and cultural background.

Torkildsen (1992) observed the nature and frequency of participation and suggested that these factors *per se,* and more, influenced participation. Table 1.16 separates influences on participation into three succinct areas. The factors that have been highlighted in bold are those that are perceived to be the most important in terms of dictating the nature and frequency of participation.

DISCUSSION

What factors or issues prevent you from participating in leisure activities? List them.

What about your parents or guardians? Are their reasons for not participating different to yours?

PERSONAL	SOCIAL AND CIRCUMSTANTIAL	OPPORTUNITY
Age	**Occupation**	Resources available
Stage in life cycle	Income	**Facilities – type**
Gender	**Disposable income**	**and quality**
Marital status	Material wealth and	Awareness
Dependants (and their	goods	**Perception of**
ages)	**Car ownership**	**opportunities**
Will and purpose in	**and mobility**	Recreation services
life	**Time available**	Distribution of
Personal obligations	**Duties and**	facilities
Resourcefulness	**obligations**	**Access and**
Leisure perceptions	Home and social	**location**
Attitudes and	environment	Choice of activities
motivation	Friends and peer	**Transport**
Interests and	groups	**Costs: before,**
preoccupations	Social roles and	**during and after**
Skill and ability – physical,	contacts	Management –
social and intellectual	Environmental factors	policy and support
Personality and	Mass leisure factors	Marketing
confidence	Education and	Programming
Culture born into	attainment	Organisation and
Upbringing and background	Population factors	leadership
	Cultural factors	Social accessibility
		Political policies

TABLE 1.16 *Factors that dictate nature and frequency of participation*

ACTIVITY

Understanding the development of the industry

You are currently employed within a sector of the leisure industry and have been asked to focus on one leisure activity, pastime or pursuit from within the entire leisure and recreation spectrum.

Your employer has asked that you prepare a report that details the growth of your sector over the last 30 years. They have asked that your report be in the format of a 'time line'. Your time line needs to chart the history, growth and development of that activity, pastime or pursuit over the last 30 years.

In order to produce a comprehensive report, which will allow your employer to analyse the growth of the sector and identify the range of variables currently influencing the sector (including the customer and the competition) you, will have to consider a number of factors:

- Technological developments within your sector of the industry.
- Socio-economic developments (remember to make reference to work type and employment rates within your region, earnings and disposable income).
- Participation rates both at your organisation and at competitor organisations and over the 30-year period. Analyse these latter rates and identify whether participation trends show a general incline, decline or constant pattern.

● Competition, that is, similar services offered. Remember to identify their location and current usage.

Your time line should be chronologically ordered, that is, when charting the activity's development from the beginning of the 1960s to the year 2000, the last point on your time line should be 2000.

Your time line should include comparative statistical evidence and research in terms of costs, participation rates and growth trends.

You may wish to consult resources such as the *General Household Survey* and *Leisure Forecasts 1999 – 2003* and relevant backdated copies to compare projections with reality.

Additional tasks

Analyse the key dates on your time line. What was the significance of them?

Compare your time line with another like activity, pastime or pursuit. Are there any differences or similarities? If so, what are they?

The structure of the leisure and recreation industry

People's leisure and recreation is made possible, in part, through the provision of a wide range of resources, services and facilities. You have already considered the way in which provision within the leisure and recreation industry can be categorised or broken down. Have a look back at pages 6–20 of this Chapter to remind yourself.

Types of providers

Provision within the industry can be broken down into three main sectors and each sector is distinguished from the other based upon the ways in which the various organisations are funded and managed. Organisations can be categorised into a sector of provision based upon their philosophy of use or *raison d'etre*.

The structure of the leisure and recreation industry in the UK is both complex and diverse, as we have already established. There are many providers offering a vast array of products, services and activities.

The following definitions provide an overview of the philosophies of each sector.

KEY TERMS

Public sector: has a statutory duty to provide a range of services for the local community.

Public (local authority) sector

Public sector facilities are those that are organised, managed and funded largely by national or local government. It has a statutory duty to provide a range of services for the local community. Its emphasis is not on profit. However, it does have to be cost effective.

Local government has changed dramatically in the last 20 years and further radical changes are expected. For example, local government has become more open to contracting and competition: that is, the need to make services more efficient and councils more responsive to the people they serve.

The introduction of Compulsory Competitive Tendering (CCT) in the 1980s had a major influence on the management of facilities and services. For example, The Barbican Leisure Centre in York is owned by the City Council, yet it is operated and managed by a private organisation called Total Leisure Management (TLM).

The proposed introduction of the statutory duty of 'best value' will have an even greater impact than CCT, in that it will apply to all areas of local government service. In essence, local authorities will have to comply with 12 key principles including service planning, continuous improvement, action on 'failing' services, competition and community involvement.

The scope of recreation and leisure services within local authorities is vast. In order to structure provision in terms of products, services and activities across the sector, authorities will often identify spheres of influence. York City Council has identified ten spheres of component areas to enable them to structure and analyse their provision. You should, however, realise that some activities will be common to one or more groupings, that is, there will be some overlap.

1 Physical activity: sport, fitness and active leisure.
2 Arts, culture and entertainment.
3 History and heritage.
4 Leisure learning.
5 Community/voluntary activities.
6 Children and young people's activities.
7 Environment/open space.
8 Drinking and eating out.
9 Recreational shopping.
10 In-home leisure.

No two authorities are exactly alike either in their provision or management. Different authorities will have different spheres or elements depending upon their location, the size of their catchment area (population size), their policies and responsibilities. There will be general similarities but specific differences in what they can and do offer.

ACTIVITY

Structuring provision

You have just been given the responsibility of constructing a Leisure Plan for your local authority that will allow the authority to analyse the nature of its current provision right across the spectrum.

Your first task is to group 'like' activities, services and facilities into component areas.

What group headings or names will you use in order to structure your provision? There should be some difference between your structure and York's.

You may wish to consider what spheres of influence your own local authority uses to structure its provision.

DISCUSSION

Think about publicly owned places you visit. Should you pay to go to the park or the beach? If so, how much?

Funding

The public has free access to a large number of facilities, for which no direct payment is made, such as, libraries, playgrounds, urban parks, beaches, picnic areas and country parks.

Payment for access and use is indirect, that is, payment is made through rates and taxes, specifically council tax which is charged to each household.

For the use of other facilities such as swimming pools, sports centres, playing fields, golf courses, marinas and art centres there is a direct payment by the user, however, this is often highly subsidised.

You may find that participation costs in a similar activity at a private or commercial organisation will be higher as there is often no subsidy, as with local authority provision. Private facilities may, however, employ a range of concessions for 'under privileged' groups during off-peak times.

ACTIVITY

Leisure costs

Using your local authority as a source of reference, identify a contrasting range of activities from within their leisure and recreation provision and identify the costs associated with participation.

Now identify private organisations offering similar provision and compare and contrast the costs between the two facilities.

In order to contrast the costs specifically, you will have to identify the difference in the activity, product or service 'bought', that is, what exactly you get for your money.

Private (commercial) sector

KEY TERMS

Private sector: is profit oriented. Its aim is to achieve a significant return on any investment through the provision of leisure and recreation products and services.

Private sector facilities, also referred to as commercial organisations, are profit oriented and aim to achieve a significant return on their investment through the provision of leisure and recreation products and services. Commercial leisure is a massive industry.

Commercial providers of facilities, services and products have by far the greatest influence on people's use of leisure time. This is most apparent in leisure in and around the home and in social recreation. The holiday and tourist industry is an expanding commercial market and the continuing rise in active recreation has expanded the leisure and sports goods markets.

The last two decades in general, and the last 10 years in particular, have witnessed a significant increase in the British commercial leisure market.

Examples of provision within the sector include the following:

- active leisure and health clubs
- sports clubs (both indoors and outdoors)
- holiday villages
- golf and country clubs
- themed restaurants
- bingo
- drink and dance bars
- cinema complexes.

DID YOU KNOW?

The UK is a major leader in the European leisure industry. Seven of the top ten leisure companies in Europe are UK-based.

Source: *Leisure Forecasts, 1999–2003*

This list is by no means exhaustive and you should be aware that the commercial leisure and recreation industry is made up of many thousands of providers that range considerably in size. The industry is widely diversified and while some providers only employ a small workforce, for example one or a few full-time staff and peak-hour part-timers, the large companies predominate.

In the last ten years there has been a significant increase in the size of the national and emerging multinational companies through mergers, takeovers and diversification of interests. It is these companies that dominate the commercial leisure and recreation industry. Examples of such organisations include Whitbread plc and The Rank Group plc.

CASE STUDY *Whitbread plc (www.whitbread.co.uk/html)*

Whitbread plc originated in 1742 and was in the first instance a brewer and although today drink is still an important part of the business, Whitbread plc has diversified considerably.

The Whitbread Beer Company brews, markets and distributes a range of the UK's most popular beer brands. First Quench is one of the leading brand names in high street drinks retailing with outlets such as Thresher, Victoria Wine, Bottoms Up and Wine Rack.

The Whitbread Pub Estate incorporates a range of high street bars, cask alehouses and pub restaurants. At present, there are around 3,700 Whitbread pubs in the UK, with those managed directly by the company run by Whitbread Inns and those which are leased under Whitbread Pub Partnerships.

The Whitbread Hotel Company is the UK's second largest hotel group, operating over 250 hotels and over 16,000 rooms, with a further 37 hotels and over 3,000 rooms under development. The Company's vision for the millennium is to be 'Britain's Favourite Hotel Company', as measured by its customers, investors and employees.

The company's activities are focused primarily on a strong, branded presence in two market sectors – four-star Marriott Hotels and budget Travel Inns.

Whitbread is developing the Marriott brand further in the UK. During 1998 hotels opened at County Hall (200 rooms) in London and Manchester (150 rooms). Two major conversions were completed at hotels in Southampton and Shipley (Leeds/Bradford). A new hotel opened at Heathrow Airport (390 rooms) earlier this year.

Travel Inn is the UK's leading budget hotel brand with over 200 hotels in operation and according to its customers is 'the UK's favourite place to stay'. During the next five years Travel Inn has announced it will spend £300 million on expanding the brand. The programme will double the current number of hotels to 400 and rooms to 20,000.

Whitbread is the leading operator of private healthcare and fitness centres in the UK with both its **David Lloyd Leisure Clubs** and the extensive golf and complementary facilities on offer at Marriott.

Whitbread in the last two years have sought to consolidate their position as a market leader in active leisure provision through mergers and takeovers. They have made two significant acquisitions in the last five years. Firstly that of the David Lloyd centres. David Lloyd built twenty centres (the first in 1982 in Heston) and sold out to Whitbread who purchased David Lloyd Leisure for £201 million in 1995. Whitbread have since acquired the chain of the Racquets & Healthtrack Group for £78.3 million. These six clubs will be rebranded as David Lloyd Leisure. The move means that by the end of 1999 David Lloyd Leisure will have 47 clubs and 170,000 members, making it the UK's leading health club operator.

This is just an isolated example of the various moves made by larger operators who are continually seeking to define their market share. The implications of these types of 'buy-outs' are vast. Through the acquisition of operations that resemble their own mix of existing provision, operators are effectively ridding themselves of a competitor. That is, they are rapidly gaining sites to add to their own portfolio and achieving savings through volume. The multi-site operators can bring business within reach of many more people and can raise the profile of a sector through a united front and establishing partnerships. However, there is still a place for the individual single site operator who has found and established a niche in the market place.

CASE STUDY *The Rank Group plc (www.rank.com/rank/rank.nsf)*

The Rank Group is a leader in what they refer to as the 'leisure and entertainment industry' and operates two business streams. It:

● Provides services to the film industry

● Entertains consumers directly through its portfolio of strong leisure and entertainment brands

Its leisure and entertainment activities include Hard Rock Cafés and global rights to the Hard Rock brand, gaming, cinemas, nightclubs, themed bars, pubs, restaurants and multi-leisure centres and holiday resorts, for example Oasis Forest Holiday Villages, Butlins and Haven.

Rank also owns film processing and video duplication and distribution facilities and has a 50% investment in Universal Studios Escape (a major theme park and development) at Orlando, Florida. Rank operates primarily in the UK and North America, although it has activities in continental Europe and other parts of the world. Rank is a multinational organisation.

Its aim is to become one of the leading leisure and entertainment companies in the world. It is one of the UK's leading leisure and entertainment companies and currently employs over 40,000 people based mainly in the UK, North America and mainland Europe.

Over the last two years, Rank has undergone extensive reorganisation, having rationalised its operation to concentrate on key businesses and markets. In March 1998 Rank acquired Parkdean Holidays, a UK holiday park operator, for £38 million. In 1999, it sold its nightscene operations, Rank Entertainment Limited, to Northern Leisure Plc for a consideration of £150 million.

ACTIVITY

Provision in your local area

Ask five people, including friends, parents and tutors, (so that you may get a cross section of interests and activities) what types of leisure and recreation activities they have participated in over the last week.

It is important that you write down not only the activity but where it took place, that is, which organisation was responsible for the provision.

Can you now categorise the provider. Is it a local authority or commercial organisation? If it is a commercial organisation state whether it is part of a multinational or if it is a smaller, single site operator.

Voluntary sector

Voluntary sector organisations exist to provide a service which may not otherwise be provided by the public or private sectors.

The resources, facilities and opportunities created by the many thousands of voluntary bodies in the UK represent a sizeable portion of leisure and recreation provision across the board. Literally thousands of opportunities to participate in a contrasting range of activities have been established through voluntary provision over the years. This sector is dominated by an immense variety of clubs and associations.

Except in cases where the focus of the group or association is the conservation of buildings or land, almost all of the voluntary organisations are concerned with the interests of their members or users. In some of the larger, national and charitable organisations the voluntary sector depends heavily upon the work of unpaid volunteers.

DID YOU KNOW?

A number of examples of contrasting provision within the voluntary sector include:

- community action groups (Gingerbread)
- children's groups (Pre-school Playgroups Association)
- youth organisations (Scouts, Girl Guides)
- women's organisations (Mothers Union, Women's Institute)
- groups for the retired and the elderly (Darby and Joan clubs)
- groups for people with disabilities
- outdoor and adventure activity groups (Outward Bound, National Caving Association)
- sport and physical recreation groups
- cultural and entertainment organisations (Museum associations, Amateur dramatics groups)
- animals and pet groups (Pony Club, Cats Protection League)
- environment, conservation and heritage groups (National Trust, Friends of the Earth)
- consumer groups (Campaign for Real Ale (CAMRA))
- weight watchers groups (Slimmer's World)
- counselling organisations (Samaritans, Child Line)
- philanthropic groups (Rotary Club)
- paramedical organisations (St John's Ambulance).

This list is by no means exhaustive, but serves to demonstrate the diversity of provision within the area.

ACTIVITY

Voluntary sector provision

These are just a few examples of voluntary sector provision. Are there any categories that we have not included? If so, what are they?

Can you think of any other examples of organisations who provide within these categories based either locally, in your area or nationally?

DID YOU KNOW?

It is estimated that there are 150,000 voluntary sports clubs affiliated to the national governing bodies.

Source: The Institute of Leisure and Amenity Management (ILAM Fact Sheet August 1998).

DISCUSSION

Almost 20 years on this figure is likely to have grown dramatically. Can you identify what the most recent figures are and account for why there has been so much growth in voluntary provision?

The organisation of sport in the voluntary sector relies on the work done by unpaid volunteers, as such the value of volunteers in sport cannot be underestimated. Sport England (1997) in their Sports Council Survey of the Voluntary Sector noted that volunteers are the backbone of British Sport, making a massive 'in kind' contribution as coaches, managers and officials. In 1995 it was estimated that the total annual value of the UK sports volunteer market was over £1.5 billion. It was also estimated that there were just under 1.5 million volunteers in UK sport.

Arts, community arts and cultural activities are largely catered for through local voluntary societies, associations and groups.

Informal outdoor recreation is encouraged through organisations such as the National Trust, the Ramblers Association and local walking and cycling groups. Individuals seeking to take part in activities away from home over a period of time are sustained by organisations such as the Youth Hostel Association.

Private landowners also play a significant part in the provision of informal recreation. They own a considerable amount of the rural land which is the setting for outdoor informal leisure and recreation (including walking, biking, horse riding and picnicking). They also own and manage historic houses and country parks.

Private and institutional bodies such as landowners, employers and educational institutions make an important contribution to the provision of recreation and associated services. Many firms provide social and sporting facilities. For example, the Slazenger Sports and Social Club in Wakefield, Yorkshire has provision for hockey (a sand-based astro-turf pitch), football, rugby and cricket fields, tennis courts and also has a bar and catering facilities.

In 1981, the English Tourist Board identified the membership of 211 national voluntary leisure groups with over 8 million members collectively, of which:

- 29% belonged to youth groups
- 27% to sports groups
- 13% to conservation and heritage groups
- 8% to touring groups

- 7% to women's groups
- and 7% to wildlife and conservation groups

Over 40% of these groups had memberships of over 5,000.

Funding

One of this sector's most distinguishing characteristics is that of its constant struggle for financial security. Funds are usually generated through a variety of sources: in the first instance from its member's pockets via annual membership fees, subscriptions and participation costs or admission fees. Players in amateur sports clubs have to play for the privilege of training and competing.

Some voluntary groups are dependent upon funding by way of sponsorship from local companies and businesses that like to be seen to be actively supporting local causes. For example, Wharfedale Rugby Club who are currently in the Jewson National Division 1, are reliant upon the support of a local inn (The Old Hall) as is the case with massive numbers of sports clubs across the country. Some voluntary groups are dependent upon the sponsorship or financial backing they receive for their continued survival.

To supplement any sponsorship or grants received, voluntary associations and clubs also rely heavily on fund raising whether it be through the traditional jumble and car-boot sales, raffle draws or race nights.

DID YOU KNOW?

The Sport England Lottery Fund alone since 1994, has supported 3,019 capital projects and committed £966.25 million.

Source: Sport England Website

DISCUSSION

In your local area identify a club, group, or association that has received lottery funding.

How much did they receive? For what specific reason were they awarded the funding? Do you think the money should have been directed elsewhere in your local area?

In many cases voluntary organisations are dependent upon, public providers and public money. Charitable trusts, advisory and counselling services are often partly sponsored by local authorities. The interdependence between the two providers is part and parcel of a wider framework of public community services, including leisure and recreation. Some of the larger national organisations have charitable status that usually qualifies for government funding.

One of the biggest sources of income over the last five years for fortunate voluntary organisations has been the allocation of resources from the National Lottery. The National Lottery Act (1993) identified five areas to benefit from Lottery funding:

- sport
- the arts
- heritage
- charities
- projects to mark the year 2000, the beginning of the third millennium.

Of every pound spent on the National Lottery, around 28p goes to good causes. By October 1999, over £7 billion had been allocated to over 47,000 projects. These funds have been directed towards helping deprived groups, saving buildings and national treasures and has enabled more people to enjoy sports and the arts.

ACTIVITY

Understanding the different types of leisure and recreation provision

In order to understand leisure and recreation provision across the three sectors you are required to compare and contrast the characteristics of three organisations.

Choose one organisation from each of the three sectors:

- public
- private
- voluntary

By choosing three organisations from within the same sector, you will obtain a more relevant base for comparison and distinction, that is, similar services, different providers.

Obtain the following information which will allow you to make distinctions between the nature of provision:

- The organisation's philosophy of use, or vision/mission statement.
- A 'family tree' which shows the staff structure in terms of the type and number of employees in a hierarchical fashion.
- The organisational structure, for example, is the facility a branch of a large organisation, where is the head office?
- Methods of funding.
- Facilities, resources and activities which the organisation has available.
- Participation costs.

DID YOU KNOW?

The UK's fitness industry is valued at around £1 billion.

Source: *Leisure Forecasts*, 1999–2003

The scale of the UK leisure and recreation industry

Leisure and recreation is now one of the largest industries in the UK.

Any industry worth £1 billion is sizeable. You need to acknowledge the fact that the fitness industry is merely a bit-part of just one component area within one sector of the industry, consequently the size of the industry as a whole is enormous.

Consumer spending

In the data published by the ONS it is interesting to note that in the *Family Expenditure Survey* 1998–9, more money was spent on leisure goods and services (almost 17% of expenditure) than on anything else.

It might be assumed that this spending was in fact the 'family's' or 'individual's' disposable income. Or it might also be a reflection of the nation's growing dependency on credit that is, credit cards, 'buy now, pay later' and interest free schemes.

Table 1.17 highlights the nature of this expenditure.

	1998–9
	£ (ROUNDED UP TO NEAREST 10P)
Leisure goods and services	59.80
Food and non-alcoholic drinks	58.90
Housing	57.20
Motoring	51.70
Household goods and services	48.60
Clothing and footwear	21.70
Alcoholic drink	14.00
Personal goods and services	13.30
Fuel and power	11.70
Fares and other travel costs	8.30
Tobacco	5.80
Miscellaneous	1.20
Total expenditure	**352.20**

TABLE 1.17 *Analysis of average weekly household expenditure in the UK, 1998–9*

DID YOU KNOW?

The average gross weekly earnings of full-time adults whose pay was not affected by absence stood at £400 in April 1999.

Part-time weekly earnings rose more quickly, by 5.7% to stand at £132.

Source: Office for National Statistics, 1999

Leisure Forecasts 1999–2003, has suggested that the significant growth in leisure spending has been fuelled by the rapid growth in disposable incomes caused by seven cuts in interest rates since the middle of 1998. The cost of mortgages, which is widely acknowledged as the single largest financial outgoing an individual can commit to, is now at its lowest level for over 30 years. The implications of this are that there is more money available to spend on leisure.

ACTIVITY

Financial expenditure

Are you aware of how money is directed in your family home? How much do you suppose is spent on leisure goods and services? If you are working as you undertake this course do you know how and what you spend your money on?

It would be a worthwhile activity to consider either the nature of your spending and or the spending within the family home (if your parents/guardians do not mind sharing this information with you).

The first thing to do is consider what you mean by the term 'leisure goods and services'. Make a list of these now.

Realise that the amount of money spent on activities incorporated into this definition will vary according to each individual and each household.

You may wish to use Table 1.18 to help you in your analysis.

ANALYSIS OF AVERAGE WEEKLY EXPENDITURE FOR

	£ (ROUNDED UP TO NEAREST 10P)
Leisure goods and services	
Food and non-alcoholic drinks	
Housing	
Motoring	
Household goods and services	
Clothing and footwear	
Alcoholic drink	
Personal goods and services	
Fuel and power	
Fares and other travel costs	
Tobacco	
Miscellaneous	
Total expenditure	

TABLE 1.18 *Financial expenditure form for leisure goods and services*

DID YOU KNOW?

Nationally the leisure industry employs a workforce of just under 500,000 (1997).

Source: CIPFA estimates England and Wales

Employment rates in the industry

The leisure and recreation industry is possibly the fastest growing industry in the UK and therefore, by definition, a major job provider. The diversity of the industry, in terms of the sheer number of providers and enterprises suggests that the range of employment opportunities is vast. In 1997, it was estimated that 223,515 businesses were directly involved in leisure.

The Institute of Leisure and Amenity Management (ILAM) in providing a statistical overview of the leisure and recreation industry in 1996 identified that employment by sector, accounted for the following employment levels:

- Tourism   1,700,000
- Hotels and Restaurants 1,330,700
- Visitor attractions   354,000

- Sporting activities   218,700
- Other recreational activities   101,000
- Libraries, archives and museums   77,100
- Other entertainment activities   74,700
- Radio and television activities   49,700
- Motion picture and video activities   30,400
- **TOTAL**   **3,582,300**

It would be fair to assume that because of the dynamic nature of the industry, growth in the number of employees working within leisure and recreation has shown a steady incline, so making the leisure industry a major employer of people in the UK.

Participation trends

Recent surveys including the *New Leisure Markets* compiled by Marketscope Ltd, the *General Household Survey,* 1996 and *Consumer Trends,* 1998, show a general increase in participation in line with the following trends:

- Interest in more active leisure rather than spectating.
- Demand for family facilities and activities.
- Demand for children's play facilities.
- Concern for health and fitness, especially among children and young people.
- Growth in casual participation.
- Rising expectations in terms of quality of provision, value for money and value for time spent.
- Emphasis on social aspects of participation.
- A narrowing of the gap between men's and women's participation.
- Growing interest in heritage, especially the countryside.
- Increased awareness of the needs and rights of people with disabilities.
- Access to a wider range of sporting and leisure opportunities.

Throughout this Chapter and text are a number of statistics that reflect participation trends in the industry. Look out for these.

DISCUSSION

Think about the last activity that you took part in, preferably away from the home.

What was it? Where was it? Think about the people employed by that organisation. What were they doing? How were they responsible for making sure that the time you spent was enjoyable and productive? List the jobs that those people performed.

Working in the leisure and recreation industry

For every activity that you participate in, any facility or venue that you frequent, for every leisure pursuit that is facilitated by somebody other than yourself, consider that someone else – an individual, a group, a team of people and maybe an entire organisation is working to make it happen.

In order to analyse employment opportunities within the industry and then isolate an aspect of that provision, one that you could conceivably work within, you will have to consider a range of factors:

- the range of employment opportunities
- the nature of employment
- personal and technical skills
- how to find jobs in leisure and recreation.

The range of employment opportunities

In order to establish a comprehensive list of the employment opportunities available, it would be best to identify opportunities across the leisure and recreation spectrum.

ACTIVITY

Employment opportunities

This activity will give you the opportunity to start to think specifically about the range of jobs or professions that exist within the industry. In small groups complete the following:

- Identify one specific organisation, facility or venue within each sector of provision.
- Obtain a work chart or structure also known as a 'family tree' from that organisation which shows the range of opportunities and the hierarchies or levels at which they exist.
- Your work chart should give the full 'badge title' of each position. Where just a generic job title such as 'instructor' is given, be more specific and state the exact nature of the position, for example, fitness instructor.

Now that you have identified a range of opportunities, try and find out whether any of these positions currently exist within your local area. If they do not exist at the organisation you have focused on, then look at a similar facility.

The nature of employment

ACTIVITY

Collecting job advertisements

Collect as many different advertisements as possible that refer to positions available right across the scope of the industry. Some of these may not be suitable for you, they may not interest you or may not be in the right geographical area for you, nevertheless still collect them as we will make reference to them throughout this next section.

In order to find a range of adverts you should look at the local and national press, specialist trade and industry magazines, job boards in your school or college, local job centres, and even on the Web.

Employment opportunities within the industry are marked by some unique characteristics which we shall look at next.

Unsociable hours

The leisure and recreation industry differs from the majority of other employers in the UK in that it does not just operate a traditional working week (9.00a.m. – 5.00p.m., Monday to Friday). It is open to accommodate the needs of people outside of the working day and, therefore, operates and employs individuals outside of that time period.

The hours available will vary according to which sector of the industry is 'working'. Dance bars and night clubs can sometimes operate extended licences. Swimming pools and fitness suites are open at 6.00a.m. to allow people to exercise before work. Some pool and snooker halls in the bigger cities are now open 24 hours. Scotland's liberal drinking rules mean that some pubs are open from 6.00a.m. until 2.00a.m., that is they are closed for a mere four hours a day.

Employment characteristics

DISCUSSION

In your group, identify how many students are currently working. Find out what the nature of their work is, for example, shift work, short-term or contract work, permanent part-time or casual. Are any employed on any other basis?

Find out why they are working in that particular field. Is it dictated by need or do they have ulterior motives to pursue a career in that area?

One of the most notable employment characteristics of the industry is that it has moved away from the traditional pattern of employing predominantly full-time workers. The industry has become used to employing most notably, young people in part-time capacities. Part-time work refers to a number of different contract and non-contract positions. Some employers will employ individuals in part-time positions or on a shift basis, particularly during peak hours, to increase staff levels. Employers may also choose to employ people on a casual or needs basis only. For example, during the Wimbledon fortnight or on other prestigious sporting occasions, corporate hospitality units will contract people to work for that time span alone.

Part-time work at Wimbledon, for young people   Source: *Corbis*

Young people, particularly students, are readily available during holiday or vacation periods and at weekends, possibly through necessity rather than choice. They are flexible in their working hours and duties, and ultimately represent cheaper labour. When employed on a casual or part-time basis, employers are not obliged to pay for sick leave or reward service with paid annual leave. Consequently, however, with such conditions there is a very high turnover of staff, as employees are not obliged to show any real commitment to their employers.

Whether the position is permanent or temporary, full-time or part-time, may well depend on consumer demand, the time of year (holiday and seasonal work), current staffing levels, the turnover of staff and employee availability and capability.

Due to the nature of the industry, sectors such as the holiday sector employ a large number of seasonal staff. Some holiday villages, for example, are not open all year round (they only operate from early May until the end of September) and will then employ staff in a range of positions, as required. Other holiday villages, like Oasis in the Lakes are open all year round and employ permanent staff on a full-time contract but the number of staff employed will vary to reflect the peak and off-peak season. That is, during the traditional school holidays more staff will be employed on a casual or short-term contract to cope with extra demand.

Within the ski industry, overseas tour operators from the UK operating in Europe employ British people in a range of positions to work in aspects of the operation of the resort. The season lasts from early December until around Easter. The range of positions available may vary, but could include resort or hotel management to tour or group representative, depending on language skills, and chalet girl or boy or

Photo of ski instructor at skiing resort   Source: *Corbis*

chambermaid, bar tending, and ski technician, and guide or instructor, depending on qualifications.

Some of those in the industry, particularly tour or group representatives, will spend their winters working in the 'snow' and the summers working in the 'sun'. They may even work for the same company. Crystal and Thompson holidays are good examples of those companies who have seasonal operations.

Some of you may work within the industry either as a recreation assistant at your local sports centre, or as bartenders in bars and nightclubs. You may work as a chambermaid in a hotel or travel lodge or as a silver service waiter; others of you may even work in the retail side of the industry, perhaps in JD Sports, HMV, or a local video store. Those of you with aspirations to work in teaching or coaching may already be doing that, particularly with young children.

Employment opportunities

To consider the range of employment opportunities that exist within the industry, look back to the beginning of this Chapter to remind yourselves of the different types of organisations, facilities and venues that exist within the industry. Within these sectors there are endless opportunities that can be categorised into 'like' positions or areas of responsibility. Positions which involve reception or 'front of house' operations, sales and marketing or promotions and management and organisation are employment features of all sectors.

More specific positions include:

- **Arts and entertainments**
    - group/tour/company representatives
    - host(ess) including DJ/MC
    - bar tending and security work
    - guides
    - grounds staff and park attendants
    - librarians
- **Sports and physical recreation**
    - teaching, coaching, leadership and instructing
    - development
    - club professional
    - recreation assistants
    - exercise prescription/sports medicine/GP referral
    - journalism and photography

DID YOU KNOW?

The licensed retail industry (pub business), is losing some £300 million each year on recruiting front line staff. Staff turnover currently ranges from 90–305%.

Source: Leeds Metropolitan University

- health and fitness instructors/personal trainers
- groundsman/keeper
- sales and retail
- children's nanny/play leader
- **Heritage**
  - guides
  - group leaders
  - research
  - conservation
  - grounds keeper
- **Catering and accommodation**
  - bookings and system administration
  - group/tour/company representatives
  - bar tending and waitressing
  - chambermaid
  - kitchen staff
  - children's nanny/play leader
- **Countryside recreation (including outdoor activities)**
  - group/tour leaders
  - activity organiser
  - outdoor pursuits/adventure activities instructors and leaders
  - park keeper/ranger
- **Home-based leisure**
  - retail and sales assistants
  - technical advisors

DISCUSSION

You may well be able to think of positions that have not been included on the list. If so, start to compile your own list of the range of positions available in the industry.

As a group, think about positions available right across the industry, do not just confine yourselves to the local area. For example, if you live in the south of England, then positions such as climbing or ski instructors might not be the first to cross your mind.

You may even want to put these job adverts up on a notice board and perhaps 'map' their locations.

Personal and technical skills

The leisure industry, as one of the fastest-growing sectors of the UK economy, offers a wide range of job opportunities for people with the right skills, knowledge and personal qualities.

In most job advertisements an employer will, alongside the conditions of the post, stipulate what qualities, experience or qualifications they are looking for from prospective candidates. This is done in an attempt to ensure that the range of applicants are suitable for the position and thus save the organisation time in the selection process.

Personal qualities

Regardless of the responsibilities and salary status associated with a position, you should realise that there are certain personal qualities that an employer will look for. The range of qualities that organisations expect are often listed in the advert, examples of which are:

DISCUSSION

From job adverts that you have collected do you recognise any of these requests?

Are there any requests for personal qualities listed in the adverts that you have that are not listed here? Write them down.

- flexible approach to hours of work
- good communication, interpersonal, administrative and organisational skills
- an outstanding hard hitting all rounder who always puts the team first
- a leading player
- highly motivated and dedicated professional
- positive outgoing attitude, leadership style and people skills to match
- enthusiastic and customer focused
- hands-on experience.

Common skills

All employers require some common skills. It is expected that all employees are numerate and literate (can read and write). These are more commonly referred to as numeracy and communication skills. Individuals in today's technical world are required to be IT (Information Technology) literate.

Communication refers to your ability to demonstrate good interpersonal skills and the ability to work effectively with customers and colleagues alike. In the leisure, recreation and tourism industries and for some overseas work, as a group or tour representative or in hotels and management, a second language is required and often listed as 'essential' for any candidate considering applying for the position.

Technical skills

Alongside personal qualities, organisations will require technical expertise, skills and qualifications. Qualifications are not confined solely to academic achievements (GCSEs, A levels, undergraduate, postgraduate or equivalent level degrees) but also refer to:

- Vocational qualifications, which include NVQs and coaching qualifications.
- Individual qualifications provided by industry representatives such as ILAM, the FIA, the YMCA and others.

Technical skills are often outlined in the job advert as a requirement of the post and an organisation's expectations may read as follows:

- You will be educated to degree level or equivalent and have at least five years' experience at senior level in a community facility environment.

- Candidates should possess a sports related qualification (preferably to degree level) and a current first aid certificate.
- Experience of IT packages including Microsoft Office at an advanced level.

ACTIVITY

Personal skills audit

When applying for positions you will have to analyse your skills.

Use the following category headings to write down and analyse your skills:

- personal
- communication
- numeracy
- IT
- technical

Now that you have committed all your skills to paper look again at a range of job adverts.

Do your skills match those that the prospective employer is looking for?

If the answer is no, then keep looking until you find a job advert that does match and that you are interested in.

How to find jobs in leisure and recreation

In order to identify a range of job or employment opportunities you will have to make reference to a range of sources. These include:

- recruitment/employment agencies
- job centres
- careers service
- job fairs
- professional associations
- trade press
- web sites
- newspapers
- press articles on new developments.

FIGURE 1.4 *Selection of job advertisements in the leisure and recreation industry*

Recruitment/employment agencies

Employment agencies advertise jobs on behalf of employers. In order to ensure a quality field of applicants for the position, they must consider a number of questions including: Where will the position be most visible? How will suitable candidates find the advert? Are we targeting the ideal candidate? Often such agencies will advertise the post through a number of media in order to maximise the job advertisement's exposure, that is, to ensure it is seen by as large a group of suitably qualified potential candidates as possible.

These agencies may even be responsible for conducting the first interview on behalf of the employer and will then short list a number of suitably qualified candidates who are then referred to the organisation itself.

Some employment agencies are responsible for collating a pool or database of suitably qualified personnel for organisations to refer to when they are either short staffed or exceptionally busy.

Job centres

The Department of Employment manages job centres. The department employs trained staff whose remit is to help prospective job applicants by providing advice to identify suitable opportunities. Job centres advertise any employment vacancy and, thus, are not a specific source of leisure and recreation positions.

Careers service

The Careers Service employs careers advisors who provide advice, guidance and information primarily to pupils and students in schools and colleges around the country. Through a series of talks and more formal interviews, careers advisors work with you to identify a 'career path(s)' which best suits your aspirations, abilities and interests.

They can provide advice and details of educational courses that will give you the opportunity to gain appropriate and specific qualifications to enter your chosen profession, occupational information about jobs or youth training courses and advice on identifying and applying for a modern apprenticeship.

The Careers Service also caters for adults, in that it provides knowledge, advice and information about realistic opportunities for those people who are either returning to work or making a career change.

Job fairs

There are, at specific times of the year, job fairs which are attended by a number of different organisations looking to recruit either school leavers or graduates to their organisations in a variety of positions. School leavers are usually recruited to positions whereby they will receive in-house training with the opportunity to progress potentially to positions of seniority.

The graduate job fairs are often national events, advertised nationwide in the national press, examples of which include *The Guardian*.

Professional associations

Within the industry there are several professional organisations that provide specialist advice and information about employment opportunities and current trends, initiatives, innovations and technological developments.

Some of the major associations in the industry are listed below:

● The Institute of Leisure and Amenity Management (ILAM) is a forum for the managers of the UK's leisure resources. They provide an immense range of services including job opportunities, news, information, advice, events, consultancy, policy and training.

- The National Training Organisation for Sport, Recreation and Allied Occupations (SPIRITO) has responsibility for leading the industry in the development of a new structure of qualifications, education and training.
- The Institute of Sport and Recreation Management (ISRM) (UK) is the national professional body for sport and recreation and facility management.

Other bodies from within the industry include the:

- Fitness Industry Association (FIA)
- British Association of Sport and Exercise Science (BASES)
- Hotel and Catering International Management Association (HCIMA)
- British Institute of Innkeepers (BMI)
- English Tourism Council (ETC)
- English Heritage
- National Trust
- Area Museums Council

In terms of finding jobs, almost all of these professional associations have web sites and newsletters/magazines that detail employment opportunities.

Trade press

One of the main sources of employment advertisements is the trade press. The trade press includes magazines, journals and newspapers that are written specifically for the leisure and recreation industry and organisations within it. Alongside employment opportunities they include features and articles of current news, directories of provision, technological developments and initiatives and classified sections.

Typical trade journals include:

- Travel Industry: *Travel Trade Gazette*
                       Travel Weekly
- Leisure Industry: *Leisure Management*
                       Leisure Opportunities
                       ILAM's *Leisure News*
- Fitness Industry: *Health Club Management*, the official publication of the FIA
- Hospitality Industry: *Caterer and Hotel Keeper*
                        Hospitality, the official publication of the HCIMA

DISCUSSION

Consider your area of interest. Is there a magazine or journal that you could refer to find employment opportunities?

Some specific activities and pastimes have their own specialist magazines, for example, climbers who are interested in finding positions in instructing, climbing and absailing should look in *High!* magazine.

Employers advertise their positions through these media because they can be sure that those people who apply via this route will do so because they are interested in and understand that sector of the industry and will have appropriate qualifications.

Web sites

In the last five years, the World Wide Web has become one of the primary media for disseminating information. Most large organisations have web sites, if they do not have a web site already they will probably have one under construction. Web sites are able to incorporate all of the features included in the trade press, specialist magazines, classified sections and news updates onto one site. The information provided in a web site is ordered into an easy to read directory that allows you to access specific pieces of information within seconds.

All web sites have an Internet location address, for example, the *Leisure Opportunities* magazine is now available to view electronically at www.leisureopportunities.co.uk. The Sportsweb (www.thesportsweb. co.uk) is an example of an online recruitment agency that specialises in recruiting for the health and leisure club sector. The Active Connection also specialises in this type of recruitment (www.activeconnection. co.uk).

The English Tourism Council set up a web-based 'employment directory' called Springboard whose address is www.careercompass.co.uk. This is largely funded by employers who pay to advertise on the site. The cost is around £4,000. This might sound expensive but they are at least reaching a captive audience.

ACTIVITY

Using the Internet to find employment opportunities

Find out the web site address of organisations across the industry. In order to help your search, you may have to use one of the search engines, for instance, Yahoo or Alta Vista, to name but two. You may have to put in key words into the search engine, such examples may include 'UK+nightclubs' or 'UK+bingo'.

Now access the site and look at its directory. Are there any employment opportunities? Most web sites will have a 'links' connection that gives you the facility to link to like sites, you should explore these.

If you find any 'attractive' employment opportunities then print them off.

Newspapers

Jobs within the industry are also advertised in local and national newspapers. Positions which hold more responsibility are higher in the hierarchical levels and which command relatively large salaries, such as middle/senior management and upwards are usually advertised in the national press, such as in *The Guardian* and *The Telegraph*.

These newspapers all have web sites where the 'job sections' can be accessed. The most useful aspect of these sites is that they do not just list current jobs, but are retrospective and allow you to search for positions you may have missed from say, the weekend supplement.

Articles on new developments

The industry is dynamic and constantly changing and there seems to be a never ending increase to the range of provision currently available. Organisations are constantly looking to expand and diversify their business interests.

It is important, for those people seeking positions in the industry to be aware of new trends and developments. Such developments, particularly those that require the construction of new premises, often require new staff. Any new development in a geographical area has implications with regards to employment opportunities. It is not just the operation of the facility or venue once it has become operational, but also the construction of it that impacts upon employment levels in that area. Xscape (Figure 1.5) is a £100 million leisure centre planned for the centre of Milton Keynes.

ACTIVITY

Gaining employment in the leisure and recreation industry

Find at least three interesting job adverts that you would consider for future employment. At this stage consider opportunities from across the industry and the country. You may use any or all of the media given in this section to identify a range of opportunities available.

The job advert will give you a contact name, address and or telephone number and possibly a reference number. Obtain the details of the post by using the contacts stated in the advert. You may well have to wait a few days before you receive any information.

Upon obtaining the specifications, analyse the post to assess whether you are suitable for it, or even if it is suitable for you. Consider the following:

- Job title
- Name of organisation
- Description/outline of the responsibilities of the post
- Skills and qualifications required
- Salary/wages
- Terms and conditions of the post, particularly the length of the contract

Are you suitable for the post? Answer the question, yes or no.

Xscape Milton Keynes

A £100m commercial leisure centre is planned for the centre of Milton Keynes, with an indoor snow sports centre as its showpiece. Designed by Newcastle-based Faulkner-Browns, the centre will provide facilities for skiers, snowboarders and snow play activities. The 170 metre indoor slope will be covered with 'real snow' made in controlled atmospheric conditions - a British first. Other leisure facilities will include a 16 screen cinema, a tenpin bowling and family entertainment centre, a health and fitness club, as well as an extensive range of restaurants, bars and lifestyle shopping.

FIGURE 1.5 *Xscape Milton Keynes*

Pursuing your own progression aims

Most people will have undertaken this Advanced Vocational A Level in Leisure and Recreation because they see it as a stepping stone into a career within the leisure and recreation industry.

Some may have clear and well defined career goals, such as outdoor activities instructor, teaching, sports massage, fitness instruction or exercise prescription, hotel or entertainment's management, or tour guide. These are but a few roles within an industry of thousands more. Others of you may know that you want to work within the industry but are not exactly sure of the sector of provision, or in what capacity.

This section will help you to identify your career objectives, that is to be specific in detailing what capacity, where and for whom you would like to work.

Defining your abilities and opportunities

ACTIVITY

Finding a job to suit you

Out of the range of job adverts that you have collected and considered, select one. Select the opportunity that best matches your own aspirations, skills and abilities.

It might be that the opportunity does not match your abilities and qualifications at the moment but could well do in the future. It may match what you wish to aspire to become in the future. Do not disregard this opportunity. We will refer to that opportunity in this next section.

How to plan your own career development

It may be that the opportunity you are currently considering, requires you to have technical and academic qualifications that you currently do not possess. Do not disregard this, but consider that you may be suitable for employment for that position if you could obtain the appropriate qualifications.

Many organisations require a combination of academic, vocational and technical qualifications. Figure 1.6 provides an overview of the qualifications that can lead to employment in the leisure and recreation industry. It shows how they relate to one another in terms of equivalencies and how you can progress or move into another area of study or training.

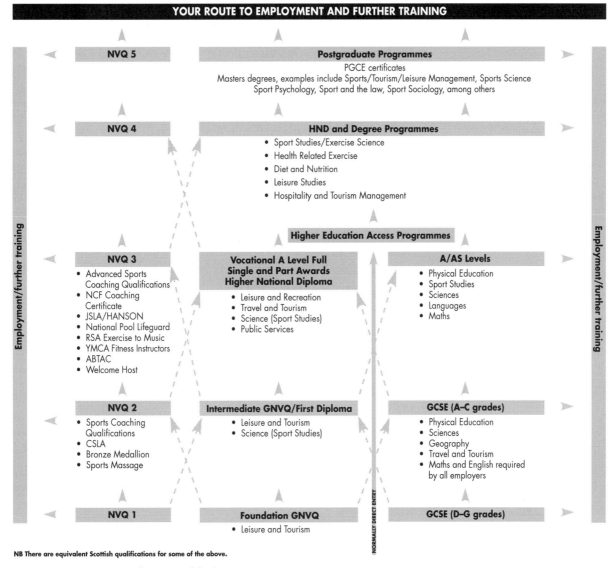

FIGURE 1.6 *Route to employment and further training*

NVQs and SVQs (Scottish Vocational Qualifications) are practical, work-based qualifications that recognise competence in particular skills. In addition to these formal and academically oriented courses many governing bodies of sport administer their own coaching awards and instructors certificates, which now have NVQ status.

Employment, training and education opportunities

There are a number of different ways in which you can train and prepare yourself for employment, and these are discussed below.

- **The academic route** – through full-time academic study, at GCSE, Advanced, Undergraduate and Postgraduate level.

  If you are considering the academic route to achieve your career goals and therefore entry into Higher Education you should contact UCAS, the University Central Application Service. Your college library will have their prospectus which details all of the undergraduate courses currently available at educational institutions across the UK.

- **Work experience** – is a valuable part of any individual's education. It can give you a taste of life in the industry or in that profession. It allows you to form opinions and may help to give your career some direction. Some colleges see work experience as an integral part of an academic course of study. Some undergraduate courses have a 'sandwich' year where there is the opportunity to work for a year in industry, sometimes overseas. From a hotel and tourism management course, students may be fortunate enough to gain work in hotels in the Far East, Hong Kong for example, or Australia and the United States.

  Employers like to see that you have undertaken placements that reflect your ambitions and goals. For example, if you wish to become a physiotherapist then you should have had some experience with a qualified physiotherapist at a clinic or hospital. Similarly if you want to go into teaching you should have gained some experience working with young children in an academic or learning environment.

- **The part-time route** – some people cannot undertake full-time academic study either because of financial or family commitments or simply because it does not suit them.

  These students undertake part-time courses of study either in the evening, at the weekend, during holiday periods, via The Open University or through other **distance learning** methods. These are correspondence courses where the learning materials are sent through the post and you are required to return completed assessments via the same method.

- **Day release** – many employers are keen for their workforce to learn new skills and will therefore encourage them to study by offering a day-release arrangement. On this basis you would spend one of your normal working days at the college. Many NVQ courses are completed in this manner.

- **On the job training** – while you are in the workplace doing a job you will learn new skills. Your supervisor, trainer or line manager will ensure that you are performing tasks in the correct way, while providing you with constant advice and guidance. There are a number of modern apprenticeships (MAs) which are three-year placements up to Level 3, that are now available within the industry whereby you will receive a minimum wage in return for education, training and accredited qualifications, usually NVQs.

Obtaining the right information and advice

You may well find that you are unsure or uncertain of your next move with regard to pursuing your career goals. You may know where you want to go but are not quite sure how to get there. Ask for advice and guidance from your course tutor or careers advisor.

Your first step is to find out what qualifications and experience you need in order to pursue a certain position or career. For example, if you want to become a teacher then you will have to go on to an undergraduate course of study (either a BA and a PGCE qualification or a BEd) for at least four years. You will have to exhibit a desire to work with children that should be reflected in the work placements you have taken up.

ACTIVITY

The qualifications and experience you need

Think about the career or job you want for yourself. Look back at the job advert you have collected. What is it? Have you sent for the job specifications? If not, do so now.

Do you know what qualifications and experience you need for the position? If so, write them down now. If not, who do you need to contact in order to find out what you need? Contact them and find out what you need.

Where are you now, where are you going?

Your next step is to compare your current qualifications with those required by the organisation.

You will need to analyse the qualifications you need in order to pursue your career goals. Make a list of your current qualifications and the qualifications you need.

Is it clear what you career goals are now?

Once you have identified the qualifications and experience you are lacking you need to set out to obtain them.

Securing work

There are a number of practical steps you can take in trying to secure work, be it permanent, full-time, part-time or even a work experience placement:

● Identify an organisation within a sector of the industry for whom you would consider working

● Identify the opportunities that are available – if there are no full-time positions, find out whether there are any part-time or casual vacancies and whether they operate some sort of waiting list? Depending on your circumstances and how much you want employment within that organisation, offer yourself on a voluntary basis. Show them how capable, dependent and diligent you are – it may well lead to paid employment

● Approach the organisation, usually in writing (a covering letter and copy of your Curriculum Vitae) explaining your current situation, aspirations and ambitions while identifying what you can give the organisation in return. Sell your enthusiastic and energetic qualities to a prospective employer

Producing a curriculum vitae

To obtain maximum visibility in the job market you need to produce a Curriculum Vitae (CV) that presents your skills, achievements and experience in such a way that it will get you into the 'yes, for interview' file as opposed to 'no, in the bin' file.

You should work on the premise that most employers during their search and selection process do not have a great deal of time available – the average time spent reading a CV is, one and a half minutes. A CV, like an application form, has a number of objectives, it is a marketing document, it is you that you are trying to sell so maximum impact is essential. A CV can be used in several ways. To:

1 Reply to advertised jobs, usually submitted alongside a covering letter, or to consolidate a completed application form.

2 Make speculative or ad hoc applications on the off chance that organisations may have vacancies.

3 Contact recruitment agencies who can then further your prospects by 'touting' your details to specific organisations with whom they are affiliated.

4 Develop contacts within a specific organisation or the industry and to get your name known.

Prior to compiling your CV you will need to identify those skills that you have developed, both within and outside of the education system, which could be relevant to the type of work which you are seeking. You should have already completed a personal skills audit.

Remember, a CV is not a place to be modest, sell yourself!

In compiling a CV you will need to dentify the skills you currently own, then list them in specific categories:

- Academic or vocational qualifications.
- Your work experience (full-time, part-time, seasonal and work placements).
- Other achievements such as, driving licence, Duke of Edinburgh's, First Aid Certificates, CSLA, sports coaching qualifications and others.
- Your abilities and leisure interests.
- If you are an athlete you may wish to have a distinct category, say 'Sporting History'.

Underneath the title Curriculum Vitae, you may wish to add a single paragraph entitled 'Profile', whereby you outline all of your best qualities, for example: 'Self motivated, positive and progressive young student having just attained an A grade profile. Hard working, conscientious and able to relate socially and professionally with colleagues. I am a successful team player.'

A CV could be structured in a number of different ways. A generic format must include the following information and could be laid out in the following manner.

Curriculum Vitae

Personal details

- name
- address
- contact telephone number(s)
- date of birth
- marital status

Education and qualifications

- Name of the most recent or current educational institution, the dates you attended and the qualifications you are about to or have obtained already and the grades achieved.

  If you are waiting for grades then simply mark them as 'due in ...' and state when expected. If there are predicted grades you could write down, mark them as 'predicted'.

- Name of any other educational establishment, say your secondary school, the dates you attended, the qualifications you obtained and the results.

You do not need to list your primary or junior schools.

Employment history

- List your current employment, the name of the organisation, job title and responsibilities.

For example:

2000 Part-time recreation assistant at The Olympia leisure centre in Wiltshire. The work involves the continual maintenance of a clean and safe environment in the changing rooms for the public

You need to do justice to the job you do, do not glorify it but explain what your responsibilities are. Do not just write, 'changing room cleaner'.

- Detail all other employment, be it part-time, full-time, seasonal or casual and work placements. Place these in chronological order with the most recent first.

Other achievements

- List these, again in chronological order of achievement and where possible, identify the dates achieved.

Leisure interests

- Do not just list these. Your interests cannot be related by a single word, explain them.

  For example:

  'I am a keen skier having been introduced to the sport by my parents when I was 9 and have now skied in seven different countries including New Zealand' or 'I enjoy outdoor activities and since leaving school have joined a mountain bike club in the New Forest'.

Referees

- Name two referees, a school contact and the other should be a work contact.
- Give their name, job title, work address and contact telephone number(s).

You must remember that your CV will be competing against dozens, possibly hundreds, of others, all of which will have like qualifications and abilities. In order to avoid the 'bin file', your CV needs to catch your prospective employer's attention.

Having your CV professionally produced may not be an option, but there are other mechanisms by which you can make your CV distinct. Word process your CV and use a professional typeface (Times New Roman or Arial). Use quality paper, perhaps of a slightly different colour to white – maybe cream or coffee coloured. Avoid offensive colours such as fluorescent pink or green. Make sure that it looks attractive, that it is easy to read and well laid out. Use no more than two pages of A4, any more and the employer may well be put off by unnecessary detail. Use power words such as *achieved, produced, established, implemented, formulated* and *independently*. Show your CV to a tutor, colleague or a careers counsellor, and have it checked for spelling, grammar and typing errors.

ACTIVITY

Constructing your own CV

You have spent time analysing your skills and experience, it is now time to place these within the structure of a CV. You do not have to use the generic format used in this text. Before putting your CV together have a look at other people's, your parents or a family member, your tutor.

When putting your CV together consider the actual positions, that is, the job adverts and specifications you have already received. Can you tailor it in any way to meet the specifications of the position?

Completing applications

It may be that in completing an application for a job you have to fill in an application form. These forms are essentially asking for the information contained within your CV. Make sure that you read the form before completing it.

Ideally you should photocopy the blank form first and complete your application in rough in order to make sure that you 'get it right' on the real form. Read the form and instructions carefully, it may ask you to complete it in block capitals or black ink. Forms which are not completed, as per the employer's instructions are often the first to head straight for the non-interview pile.

Most forms will often ask you to complete a personal statement. This is your opportunity to show your prospective employer who you are, what you can do and why you, above anyone else, are most suited for the position. A well-written personal statement may take some time and several attempts to perfect. Spending the time writing your personal statement says more than, you are 'interested in the job'. Remember each personal statement that you write should be different, it should be tailored to show that your skills and abilities can meet the needs of the organisation to which you are applying.

Preparing for interviews

Once you have been chosen or selected to go for interview you will have to prepare thoroughly. During the interview itself you may only have a few minutes to make a lasting impression. In preparing for the interview, you will have to do your homework, that is, there are a number of things that you should consider prior to the interview:

- You may well be asked to tell the interviewer about yourself. Design a three or four-sentence statement that describes your best skills and attributes, your drive, energy, enthusiasm and sense of commitment.

- Think of examples that illustrate your skills. For example, if an interviewer asks 'what are your strengths?' replying with 'I am a good leader' is not very descriptive. You need to explain this ability with specific reference to an instance you can share. For example, when you were leading a night walk during a Duke of Edinburgh expedition you were the designated map reader, responsible for navigating your way to the meeting place.This kind of response paints a picture for the interviewer of your skills in action.

- Practise interviewing with a tutor, careers advisor, parent or friend. Have them ask sample questions that you can respond to. Answering questions out loud will bring potential problems in your responses to light before the actual interview. Ask them to give you feedback on say your body language, non-verbal language or eye contact.

ACTIVITY

Your future

Through the study of this part of the text you should now be able to answer some key questions. Try and answer them with a simple yes or no.

If your answer is yes, then continue to answer the questions in more detail. If your answer is no, then you still need more help, advice, guidance and clarification in defining your career goals, ambitions and aspirations:

- Do I know what my strengths, weaknesses and interests are?
- Do I know what sectors of the industry I want to work in and what are available to me?
- Do I know what job opportunities there are, both for part-time, full-time, casual and permanent employment?
- Do I know what I have to do in order to pursue my career goals?

ASSESSMENT EVIDENCE

As part of the Investigating Leisure and Recreation Unit you are required to produce a range of assessment evidence.

The Unit specifications state that you need to produce the following:

● An investigation into the UK leisure and recreation industry.

● An investigation into employment opportunities in the leisure and recreation industry.

1 Investigation into the UK leisure and recreation industry

You have been commissioned by the Industry Standards Research Council to conduct an investigation into the recent history of one aspect of the leisure and recreation industry. They have suggested that your research may focus on one aspect of provision, that is, an activity, pursuit, pastime or sector within the industry. Examples you may wish to focus your research on could include activities such as squash, mountain biking, or more passive pursuits such as computing and IT. You may choose to focus on a broader remit, on provision such as home-based leisure, the video industry or on the recent advent of theme bars. These examples are not exhaustive and exist merely as a guideline for areas of study.

In order to conduct a thorough investigation into the history of your choice of provision, you will need to consider the growth of that provision and identify the range of variables currently influencing that provision (including the customer and the competition). You will need to identify how your example of provision relates to and compares with other provision within the industry. Your investigation should:

● Include a full description of provision within the industry, more specifically identifying how your focus provision compares with the leisure and recreation industry generally.

● Account for the rapid development of that provision since the 1960s. You should consider technological and socio-economic developments.

● Identify the scale and significance of that provision in relation to other aspects of areas of provision within the industry. You may wish to make reference to participation rates over the 30-year period and identify whether participation trends show a general incline, decline or constant pattern. You should also refer to its economic and social significance.

● Identify whether provision within your area of focus is led mainly by the commercial, public or voluntary sector.

- Comment on the future for that provision in relation to the industry generally and identify the factors or variables that may impact upon its development in the future.

Conducting your investigation

In conducting your investigation you must consider that:

- Your investigation should be well structured, designed and professionally conducted.
- Findings may be presented in either a report, written document or oral presentation.
- Findings must be objective, supported by valid evidence, data and statistics.
- You must make accurate comparisons and distinctions between provision in your focus area and provision generally within the industry.
- Findings should be reinforced with industry-led examples where appropriate.

2 Investigation into employment opportunities in the industry

You are required to produce an investigation into a range of employment opportunities, ones conceivably that you would consider applying for and taking up, if employment were offered to you. Equally you may find a range of positions attractive, ones for which you are not yet appropriately qualified but could be with the correct training and education. Do not disregard these opportunities.

There are three distinct stages to this investigation:

1 In order to identify a range of positions you should consider opportunities from across the leisure and recreation spectrum. You will have to consult a variety of sources in order to find those opportunities (these are listed on page 51 of this Chapter). These opportunities should reflect diversity in order to allow you to make an informed choice about appropriate progression.

2 You should consider opportunities from a range of contrasting organisations which reflect different employment and career opportunitiues. You may find a temporary position aboard a cruise liner as attractive as a job which offers life long opportunities and progression for the 'right person'. In order to assess the merits of each position you should obtain the specifications, details and requirements of the post.

3 You should be able to evaluate the merits of the position and clearly explain why and how that position matches your personal circum-

stances, abilities and aspirations. You should produce and tailor a Curriculum Vitae in order to make a realistic application.

Key Skills

In completing the assessment for this unit, you can achieve the following key skills. These will be accredited at the discretion of your tutor on the basis of the quality of work you submit.

COMMUNICATION, LEVEL 3

C3.2 Read and synthesise information from two extended documents about a complex subject. One of these documents should include at least one image.

C3.3 Write two different types of documents about complex subjects. One piece of writing should be an extended document and include at least one image.

2

Safe Working Practices in the Leisure and Recreation Industry

Aims and Objectives

Through the study of this Unit you will have the opportunity to:

- **consider the emphasis placed on safe working practices and the importance of working within the law**
- **research the range and significance of Health and Safety legislation and regulations imposed on organisations in order to ensure a safe working environment**
- **understand the principle of risk assessment in terms of identifying actual and potential health and safety hazards**
- **understand the need to ensure a safe and secure working environment**
- **identify the measures organisations must have in place to ensure security in leisure and recreation**

❝I was at the front of the channel, and could see that people were being crushed and were suffering. I ask, pleaded, with a copper to open the gates. I received no response. Some who tried to climb out were pushed back in, maybe to die!❞
(Hillsborough Survivor)

On 15 April 1989, 96 Liverpool fans lost their lives and many more were injured as 5,000 football fans attempted to enter the Leppings Lane terraces at Sheffield's Hillsborough Stadium.

Tragedies such as this across Britain's sports arenas have been thrust into the public eye as a result of the massive media coverage afforded each of these events and witnessed by those who were there. In response governing bodies have been forced to take action to prevent further incidents, but still we grieve as such accidents continue to happen.

The purpose of this Chapter is to draw your attention to the real meaning of health and safety and its implications in the world of sport and recreation.

Introduction

An essential function of all leisure and recreation organisations (public, private and voluntary), is the provision of a safe, controlled and managed environment for its staff and customers.

The leisure and recreation industry incorporates a wide and diverse field of activities, spanning organised games, rambling, parachuting, water sports and much more, as investigated in Chapter 1. The health and safety of those employed to supervise or provide these activities is protected through health and safety legislation. This legislation also places a 'duty of care' on employers and providers to ensure that members of the public are not put at risk as a result of the work or conduct of their employees.

Because of the wide and diverse nature of the leisure and recreation industry each organisation, each facility or venue and each sport is responsible for its own unique health and safety requirements – motor racing is one such example.

CASE STUDY *Motor racing*

For 12 years the sport of Formula One Motor Racing had experienced a relatively safe period, but the 1994 season brought with it tragedy. The deaths of Roland Ratzenberger and Ayrton Senna during the same weekend at the San Marino Grand Prix (Imola), sent shock waves through the motor racing world and the governing body, International Motor Sport Federation (FIA).

Despite the meticulous planning and preparation and the existing safety codes within the sport, the Tamburello Curve at Imola proved to be fatal. A sport, which had experienced no fatalities since the death of Ricardo Paletti in Montreal 1982, was now suddenly faced with a double tragedy.

Sport can be inherently dangerous, whether you are competing or spectating:

- In 1995 during a cricket match between India and New Zealand, a wall collapsed at the Nagpur cricket ground, killing eight fans and injuring 50
- The infamous 1933 Ashes Test Series between Australia and England, known for 'Body-line' bowling instigated by Douglas Jardine with Harold Larwood as his strike bowler, caused controversy about gentlemanly conduct and ethical spirit within the game
- In the world of athletics, the South African born British athlete Zola Budd, notably remembered for the collision with Mary Decker in the

DID YOU KNOW?

Managing Health and Safety in Swimming Pools 1999, **published by the Health and Safety Committee (HSC) and Sport England, with support from the Scottish, Welsh and Northern Ireland sports councils, replaced the previous guidelines of 1988.**

Olympic 3,000 m, was constantly followed by anti-apartheid protesters, who even stepped out in front of her while she was racing.

- Equestrianism is notorious for accidents, injuries and a significantly high incidence of horse fatalities. During one event alone, Badminton 1992, three horses were reported to have died while attempting the cross-country course in appalling weather which had made the ground treacherous. Indeed, it was likened on the day to attempting to ride a horse on an ice rink. Four riders died during the 1999 season with the most recent being 38-year-old Simon Long, who died after his horse fell at a fence during the Burghley Horse Trials in September 1999.

- Accidents are not just limited to land-based sports, water provides its own dangers. During the 1993 British Grand Prix of the world power boat championships, six competitors were taken to hospital as a result of accidents including running aground on rocks and barrel-rolling at 130 miles an hour.

In order to consolidate your understanding of the range of provision within the industry, the following facilities are included:

Sports and leisure centres

Sports and leisure centres provide a variety and mixture of both wet and dry facilities, including a range of equipment requirements, all of which

Crowded arenas pose many health and safety issues

Source: *Corbis*

may expose participants and employees to potential risks. Water facilities provide their own high-risk situations. Updated 1999 regulations covering the management of swimming pools provide guidance about these risks.

Indoor entertainment complexes

Indoor entertainment complexes include facilities such as sports stadia, theatres, concert halls, conference facilities and cinemas, all accommodating large volumes of people at any one time. The implications of housing thousands of people at any one time can cause significant health and safety concerns, for example, the Hillsborough disaster which no one could have foreseen at the time.

Outdoor activities/adventure sports

All staff must be fully trained and qualified in their area of expertise and delivery. Sports and activities such as rock climbing, mountaineering, sailing and canoeing pose potentially dangerous situations and the hazards and risks inherent within some of these activities could prove to be life threatening. The provision of these and other activities to persons under the age of 18, governed by legislation since 1996, now requires the provider to obtain a licence from the Adventure Activities Licensing Authority. The call for provision of such legislation was a direct consequence of the Lyme Bay canoe tragedy.

Voluntary organisations

The ad hoc nature of some voluntary leisure and recreation provision can lead to gaps and infringements of the health and safety regulations. However, all providers, even those whose activities are run solely by volunteers, for example sports clubs, are still required to provide a duty of care towards the participants. Some organisations such as English Heritage and The National Trust put health and safety high on their priority agenda.

Transport operators

Trains, airlines, ferry companies, bus and coach companies all have a duty to ensure that their vehicles and equipment are safely maintained and in full operational condition and that emergency facilities and procedures are clearly understood and enforced. For example, in the Zeebrugge ferry disaster, the passenger ship the *Herald of Free Enterprise* contravened all existing regulations when she left port with her bow doors still open.

Catering facilities

Alongside the immense variety and number of restaurants, bars and clubs that exist within the industry there are a significant number of leisure and recreation facilities and services which include a catering division or centre. Regardless of the size of the facility, personnel who come into contact with food products destined for the public, must follow a number of food storage and handling guidelines, regulated by the Food Safety Regulations 1995.

DID YOU KNOW?

A pub on church grounds is not allowed to open on Sundays.

ACTIVITY

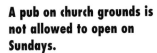

A risky business

For each of the leisure and recreation groupings defined, identify either a local or known provider and highlight the potential health and safety risks and concerns.

Produce a table fully illustrating your findings and group together the most significant and frequent risks.

Plot your results in a graph and compare.

Questions to consider

Which organisations, activities or sports present the greatest risks and potential hazards and why?

Working within the law

The Health and Safety Executive estimates that the annual cost to UK industries from working unsafely is between £11 and £16 billion with most of these costs being uninsured. Although most leisure and recreation facilities and providers address health and safety issues, the potential loss either financially or through image, prestige, or customer loyalty and trust can be great.

There are a number of insurance companies, commonly referred to in the United States as 'ambulance chasers', which offer facilities to actively chase compensation from other companies for negligence on a 'no win, no fee' basis. This concept is becoming ever more popular with the advent of e-mail and e-commerce. It is imperative that those individuals within the industry responsible for the provision of health and safety arrangements (usually a management concern), communicate these throughout their organisation. Poor communication and management control can lead to detrimental effects and repercussions on the:

- Organisation
- Staff
- Customers
- Environment

The incidence of fatalities within organisations is shown in Figure 2.1.

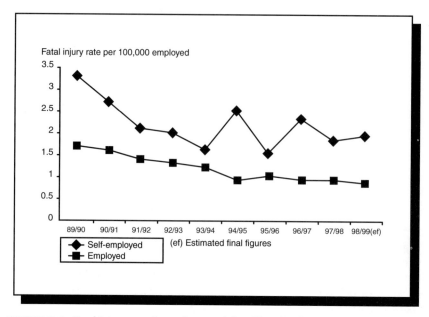

FIGURE 2.1 *Fatal injury rates for employees and the self-employed 1989/90–1998/99*

Source: *HSE Safety Statistics Bulletin*

The graph suggests that the rate of fatal injuries occurring at the workplace is visibly decreasing during the period 1989/90 – 1998/99. The rates are the lowest since the introduction of RIDDOR (Reporting Injuries, Diseases and Dangerous Occurrences Regulations) in 1986, however these rates are distorted since the revision of RIDDOR in 1995.

ACTIVITY

Is every tragedy an accident?

In recent years there has been a spate of tragedies, some of which are listed below, you are required to investigate one of these tragedies:

- 2 January 1971:   Ibrox Park stadium collapse
- 12 May 1985:   Bradford City football stadium fire
- 29 May 1985:   Heysel stadium
- 22 August 1985:   Manchester Airport fire
- 6 March 1987:   Herald of Free Enterprise sank
- 19 August 1987:   Hungerford shooting
- 18 November 1987: King's Cross underground station fire
- 15 April 1989:   Hillsborough football stadium disaster
- 1 May 1994:   San Marino Grand Prix Ayrton Senna death
- 30 July 1994:   Benetton pit fire

Questions to consider

Identify the possible causes and the people affected by these incidents, for example, the general public, participants and the providers.

How could such accidents have been avoided? What action has been taken since these events to reduce further risk?

The organisation

With so many high profile health and safety incidents reaching the many modes of media today, leisure and recreation providers cannot neglect health and safety issues and treat them simply as an additional task or system to conform to. Health and safety needs to underpin the decision making process within all industries, and with today's organisations welcoming more and more freelancers/contractors within their environment and attracting greater numbers of customers, a coherent and well practised health and safety policy needs to be in place and strictly adhered to.

It is the employer's responsibility to identify and control actual and potential risks to health and safety that arise from the work or environment. Employers are also bound by law to make provision for employee welfare. Their arrangements and considerations must take into account the following:

KEY TERMS

Risk: A risk entails the likelihood of injury, damage or harm arising, taking into account any preventative measures already in place.

Source: *AMT International*, 1996

- Which employee is responsible for which type of work and the risks associated with that position
- The training requirements and needs of employees in order to perform their roles competently
- The supervision of staff in the performance of their duties and the extent to which supervision is required
- The equipment within the organisation, that is, its purpose and use and who is responsible for its operation
- The type of protective clothing required and its condition
- Material specification and the working environment

These regulations are listed in the Health and Safety at Work Act 1974, which is looked at in more depth later on in the Chapter.

All organisations should be aware that non-compliance or negligence on behalf of the employer can lead to temporary closure of the facility or worse, which will result in a poor reputation and a possible increase in insurance premiums.

The staff

Employees have a responsibility and duty to take care of themselves and other people who may be affected by their work or conduct, as well as cooperate with their employers. It has been suggested that the employer is legally responsible for, and obliged to set up and monitor, the operation of health and safety systems and procedures. Once these are in place, the employee is required to adhere to these regulations and act in a responsible manner.

The conduct of an employee directly affects the safety of the customer or user. Employees must ensure that they cooperate with the employer and the stated rules and regulations to ensure a safe environment for themselves and the customers.

Customers

Employers should have in place mechanisms that identify hazards or potential risks to all people within or who enter their organisation. The interpretation of legal and regulatory requirement infers that the safety of all customers and visitors to leisure and recreation sites is an organisation's top priority. Customers should be given the opportunity to voice their opinions on the quality of service provided and the level of health and safety measures. These comments can prove to be invaluable to the employer and employee, sometimes highlighting possible risks and accidents before a serious incident occurs.

The increase in personal injury claims against organisations, such as those received by Claims Direct, indicates the changing nature of society and underlines the importance of the provision of protection towards leisure and recreation users. Insurance companies acknowledge that prevention is better than cure and that measures like this will enhance the reputation of the company and provide the customer with a much better experience and a higher level of customer service.

The environment

Potential damage to the environment by organisations and their associated activities must be measured. Often public rights protesters and action groups highlight possible environmental impacts likely to be caused by the introduction of a new leisure and recreation facility. For example, 'Swampy' became nationally recognised as the spokesperson against the Newbury by-pass and the destruction to the environment, which would be caused by this development. Changing farming methods (intensive farming) and the use of the public footpath system around Britain by the Ramblers Association provide many case studies highlighting the conflict between industry and recreational use of land.

These and many other factors need to be considered, including noise and air pollution, traffic congestion, erosion of the natural environment, and waste disposal, for example, toxic substances. The reclamation of 'Brown Sites' which can be seen as a positive benefit of re-utilising old industrial grounds, can generate numerous health problems. Examples include housing developments being built upon old chemical waste sites. Developers may need to carry out an environmental impact assessment before commencing their project to identify potential hazards and develop contingency plans.

Strict measures against these need to be implemented and monitored, based upon the advice of agencies such as the Health and Safety Executive, local Environmental Health Department and the National Rivers Association.

ACTIVITY

Public safety

Examine Table 2.1 below.

The figures relate to injuries reported to local authorities by employers and others under RIDDOR (Reporting Injuries, Diseases and Dangerous Occurrence Regulations)

KIND OF ACCIDENT	1991/92	1992/93	1993/94	1994/95	1995/96	1996/97	TOTAL
Contact with moving machinery or material being machined	–	1	–	1	1	6	9
Struck by moving inc. flying/ falling object	4	3	4	8	6	68	93
Struck by moving vehicle	16	20	7	4	6	30	83
Strike against something fixed or stationary	4	13	12	16	20	113	178
Injured whilst handling, lifting or carrying	–	–	7	11	6	9	33
Slip, trip or fall on same level	156	317	325	364	387	448	1997
Fall from a height	68	182	172	247	263	341	1273
Drowning or asphyxiation	–	4	3	2	3	1	13
Exposure to or contact with harmful substance	–	2	–	–	2	11	15
Exposure to fire	2	1	–	2	–	1	6
Injured by an animal	4	7	3	5	5	28	52
Other kind of accident	12	24	9	16	9	21	91
Total	**266**	**574**	**542**	**676**	**708**	**1077**	**3843**

Under RIDDOR 95 a non-fatal injury to a member of the public was widened to include such things as 'taken to hospital'

TABLE 2.1 *Major injuries to members of the public by kind of accident, 1991/92–1996/97*

Source: *HELA 1998, GSS*

Identify the kinds of accidents that occurred and discuss how these may have happened and how they could have been avoided.

Using the data from the above table, construct a graph to analyse the trend in injuries to the public from 1991/2 – 1996/7.

Questions to consider

Discuss the health and safety aspects of residents living adjacent to a major airport. What regulations does the airport need to consider?

Provide examples of measures taken to reduce the risk and discomfort towards the local population.

Health and safety legislation and regulations

Accidents do not just happen. They can be prevented and should be prevented.

The workplace or any entertainment facility, for example sports stadium, theatre and recreation environment, should not present a high risk of injury. However, this is not always the case. This was highlighted earlier in the Chapter, by one of the worst days in the history of Merseyside. Liverpool was set to play Nottingham Forest in the semi-final of the FA Cup at the Hillsborough Stadium. As thousands of fans gathered outside, the gates opened allowing many supporters into an already crowded Leppings Lane End. Many investigations into the incident have revealed inconclusive reports as to the actual occurrences, but the facts speak for themselves, as 96 Liverpool supporters died that day, crushed by the shear volume of people.

Health and safety is common sense, we can *all* be aware of hazards and follow established safety rules and regulations. Accidents can be avoided.

Health and Safety in the leisure and recreation industry is maintained though a range of practices and procedures. Legislation, mainly coming from from the Health and Safety at Work Act 1974 (Health and Safety at Work (NI) order 1978), govern these procedures and set the guidelines for leisure and recreation managers and providers. The collectively known 'Six Pack Regulations', introduced in 1992 are now all in place and they play a major role in the implementation and enforcement of health and safety law.

Role of agencies who enforce legislation

There are a number of agencies, as well as local authorities that are involved in the provision and enforcement of legislation and regulations.

Health and safety commission (HSC)

The introduction of the Health and Safety at Work Act 1974 (came into

Health & Safety Executive logo

The HSE carried out a full investigation into the Ladbroke Grove Rail disaster in 1999.

effect 1975) modernised all existing health and safety laws, and created the Health and Safety Commission, which has overall responsibility for the control and development of health and safety in Britain (commonly known as HSW Act). The HSC oversees the health, safety and security of people at work and protects the general public from risks to their health and safety outside of the workplace.

Health and safety executive (HSE)

The HSE are under the control of the HSC, and their responsibility is to enforce the HSW Act. They have the right to enter workplace premises at any reasonable time and carry out a full examination, including interviewing employees, taking samples of products, photographs, and in the case of imminent danger, they have the right to seize any substance or article and destroy it or make it harmless.

If contravention of any of the HSW procedures is discovered the HSE inspector can take any of the following actions:

- **Give advice** – it is better to prevent accidents, than to prosecute. Enforcement officers will give advice and guidance on improving work Health and Safety.

- **Serve an Improvement Notice** – if a contravention of the act has occurred an improvement notice can be served, giving a limited time period during which the appropriate action should be taken for compliance with the contravention.

- **Serve a Prohibition Notice** – in dangerous circumstances, a person issued with a prohibition notice must stop work straight away, until the specified action required to remedy the situation is completed and the risk is rewarded.

- **Prosecution** – further to the advice, Improvement Notice or Prohibition Notice, employees, employers and the self-employed found to be contravening the Act or any of its regulations may be prosecuted, resulting in a fine and or possible imprisonment.

The maximum fine for a case heard in the Magistrates court is £20,000, for cases in higher courts, the fine is limitless. Imprisonment for up to a maximum sentence of two years may be served.

On 5 March 1999, Dunlop Tyres Ltd were fined £100,000 and ordered to pay £2,855 in court costs following the death of an employee who became entangled in heavy machinery at the Dunlop Erdington site. Dunlop Tyres Ltd contravened Section 2(1) of the Health and Safety at Work Act which states that:

❛It shall be the duty of every employer to ensure, so far as is reasonably practicable, the health, safety and welfare at work of all his employees.❜

Following the collapse of tunnels at Heathrow Airport's Central Terminal Area, part of the Heathrow Express rail link project, Balfour

Beatty Civil Engineering Ltd were fined £1.2 million. The biggest single fine for offences under the HSW Act.

Local authority

Local Authority Environmental Health officers work in parallel with HSE Inspectors, dealing with health and safety issues in shops, offices, the catering and hotel industry, leisure and services sector premises. They have the authority to carry out inspections using the same procedures as the HSE.

Where an individual premises carries out more than one activity, for example, a railway station, which includes retail, catering and transport, then this crosses the governing boundaries of both the HSE and LA. It is the main activity that determines the appropriate authority. An exception to this rule is that the HSE is the enforcing body in respect of all previously occupied facilities or those controlled by local authorities themselves, for example, local authority sports centres.

Health and safety law

There are two different types of law that you should be familiar with:

CIVIL LAW	CRIMINAL LAW
Employers have a duty to their employees to provide a reasonable standard of care. If a person is injured at work and feels it is the employer's fault, the employee can take the employer to court and sue for damages	This is set by Parliament. If a person breaks the law they can be punished. The police have the power to arrest suspected criminals and take them to court. In the area of occupational health and safety it is the Health and Safety Executive Inspectors and local authority Environmental Health Officers who can prosecute companies and individuals

Source: IEHO – *Basic Health and Safety at Work,* 1993

Legislation governing health and safety, can be divided under four main headings:

1 Acts of Parliament.
2 Regulations made under the Act.
3 Approved Codes of Practice.
4 Guidance.

These are discussed further following.

Acts of Parliament

Acts of Parliament are law, and must be adhered to. Government lawyers draft a Bill, which then proceeds through the following stages in Parliament:

- First Reading
- Second Reading
- Committee Stage
- Report Stage
- Third Reading
- House of Lords (who can delay a Bill for up to one year)
- Royal Assent

The Bill then becomes Law.

The HSW 1974 is an enabling Act and is supported by Regulations, Approved Codes of Practice (ACOP) and other guidance material.

Regulations made under the act

Regulations made under the original Act are generally compulsory, and must be obeyed and carry the same penalties as the act. However, regulations such as Manual Handling Operation Regulations 1992, Safety Representation and Safety Committee's Regulations and the Safety Signs and Signals Regulations 1996, lay down a bill for rights which may be claimed by those for whose protection they have been enacted.

Approved codes of practice (ACOP)

Approved codes of practice provide practical guidance about how to comply with the legal requirements of the Act and related legislation, including Regulations. No one can be prosecuted for failing to follow the guidance. However, if a breach of the code is alleged, then it is up to the defendant to demonstrate how they have satisfactorily complied with the requirements in some other way.

Therefore it is good practice to actively follow the respected ACOP, as auditable evidence will be far more easy to produce in a Court of Law if legal proceedings are taken against any breach of requirements.

ACTIVITY

Always read the instructions first

Every sports facility will have a number of accepted codes of practice established and incorporated as standard working practices. These codes will relate to the range of activities offered.

Investigate the ACOP within your local sports facility.

What advice does the code give concerning the following sporting activities:

- trampolining
- swimming
- athletics

Guidance

The HSE publish guidance notes refer to procedures on how to deal with various Health and Safety Activities, for example, *Health and Safety at Motor Sports events: A guide for employers and organisers*. This was brought out in January 1999 and looks at legislation safety issues such as:

- pre-event planning
- track or course design
- safe storage and use of fuel
- first aid procedures
- spectator safety

The guidance notes are not mandatory but are based on practical experience and historical events, indicating the way in which the enforcing authority (HSE and LA) expect the employer/organiser to meet the Health and Safety requirements.

The above guidelines do not cover Formula One events, the Fédération Internationale de l'Automobile provides such guidance. In the aftermath of the Imola tragedy, the £1 million facelift on the Silverstone track prior to the British Grand Prix July 1994, turned it into one of the safest Formula One circuits in the world. Work which took only 18 days to complete included the introduction of bigger gravel traps and run-off areas. Four of the fastest corners were made tighter, thus forcing drivers to slow down, making the whole track slower but more exciting as the opportunity for over-taking increased.

Damon Hill's track record of 1 minute 22.51 seconds in 1993 was never challenged by Michael Schumacher's qualifying time of 1 minute 26.32 seconds in 1994, clearly demonstrating the effects these modifications had on the track, not to mention the changes imposed upon car dynamics.

Duty of care

Common Law imposes on all of us a duty to try and avoid injuring each other, whether employees, employers, sporting or social activities, even at home. Figure 2.2 shows the causes of child fatalities in the home.

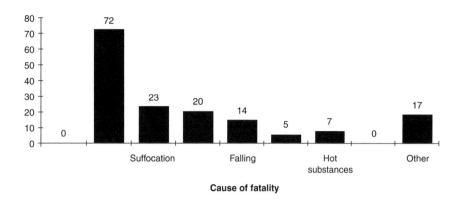

FIGURE 2.2 *Number of recorded child fatalities in the home, 1994*

Source: Data adapted from Home Accident Death Database (HADD), 1994

A duty of care insists that:

❝You must take reasonable care to avoid acts or omissions which you can reasonably foresee would be likely to injure your *neighbour.*❞

Your neighbour is further defined as:

❝Someone who is so closely and directly affected by my act that I ought reasonably to have them in contemplation as being affected when I am directing my mind to the acts or omissions which are called into question.❞
(Lord Aitken in the case of Donoghue vs Stevenson, 1932)

ACTIVITY

A case to study

Read the following case studies and discuss the outcomes.

Woodridge vs Summer, 1963

During a competition at the National Horse Show, the plaintiff took up a position at the edge of the arena, a suitable place to take photograph. Work of Art, a competing horse, ridden by Ron Holladay, came down the far side of the course, rounded the head at high speed, then galloped, apparently out of control down the edge of the course, where the plaintiff was standing. In fright, the plaintiff attempted to pull another spectator out the way of the oncoming horse, but he fell back into the horse's path and was seriously hurt.

Amazingly, the horse returned, and won!

The resulting court case held that the rider had been negligent in allowing the horse to go so fast, and in attempting to bring the horse back on course, when there were people in the way. This demonstrates a duty of care to his neighbour, that is, in this case, spectators in close proximity.

Denier vs Heaney, 1985

A group of tourists go on a day outing to Mallorca's Santa Ponsa go-kart track, the plaintiff is very unsure of himself in the go-kart, and very slowly crawls around the edge of the track. The defendant, who seems far more experienced or confident, is going as fast as possible, similar to many other participates at the time. The defendant makes an error of judgement and collides with the plaintiff, who suffers a hand injury.

The defendant was held liable for £5,500 plus costs.

Questions to consider

Do you agree that the defendants displayed duty of care, or were they being negligent?

Employer/employee responsibilities

Health and safety at work act 1974 (HSW)
The act was introduced in 1974 and replaced numerous laws dating back to the first occupational health and safety legislation in 1802. The act clearly states that 'we' all have a duty and responsibility for health and safety, it is an essential element of work, not an option.

The act pertains to everyone at a workplace, including neighbours, passers by and customers (that covers all people using a sports centre or stadium), but excluding staff in domestic premises and some of the armed forces. The 1974 Act provides legislation for the protection of almost 8 million people in occupations that had previously not been covered, including the self-employed, education, areas of the Leisure and Tourism industry, and the Health Service.

DISCUSSION

What is the difference between Civil and Criminal Law?

The purpose of the act is not to give step-by-step instructions, but to encourage and stimulate high standards of health and safety and to protect people from coming to harm.

Unlike Civil Law, which only comes into force as a result of an injured party taking action after an accident or dangerous occurrence, the Health and Safety at Work Act 1974 provides the legislative framework and the appropriate tool towards accident prevention.

Duty of employers
The majority of the responsibility for health and safety in the workplace is placed upon the employers. As far as is reasonably practicable, it is the duty of the employer to oversee the Health, Safety and Welfare of all those within the workplace. This duty extends to all people who may come into contact or be affected by the operation *and* running of the organisation or facility, for example contractors, freelancers, customers, guests and other members of the general public.

To achieve this, employers must comply with the stipulations of the Act and are obliged to provide the following:

1 Safe plant, machinery, equipment and appliances, including safe methods for handling, storing and transporting of material.
2 Ensurance that work systems and practices are safe.
3 Monitoring the health and safety of the work environment.
4 Provision of a written health and safety policy if they employ five or more people.
5 Provision of adequate information, training instructions and supervision to all staff in matters relating to health and safety.
6 Provision of safe access to and exit from working premises.

Duty of employees

Under the HSW Act, employees have the duty to:

1 Take reasonable care of themselves and anyone else who may be affected by what they do at work.
2 Cooperate with the employer with health and safety issues at all times.
3 Not interfere with, either intentionally or recklessly, or misuse anything intended for health and safety welfare, for example fire extinguishers, alarms, buoyancy aids.

If an employee's actions cause someone to have an accident, the employee could be held responsible and prosecuted.

European union (EU) directives

The 'Six Pack', a set of six health and safety at work regulations came into effect in 1993, as part of the continuing modernisation of the UK law. This modernisation involves the replacement and updating of previous confusing and outdated legislation. The EU directives are part of the move towards a single European market.

Modern laws, for example, COSHH (Control of Substances Hazardous to Health) have not been significantly affected by regulations, and the changes to the UK Leisure and Recreation industry should not be too immense if they are currently complying with the HSW Act.

Health and safety management

The Management of Health and Safety at Work Regulations 1992, require a risk assessment to be undertaken to identify the hazards and take the necessary steps to reduce the risk of an incident (refer to Risk Assessment on page 105). Further to these requirements the 1992 regulations enforce the legislation laid down by the HSW Act, as identified earlier.

Employers are obliged to assess the risks at work and take measures to prevent or reduce them. That is, the

● Provision of effective health and safety management arrangements, for example, the production of a health and safety manual.

- Designation of competent personnel for health and safety purposes, for example, designated health and safety officer.
- Provision of staff training, for example, first aid certificate or RLSS Pool Lifeguard Award.
- Consultation with their employers or representation of union representative, for example, a health and safety committee.
- Implementation and training and emergency arrangements, for example, fire drills, bomb alerts and evacuation procedures.

Under these regulations, the employers and the self-employed, have to make a suitable and sufficient assessment of the risks to anyone who might be affected by the work activity. Arrangements need to be introduced, that is, the planning, organisation, control, monitoring and review of protective and preventative measures.

Upon recruitment employees must receive adequate health and safety training, which should be periodically updated to take account of new or changed risks. This training must take place during work hours. These arrangements also need to be extended to temporary workers, for example, contractors. It is the organisation's responsibility to ensure that all individuals receive appropriate information and instruction, including identification of 'nominated' persons for emergency procedures.

ACTIVITY

Comparative safety

Investigate the emergency procedures at your school or college, compare them with the procedures at a local sports centre.

Do they follow the same basic procedures, for example, for fire drills or bomb scares.

Workplace conditions

The Workplace Regulations (Health, Safety and Welfare) 1992, force employers to accept responsibility for workplace conditions and in doing so stipulate broad areas for both physical and personal comfort. Employers are expected to adhere to these stipulations. The six areas of focus are discussed here:

1   The temperature within indoor workplaces must be kept reasonable within every room inside which people are employed to work. A minimum temperature of 16 °C (60 °F) needs to be attained within the first hour of work. The word reasonable is used, as some work areas, for example swimming pools, or areas which include computers, photocopiers and other electronic equipment, are normally much higher, if not double. If people work outside or in work areas that require temperatures to be kept high or low, special clothing is required, as stipulated in the PPE Work Regulations 1992. All rooms also need to

maintain a constant flow of clean, ventilated air, and should be well lit, wherever possible using natural light so as to reduce eye fatigue, headaches and possible drowsiness.

2 Employees come in all shapes, sizes, height, weight and strengths. The workplace environment and the equipment within it must be designed to suit the work that is taking place, and decrease the risk of injury to employees. Swivel chairs must have five feet to ensure stability and work benches should be designed to allow a comfortable sitting position, with plenty of leg room. Overcrowding can lead to high stress levels, thus adequate space needs to be provided.

3 The workplace regulations state that there should be enough floor area, light and unoccupied space to ensure health, safety and welfare. At least 11 cubic metres per person is recommended, this excludes any space above three metres from the floor.

4 The passage of pedestrians and vehicles across all floors, passageways and stairs must be kept in good repair. All stairways must be fitted with guard-rails and free from obstruction, and areas in the proximity of any machinery must be securely fenced and adequately guarded against possible injuries.

5 General facilities such as toilets (separate male and female are normally expected) should be kept clean and well maintained, and drinking water and hand washing facilities with hot and cold water must always be available.

6 Other areas required include rest facilities, which should have smoke-free zones and facilities for pregnant woman and nursing mothers. Housekeeping is paramount, to ensure compliance with all of the above. Premises should be kept reasonably tidy and equipment stored correctly including clothing.

DISCUSSION

Read the passages concerning workplace conditions and highlight the major areas of concern.

Divide these areas of concern into four distinct areas.

Think about your workplace or workspace. Are there any of these four areas which need attending to? What are they? What needs to be done?

ACTIVITY

Workplace design

Outline the layout and design of your classroom or other work space, perhaps the space in which you operate at your workplace.

Can you redesign the space to create a better working environment. In planning a new work area you will need to commit a range of ideas to paper before deciding on one that could work.

Present your findings to the group. You will need to be able to explain and justify the design of the new workplace.

Manual handling of loads

In the UK, it is estimated that approximately 54 million working days are lost through injuries to the back, and the annual cost to society in terms of lost output and medical treatment has been estimated at between £110 m – £130 m (IEHO93).

Research undertaken by Professor Frostick in 1999 and funded by the

HSE concluded that manual handling injuries are not typical in the leisure context, suggesting that the working environment, for example construction and manual work, and work practices play a significant part in their causation, yet manual handling provides many risks within leisure and recreation.

ACTIVITY

Too heavy to handle!

In groups, select a sector of the leisure and recreation industry on which to focus.

List situations which would require the lifting or handling of heavy, difficult or awkward objects, for example, luggage, stationery equipment, gas cylinders, liquids, barrels and in some instances, people.

Discuss the precautions which could be taken to eliminate the risk of injury and avoid employees manually handling heavy loads.

Where employees cannot avoid the handling of heavy goods, design a step-by-step guide of how to lift and avoid injury. Often instructions can be just as useful in pictures or images as this gives the reader a mental picture of how to do it.

DID YOU KNOW?

Manual handling regulations do not set exact limits, such as the load an individual can lift, their objectives are to reduce the incidence of lifting injuries.

The Manual Handling Operations Regulations 1992, has been consolidated by the more recent Provision and Use of Work Equipment Regulations 1998 (PUWER98) and Lifting Operations and Lifting Equipment Regulations 1998 (LOLER98). These apply specifically to work equipment used in all industry sectors ranging from construction, agriculture, health care and education. They stipulate that as far as is reasonably practicable, employers should avoid the need for employees to manually handle loads (baggage) at work which involves a risk of being injured. In order to achieve this, employers must make suitable and sufficient assessment of any manual handling operation. If it is not possible to avoid the handling operation, which may involve a risk of injury, the employer is required within 'reasonable practicalities', to reduce the level of risk.

The employer's assessment of manual handling operations, should consider the following:

- Task
  - Posture
  - Repetitive handling
  - Recovery time
  - Distance covered, carried
  - Distance held from trunk

- Load
  - Size
  - Shape
  - Weight
  - Location of handles (if any)

- Environment   – Constraints on posture
                     – Ground/floor surface
                     – Lighting, weather

- Individual Capability – Need for training
                         – Physical characteristics

- Other factors   – Protective clothing

The continual and repetitive actions carried out by checkout operations, have been linked to an estimated 1–2 million people being affected annually with musculoskeletal disorders. The main findings of the research conducted by the HSE in 1998 highlighted that belt-scan checkouts tended to be associated with fewer musculoskeletal disorders than those involving trolleys, tills and packing. These statistics have been the evidence base for the development of workstations within our supermarkets.

 **DID YOU KNOW?**

Personal Protective Equipment (PPE) at Work Regulations 1992 stipulates that high visibility clothing is mandatory for workers around aircraft.

PPE are always the last line of defence.

Personal protective equipment (PPE)

The PPE at Work Regulations 1992, outline the employer's last line of defence against risk within the workplace.

PPE includes most types of protective clothing and equipment such as safety harnesses, life jackets, high visibility clothing (HV), head, foot and eye protection. The type of PPE a person uses will depend upon the task, environment and potential risks associated within the situation.

Formula One motor racing dramatically exposed to the world the importance and life saving potential of PPE, following the controversial rule change during the 1994 season, which lifted the refuelling ban, (a practice that had been banned in Formula One since 1983). A horrific pit lane fire during the German Grand Prix engulfed Dutch driver Jos

Formula One pit fire   Source: *actionplus*

Verstappen along with five further team mechanics from the Benetton Pit Crew, all of whom amazingly escaped with only superficial burns, due to the efforts of other colleagues and the protective fire-proof clothing. Since this incident further safety precautions concerning protective clothing have been enforced by the FIA (Fédération Internationale de l'Automobile).

ACTIVITY

Dressed for the occasion

Look at the following sport and recreation activities. Choose two sports from each column and list the protective equipment required.

Archery	Rugby League	Association Football
Water Polo	Swimming	Horse Riding
Motor Cycling	Cycling	Mountaineering
Scuba Diving	Sailing	Abseiling
Canoeing	Clay Pigeon Shooting	Cricket batsman
Formula One	Bobsleigh	Parachuting

Some of the items you will list are not covered by the PPE regulations, however, they are taken for granted within the sport, yet participants rarely consider the safety aspects associated with them.

If you cannot think of what the safety clothing and equipment is then refer to photographs of that particular sport or activity to help you. You may also wish to contact the governing body of that sport, who would identify the safety clothing and equipment a participant requires.

Personal protective equipment, i.e. ear protection, gloves, etc

If PPE is an essential element of your work, such as high-visibility clothing, fire protection, ear and face guards, the employer must supply these free of charge. They also have a duty to:

- Ensure all PPE issued is suitable for the risk involved
- Maintain PPE in a clean state and working order, checking each item before issue
- Provide storage facilities for PPE when not in use
- Provide adequate information, instruction and training for use of PPE
- Supervise and ensure PPE is used correctly at all times when practicable

The control of substances hazardous to health regulations (COSHH)

Under COSHH, employers must assess the risk of exposure to all hazardous substances, which could be in the form of liquids, solids, dusts, powders and or gases. Employers must take steps to prevent employees or other persons being exposed, and if this is not possible, work practices must be introduced to limit the exposure time or intensity.

DID YOU KNOW?

There are around 2,000 cases of accidents involving chemicals at work reported every year.

Source: RoSPA *Occupational Safety Facts,* 1999

The COSHH regulations define 'hazardous substances' as ranging from very toxic, toxic, corrosive to irritant. The two main objectives of COSHH are to increase awareness of the hazards posed by chemicals and to promote their safe handling and storage.

A COSHH assessment follows the same principles as a Risk Assessment (see page 108), as employers must take the following steps:

1 Identify hazardous substances.
2 Identify who is at risk.
3 Evaluate the risk.
4 Introduce control measures.

ACTIVITY

The Acid Test

As the manager of a privately owned Health and Fitness Club, you have identified a range of substances. Carry out a COSHH assessment following the four steps above for each one:

- chlorine for the swimming pool
- toner for the photocopier
- creosote for external wood work
- scuba equipment
- mercury in blood pressure gauges
- weed killers and insecticides

The Signpost to The Health and Safety (Safety Signs and Signals) Regulations 1996, make it a requirement for all containers of dangerous substances to use the appropriate warning signs as illustrated in Figure 2.3.

TOXIC

CORROSIVE

HIGHLY FLAMMABLE

HARMFUL

OXIDISING

EXPLOSIVE

FIGURE 2.3 *Safety signs*

ACTIVITY

Control of chemicals

Contact the manager or Duty Officer at your local swimming pool. Investigate how they control the chemicals associated with the pool water, and what dangers are associated with the incorrect usage of these chemicals.

Work time regulations

The leisure and recreation industry is renowned for its long and unsociable working hours, one notable example, are Chefs within catering establishments. Originating from the 1993 European Community Directives, the Working Time Regulations came into force on 1 October 1998.

The 48-hour a week rule identified within these regulations has caused many misconceptions, as working time should be looked at over a 17-week period, during which the weekly average for any employee must not exceed 48 hours, although it is possible for an employee to voluntarily opt out of the regulation and have their employment contract amended accordingly.

The regulations also make provisions for breaks, with a 20-minute break away from the normal work station being stipulated for all employees whose daily working time exceeds 6 hours.

It is important for all leisure and recreation providers to implement and record these regulations. Other conditions, including holiday entitlement and health assessments for night workers, should also be recorded. Auditable records of the implementation of regulations prove responsibility to the HSE, who have the same powers of prosecution as under the HSW Act.

The flexible nature of the leisure and recreation industry will be affected by these regulations. In order to comply with the regulations, managers will need to plan carefully their current staffing rotas and make the necessary adjustments.

ACTIVITY

Still on duty

You are the manager of the local swimming pool which is open to the public from 7.00 a.m. to 8.00 p.m. seven days a week.

Using the regulations concerning maximum working hours and legally enforced breaks away from the work station, work out a rota and establish how many employees you will require to staff the following positions:

- minimum of two lifeguards on duty at all times
- receptionist
- male and female basket room attendants
- duty manager

Health and safety (first aid) regulations 1981

In terms of employer responsibility to employees and customers ensuring their own health and safety, this is probably the most important piece of legislation. These regulations set down the legal requirements of employers to provide adequate first aid provision for both employees and participants, that is, guests, visitors and spectators.

In high-risk occupations, a trained first aider is required if there are over 50 employees. In the case of leisure and recreation facilities, such as, sports stadiums, concerts and other venues which attract high volumes of people, the arrangements for first aid should take account of this. Often the organisers of large events will invite medical organisations such as the St Johns Ambulance to attend.

Under RIDDOR 1995 the Reporting of Injuries, Diseases and Dangerous Occurrences Regulations, an employer has the duty to inform the HSE or Local Authority of:

- fatal injuries
- non-fatal injuries, including major injuries such as dislocation of the knee, hip or shoulder and fractures, excluding fingers and toes. It also includes any injury resulting in an inability to do normal work for more than three days, with respect to employees.

Medical organisations are essential in mass participation events   Source: © *actionplus*

Health and Safety at Work Act 1974
The reporting of Injuries, Diseases and Dangerous Occurrences Regulations 1995

HSE
Health & Safety
Executive

Report of an injury or dangerous occurrence

Filling in this form
This form must be filled in by an employer or other responsible person.

Part A

About you

1 What is your full name?

2 What is your job title?

3 What is your telephone number?

About your organisation

4 What is the name of your organisation

5 What is its address and postcode?

6 What type of work does the organisation do?

Part B

About the incident

1 On what date did the incident happen?

         /   /

2 At what time did the incident happen?
(Please use the 24-hour clock eg 0600)

3 Did the incident happen at the above address?

Yes ☐ Go to question 4

No ☐ Where did the incident happen?
   ☐ elsewhere in your organisation - give the
     name, address and postcode
   ☐ at someone else's premises - give the name,
     address and postcode
   ☐ in a public place - give details of where it
     happened

If you do not know the postcode, what is
the name of the local authority?

4 In which department, or where on the premises,
did the incident happen?

Part C

About the injured person

If you are reporting a dangerous occurrence, go
to part F.
If more than one person was injured in the same incident,
please attach the details asked for in part C and part D for
each insured person.

1 What is their full name?

2 What is their home address and postcode?

3 What is their home phone number?

4 How old are they?

5 Are they
   ☐ male?
   ☐ female?

6 What is their job title?

7 Was the injured person (tick only one box)
   ☐ one of your employees?
   ☐ on a training scheme? Give details:

   ☐ on work experience?
   ☐ employed by someone else? Give details of the
     employer:

   ☐ self-employed and at work?
   ☐ a member of the public?

Part D

About the injury

1 What was the injury? (eg fracture, laceration)

2 What part of the body was injured?

FIGURE 2.4 *Form F2508 used for reporting injuries or dangerous occurrences*

3 Was the injury (tick the one box that applies)

☐ a fatality?

☐ a major injury or condition? (see accompanying notes)

☐ an injury to an employee or self-employed person which prevented them doing their normal work for more than 3 days?

☐ an injury to a member of the public which meant they had to be taken from the scene of the accident to a hospital for treatment?

4 Did the injured person (tick all the boxes that apply)

☐ become unconcious?

☐ need resuscitation?

☐ remain in hospital for more than 24 hours?

☐ none of the above.

Part E

About the kind of accident

Please tick the one box that best describes what happened, then go to Part G.

☐ Contact with moving machinery or material being machined

☐ Hit by a moving, flying or falling object

☐ Hit by a moving vehicle

☐ Hit something fixed or stationary

☐ Injured while handling, lifting or carrying

☐ Slipped, tripped or fell on the same level

☐ Fell from a height

How high was the fall?

| metres |

☐ Trapped by something collapsing

☐ Drowned or asphyxiated

☐ Exposed to, or in contact with, a harmful substance

☐ Exposed to fire

☐ Exposed to an explosion

☐ Contact with electricity or an electrical discharge

☐ Injured by an animal

☐ Physically assaulted by a person

☐ Another kind of accident (describe it in Part G)

Part F

Dangerous occurrences

Enter the number of the dangerous occurrence you are reporting. (The numbers are given in the Regulations and in the notes which accompany this form)

Part G

Describing what happened

Give as much detail as you can. For instance

- the name of any substance involved
- the name and type of any machine involved
- the events that led to the incident
- the part played by any people.

If it was a personal injury, give details of what the person was doing. Describe any action that has since been taken to prevent a similar incident. Use a separate piece of paper if you need to.

Part H

Your signature

Signature

Date

| / | / |

Where to send the form

Please send it to the Enforcing Authority for the place where it happened. If you do not know the Enforcing Authority, send it to the nearest HSE office.

For official use

Client number	Location number	Event number	☐ INV REP ☐ Y ☐ N

FIGURE 2.4 *(Continued)*

DISCUSSION

Reporting only 40% of injuries is very low, why do you think employers neglect the other 60%?

DID YOU KNOW?

Multiple injuries, fractures and concussion or internal injuries are the three most common types of fatal injury.

Source: HSE, 1999

Form F2508 (Figure 2.4) must be used for reporting these injuries and/or dangerous occurrences and sent to the HSE within ten days of the injury. Form F2508a needs to be completed in the case of an outbreak of work-related disease.

The 'key facts sheet' on injuries within the consumer and leisure service industry reported to local authorities 1991/92 to 1996/97, highlights a number of statistics . During this period there was a total of 2,674 non-fatal injuries to employees, from which 715 were major injuries within the sport and recreation industry alone. A further 3,594 non-fatal injuries to members of the public were reported.

The most common non-fatal injury to an employee resulted from a slip or trip either from a slippery surface, or obstructions, and importantly 78% of these injuries involved fractures mainly to the arm, shoulder or collar bone. The same trends are observed within injuries to the general public. The figures look high, but a labour force survey carried out by the HSE indicates that employers only report approximately 40% of non-fatal injuries to employees to the Local Authorities or HSE.

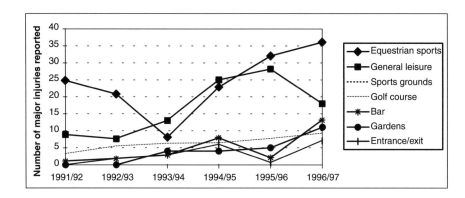

FIGURE 2.5 *Major injuries to employees 1991/92–1996/97*

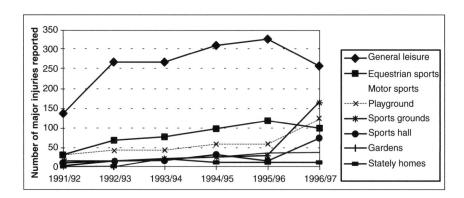

FIGURE 2.6 *Major injuries to members of the public 1991/92–1996/97*

Source: Graphs adapted from Government statistics in the HSE 1998 Key facts sheet on injuries within the consumer/leisure service industry reported to local authorities 1991/92–1996/97

DID YOU KNOW?

During the period 1991–97, 26 fatal injuries in the sport and recreation industry were reported to the HSE.

Source: HSE, 1999

Figures 2.5 and 2.6, adapted from the HSE Key Facts Sheet, illustrate the trend and quantity of reported major injuries to both employees and the general public within the sport and recreation industry.

Fatal injuries reported within the same period, spanning the consumer and leisure service industry are very low considering that in 1996/7 there were approximately 188,000 consumer/leisure service premises, employing around 896,000 people, attracting larger numbers of the general public each year. Does one assume that employers are rigorously enforcing legal and regulatory requirements or are they just lucky?

Indeed, the HSE report that under (RIDDOR 1985–95), businesses involved in sports and leisure activities, events, consumer activities such as hairdressing and laundries, and religious institutes, only 37 fatal injuries to either employees or self-employed members of the public had been reported.

Sport and recreation activities accounted for 26 of these fatalities. Of the 21 accidents involving the general public, circumstances surrounding the fatalities included:

- Falling from a height, for example, from a horse or pony.
- Being struck by a motor vehicle or other moving object.
- Drowning in swimming pools.

These reported figures are very low, as tragedies such as Lyme Bay, Hillsborough, Bradford and the Apex Cheviot Motor Rally alone account for 157 fatalities during the period 1985–2000.

Specific legislation affecting the leisure and recreation industry includes:

Adventure Activities Licensing Regulations 1996

Government regulations and legal requirements governing the duties and responsibilities of providers within the Outdoor Activities Industry were introduced in the wake of the of the Lyme Bay tragedy. Four sixth formers from Plymouth died after their canoes were swamped during a two-mile paddle across Lyme Bay towards Charmouth. They were killed during an organised school canoeing adventure expedition. Four other school friends, their teacher and two canoe instructors, were all rescued from the water after the four died from hypothermia and exhaustion.

CASE STUDY *The Lyme Bay canoe tragedy – what happened?*

At 10 a.m. on a sunny Sunday morning, two relatively insufficiently qualified canoe instructors who had only passed the British Canoe Union (BCU) one-star performance test, led a party of eight from the Southway Comprehensive School, Plymouth, on a two-mile paddle across Lyme Bay. The waves were about one metre high capped with white foam being whipped up by the Charmouth Funnel, a locally known phenomenon built up by wind being blow down through a gap in the hills.

Within the first 90 minutes the group, for whom this was their first experience of canoeing, having only had one basic lesson in the centre's swimming pool that morning, soon started experiencing difficulties out at sea. The Mirage Scout canoes, designed for river and surf and not novice sea tours, lacked decklines and ropes on the bow and stern which are used to assist righting canoes after capsizing. This made the boats difficult to handle in the sea conditions, in fact the accompanying teacher found it very difficult to keep his balance and kept capsizing. Without the provision of spray decks, water easily seeped into the canoes. Despite the efforts of the two instructors who attempted to raft the canoes together in pontoon fashion in order to stabilise the crafts, the Charmouth Funnel forced them to drift out into the open sea. Once in the open sea the increasingly bigger waves and swell swamped them and gradually all the canoes either sank or capsized, leaving the party of ten stranded and supported by life-jackets only.

One of the drifting canoes was spotted by a local fisherman, who hauled it aboard his boat and immediately radioed the coastguard at Weymouth. The coastguard had not been notified in advance of any trip across the bay, therefore was unable to recognise the scale of the tragedy, nor did the canoe have any distinguishing markings linking it to the St Albans Centre. Despite the party missing their 1.00 p.m. estimated arrival time at Charmouth, the Harbourmaster at Lyme Regis failed to report this to the coastguard until they spoke at 3.16 p.m. as the coastguard phoned around attempting to locate the owner of the canoe. By this time the party had been out at sea for approximately five hours in total. They were struggling for their lives, with the instructors battling against the elements trying to boost moral and resuscitate those who had fallen unconscious. It was not until about 5 p.m. that the first Sea King Rescue Helicopter spotted some of the empty canoes some three miles off-shore and the rescue began.

The manager of the St Albans Centre and the managing director of Active Learning and Leisure (operator of the centre), were both charged with the unlawful killing of the teenagers.

Although this was a very sad and tragic incident, the industry has a lot to learn from this, and can use this as a stepping stone forward in the delivery of safer adventure activities and reduce the risks involved. Under the provision of the 1996 Act, providers must obtain a licence from the Adventure Licensing Authority, especially if they cater for under 18-year-olds, in activities such as caving, climbing, trekking and water sports.

ACTIVITY

A tragic way to learn

Study the Lyme Bay case study and supplement this by further research. Identify the areas that possibly contributed towards the tragic events that occurred. How could these have been avoided?

Research the Adventure Activities Licensing Regulations. What stipulations do these now impose upon organisations offering and delivering such activities?

DID YOU KNOW?

1 October 1999 saw the introduction of the new statutory 'Health and Safety Law' poster and leaflet, which all employers in the UK need to provide for their work force.

Between 1997 and 1999, some 900 licences have been issued across England, providing evidence of a proven level of health and safety.

Before embarking upon an activity, it is wise to check if a licence for the respective activity is required and if the provider possesses such accreditation and the instructor or leader, the appropriate qualifications.

Below is an extract from the Canoe Outfitters of Florida (COF), who run a canoe rental project along the Loxachatchee River through Palm Beach County's Riverbank Park.

This extract is part of a disclaimer which is designed to remove any responsibility from the COF for accident and injuries sustained during participation:

6I realise that risks from storms, lightning strikes, alligator attacks, overturning of boats and other dangers exist in my participation of boating activities made available by COF ... I agree to indemnify COF ... from any and all contract or negligence claims and suits for bodily injury, property damage, wrongful death or otherwise which may arise from my participation.9

Disability Discrimination Act 1994

The Disability Discrimination Act has been established in parts. Part 3 of the Act came into effect in October 1999, requiring all service providers to make 'reasonable adjustments' to operations, if people with disabilities were having difficulties in accessing their services. These adjustments could include auxiliary aids or services such as audio tapes, Braille, large print and the provision of sign language interpretation. However, the definition of reasonable is open to interpretation, as factors such as potential effectiveness, practicability, disruption and costs need to be taken into account before adjustments are made.

Children's Act 1989

The Act came into force in 1991, replacing approximately 50 other Acts of Parliament. The main implication of the Act upon local authorities is that they need to plan for children and ensure that there are sufficient services and support systems for children and their families.

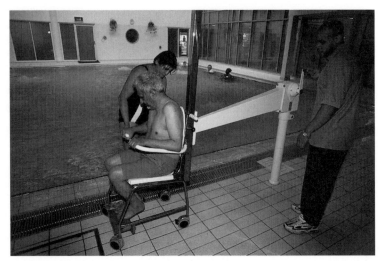

Facilities such as these are ideal for people with disabilities, however, they are not always feasible at all leisure facilities.   Source: © *Paul Doyle/Photofusion*

Local authorities have to carry out four main duties:

1 Provide information, advice, guidance and support.
2 Publish approved codes of practice (ACOP).
3 Review codes in light of new legislation.
4 Register and continually monitor activity schemes against compliance with regulations.

The leisure and recreation industry provides a vast range of children's services, including play groups, crèches, holiday schemes, sports centres and outdoor activities, among others. All provision for children needs to be monitored. The providing organisations and the people actively involved may need to be reviewed, inspected and monitored. Indeed, many children's play providers, especially holiday schemes, need to change their recruitment practice and review their facilities, staffing and programmes in order to comply with the Act.

Wiltshire County Council Social Services Code of Practice for 'Out of School and Holiday Care' for 5–8-year-olds clearly outlines the standards required by providers in order to become a registered provider. The ACOP covers the areas that are listed in Table 2.2.

Groups should ensure that proper recognition is given to the multi-cultural nature of our society and to equal opportunity for all. Equal opportunity considerations are relevant to all aspects of group functioning, including employment, the selection of play material and books and the conduct of the group (for example, avoiding racially offensive language). All children must be cared for with equal concern and with due regard shown to their religious persuasion, racial origin and culture. Failure to do so may provide grounds for cancellation of registration.

STANDARD	RANGE
Quality of play provision and care	ages, discipline, special needs
Staffing	numbers, qualifications, employers liability, suitability
Suitability of premises	space, storage, heat, light, ventilation
Safety	fire precautions, exits, evacuation drill, accidents
Health and hygiene	cleanliness, toilets and washing facilities, diet
Records	daily registers
Insurance	
Child protection	

TABLE 2.2 *Extract of approved code of practice employed by Wiltshire County Services*

Data Protection Act 1998

The Data Protection Act 1998 came into force in 1999, replacing the previous 1984 Act. All automated processing of personal data will need to comply with the act before the end of 2001. The impact of this should not burden leisure and recreation providers in any great way, as many of the requirements of the 1998 Act are substantially the same as those of the 1984 Act. The Act is designed to protect individuals' rights to privacy.

As with the 1984 Act, there are eight Data Protection Principles, these are:

1 Personal data shall be processed fairly and lawfully.
2 Personal data shall be obtained only for one or more specified and lawful purposes, and shall not be further processed in any manner incompatible with that purpose or those purposes.
3 Personal data shall be adequate, relevant and not excessive in relation to the purpose or purposes for which they are processed.
4 Personal data shall be accurate and, where necessary, kept up to date.
5 Personal data processed for any purpose or purposes shall not be kept for longer than is necessary for that purpose or those purposes.
6 Personal data shall be processed in accordance with the rights of the data subject (person).
7 Appropriate technical and organisational measures shall be taken against unauthorised and unlawful processing of personal data and against accidental loss or destruction of, or damage to, personal data.
8 Personal data shall not be transferred to a country or territory outside the European Economic Area, unless that country or territory ensures adequate levels of protection for the rights and freedoms of data subjects in relation to the processing of personal data.

 **DISCUSSION**

Store cards and loyalty cards are used by many leisure and recreation providers, such as supermarkets, sports centres and retail outlets. Other than promoting their services for what other uses do the providers utilise the information obtained by these cards?

ACTIVITY

Data protection

Make a list of all the occasions you can think of where a leisure and recreation facility may need to hold personal details of staff or customers.

What sort of details would they require and for what purpose?

Safety at Sports Grounds Act 1975

Introduced as a result of a stadium disaster which killed six spectators at the Ibrox Stadium, Glasgow in 1971, the Act is now applicable to all stadiums. Further regulations have been made following more recent disasters such as the Bradford City Fire, Hillsborough and Heysel Stadium incidents. Legislation controls conditions such as terracing design, seating capacity, safety barriers and crowd density.

Following one of the worst tragedies in the history of British football, at the Hillsborough Stadium on 15 April 1989, Lord Justice Taylor was commissioned to investigate the events that occurred at Sheffield Wednesday's football ground, and make recommendations concerning the safety at sports events and the requirements of further crowd control mechanisms. This became known as the Taylor Report 1990. The Taylor Report was indeed the ninth commissioned inquiry into ground safety and crowd control at football matches, following previous reports by Lord Wheatley who introduced the Green Guide on Safety and the Safety at Sports Grounds Act following the events mentioned above at Ibrox, and the Popplewell Inquiry which investigated the deaths of 56 fans at the Bradford City fire.

Taylor's report had a huge impact upon the sport of football and the management of crowd safety at sports events in general. In the initial Interim Report 1989, Lord Taylor made over 40 recommendations, aimed at league clubs, highlighting the practical measures needed to reduce the prevalence of injuries at sports grounds. These included:

- Restrictions on the capacities of self-contained pens.
- A review of all terrace capacities, with an immediate 15% reduction in all ground capacities.
- The opening of perimeter fence gates.
- New provision for first aid.

Lord Taylor's Final Report 1990, looked at the basic problems facing British football. Taylor identified the impact of the media and the links with football hooliganism and the possibilities of alcohol as a cause of disorder.

One of the most influential recommendations involved the gradual replacement of terraces with seated areas, aimed at 100% compliance by all four football divisions by the year 2000. Obviously this has not totally come to fruition, although Premier League clubs began the transition, with Anfield, Liverpool Football Club's home ground, being one of the first to announce their plans. Indeed, the combined development of Anfield and Ibrox, two stadiums which witnessed two of the most horrific disasters totalled approximately £22 million, by 1993 the renovations to the Ibrox stadium had reached £28 million alone.

The financial burden associated with such dramatic changes was felt by all but the largest clubs, and indeed even today lower league clubs struggle to improve the standards of their facilities in order to comply with the stringent rules associated with entry into higher leagues. To alleviate some of the financial constraints, back in March 1990, the then Chancellor of the Exchequer, John Major, cut the tax levied on football pools by 2.5%, thus releasing approximately £100 million over a five-year period to the redevelopment of football grounds. This was further enhanced by the Football Trust's decision to provide maximum grants of £2 million per club up to a total of £40 million, over the same five-year period. Within four months, the Football Trust had contributed £7.73 million towards ground improvement projects and in total received 120 applications.

Other recommendations made by the Taylor Report suggested that no perimeter fencing should have spikes on the top or be more than 2.2 metres high, ticket touting should be made illegal and laws should be brought into force dealing with racist chanting and taunting inside football grounds.

DISCUSSION

Who is the current Minister for sport?

One final recommendation defused a major issue stemming from the Football Spectators Act 1989, which was the motion brought forward by the then Minister for Sport, Colin Moynihan, concerning the introduction of compulsory membership or identity cards for all spectators at league games in England and Wales. Taylor dismissed this.

ACTIVITY

Stadium designs

Investigate how stadium designs have changed since the unfortunate occurrences of the Bradford City Fire and the recommendation and conclusions drawn from both the Popplewell and Taylor Reports.

What impact has this had on Premier League teams, in terms of crowd capacity, seating, security, terracing?

Food Safety Act 1990

There are numerous legislative items aimed at regulating the food industry, such as the Food and Drugs Act 1955, the Food Act 1984 and the Food Safety Act 1990. Under the last Act, it is an offence for any food retailer 'to sell for human consumption any food which is rendered injurious to health or unfit for human consumption, or is so contaminated that it would not be reasonable to expect it to be used for human consumption in that state'.

Local authorities enforce the Food Hygiene Regulations 1995 via inspectors, who cover the full leisure and recreation range from hotels, bars, clubs, sports facilities and restaurants. They have the right to enter the premises at any reasonable hour to check compliance.

CASE STUDY *Contravening food hygiene regulations*

A caterer was jailed for four months after a wedding reception caused 224 guests to suffer from salmonella. The cause of the outbreak was due to a mayonnaise-based seafood salad being left standing for several hours on a hot summer's day inside the marquee. A Scottish butcher was fined £2,250 after admitting that his company had failed to comply with the regulations. Twenty people died from this well publicised E.coli outbreak, though lack of evidence cleared the butcher of the accusations of wilfully and recklessly supplying the meats responsible for the outbreak.

The Food Hygiene Regulations define alcohol as food, therefore publicans and all food handlers must receive proper health and safety training, as well as training in the safe preparation of foods.

Licensing laws
The Leisure and Recreation industry is an entertainment industry, with most facilities including hotels, restaurants, social clubs, sports clubs, leisure centres and theatres wishing to offer numerous activities for which a licence or licences will be required.

Examples of the types of licence that a leisure provider may require are listed below.

Public Entertainment Licence (PEL)
This Act applies to any facility or organisation that wishes to provide recorded music such as during the interval at a football match, in social areas of sports clubs e.g. bars, fitness areas or swimming pools.

Liquor Licences
It is almost an impossibility to attempt to embrace within this chapter the full extent of this area of licensing within the leisure and recreation industry. Different types of certificates exist for registrations as well as types of licences, such as, occasional, special or extended. Since the

Licensing Act 1964, which controls the sales and consumption of alcohol, further regulations have come into force directly related to the sale and consumption of alcohol during sporting events.

The Sporting Events (Control of Alcohol) Act 1985 as amended 1986

This creates a network of prohibitions across England and Wales against the transportation and consumption of alcohol at sporting events. Even under these provisions it is difficult to prescribe a hard and fast rule concerning alcohol at sporting events. Although consumption of alcohol is banned from sporting terraces, the sale and consumption times at sports events are still dependent on the local licence and the set up of the facility, for example, a social club or a sports club. In some sporting arenas it is possible to purchase and consume alcohol throughout the whole duration of the event, within a restricted area, while at others the sale and consumption of alcohol is prohibited until after the sporting event has ceased.

Hazards and risk assessment

KEY TERMS

Hazard: is anything that could cause harm to anyone, e.g. chemical, equipment, surface, personal competence, environment.

Risk: is the chance that anyone could become harmed by a hazard.

As a leisure and recreation provider, you are continually faced with the prospect that your worst nightmare can come true, as recently occurred at the North Gate Arena, Chester in 1998.

Although all staff were exonerated by the resulting inquest, lessons were learnt by all, not least the need to test, review and evaluate all emergency procedures and potential hazardous environments. If you turned this around, and made it essential that these checks and procedures were carried out on a continuous and ongoing process, then the possibility of further injuries and deaths would be decreased. This is called **risk assessment**.

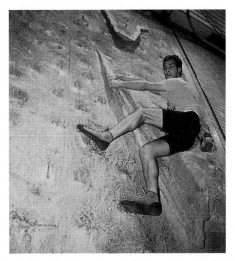

Some sports present far higher risks than others. Full instruction must be given and the correct safety gear must be used at all times.   Source: © actionplus

KEY TERMS

Risk assessment: is the careful examination of the potential of risk within the workplace (sporting activity), and the identification of precautions required to reduce these risks.

The leisure and recreation sector carries numerous risks and potential risks, due to its diverse range of settings, including land-based activities such as rock climbing, water-based activities such as water skiing and jet ski, airborne activities such as hang-gliding and facility-based activities. Each environment provides its own risks and hazardous situations.

Alice Reed, a 17-year-old girl, was skiing in the Austrian Alps with friends and found herself caught up in an avalanche that savagely buried her alive. Luckily, Alice was able to clear the snow away from her face and managed to protrude her left hand out of the snow, enabling rescuers to located and dig her out. A lucky escape!

Health and safety law in the UK and the European Union (EU) is now based on the principle of risk assessment.

The onus is on employers to assess health and safety hazards and risks and then take appropriate measures to remove or control them. Within sport it is virtually impossible to remove all risk, so proper control of risk wherever 'reasonably practicable' is essential to comply with the law.

The ever increasing demand for white-knuckle experiences and extreme sports, is pushing risk assessment to the limits. Some sections of society require the thrill of risk to stimulate them, other more commonly practised sports do not provide the buzz. Participation in sports such as sky surfing, bungee jumping and platform diving, require high levels of safety precautions.

In response to a number of deaths, including 18-year-old British holiday maker Tracey Slatter, the Spanish Government introduced controls on Wet-Biking (Jet Ski). A 200 metre wet-bike exclusion zone has been instigated on all beaches, and speed restrictions have been applied during the launch and landing periods during which wet-bikers pass through normal bathing zones. Two further deaths of British wet-bikers occurred within two months of Tracey's death, calling for the British Government to follow the Spanish and impose regulations on this sport, including essential training and zoning.

ACTIVITY

Beyond all limits

Rearrange the following sports and activities in order of risk, with the highest risk first:

Skydiving, American football, course fishing, Formula One, rock climbing, hang-gliding, jet skiing, football, DIY, canoeing, sailing, swimming, marathon running, skiing, Scuba diving, horse riding.

Compare your results with the rest of your group. Justify your reasoning for the order of placing these sports within your list.

Investigate two activities from the above list through newspaper articles and the Internet, and compare the number of recorded accidents, injuries and fatalities.

What were the main causal factors contributing to these incidents?

Do you think that certain incidents could have been prevented?

Hazards

The wide ranging nature of the leisure and recreation industry means that each sector of the industry will have its own particular hazards. A swimming pool has different hazards from a rock concert, yet both need to be analysed and assessed in the same way. A girl came close to death, at her local indoor swimming pool in Birmingham, when her long hair became trapped in the filtration duct on the pool floor. If it had not been for the actions of the quick thinking lifeguard who gave her air through resuscitation under the water, until a pair of scissors arrived to cut her free, she would have died. A participant of an aerobics class sued a sports centre, claiming that the dance floor had caused his injuries as he slipped while performing aerobic exercises. The floor itself was highly polished, and was used for a number of other activities. However, the judge decided that the polished floor was not reasonably safe for this particular activity and awarded the plaintiff damages for his injuries.

Cases such as these highlight the difficulties of risk assessment within the sport and recreation environment. With regard to the second example, although other activities had used the floor in a reasonably safe environment, the floor proved to be unsafe on this occasion, emphasising that operators of recreation activities cannot assess the risk of their premises in general terms, but need to assess the level of risk for every activity, assessing whether the premises are reasonably safe for each type of activity.

In the case regarding the swimming pool, the need to review and develop staff expertise is an essential criterion of risk assessment. It would have been difficult to have foreseen this particular incident and potential hazard. However, the training and skills of the staff prevented an almost certain fatality. A systematic approach towards the training and development of staff is essential for risk assessment, as the high turnover of staff associated with the leisure and recreation industry provides organisations with an ongoing issue of HSW Act regulation compliance, that is the training requirements and needs of employees in order to perform their roles competently.

The degree to which an organisation is exposed to hazards is dependent on a range of factors, for example its scale of operation, location and the sector in which it operates.

Risk

The degree of risk can be divided into three levels:

1 **Low:** safe condition with safety measures in place, for example, one-to-one tuition between a participant and fitness instructor in a gym, where adequate health records have been maintained.
2 **Medium:** acceptable risk, however attention must be given to ensure safety measures operate. For example, public swimming pool with a water flume: sufficient staff on duty patrolling not only the main pool but also all aspects of the flume including entry and exit points.
3 **High:** where safety measures are not fully in operation. Requiring immediate action. For example, an un-patrolled area of beach, where a combination of bathers, surfers and water skiing activities exists.

Risk assessment

The Health and Safety Executive has produced a document identifying five steps to risk assessment.

You do not need to be a health and safety expert to carry out the five steps to risk assessment, however, if you feel that you require assistance, the HSE provides a number of further leaflets and training material designed to assist you. However, it must be remembered that ultimately, it is you as the manager/safety manager who is responsible for ensuring that the risk assessment is adequately done.

The HSE advises the following steps:

Step one – look for the hazards

Walking around a swimming pool you observe a number of hazards. Concentrate on the more significant areas, such as slippery areas, broken tiles, blind spots, inner surface of flumes, chemical concentration, clarity of pool water. Discussing such areas of concern with other personnel working within the area, e.g. lifeguards, may identify further hazards and put others into perspective. Also referring to accident report books will highlight consistent hazards. Be sure to check all areas, as a general risk assessment may not be sufficient.

Step two – decide who might be harmed and how

Steps into the pool may cause difficulties for pregnant women, the elderly or people with disabilities. Are the directions towards the shallow end sufficient to guide young children and weak swimmers to a safe entry point? Are spectators able to gain suitable vantage points without putting themselves into danger? Are all lifeguards suitably trained and work reasonable shifts without causing undue fatigue?

Step three – evaluate the risks and decide whether existing precautions are adequate or whether more should be done

Handrails and steps conform to guidelines and observation has proven facilities are proficient, no further precautions required, however unable to eliminate hazard thus lifeguards are trained to continually monitor steps area. The deep and shallow ends of the pool are clearly identified, although the changing rooms enter pool side at deep end. Recommendations required to control the risk and prevent access to the hazard (entering water at deep end), e.g. railings to be erected to form a barrier between entrance point and water, further signs required to direct all swimmers to the shallow end. Lifeguards were showing signs of complacency, rearrange the rota ensuring a 20-minute shift system, thus reducing the exposure to risk.

Step four – record your findings

As most swimming pools have more than five employees, there is a necessity to record the findings of the risk assessment. The recordings will need to demonstrate that a thorough check has been carried out, that all potentially affected people have been consulted and that all precautions have been made, leaving only low-risk situations.

Step five – review your assessment and revise it if necessary

It is good practice to review your risk assessments, to ensure that the precautions are still in place and effective, also it is essential to consider new risks as changes occur, such as the introduction of a wave machine.

Swimming pools can be high-risk areas, the introduction of other facilities increases the level of risk and supervision required.   Source: *Corbis*

ACTIVITY

Too risky!

Visit your local leisure centre or entertainment facility. Carry out a risk assessment for one activity area using the example assessment form (Figure 2.7) or design your own. Be sure to establish what activities the area is used for and the types of users.

Do you consider the area to be a high- or low-risk area? Discuss your findings with the group.

Sample Risk Assessment Form

Name of Company	Risk assessment carried out by	Reason for assessment
Activity Area	**Date**	**Proposed assessment review date**

Step One Areas of significant hazard	
Step Two People who are most likely to be at risk from the significant hazards, e.g. staff or public	
Step Three Existing controls and proposed new controls identified via Step two	
General comments and overall review	

Signature _____

Position _____

FIGURE 2.7 *Example assessment form*

Ensuring a safe and secure working environment

It only takes a split second to cause an accident. Eddie Kidd, Britain's answer to Evil Kinevil, had mastered the art of handling a motor cycle to achieve many world records, yet one lapse in concentration and misjudgement wrecked his career as a motor cycle stunt man and left him with severe disabilities.

If such tragic occurrences can happen to a highly trained individual within a perfectly controlled environment, then accidents can happen anywhere.

The managers and owners of all leisure and recreation facilities have a duty to provide a safe and secure environment for their staff and visitors. By complying with current legislation such as the Health and Safety at Work Act and the associated regulations, all organisations within the Leisure and Recreation industry should provide a safe working environment for all parties involved. By carrying out regular and detailed risk assessments, hazards should be identified and risks limited to low levels. However, it is virtually impossible to eliminate all aspects of risk, but the employer has to demonstrate due diligence towards the management of health and safety policies and procedures and ensure that all involved are aware, understand and cooperate. For example, employees and or guests including visitors, participants or spectators, may see the facility as operating in a safe and secure working environment. But unfortunately, as is observed on many occasions, this is not always the case.

This Chapter has highlighted the need for all leisure and recreation facilities to implement the following throughout their organisation.

The fate of Eddie Kidd demonstrates that, even under the tightest controls, tragic accidents can still happen.   Source: *PA Photos Ltd.*

Regular facility inspections

Although activity specific risk assessments are now a requirement under health and safety legislation, continuous maintenance checks and procedure audits are essential to maintain a high standard of health and safety. Quality assurance programmes, such as ISO9002, provide an audit trail enabling managers to trace the origin or cause of individual incidents.

Staff training

Staff training is essential, not only to teach how to avoid accidents, but also how to deal with accidents and emergencies, for example, fire and bomb evacuation drills, or hostage situations. Basic first aid knowledge in some organisations is mandatory, as the actions taken during the first few minutes after an accident can mean the difference between life or death. Likewise, employers must ensure that the training is continually updated in line with new legislation.

Implementation of health and safety legislation and codes of practice

As with training needs, health and safety legislation and approved codes of practice are continually being updated. The law does not recognise ignorance, if the law exists you are expected to follow it. Figures from RoSPA indicated that during 1994–5, there were some 376 fatalities and over 1.5 million injuries occurring in the workplace alone. Might this suggest that the safe working practices are not stringent enough or that in some cases procedures have not been followed?

Swimming pools provide particular dangers, although they do have a good safety record in comparison with other recreational water areas, such as rivers, coastal regions and even the home bath. In 1997 swimming pools represented only 5% of all drowning recorded in the UK with the other three areas representing 30%, 24% and 6% respectively, (RoSPA, 1999).

Managing Health and Safety in Swimming Pools 1999, issued jointly by the HSC and Sport England and supported by the sports councils for Scotland, Wales and Northern Ireland, is a guidance document aimed at ensuring high health and safety standards. The policy consolidates the provisions of the 1988 guidelines and gives practical and sensible advice to all pool providers other than domestic provision, so that they can comply with existing legislation and reduce the number of fatalities and injuries to swimmers. All pool operators must have clear, written safety procedures, controlled access and emergency arrangements. These must

It is essential that staff are trained in rescue, resuscitation and first aid and are able to respond immediately to emergencies in a swimming pool.   Source: © *Dave Thompson/Life File*

include signs indicating no supervision (if appropriate), depth of water, an alarm system with instruction to summon help when required, suitable rescue equipment and, at all times, fully trained staff capable of rescue, resuscitation and first aid.

Seeking advice and guidance

The Health and Safety Executive(HSE), under the control of the Health and Safety Commission (HSC), have a network of regional offices around England, Scotland and Wales, all of whom are able to advise and provide guidance on issues relating to health and safety issues at work. They provide a range of information leaflets covering specific areas of the Health and Safety legislation and how to implement these regulations within the workplace. Alternatively, their web site, www.hse.gov.uk gives updated information with new regulations and EU directives on health and safety. Alternatively, contacting your local Environmental Health Department will allow you access to information on other issues including pollution, food hygiene and COSHH.

The Royal Society for the Prevention of Accidents (RoSPA), a charitable organisation working on behalf of all organisations, provides a readily available source of information and statistics covering occupational health issues, road safety, water safety and product safety. Their web site is well worth a visit. Log on at www.rospa. co.uk.

Professional bodies and quangos are also useful sources of information and publications of health and safety documents, such as Sport England or respective sports councils in Wales, Northern Ireland and Scotland, the Institute of Sport and Recreation Management and the Institute of Leisure and Amenity Management often provide seminars and workshops on the implication and implementation of health and safety legislation.

Budget for health and safety

With the continual process of health and safety legislation and the requirement of compliance, leisure and recreation organisations need to budget for this in the same way they would for any other aspect of the business, such as capitation or staffing. The cost of a typical professional training day can amount to between £150–£180 per delegate per day. Staff development does not come cheap, therefore an in-house training mechanism may prove to be more cost-effective.

As stipulated in the HSW Act, the employer must provide for the training needs of its employees to enable them to perform their roles competently. This is only one aspect of budgeting, imagine the cumulative costs of facility and equipment requirements, repairs and maintenance, compliance with new standards and legal costs. Health and safety measures must be taken seriously as they can be the pivotal point of the success or loss of the business.

Dealing with staff and visitors with special needs

❝As I stepped off the plane clutching my three medals, two golds and a silver, I noticed the silence as not one photographer was there to meet us. But it did not bother me, as I was proud to be British and proud of my achievements.❞

(British Field Event Athlete after the Para Olympics in Seoul, 1988)

The Disability Discrimination Act requires all service providers to make 'reasonable adjustments' to operations if people with disabilities are having difficulties in accessing their services. These adjustments could include auxiliary aids or services such as audio tapes, Braille, large print and the provision of sign language interpretation. However, the definition of reasonable is open to interpretation, as factors such as potential effectiveness, practicability, disruption and costs need to be taken into account before adjustments are made.

Staff should be trained to work with people with all forms of disability, and all people should be given the opportunity to take part in all sports where reasonably practicable. It is worth noting that British athletes also win medals at the Para Olympics, though recognition of such feats of sporting prowess is rarely given as much media coverage as other mainstream sports.

ACTIVITY

We are all on equal terms

The Para Olympics always takes place immediately after the Olympic Games, yet does not attract the same media attention.

List the sports that are included in the event and research the adaptations that have been made.

How do the safety regulations differ from mainstream sport?

It is important to remember that ensuring health and safety in the leisure and recreation workplace is a continuous process, needing the support and commitment of all those working for the organisation.

ACTIVITY

Anticipating hazards

The typical sports and leisure centre caters for a variety of activities and customers. Each activity will raise differing hazards and safety precautions. A typical centre will have the following facilities:

- main entrance
- wet sports area
- dry sports area
- changing facilities
- spectator gallery/refreshment facility

Take a look at the common hazards associated with each area, add further examples if you can, then list the type of accidents that may occur due to the presence of these hazards. Use the proforma below to help you.

Main entrance	Injuries/accidents occurring due to hazards
Steps or inappropriate slope	
Unstable hand rail	
Inappropriate queuing facilities	
Wet sports area	**Injuries/accidents occurring due to hazards**
Slippery surfaces around edge of pool	
Inaccurate depth signs	
Faulty alarm system	
Inadequate lifesaving equipment	
Untrained staff	
Unsafe diving boards	
Inadequate zoned area around exit point of flume	

Poor quality water, e.g. unable to see bottom of pool	
Dry Sports areas	**Injuries/accidents occurring due to hazards**
Slippery surfaces	
Equipment left unattended, e.g. trampoline	
Poor lighting	
Poor ventilation	
Inadequate supervision in weights room	
Damaged equipment	
Changing facilities	**Injuries/accidents occurring due to hazards**
Slippery floors	
Broken tiles and mirrors	
Food and drinks littered on floor	
Cleaning materials and equipment left out	
Scalding water	
Unhygienic toilets	
Individual hand towels	
Spectator gallery	**Injuries/accidents occurring due to hazards**
Inappropriate emergency exits	
Low railings	
Damaged seats	

RoSPA, a registered charity that works across all industries, including central and local government, and public private sectors, has researched and lobbied for safe practice not only in the workplace but also in the home and on the roads. Table 2.3 shows statistics corresponding to these three areas. Their work has covered issues and aspects including road safety, occupational health and safety, safety education, water and leisure safety and product safety.

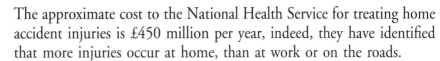

DID YOU KNOW?

The biggest single cause of accidents is human error, and more people are injured in their homes than anywhere else.

DID YOU KNOW?

A visit to the RoSPA web site at www.rospa.co.uk, is well worth it. It contains useful facts, figures and articles relating to safety.

LOCATION	KILLED	INJURED
Home 1995	4,066	2.7 million
Road 1996	3,598	316,704
Work 1994–95	376	1.5 million

TABLE 2.3 *Accident statistics from RoSPA*
Source: *RoSPA Guide to Home Safety Projects*

DID YOU KNOW?

Children aged 0–4 years old account for the largest proportion of accidents.

Source: Consumer Safety Unit, 1995

DID YOU KNOW?

Around ten children die as a result of falls each year.

Source: Consumer Safety Unit, 1995

The approximate cost to the National Health Service for treating home accident injuries is £450 million per year, indeed, they have identified that more injuries occur at home, than at work or on the roads.

Accidents in the home

There are three main categories of accident which account for the majority of all accidents within the home:

1 Impact: mainly through falling or falling objects, the elderly are particularly at risk from these types of injuries

2 Heat: scalds and burns from a 'controlled' source, e.g. a kettle, or oven are very common. Home fires are also caused by similar factors including faulty appliances.

3 Through mouth/foreign body: young children, especially 0–4 age group, are at risk from suffocation, accidental poisoning and choking on objects which they put in their mouths

With such a high prevalence of accidents and injuries occurring within the 'safety' of the home, it is important for all people to carry out their own personal risk assessments to limit the risks to which they expose not only themselves but also other members of the family and visitors.

The Toys' Directive introduced into British law via the Toys (Safety) Regulations 1995 under the Consumer Protection Act, stated all toys are subjected to stringent safety requirements covering their flammability, toxicity, mechanical and physical properties. If in doubt about the safety of a toy then look for the official European Community (CE) symbol, as this indicates that the manufacturer claims the toy meets the European requirements of the EC Toy Directive. Alternatively look for the 'Lion Mark', the symbol of the British Toy Manufacturers Association, which assures the toy meets the safety standards. Toys without these logos are still available on the market but are illegal.

However, even if toys are safe and fit for their purpose, the environment and the manner in which these toys are played with can contribute to the incidence of accident. Risks can be limited by keeping floors and walkways free of toys and obstructions that can be tripped over, as 39% of all non-fatal accidents in the home involve falls and trips of some kind.

ACTIVITY

Safety in your home

List the accidents that have occurred in your household, categorise the accidents into indoor and outdoor accidents.

Collect and compare your list with other members of your group.

From the two groupings (indoor and outdoor), further divide them into the three distinct causes of accidents in the home as identified by RoSPA, that is, impact, heat, through mouth/foreign body. Graphically illustrate your findings using charts.

Identify the three most common accidents. Discuss the causes and explain how these could have been avoided or at least reduced.

Security in leisure and recreation

All leisure and recreation organisations have measures in place to identify security hazards and take steps to minimise security risks.

The increasing development of the use of IT systems within the sector has brought about a wealth of security concerns and with the advent of shopping on-line and Internet banking, information stored by company data bases needs to be kept safe and secure.

The Millennium Bug

Millennium bug
act now!

As the millennium approached, thousands of companies across the world faced a problem, The Millennium Bug. The basic issue was that their computers and other date dependent applications were programmed to display the year in two-digit date fields, thus 2000 would be read as 00. But the date problem did not simply stop on 1 January, as 2000 is a leap-year, hence has 366 days, which potentially caused further issues, with possible melt down (systems crashing) dates of 01 February, 29 February and 31 December 00 targeted.

The 'bug' might sound harmless, but had numerous health and safety implications:

● The malfunction or failure of safety related systems, for example, alarms, security and temperature control.
● Malfunction of embedded microprocessors in equipment, for example, the failure of systems, membership data bases.
● Failure of systems to respond correctly to programmed instructions, for example, banks, energy suppliers.

The resultant effect would have been an unsafe working environment and possible closure of business.

The Health and Safety at Work Act 1974, and other regulations stipulate that employers are legally obliged to ensure the safety of their employees, thus management of the Millennium Bug became of paramount importance during 1999. These other regulations are:

● Management of HSW Regulations 1992, which impress a duty on employers to assess the risk to health and safety.
● Provision and Use of Work Equipment Regulations (PUWER) 1998 requiring that all control systems of work equipment are safe, and the failure of any one part does not lead to unsafe conditions.

- Lift Regulations 1997 require that no lift be put into service unless it satisfies the relevant essential health and safety requirements, including the Supply of Machinery (Safety) Regulations 1992.

The J Sainsbury Group incorporating Sainsburys supermarkets, Homebase, Savacentre, Sainsbury's Bank and US-based shops estimated overall cost for compliance at £75 million. In fact, the *Sunday Times* (9 January 2000) stated that up to £360 billion is believed to have been spent worldwide tackling the 'bug'. During the week leading up to the Millennium, even Harrods refused to accept credit cards, as a precaution against loss of revenue.

In fact only a minority of incidents were reported, such as the failure of the tidal gauge at Portsmouth Harbour and Portman Building Society sending out statements informing savers of interest rates in January 1900, incidents far from the anticipated worldwide power failures, total computer system crashes and food shortages.

Security

The degree to which an organisation is exposed to security risks is dependent on a range of factors, for example its scale of operation, location and the sector in which it operates. It needs to be able to protect employees and customers against all forms of loss from a range of sources. Within the leisure and recreation industry, security measures need to cover, People, Property, Money and Information against factors such as Violence, Theft, Fraud, Sabotage and Accidental damage.

Security of people

In compliance with the HSW Act, the employer has a duty to protect all people from acts of danger, this includes violence.

The leisure and recreation industry is a service, dependent on contact between people, and at times people are likely to encounter uncomfortable situations including verbal and threatening behaviour, sometimes even violent actions. The Taylor Report identified an area of verbal abuse, which recommended control through legal policy. It was referring to the verbal attacks and visual displays that football players and referees receive from chanting crowds. Examples of visual displays of threatening behaviour have included the waving of inflated bananas.

In the work place, whether a sports centre, sports stadium, retail outlet or entertainment facility, the manager needs to minimise the risk of such violence. The HSE recommends a seven-point plan aimed at reducing the prevalence of violence at work.

Step One	Establish if there is a problem. Sometimes problems or issues among staff or between customers are not always visible until they erupt. Cantona's attack on a spectator was allegedly provoked by the constant verbal abuse by the spectator towards the football star.
Step Two	Ensure all incidents are recorded. The use of closed circuit television (CCTV) enables the police and sports clubs to monitor and record the actions of suspected ringleaders involved in sports violence known as hooliganism.
Step Three	Classify all incidents. Violence such as verbal abuse will need to be carefully considered in the context in which it was given.
Step Four	Search for preventative measures. If theft from changing facilities is occurring, is there any way of ensuring continuous staffing or a new security system, e.g. individual lockers rather than baskets as commonly used in swimming pools?
Step Five	Decide what to do. The identity card system, proposed to control and monitor football spectators, was eventually rejected by the Taylor Report as an inappropriate measure. Further policing and training took place to replace this original concept.
Step Six	Put measures into action. Policies and procedures must be documented and all employees and users informed about them. For example, most retail outlets will have a customer service policy which is used to defuse what can become a very difficult situation between staff and customers.
Step Seven	Review and evaluate policy. As you will have learnt throughout this chapter, legislation and regulations are continually being revised and updated. For example the Managing Health and Safety in Swimming Pools 1999 regulations replaced the previous Safety in Swimming Pools 1988 document.

Under the Occupiers Liability Act, Cunningham and Others v Reading Football Club Ltd 1991, saw £250,000 worth of damages being awarded to the police officers who were injured by soccer hooligans during a top of the table battle between fourth division team Reading and Bristol City.

Any individual who chooses to play any physical sport such as football or rugby, has to accept that there is an inevitable risk involved, however, any one player does owe a duty of care towards another player, either amateur or professional. Indeed, a player acting recklessly or intentionally causing an injury, provides a case of negligence. Therefore, if a player inflicts an injury on another player or spectator in a wholly unacceptable manner, either with recklessness or intent, then the injured party, by law, has the right to claim compensation. One classic instance was that of Eric Cantona who kicked out at a fan who was goading him.

Physical violence on the sports field has begun to enter the world of sport more and more, some of the most publicised incidents include Elliott v Saunders and Liverpool FC 1994 and O'Neill v Fashanu 1994. O'Neill received a £70,000 out of court settlement, following his collision with John Fashanu, during his debut match for Norwich City in October

1994. The settlement was only awarded after the allegation of assault was lifted, but significantly not negligence.

The door to sports injury litigation may seem wide open after cases such as this, however, the Elliott v Saunders and Liverpool FC case, which took place only a matter of months prior to O'Neill's case, saw Elliot suffer similar injuries which have practically ended his football career. A decision was found against the plaintiff (Elliot).

DID YOU KNOW?

The report *Policing Football Hooliganism* estimates the cost of policing Saturday football matches in England and Wales on an annual basis extends to £22 million, utilising 5,000 police officers each week.

Part One of the Football Spectators Act 1989, proposed the introduction of compulsory membership or identity cards for all spectators at league, cup and international matches held in either England or Wales. This proposal was initially designed and piloted by a few clubs, Luton Town being one of them. They were looking to facilitate the identification and ultimate exclusion of suspected hooligans, or spectators who had previous records of causing violence or damage at sports events. The introduction of such a scheme, however would have incurred further costs on clubs and ultimately the supporters, but would have also contributed to greater queuing, congestion and confusion at the turnstiles. The Taylor Report 1990, recommended that the scheme be put on hold, as it did not directly assist in the control of current factors associated with crowd disorders. For example, it would not have helped prevent such disasters as Hillsborough, which was not caused by violence.

The second part of the Act was concerned with the control and restriction of football fans travelling abroad, indeed, following riotous occurrences abroad, all English football teams were banned from playing in Europe for two years. This had a devastating effect upon the then First Division clubs and the financial awards available to them from European competition.

Security of property

Buildings, facilities and equipment used in a leisure and recreation environment are exposed to a number of threats, largely from theft, but also from damage or sabotage. For example a coded bomb scare at the 1997 Seagram Grand National caused the historic event to be evacuated and postponed until the following day. This incident was an excellent public display of well rehearsed and organised emergency procedures.

Theft from buildings of equipment, facilities or petty theft of personal items either from staff or customers, can be deterred by a number of basic security provisions, including:

1   The use of closed circuit television (CCTV), not only as a deterrent, but also as a tool to provide recorded coverage of proceedings to enable the police or organisation to identify potential incidents and deal with them immediately, as used at sports grounds. Or the use of footage for reference purposes. CCTV can be used to monitor access

areas such as entrances and exits, car parks and terracing, protecting staff as well as customers, and further enhanced by the employment of security staff.

2 Fitting security locks to all external doors and windows is essential, but high risk areas such as bars, equipment stores, single person areas, e.g. night shift at a petrol station, need to have further protection including bars or shutters across windows and doors, and the installation of light beams and pressure-sensitive equipment that activates alarm systems when breached.

3 The introduction of membership schemes and cards, although rejected by the Football Association, provides sports centres and health club operators with a control system whereby they can check the details of all people on site and deny access to others. Often the membership card will contain a swipe mechanism that has a different locking code for each individual member, which can be changed automatically on a regular basis providing a securer system without the need for the use of a key. A majority of hotel chains, such as Sheraton, use this system whereby a central computer processes a new pin number for each guest.

4 The changing facilities in sports and leisure centres have a high incidence of theft. Some centres operate a basket system, manned at all times and often working between rooms. Others provide individual lockers.

DISCUSSION

Discuss the implications of using either of the two changing facilities systems. Which one is the most secure and why?

Security of money

The leisure and recreation industry is essentially a service provider, involving the transaction of payment. Although it is usual to pay in cash rather than by cheque, the trend today is steadily rising towards the use of credit/debit cards.

Within the industry, the opportunity for theft is high from the many financial transaction points that exist. Some of these are listed below:

● entry points to events
● refreshments
● gambling and betting
● transport and taxi fares
● paying for rides at amusement parks

Leisure and recreation operators are introducing more secure methods of payment in order to reduce the risk of theft and fraud by staff and visitors, for example, entrance tickets to Lego Land can be ordered and paid for over the phone, enabling you to collect the tickets and gain the advantage of priority entrance, avoiding the need to queue. Likewise the booking office at Wembley Arena will accept card payments and post tickets to you. Some health clubs run membership schemes which bill the customer on a monthly basis, thus reducing the need for cash payment at the initial points of transaction. Even Tesco petrol stations have introduced pay at the pump facilities, improving the security both for customers and staff.

However, the increase in automatic transaction systems and the use of credit cards has led to the increase in cases of fraud. One of the most publicised cases of fraud resulted in Nick Leeson being jailed for up to 6½ years.

The Times newspaper, 2 December 1995, described the sequence of events:

❝Nick Leeson is accused of forging the signature of a director of a Wall Street stockbroking firm in an $81 million (£52 million) transaction, according to the public prosecutor in Frankfurt. Giving details of the allegations that led to Mr Leeson being jailed pending extradition proceedings to Singapore, it was disclosed that the 28-year-old banker supposedly forged the signature of Richard Hogan of Spear, Leeds and Kellogg. Hans-Herman Eckert, the prosecutor, said a copy of the document, sent from Singapore, purports to say that Spear, Leeds and Kellogg transferred 108 million marks to Baring Futures in Singapore for derivatives trading on the Nikkei 225 stock market index. The prosecutor's office said that the Singapore Justice Department alleges that Mr Leeson used the document as collateral to obtain a loan from Citibank in Singapore. This money was then allegedly used to conduct the trades that led to Baring's collapse last week.❞

Security of information

The two main security risks to information come from theft or fire. During the 1970s and early 1980s, the majority of information and data was stored on paper. Currently this has changed as most information is received and stored electronically. While this change has not reduced the risk from theft or fire, it has dramatically improved the processing and transportation of information and data. However, due to its own success and innovation, it creates further risks.

The Data Protection Act 1999 provides legislative protection against the unlawful use and/or loss of information stored electronically.

ASSESSMENT EVIDENCE

This Unit is assessed externally. For the assessment you are required to demonstrate your understanding of how two leisure and recreation facilities or events manage their health, safety and security responsibilities, including how they:

- meet the relevant legislaton and regulations
- ensure a safe working environment for staff and visitors
- ensure security for staff and visitors
- carry out risk assessment.

The following Case Study provides a sample assignment, based on the external assessment procedures used by the Edexcel Awarding Body. Tutors could use this as a practice or mock exam during January if the centre is entering the June Test series.

A period of 2 hours 30 minutes is recommended for the assessment question, reflecting the time allocation used in the external assessments.

Carn Braith festival of sport

The town

Carn Braith, with its beautiful scenic views, undulating landscape and breathtaking coastal paths, is a former industrial town set in the heart of Cornwall. Formerly dependent on the tin industry, tourism is now the major provider of employment in the area. Carn Braith and its surrounding villages make for a delightful holiday town.

The area is known for its sporting prowess, in particular its rugby, with its local side regularly competing in the national finals. However, a strong athletic fraternity exists, further enhanced by the development of a new athletics track built last year at the foot of the Carn – the hill from which Carn Braith takes its name – within the grounds of the existing leisure centre.

The festival of sport

Every year for the past 20 years, Carn District Council, via the Sports Development Unit, have organised a successful Festival of Sport. This year to celebrate the anniversary of the track, they plan to include a mini biathlon (cycling/running) event hopefully attracting 300 competitors, with the running stage of the race finishing down the home straight.

The management team

Roger Plank, the Senior Sports Development Officer, appointed last year when the track was first opened, is chairing the organising committee. Although he has organised many sporting festivals before, Mr Plank is a rather retiring character, who does not like to take front stage, and therefore delegates areas of authority to all members of the ten-strong committee, thus, enabling him to coordinate the project from a distance.

In the past this has presented difficulties. For instance, when a problem arose with the accommodation of athletes at the South West Special Olympics, an event Mr Plank himself had previously organised, his distant approach to management was emphasised as he could not be contacted and the issues were not resolved adequately, resulting in the athletes having to share facilities over the weekend.

The festival

The Carn Braith Festival of Sport includes a variety of sports such as swimming, five-a-side football and indoor rowing and hockey. All take place inside the Carn Braith Leisure Centre.

Outside on the infield area of the athletics track, many stalls are set up on the day and run by volunteers from the village. These include cake stalls, home-made sandwiches and burgers, ice-cream delis and refreshments, such as tea urns, providing a self-serve facility.

The atmosphere for the day will be pumped up by live bands playing on a temporary stage constructed by volunteers out of old beer barrels, scaffolding and planks of wood; the spaghetti of wires hidden around the back under plastic sheeting linked to the generator providing the perfect place for children to play.

The mini biathlon

Both sections of the mini biathlon follow the same loop around the village, winding their way around the narrow country roads and through the village, which has a one-way system, until they enter the grounds of the sports centre via the main entrance located adjacent to the finish line on the track.

The transition area, where competitors leave their bikes to continue with the running section, is located behind the Porta loos, as these provide a good enclosure area. The runners will then leave the arena via the same entrance gate and continue on a further loop, before entering the arena again to complete one lap of the track, where on finishing they are presented with a commemorative medal and provided with water served out of large drums using plastic cups. They will then be encouraged to walk over to the stalls on the infield if they require anything to eat, such as sandwiches. The changing facilities for the event are located inside the sports centre.

Roger Plank has arranged with the local Rotary Club, for the Rotarians to act as marshals around the proposed course. He has asked if any of them has a first aid qualification, as he wants some marshals to take on the role of first aiders at various points throughout the route.

In order to generate an atmosphere along the route as well as inside the arena, letters have been sent to local pubs along the route, encouraging them to hold further events providing viewing points for spectators of the event.

At the end of the day, Sebastian Coe will be presenting prizes at an awards ceremony, held on stage in the arena.

Carn Braith mini biathlon event

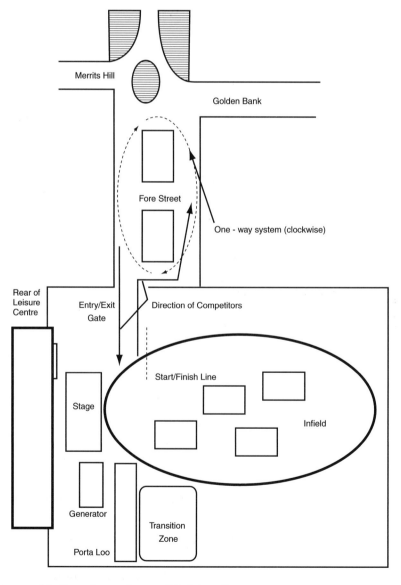

Diagram of the Sports Area at the rear of the Leisure Centre

Carn Braith Leisure Centre

Inside the Leisure Centre many other activities are scheduled to run, including the summer play scheme, which takes over the under-utilised squash courts and runs every year during July and August catering for 5–8-year-olds. The rest of the Leisure Centre consists of a 25-metre swimming pool, a multi-purpose sports hall with five badminton courts, a bar area, wet and dry changing facilities, a reception area, manager's office and plant room.

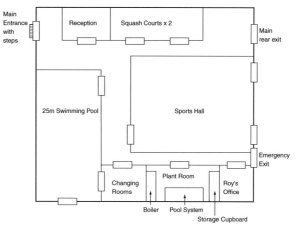

Internal diagram of the Centre

Staff responsibilities

During the year, the Centre is run on a skeleton staffing structure, with Roy Albany the manager, and Helen the administrator. Helen has recently handed in her notice as her job has not fulfilled her needs and expectations of development and training. During the five years she has been employed at the Centre she has been working with the same computer facilities, working in DOS. Three further full-time staff include two recreation assistants Gary and John, employed to cover the pool and sports hall, and one pool plant operator, Howard.

During the summer months to cover the extra demands, such as the play scheme and the sports festival, school leavers are employed on an hourly basis, supplemented by volunteers from the user groups, for example parents. They are given the same responsibilities as the full-time employees including cashing up and locking the facilities at night, especially after the weekly pool competitions held in the bar most Thursday nights, which often continue until well after midnight.

Storage

Over the years, the sports development unit has used one of the cupboards in the plant room to store equipment, such as fold-away tables, clothes, flags, posters, signs and barrels which are all neatly stacked on top of one another almost touching the ceiling. Space in the facility is limited, so other materials such as paint, weed killers, aerosols, adhesives and other cleaning products used throughout the centre are also stored in the cupboard. This makes the area very cramped and stuffy, especially with the main boiler for the sports centre being located directly opposite and adjacent to the pool pump system.

Facility inspection

As the children's play scheme is registered with the Social Services, Carmel, the under 8's officer from Social Services, visits each year and carries out an inspection of the facilities and provisions. Following her visit last year, she has requested that Peter, an officer from the Council Health and Safety Department, accompanies her.

On the day of the visit, one week prior to the Sports Festival, the two officers observe the following:

- As they walk up the two entrance steps, the officers are impressed by the highly polished chrome fittings around the door and the gleaming polished floor throughout the reception area. They are greeted by Helen who is working her last day before leaving to work elsewhere, as she turns down her CD player, which is also connected to the Centre's public announcement system. She attempts to print off identity tags, but due to a computer failure all the details are lost and the two officers enter without needing to sign in. Before they are out of ear shot, Jason, a part-time member of staff, rushes in and asks Helen if anyone had handed in his school jumper which he left in the bar last night before locking up after the pool match.

- As they enter Roy's office, he greets them with a smile and boasts about taking the sixtieth booking for the children's play scheme. As the scheme was his venture, Roy is proud of its success and makes a comment about how excited the children are about using the trampoline. His office is in a mess with insurance certificates and health and safety posters stacked on the end of his desk, but he assures the officers that he was about to display them but with all the organisation of the Sports Festival going on at the moment, he just had not found the time.

- The phone rings, it is Helen on Reception: she reports that an accident has occurred in the sports hall. Roy asks her to call John away from pool-side as he is the appointed first aider, to deal with the injury and to complete the F2508 if required.

- They leave the office and pass the sports hall. Roy is happy to see that John had successfully dealt with the injured person who had suffered concussion after slipping on the floor, banging his head on the badminton stantion and knocking over the glass of water he had on the side line. The sound of the ambulance can be heard in the background. The safety officer is pleased to note that all around the hall and corridors of the sports centre, appropriate safety and prohibition signs are displayed, but does question the reasoning for the fire exit at the rear of the sports hall being locked.

- Finally, both officers go their separate ways. Carmel is attracted to the sound of children's screams coming from the squash courts, where she observes 28 children playing games in the confines of one court, while Peter, the safety officer, inspects the plant room where he observes a room as described earlier. After stubbing his cigarette out on the floor, Howard the plant operator, shows Peter around.

Carn Braith case study question paper

1 During the organisation of the Sports Festival, Roger Plank will need to obtain permission from a number of authorities. Name three of these authorities, the permission required and the reasons for this.

2 Identify any major hazards which may arise from the running of the mini biathlon. How could these be reduced or eliminated?

3 Roger is hoping that by using the Rotarians as marshals, the biathlon route will be easy to follow and safe, as he hopes that some of the marshals hold first aid certificates. Is Roger safe in his assumptions? Should the marshals take any safety precautions, if so explain what and why?

4 Suggest a communication strategy that will ensure rapid response to emergencies, incidents and the general running of the event.

5 Security will be a big issue with the biathlon, especially as the transition area will contain up to 300 bicycles. Suggest how this could be monitored. What other security issues should be raised?

6 The activities on the infield present a number of health hazards. Identify three hazards and how you would minimise them.

7 Other than the first aid provisions required for the biathlon, what first aid precautions are required in the sports arena? Name five first aid incidents that you would expect to occur on the infield and entry/exit point to the area.

8 On behalf of Peter, the Health and Safety Officer, carry out a risk assessment of the Carn Braith Sports Centre as you have seen it during your visit.

9 Write a report, outlining the area of misconduct that you have observed. Identify Roy's statutory responsibilities, providing examples of failure. List the pieces of legislation that he has contravened and advise him on any other areas of bad practice that you observed. On a positive note, outline the good practice that you observed.

10 Carmel, the Social Services Officer, has drafted a report outlining her observations of the provisions made for 5 – 8-year-olds. What do you think are the major issues that she observed?

Key Skills

In completing the assessment for this unit, you can achieve the following key skills. These will be accredited at the discretion of your tutor on the basis of the quality of the work you submit.

COMMUNICATION, LEVEL 3

C3.2 Read and synthesise information from two extended documents about a complex subject. One of these documents should include at least one image.

CHAPTER 3

The Sports Industry

Aims and Objectives

Through the study of this Unit you will have the opportunity to:

- **investigate the complex structure of the sports industry**
- **realise that the industry has an immense impact on people's lives through the media as well as participation**
- **investigate the structure, economic impact, organisation and funding of the sports industry**
- **examine the relationship between sport and the media**
- **identify current trends within the industry and the relationship between sport and the mass media**

Introduction

DISCUSSION

How much contact have you had with the sports industry over the last month in terms of sports you have watched live, or on television? Have you participated in sport? Have you bought any equipment?

What about your class mates? Ask them the same questions.

The sports industry is vibrant, dynamic and constantly changing. It is also incredibly diverse, encompassing everything from fashion tracksuits to betting on the Derby, from health and fitness clubs, to modern sports grounds incorporating state-of-the-art hospitality and media facilities. In the midst of the technological and media revolutions that are changing our lives, sport is at the forefront, whether it is shopping on the Internet for a track suit, computerised fitness assessments at the local gym or pay-per-view TV for a major sporting event.

ACTIVITY

Investigating sport

As part of the assessment of this Unit you are required to produce a thorough investigation into two sports, you should identify which sports you want your investigation to focus on now.

The nature of the sports industry
Sporting goods – the fashion of our times

The increase in the popularity of sport and leisurewear is one of the major fashion trends of recent years. Around this growth has emerged a range of high street chain stores – such as First Sport, JD Sports, and JJB Sports – that all compete for a share of the highly competitive leisurewear market.

The emphasis of sports retailing has moved away from selling simply sports clothing and equipment to catering for a far wider leisurewear market. This has been reflected in the growth of merchandise such as replica shirts, fashion training shoes and leisure clothing and the emergence of retail park sports superstores.

The brands of major producers such as Adidas, Nike, Reebok and Umbro have become household names and their imaginative marketing has helped to make their logos instantly recognisable. Of course sports wear companies need to consider carefully their image and their market placement. A large part of the attraction of leisurewear is the active or sporting image that comes with it. For this reason leisurewear companies continue to market their products predominantly in an active sporting context even though in reality they are appealing to a far wider base of customers, many of whom are not necessarily active sports participants.

Companies that produce sports goods communicate their sporting appeal to us in many ways.

- Leisure companies sometimes use sporting super stars to help advertise their products. Over recent years Nike have used footballers such as Eric Cantona and Ian Wright. Ronaldo and the Brazilian team were used for the television advertising campaign around the 1998 World Cup.

Tim Henman illustrates how merchandising helps sell sports goods   Source: © *actionplus*

DID YOU KNOW?

In the 1998/99 season Manchester United earned almost £21.6 million from merchandising and Arsenal almost £6.4 million through retail income, amounting to around 19% and 13% respectively of total turnover.

Source: Annual Reports MUFC, 1999, AFC 1998–9

- Some advertising campaigns deliberately show 'grass roots' images of people using their products in order to portray the company as a manufacturer of active sports wear in tune with all levels of sport.

- *Product endorsement* is a powerful way of selling a brand name. When a sports star enters a playing arena wearing a certain type of footwear or using a certain piece of equipment, it is the highest possible recommendation. The image and the profile of a sports product benefits enormously when it is used or worn by major sports stars, particularly when they win! There is keen competition to have leading and successful sports celebrities using and endorsing products, such as the tennis rackets used by the top seeds at Wimbledon.

- *Merchandising* is now at the forefront of almost all professional sports clubs. Within a ten-year period the club shop has been transformed from a small, discrete trading outlet, often in a side stand, to a modern, spacious, front-of house-store or superstore. Fans are now able to buy anything from club pillowcases to wallpaper, all emblazoned with the club colours and logo. The 1990s saw a phenomenal growth in the sales and popularity of replica kits. While football led the way, Rugby League, Rugby Union and Sunday League Cricket kits all became widely available and a replica shirt has become a major fashion accessory for spectators at football grounds.

  Merchandising is now a significant part of the income for many clubs and many are now opening shops and retail outlets away from their grounds in places such as high streets and shopping malls. However, the high income to be earned by sports clubs from merchandising led to criticism in the 1990s that some clubs were changing the design of their kits every two or three years at short notice in order to reduce the life of the products they sell. As a result, one of the proposals put forward by the Football Task Force was the introduction of published policies on the timings of kit changes.

Not just fashionable at sports grounds – replica kits are now worn everywhere

Source: © *actionplus*

Sports goods companies become involved with sponsorship in a variety of ways. This can range from Adidas providing the kits for the Great Britain team in the Sydney Olympics, or the support by JJB Sports of both Orrell Rugby Union and Wigan Rugby League Clubs and Wigan Athletic Football Club. However, there is intense competition to provide sponsorship for sport and it is quite common to see financial support coming from all sectors of the economy, such as the Allied Dunbar Rugby Premiership or the Axa Sponsored FA Cup.

Some companies or brand names are best known to the competitors who participate in particular sports. For example:

● Gunn and Moore cricket equipment
● Mitre footballs, boots and shin pads
● Slazenger or Wilson tennis or squash rackets
● Carlton badminton rackets and shuttlecocks
● Speedo Swimwear

ACTIVITY

Spot the brand names

Look through the sports pages of some national newspapers. Make a list of all the sports goods companies that you can see being endorsed either by people wearing branded sports clothing or using branded sports equipment.

CASE STUDY *The sports goods retail sector*

The sports retail sector is a highly competitive, dynamic and fast moving industry that has undergone rapid changes during the 1990s. Three of the main players are examined below:

1 JJB Sports added to their existing 202 stores by acquiring the 254 stores of Sports Division in 1998. By the end of 1999 they were trading from a total of 471 stores consisting of 270 high street stores, 185 superstores and 16 small concessions. The company has grown rapidly since 1995 when JJB were trading from just 126 stores, with a turnover of £60.51 m.
2 Blacks Leisure Group are also a major player and First Sport is probably one of their better known trading outlets. They also have interests in FILA UK. In 1999 their Retail Division was trading from 182 stores of which 124 were First Sport, 40 were Blacks Outdoor and 18 were Active Venture outlets.
3 JD Sports were trading from over 120 stores in 1999 of which 17 were edge of town or out of town stores.

The combined turnover, or income, of JJB Sports and Sports Division has clearly made them a major player in the sports goods retail sector at the beginning of the twenty-first century, as can be seen in Table 3.1.

JJB Sports (incl. Sports Division)	**£372.98 m**
First Sport	£99.30 m
Blacks Outdoor	£27.50 m
Active Venture	£11.70 m
Blacks Leisure (Retail Division)	**£138.50 m**
JD Sports	**£142.60 m**

TABLE 3.1 *Turnover of sports goods retailers, 1999*

The turnover for sports retail chains comes from four main categories:

1 footwear
2 clothing
3 replica
4 equipment and accessories

A brief analysis of the product mix of some of the companies in Table 3.2 below shows the strength of clothing and footwear, although you may be surprised that the contribution from replica kits is not higher, given their visual prominence in many modern sports stores.

	JJB	SPORTS DIVISION	FIRST SPORT
Clothing	43%	49%	50%
Footwear	30%	33%	40%
Equipment and accessories	13%	18%	6%
Replica	14%	*	4%
Total	100%	100%	100%

* very small figure included in clothing

TABLE 3.2 *Product mix of sports goods retailers, 1999*
Sources: Adapted from Annual Reports of Blacks Leisure Group, JD Sports, JJB Sports, 1999

ACTIVITY

How much were those trainers?

Conduct a quick survey among people you know. Ask them how much they have spent on each of the categories of sports goods over the last 6 months.

How do your results correspond with the figures in Table 3.2?

National sports facilities

❝The new Millennium Stadium in Cardiff, Hampden's Field of Dreams, Belfast's Odyssey and other impressive sports facilities are part of Britain's £5 billion millennium programme – the biggest of its kind in the world. These are the cathedrals of sport – meccas for the sports enthusiast.❞

– The British Tourist Authority

Major sporting grounds are an important and much loved part of our national heritage. Venues such as Wembley, Old Trafford, Murrayfield, Twickenham, Lords and Headingley are known by sports enthusiasts across the world. Race tracks such as Silverstone and Brands Hatch, race courses such as Aintree, Ascot and Newmarket, golf courses such as St Andrews and the tennis championships at Wimbledon are internationally famous sporting venues that are steeped in tradition. They are, in short, an important part of our culture, our sporting lives, our heritage and our living history.

Forces for change in the 1990s

In 1990 most sports grounds were still of pre-war origin, frequently characterised by inferior sight lines for spectators, stands with pillars that obstructed spectator view and inadequate transport, toilet and refreshment facilities. For many dilapidated facilities the future was uncertain. The 1990s saw a radical improvement in the standards of sporting accommodation.

The disasters at Ibrox, Bradford and Hillsborough between 1971 and 1989 highlighted the need for new investment in our sports stadiums. Many sports grounds were out of date, unsuitable to cater for modern customer needs and expectations, others were tragically not safe.

At some grounds, such as Stamford Bridge Chelsea, new stands were built in the 1970s and 1980s with improved safety and better spectator facilities but they were often isolated attempts at modernisation and were frequently out of character with the rest of the stadium in which they were set. It was not until the 1990s that the rebuilding of our major spectator facilities began on a larger scale. There were four main forces behind this:

1 In the wake of the Hillsborough disaster in 1989 where 96 football supporters were crushed to death, the Lord Justice Taylor Report was commissioned. It recommended the introduction of all-seater football grounds in the top two English divisions by the beginning of the 1994/95 season with a similar approach to be adopted in Scotland. This not only forced change in football but acted as an impetus for change in sports facilities in general.

2 This coincided with a new generation of stadium design and media technology and a growing awareness that stadiums in the UK were falling behind facilities elsewhere. Expectations and standards had changed and the televising of events such as the Italia '90 World Cup, and the Barcelona and Atlanta Olympics, portrayed facilities from around the world that made facilities in the UK look very dated by comparison.

3 Dilapidated and run-down stands offered limited scope for extra income and many grounds were unable to respond to the growing opportunities and demand for corporate hospitality, package entertainment, banqueting and conferencing, merchandising, modern refreshment outlets and media facilities.

4 The arrival of the National Lottery in 1994 provided further impetus. The Lottery helped fund the new Wembley Stadium and provided £46 million through the Millennium Commission towards the construction of the Millennium Stadium in Cardiff. (Source: Cardiff Research Centre *Economic Impact of Millennium Stadium.*)

Developments for the twenty-first century

The latest generation of major facilities have clear sight lines for spectators, wide selections of refreshment outlets, wider concourses and increased standards of customer comfort. New grounds aim to be not only customer friendly but also customer enticing. Many new stadiums have modern executive and corporate hospitality facilities, ancillary facilities such as bars, games rooms and restaurants and space-age media facilities that will enable them to become major broadcast venues in the age of digital communications and pay-per-view television.

Almost all major sports have improved their facilities and at the turn of the century this process looks as though it will continue.

Rugby Union – In 1999 the magnificent 73,000 capacity £121 million Millennium Stadium in Cardiff with its revolutionary moving roof was opened for the Rugby World Cup. Twickenham and Murrayfield have also undergone major renovation in recent years and are now arenas fit for major rugby spectacles in the twenty-first century.

Rugby League – Traditionally, Wigan Rugby League Club and Wigan

Football Club played at separate grounds that had originally been built at the turn of the last century. In 1999 the impressive 25,000 seater JJB Stadium was opened at a cost of £32 million for both clubs to share, featuring, among other things, facilities for conferencing and banqueting. Attached to the stadium is the Soccer Dome with 20 indoor 5- and 6-a-side soccer pitches.

Tennis – In 1997 the new Number 1 Court was opened at the All England Club, Wimbledon, with a capacity of over 11,000 to replace the familiar old stands that had been there since 1924.

Cricket – The New Stand at Lords was opened in 1998 with modern hospitality and executive facilities.

Football – In England and Scotland during the 1990s over 40 clubs converted their grounds to all-seater stadiums, many building magnificent new stands to accommodate this change. Some clubs such as Derby County, Middlesborough, St Johnstone and Sunderland have constructed entire new grounds on edge of town sites that are more suitable to the demands of the twenty-first century and more accessible by car than the inner city sites that were often selected in Victorian times.

Horse racing – In the 1990s racecourses such as Kempton Park, Epsom, Goodwood, Newbury and Cheltenham have all constructed new stands

Images of sports venues: Rugby Union (Murrayfield); Cricket (Lords)

Source: © *actionplus*

to cater for the demands of the modern spectator. At Newmarket the main grandstand was rebuilt at a cost of around £16 million complete with full range of modern facilities.

ACTIVITY

Structural changes at sporting venues

Using the two sports that you have identified as the basis for your investigation, find out the names of as many venues as you can where these sports take place and any recent changes to their major facilities.

The governing body website should be a good start.

CASE STUDY *Aintree racecourse*

By the mid-1970s attendances at the Grand National were declining.

During the 1980s the situation did not improve and the future of Aintree was uncertain with modernisation required but without the long-term financial resources to see this through. The facilities were not ready for the modern leisure market and many of the stands needed updating. For a long time it seemed that every Grand National at Aintree would be the last.

However, around the end of the 1980s the tide turned, helped through sponsorship that gave financial stability and a massive outpouring of public support. In 1992 the new Queen Mother Stand was opened at a cost of around £7 million and in 1998 the new four-tier Princess Royal Stand followed, with the help of European funding at a cost of almost £10 million. Both these stands have modern facilities for increased spectator comfort and corporate hospitality. In 1999 50,000 people attended the Grand National and a further 40,000 attended on the Thursday and the Friday helping to establish the event as a three-day racing festival.

DISCUSSION

Improved facilities can mean higher pricing and spectator space taken up for corporate hospitality. This can mean that some keen sports fans cannot afford to spectate or have greater difficulty obtaining tickets. Is it right that sports clubs should aim to maximise income or do they owe some loyalty to their fans?

Local facilities

Just as major sports facilities can be a source of national pride so local sports facilities can be a source of civic pride. Local sports facilities provide an invaluable contribution to our health, our communities, our development as individuals and our quality of life.

The range of local sports facilities is vast, from the local voluntary sector bowls club with its small clubhouse, to the local swimming baths, health club, playing fields or semi-professional football team.

Development of local facilities

In 1970 local authority sports provision still mainly consisted of traditional swimming baths and playing fields. Since that time there has been an explosion in public sector sports facilities with the construction of modern leisure centres. The late twentieth century also saw the growth of dual use facilities, particularly where leisure departments used school facilities for evening and weekend community programmes. In the private sector one of the main developments was the growth of health and fitness facilities and private gyms.

At the beginning of the twenty-first century the National Lottery is providing a massive impetus for a new era of growth in local sports facilities. As lottery money often only provides part of the funding there will also be a spurt in partnership funding where agencies, such as schools and local authorities, join forces in order to build or renovate a centre.

From sports centres to leisure centres

When new facilities were opened in the 1970s they were called sports centres, by the 1990s they were commonly referred to as leisure centres. This change in terminology is highly significant and demonstrates that sport is now only part of the story in the modern leisure centre. Sport has to compete for time, space and resources against other forms of physical recreation such as aerobics and dance movement and against other leisure demands such as children's pool parties and pensioners' tea dances.

There has been an increasing emphasis on recreational fun and personal well being. This has led to the growth of fitness rooms, personal training,

Sports centre in London showing fitness suite   Source: *Corbis*

GP referral schemes and alternative therapies such as reflexology or aromatherapy.

This does not, however, always follow the interests of sports governing bodies or the traditional sports. For example in the 1990s there was concern that the growth of leisure pools with slides and wave machines would not only be detrimental to sports such as swimming, diving and water polo, but also to the wider social issue of providing facilities in which to teach children to swim.

Playing fields

Playing fields are one of the most important areas of our local provision and provide a vital contribution to our quality of life. They give children a place to play and are used for both structured sport and simple free-spirited play. In many urban areas playing fields are 'the lungs of our cities' and contribute to our physical health and personal well being.

In 1993, according to English Sports Council (Sport England) there were almost 78,000 pitches in England alone, allocated as follows:

- Football – 39,000
- Rugby – 8,000
- Cricket – 11,730
- Hockey – 8,000
- Rounders – 11,500

Over recent years there has been tremendous concern that playing fields are being lost to developments, such as new housing estates and supermarkets. There are also fears that too many schools have been selling their playing fields in order to raise money for other areas of development or building on their playing fields due to lack of space. See page 173 for more information on the National Playing Fields Association.

Playing fields are an important leisure facility   Source: © *actionplus*

ACTIVITY

Local sporting venues

Find out where the two sports you are investigating are played near you. Make a list of these venues.

Management and maintenance of facilities

National and local developments

There would be little point in providing wonderful national and local facilities if they were not managed properly. During the 1990s the management of facilities became more customer focused and the expectations of spectators and sports participants changed.

At the local level Compulsory Competitive Tendering led to opportunities for private sector companies to manage local authority leisure facilities. Consequently there was an expansion in private companies specialising in facility management. This does not only happen in public sector facilities. Sometimes private sector companies who have sport facilities will recruit private sports operators to run the facilities for them. Companies that specialise in running leisure facilities have now become an important and significant component of the sports industry.

At the national level the management of our top sports grounds is changing. Before the 1990s the emphasis was frequently on crowd control and crowd management rather than on customer service and comfort. At the turn of the century there is a realisation that crowd control, stewarding and customer service are all part of the same package and increasingly emphasis is being placed on customer service and meeting customer expectations. This includes both providing better customer facilities and providing better trained staff who are able to assist spectators as well as control crowds. Indeed the Taylor Report required football grounds to provide sufficient and trained stewards. Stewarding and crowd control are now part of a bigger customer service picture.

Quest

During the 1990s many sports facilities obtained quality standards, such as ISO 9000. However while these were often useful they were general quality standards and were not specific to the management of sport and leisure facilities. As a result Quest has been developed as a new quality initiative for the management of sports and leisure centres.

Sports coaching

❝We exist to support the person with the most difficult job in sport –

DISCUSSION

'At the elite level, in recognition of the vital contribution that coaches can make to a team or individual's success there have been further developments to help coaches to maximise their potential. The High Performance Coaching Programme is a scheme that aims to help our elite coaches to become truly world class by creating an individual development programme for each coach. By 1999 over 80 coaches had been assessed.'

Source: Sport England Fact Sheet 18, November 1999

Consider the statement above. Is elite level coaching more important than grass roots level coaching?

the coach. We know that behind every successful performance is a dedicated coach. *

– National Coaching Foundation

Coaching

Coaches work at all levels of sport from preparing athletes for Olympic competition to teaching youngsters how to play a sport for the first time. Many coaches are part-time, working freelance or for a couple of sessions a week in voluntary sector clubs, schools or in leisure centres. At the top end of the spectrum coaches can be found working for national squads and professional sports clubs. Governing bodies also employ coaches, usually to develop their sport, increase levels of participation and improve performance.

The skills and knowledge required to train a professional athlete are very different from those required to coach at grass roots level. Governing bodies have a hierarchy of coaching awards progressing from introductory level to coaching international stars. The vacancies for full-time coaches are limited and many of the coaches who work with professional sports people would themselves have reached a high level of performance when they were competing.

Coaching has developed enormously over recent years and the advent of vocational sports qualifications has standardised the levels of skills and knowledge needed to become a coach across different sports. Many coaches now attend courses run by organisations such as the National Coaching Foundation, covering general issues that cut across sporting boundaries, such as nutrition, injury prevention, sports psychology and coaching children. By 2012, SPRITO would like to see coaching as a recognised profession.

ACTIVITY

Coaching structures

Visit the web site or make contact with the national governing bodies of the two sports you are focusing on for your investigation.

Find out about the coaching structure that they currently have in place. Does this structure cater for both grass roots and elite participation? How? Obtain a copy of the structure.

Do they have a coach education programme? What is it?

Leadership

❝Everyone on the world can make a difference. Just remember, there are leaders and followers in the world; take a Sports Leader Award and make sure you're not a follower. ❞

– Linford Christie MBE (*Sports Trust Report*, 1998–9)

DID YOU KNOW?

Of the different Sports Trust awards the Community Sports Leaders Award is by far the most popular. In 1998/99 there were over 26,000 people entering this award comprising over 60% of the total of 43,000 who entered the awards scheme.

Source: *Sports Trust Report and Accounts, 1998–9*

In a strict sense leadership and coaching are different things although there is clearly an overlap. Leadership courses aim to equip young people to organise, plan, communicate and motivate and to provide safe environments for people to participate in sport. Sports leaders can be found in a wide variety of situations from youth and football clubs to outdoor adventure sports.

One of the main organisations involved with sports leadership is the Sports Trust. They offer four leadership awards:

1 Junior Leaders Award
2 Community Sports Leaders Award
3 Higher Sports Leaders Award
4 Basic Expedition Leader Award

Sports development

‘ The practice of sport is a human right. Every individual must have the possibility of practising sport in accordance with his or her needs. ’

– The Olympic Charter (Fundamental Principle No. 8)

Background

The early 1980s saw a rapid increase in commitment to sports development by local authorities. Inspired by events such as the Sports Council Sports For All campaign, many local authorities began to set up sports development departments and Action Sports initiatives, where sports leaders would conduct outreach work in local parks and play areas. This early form of sports development soon became more formalised and soon sports development teams became an accepted and common part of leisure services departments.

During the mid-1980s one of the cornerstones of the Sports Council's development initiatives was to increase participation. The campaigns focused on a number of distinct target groups:

- women
- ethnic minorities
- disabled
- youth
- over fifties
- rural communities

These campaigns were later consolidated and reinforced by others such as Ever Thought of Sport, which aimed at stimulating youth participation. This approach formed the basis of a large amount of sports development for many years and helped to shape the way that modern sports development has evolved.

Today a more holistic approach is required that does not place such emphasis on targeting specific groups. The key terms now are equity, equality of opportunity and inclusivity, that is, the tackling of barriers that lead to social exclusion in sport.

Sports development and local authorities

The nature of sports development varies enormously from area to area depending on the local situation, the objectives of the organisation and the sports that are targeted for development. For example, a very different approach would be needed to develop tennis in an affluent suburban area than would be required in an inner city area where there was little tennis tradition or infrastructure. The starting point, the local resources and the attitudes and levels of experience of participants would be completely different.

Although sports development departments vary enormously in their work, they may undertake projects such as:

- Running sports leadership and coaching courses to enable new generations of qualified coaches to pass on their skills and knowledge.
- Setting up clubs, either by providing leadership or by helping new voluntary sector clubs to develop themselves.
- Running introductory sessions or come-and-try days, particularly among low participation groups.
- Helping to develop new facilities.
- Liaising with governing bodies to develop sport in their area.
- Supporting or organising tournaments, coaching programmes and teams.
- Supporting voluntary sector clubs through publications, giving advice or through supporting local sports councils.
- Working with local schools and in after school clubs.

Although local authority sports development departments were not subject to Compulsory Competitive Tendering they are subject to Best Value.

Governing bodies and sports development

Sports governing bodies take a keen interest in developing their own sport and many employ sports development officers to work locally to develop their sport at the grass roots level. These sports development officers are frequently based at regional or county level and their work often involves liaising with local authority sports development officers in order to set up initiatives in that local area. Depending on the sport that they are working in they may also work with schools to promote interest and achievement in their sport or set up coaching programmes and squads through which youngsters can progress.

Governing bodies sometimes encourage children and schools to take up mini games that are more suitable for youngsters. Such games help children to learn about a new sport in circumstances that make it fun, rewarding and challenging such as Short tennis or Mini Soccer.

CASE STUDY *Kwik cricket*

'Since it was introduced in 1988, Kwik Cricket has become a byword for fun in sporting education with more than half of all primary schools in the UK now playing the game. Resembling cricket but without complex rules and the hard ball, Kwik Cricket was devised by the Test and County Cricket Board – the forerunner of the England and Wales Cricket Board – and the National Cricket Association after years of detailed product development and research in consultation with cricket coaches, education authorities, teachers and, most importantly, the children themselves. The result is an easy to understand, fun activity which appeals to hundreds of thousands of boys and girls aged five upwards.

More than 42,000 Kwik Cricket kits have been sent out and demand remains high'

Source: *www.lords.org.uk*

Sports development in the twenty-first century

Currently, there are a variety of forces acting on sports development.

The allocation of lottery money for revenue projects means that there are new opportunities such as setting up programmes linking voluntary sector clubs to school activities through the New Opportunities Fund or working with clubs to prepare funding applications to support their activities.

Following disappointing performances by national teams across many sports during the 1990s and particularly the poor haul of medals at the 1996 Atlanta Olympics, there is increasing awareness that as a nation we should do better. The development of programmes to support excellence and to nurture potential talent has been brought to the fore with programmes such as the World Class performance and Sport England's 'More Medals' campaign.

This is not to say that grass roots participation is not being encouraged. However, in the early 2000s the emphasis in encouraging sports participation is often either on promoting mass participation as a foundation for later, medal winning, excellence or on participation as a means of tackling social exclusion in society as a whole.

In 1999 the National Association of Sports Development Officers was launched in Nottingham with the aims of raising the profile of sports development, sharing good practice and representing the views of those involved in sports development.

Sports tourism

❝Sport and tourism, Britain's perfect match❞
— The British Tourist Authority

Sports tourism has existed since the ancient Greeks travelled to the Olympics in 776 BC. In the UK today it is a massive industry and encompasses both those who travel to participate in sport and those who travel to watch sport. Every week thousands of fans travel around the country as domestic tourists supporting their teams. Package holidays now abound for people to go to see World Cups, Olympics, Test Matches, Champions League matches and other prestigious sporting occasions. It is estimated that 5,000 people travelled from the UK to see Lenox Lewis fight Evander Holyfield in Las Vegas in 1999.

New developments

In January 2000, in recognition of the substantial role that sport plays in tourism, the British Tourist Authority set up the Sports Tourism Department to implement a sports tourism strategy in the new century. Under the banner heading 'A Sporting Chance for Britain', the British Tourist Authority sums up its vision:

❝Visitors also come to Britain for sport. And they come in their millions – to watch, to play, to visit famous sporting venues and to enjoy a wide variety of leisure and recreational activities. But, with our sports tourism excellence and even greater sports tourism potential, Britain could be attracting even more sports tourists. This is our challenge and our opportunity. We have a unique turn-of-the-millennium chance to propel British sports tourism ahead of the competition, and fight off the threat we face from foreign sporting destinations.❞

A significant component of the strategy for sports tourism is the staging of major international sporting events. At the period around the turn of the millennium the UK will have hosted:

- 1996 European Football Championships
- 1999 Cricket World Cup
- 1999 Rugby World Cup
- 2000 Rugby League World Cup
- 2000 UCI World Track Cycling Championships
- 2000 XVII Commonwealth Games in Manchester

There are also bids under way for the IAAF World Athletics Championships, the FIFA World Cup and aspirations towards a sustained Olympic bid, possibly for the year 2012.

In order to maximise the potential of sports tourism the key is to make major sports events a magnet for tourists visiting the area and also to use the event to promote tourism in the wider region, not just around the stadium on the day of the event.

CASE STUDY *Horse racing: the Cheltenham Gold Cup*

During the Cheltenham Gold Cup Week it is estimated that the normal population of the town of 100,000 doubles. Accommodation is scarce and many people book up a year in advance. During this famous racing festival it can be difficult to find somewhere to stay as far away as Evesham which is 15 miles away. To help cope with the accommodation demand for the week, Cheltenham Borough Council runs a service which facilitates sports tourists to rent places in private homes. Traditionally many of the visitors to the Gold Cup come from Ireland.

CASE STUDY *The Rugby World Cup and the Millennium Stadium*

In 1999 Wales hosted the Rugby World Cup at the new Millennium Stadium in Cardiff with other matches played in England, Scotland, Ireland and France. Based on the previous World Cup in 1995 in South Africa it is estimated that the 1999 tournament may have grossed as much as £800 million. Six games were held in the Millennium Stadium attracting about 400,000 people. It is estimated that this could have injected around into £45 million into the Cardiff economy with a further £15 million from related tourism such as the 3,000 media personnel who covered the 5-week long tournament and the additional fans who arrived in the city just to just soak up the atmosphere.

The Millennium Stadium will also bring sustained tourism benefits to the city with a possible 600,000 visits a year to see sports events plus a further 100,000 visits to other attractions on the site such as the Virtual Rugby Museum, the Visitors Centre and banqueting. In all, the new stadium could generate an extra £19 million annually into the Cardiff economy, a massive increase over that which could have been generated by the old national stadium.

Source: *Cardiff Research Centre Economic Impact of Millennium Stadium*

Professional sport

Background

Top sports stars can earn millions of pounds a year not only through their sporting performances, salaries and prize money but also through

DISCUSSION

Name 12 professional athletes or sportspeople.

How many of them are football players? How many different sports are represented in your choices of athletes?

DISCUSSION

Do you think that the prize money at the Wimbledon tennis championships should be the same for women as for men?

DID YOU KNOW?

Professional Football Clubs are not clubs at all but companies.

The last major professional 'football club' in England was Nottingham Forest which became a limited company in 1982 and is now a Plc.

DISCUSSION

Baron de Coubertin, the Frenchman who founded the modern Olympics in Athens in 1896 said 'It is not the winning but the taking part that matters.' Do you agree?

DID YOU KNOW?

Since 1994, the Sport England Lottery Fund has supported 3,019 capital projects and committed £966.25 million.

Source: Sport England web site (www.english.sports. gov.uk/info/about.htm)

product endorsement, media work and advertising fees. Today, mass exposure through the media has meant that top performers are more than sports stars, they are national and international celebrities.

In some sports the introduction of professionalism, and hence payments to players, has come only very recently. Football still had a maximum wage until the early 1960s and tennis only legalised Open Tournaments where professionals could play in 1967. More recently athletics only began on the road to professionalism in the 1980s and Rugby Union in the 1990s.

Professional or semi-professional?

‘Without the lottery funding I would be stuffed’

— Steph Cook, Modern Pentathlon Relay World Champion
from *UK Sport Annual Report*, 1998–9

Earning millions of pounds a year, however, is not the norm for the majority of professional athletes and many need to supplement their income from other sources in order to continue. For those who need to train and compete full-time, such as potential Olympic athletes, the problem of finding funds to finance their training can be crucial to their success and for many the only hope until recently was sponsorship.

The World Class Fund was established to provide a financial boost to the training of British teams and athletes. However, existence of the Fund does not mean that all semi-professional sports people can automatically turn professional, as even with this support many athletes will still need to work to supplement their income.

CASE STUDY *Lottery funding allows athletes to reach their potential*

MIRIAM BATTEN, ROWING

'In the pre-lottery days she worked part-time at Debenhams then rushed to the Amateur Rowing Association's Headquarters at Hammersmith to fit in a training session in the afternoon and another in the evening. In such circumstances, her highest achievement was a bronze medal in the 1991 World Championships. As a full-time squad athlete she won silver in 1997 and Gold in1998 in the double sculls.

Source: *Sunday Times* March 1999 from Sport England Lottery Fund Strategy 1999–2009

Martine Hingis: young sporting person in action

DISCUSSION

Why are the home nations not more successful when it comes to major international events such as football world cups, cricket test matches and the Olympics?

JENNY COPNALL, CROSS COUNTRY MOUNTAIN BIKER

Talking about the (World Class) Programme Jenny commented 'Having proved my potential with two national championship medals, the next step is the world podium. The Programme has arrived at an ideal time for me as a developing rider and the goals of improved international performance and future Olympic medals tally with my own aims.'

With the World Class Performance Programme to help her, Jenny says, 'I hope to be serving up fewer pizzas in my spare time and more podium placings.'

Source: *UK Sport Annual Report, 1998–9*

Sports-related gambling

Traditionally the major sports for gambling were horse racing and greyhound racing and these sports are still of vital importance to the gambling industry. Originally business was mostly done at the track or the course as the high street betting shop is a relatively new phenomenon only emerging since the Second World War. Since their arrival, names like William Hill, Ladbrokes and Coral have become common place in the high streets of most towns. Most sports betting is done by regular or recreational gamblers with the rest of the population taking part in big events such as the Grand National and the FA Cup Final.

CASE STUDY *The football pools*

One of the main forms of mass gambling is the football pools. For 70 years until the advent of the National Lottery the football pools were the best hope for many to get rich quick. Their place in the sporting world is well established and is demonstrated by the TV announcing the pools results and forecasts along with the football results every Saturday. There are three main pools companies: Littlewoods founded in 1923, Vernon founded in 1925 and Zetters founded in 1933. The Pool Promoters Association exists to represent the interests of the pools industry. The advent of the National Lottery has had a devastating affect on the pools with the amount of money staked now is only a fraction of the amount that it was at the outset of the National Lottery in 1994 (Table 3.3).

Amount (millions)	£773	£839	£869	£937	£823	£556	£427	£319	£237
Year	90–91	91–92	92–93*	93–94	94–95	95–96	96–97	97–98*	98–99

*53-week season

TABLE 3.3 *Amount staked on the pools*

The football pools must donate a proportion of their money to the Football Trust to go towards investment in football stadium redevelopment.

Source: The Pools Promoters Association

 DID YOU KNOW?

Littlewoods Pools was started in 1923 by three Manchester telegraphists as a part-time venture. During the early days 10,000 coupons were distributed at a major football match in Hull with only one returned. After early losses two of the three could not continue. John Moores decided to go on and became a millionaire before he was 35.

DISCUSSION

Horse racing, greyhound racing and betting shops should not operate on Sundays. To what extent do you agree or disagree with this statement?

Changes in sports gambling at the turn of the century

At the beginning of the twenty-first century changes are taking place that are significantly changing the face of sports gambling. The origins of modern sports gambling can be found on the racecourse and there is now a growing trend to encourage gambling at a wide variety of sporting events. The concourses of many new football stands now have easily accessible betting outlets beside refreshment stalls, as the sports gambling industry aims to become more available and accessible to a wider customer base.

Spread betting is now very popular where rather than just betting on a result, such as a team winning the cup, your success is spread over a range of possible different outcomes.

New technology now means that it is no longer necessary to go to a betting shop or a sports stadium to gamble. The growth of information technology and the development of widespread telephone payments means that the sports gambling industry may look very different in 10–15 years' time compared with the beginning of the twenty-first century.

Phone betting and Internet betting are now easily accessible and it has never been easier to gamble without leaving the home. The ability to make long-distance payments, either by phone or by the Internet, has led to betting with offshore companies in places such as Gibraltar, who can offer significant tax advantages to gamblers. The growth of Teletext and the Internet has also helped the spread of information so that gamblers can keep abreast of developments from home. It may be that the high street betting shop will not survive in its present form in the next 20 years or so.

Sports medicine

Sports medicine is now as advanced as our scientific knowledge will allow. It is not only about injury recovery and rehabilitation – although this is a vital component – it is also about harnessing the most advanced scientific and medical knowledge to give elite athletes the best chance possible. Letty Wevers, the Senior Physiotherapist for the British Amateur Gymnastics Association explains the importance of both physical and psychological preparation and well being:

❛It's a very important part of the process. The gymnasts train very hard and put an awful lot of pressure on their bodies and minds. We try to speed up their recovery rate after training so they rest before the next session. We try to keep them happy.❜

– *UK Sport Annual Report*, 1998–9

Sports medicine also exists at the grass roots level. In some areas sports injury clinics can be found in sports clubs, and in most areas physiotherapists are available who specialise in sports injuries.

Recent years have seen greater awareness by sports people at all levels of the roles and importance of correct preparation for sport, nutrition and sports psychology. Along with this growing realisation and body of knowledge, the number of sport science degrees has increased significantly in the last 15 years and they are now available at universities all over the country.

Sports science and medical organisations

In 1992 the National Sports Medicine Institute of the United Kingdom was founded. It exists to provide a focus for all those involved or interested in sports medicine including doctors, physiotherapists and nutritionists. Its field covers areas such as sport and exercise, medicine, physiotherapy, physiology, nutrition and psychology.

The British Association of Sport and Exercise Sciences (BASES) aims to 'develop and spread knowledge about the application of science to sport and exercise'. BASES is the professional association providing for people who have an interest in sport science and can provide information on conferences, sport science degrees, career opportunities for sport science graduates and accreditation for sport and exercise scientists.

Health and fitness

One of the main areas of growth in physical recreation is the growth of the health and fitness industry. Since the early 1980s there has been an explosion in this whole area and a modern fitness area is now a vital part of a leisure centre.

The first sign of the change in public demand and attitudes was the growth of aerobics and this spread to other forms of exercise class such as step aerobics, boxercise and 'legs, bums and tums'. The growth of this form of exercise was important in that it stimulated the increased participation of women in active leisure. However, many people prefer to train alone or require personal monitoring and feedback of their progress in order to maximise results. In response to this demand personal fitness trainers are available to act on this one-to-one basis.

CASE STUDY *Holmes Place Health and Fitness Clubs*

Holmes Place operates health and fitness clubs, most of which are around London and the South East. They offer fully equipped gyms with trained instructors, a range of exercise classes (such as Tai Chi, Yoga, Body Pump, Step), sauna and steam rooms, body and skin care treatments and restaurant and bar facilities. Some clubs have heated swimming pools, jacuzzis and crèche facilities. Each member is given a personal assessment to form the basis of their programme and personal training is available at additional cost. By mid-1999 they were operating 37 clubs and had a membership of over 96,000. Their half-yearly turnover at June 1999 was over £26 million.

Source: Interim Report 1999, via web site

DID YOU KNOW?

In 1998 there were 2,500 private health and fitness clubs in the UK.

Source: Sport England Fact Sheet 17

There has been a corresponding growth in fitness rooms and the emphasis has been more and more on cardiovascular machines, such as fitness bikes and rowing machines and away from the traditional weights type of gym. To cope with this demand many centres have converted squash courts and ancillary halls into fully equipped fitness rooms.

At the turn of the century the trend continued towards more of this type of provision with customer expectations also requiring services such as fitness assessment and supervised fitness programmes. The modern fitness room is spacious, has trained staff who can offer a range of services, has modern user-friendly equipment and is comfortable. Fitness rooms that do not meet these criteria are failing to respond to the challenges and customer expectations of the new century.

Picture of inside a luxury health club

Source: © *actionplus*

GP referral schemes

While it has long been known that an active lifestyle can keep you healthy, the medical profession has been slow to pick up the practical applications of this when it comes to using exercise as part of a therapy. Consequently, although the medical knowledge has been there for some time, it is only in recent years that doctors have been able to give patients 'exercise prescriptions' on a more widespread basis, for ailments such as obesity and stress.

Under the GP referral scheme, a patient gets referred to a leisure centre where a qualified member of staff places them on an appropriate exercise programme under supervision. Despite the medical benefits of such a partnership between the medical and leisure professions, GP referral schemes are not currently in operation in all local authorities.

Outdoor and adventure activities

The range of outdoor and adventure activities is enormous. The Outdoor Pursuits Division of the Central Council of Physical Recreation contains over 40 organisations ranging from those involved with adventure style sports, such as the British Mountaineering Council and the British Hang Gliding and Paragliding Association, to other outward bound bodies such the Ramblers Association, and the Duke of Edinburgh Award. Apart from these air-based and land-based activities, water recreation is also a significant aspect of outdoor activities. Organisations in this area range from the British Sub-Aqua Club to the National Federation of Anglers.

People often take part in outdoor pursuits as a recreational escape from the cities and the pressures of modern life. A large part of the attraction

Enjoying the great outdoors   Source: © *actionplus*

of activities such as pony trekking or rambling, is the enjoyment of the great outdoors and to find peace and distraction away from the stresses of modern living. Other people prefer more adventurous or active sports such as bungee jumping, hang gliding or scuba diving.

The industry that has developed around adventure activities and outdoor pursuits is obviously skilled and specialised yet comparatively small. It is also composed of people from a variety of different organisations, from rural local authorities running outdoor water sports centres, to organisations such as the Youth Hostels Association which provides accommodation.

There has also been a realisation among many businesses that outdoor adventure activities can help their staff with team building and the developing of personal skills, such as communication, decision making and self-confidence, and it is not uncommon for businesses to send their staff on outdoor or adventure weekends.

Adventure in the city?

A recent trend has been the increase in the number of opportunities for people to take part in outdoor adventure type sports in cities. Venues such as artificial ski slopes, water sports on urban canals, rivers and docklands and climbing walls have emerged in many urban areas and water-based recreation is now a feature of many dockside urban redevelopments.

 DID YOU KNOW?

For every £1 of central and local government support received, sport gives back £5 to the taxpayer (not counting the invisible benefits of reduced use of the health service, sports tourism and greater fitness in the work place).

Sport is also a major employer. According to Sport England it is estimated that sport provides over 400,000 paid jobs and the voluntary sector the equivalent of a further 108,000 full-time jobs.

Source: Sport England Fact Sheet 17, Oct 1999

The scale of sport and its contribution to the UK economy

Sport is a multi-billion pound business that emerged as a major sector of the economy in the last third of the twentieth century. People work in the sports industry in a variety of ways: as coaches, sports centre staff, sports retail assistants, and a very few as professional sports people. Sport is big business and it impacts on all our lives. The statistics below show the enormity of the sports industry at the start of the twenty-first century:

- Consumer expenditure on sport in the UK was estimated to amount to £10.4 billion in 1995, equivalent to 2.24% of total consumer expenditure.

- Sport is worth £8 billion to the UK economy, representing approximately 1.7% of GDP.

- In 1998 consumer spending on active sports amounted to £5.53 billion.

• In 1995 consumers spent an estimated £3,125 million on sportswear and £1,935 million on sports participation.

Source: ILAM Fact Nov'98 sheet from Marketscape Ltd. 1997

Participation

There are few people who have not heard the message that an active lifestyle helps to keep you healthy. However, for many people lack of time, money, access or simply confidence to get started means that they are among those who still remain inactive.

It is estimated that 10% of the population visit a leisure centre once a week and a really keen 1% visit a leisure centre once a day! Around 29 million people in the UK over the age of 16 regularly take part in exercise. Table 3.4 shows adult participation rates.

ACTIVITY	PARTICIPANTS (%)
Walking/Rambling	44.5
Swimming	14.8
Keep Fit/Yoga	12.3
Snooker/Pool/Billiards	11.3
Cycling	11.0
Weight Training	5.6
Football	5.8
Golf	4.8
Running/Jogging, etc.	4.5
Tenpin Bowling/Skittles	3.4

TABLE 3.4 *Adult monthly participation by activity*

Source: © Crown Copyright (Office for National Statistics *General Household Survey*, 1996)

ACTIVITY

Participation trends in sport – what do you know?

Conduct a quick survey asking people to list what they think are the top 10 sports in order of participation. Look at your findings and compare them with Table 3.4. What has emerged from your survey? Why do you think your respondents have got the wrong idea about the popularity of certain activities?

Clubs and memberships

In 1995 there were an estimated 150,000 sports clubs in the UK. Table 3.5 details clubs and membership numbers.

 DID YOU KNOW?

The leading three sports among school children outside of lessons in the mid-1990s (participating at least ten times in previous 12 months) were:

1 Cycling: 57%
2 Swimming: 50%
3 Football: 37%

Source: *Social Trends*, 1998

SPORT	MEMBERS	CLUBS
Football	1,650,000	46,150
Billiards/Snooker	1,500,000	4,500
Golf	1,217,000	6,650
Squash	465,000	1,600
Bowls	435,000	11,000
Sailing	450,000	1,650
Angling	392,000	1,750
Rugby Union	284,000	3,250
Lawn Tennis	275,000	2,800
Swimming	288,000	1,950

TABLE 3.5 *The ten leading sports in terms of club membership*

Source: Sport England from Keynote, *UK Sports Market 1996 Market Review*

The organisation and funding of sport

The sports industry consists of a diverse range of organisations, from government agencies to small voluntary sector sports clubs, from public sector facilities to private sector racket clubs and professional sports clubs. The means of funding such a variety of bodies is as diverse as the nature of the organisations themselves.

Sponsorship

It is impossible to be interested in sport and to be unaware of sport sponsorship. Sponsors' names appear on clothing, on advertising hoardings and perhaps most powerfully of all, company or brand names replace or become associated with the names of tournaments, for example, the Nat West Cricket Finals or the Worthington Cup in football.

Sports sponsorship spending has increased from £265 million in 1994 to an estimated £347 million in 1998 and sponsorship of sport far outstrips sponsorship of the arts. Table 3.6 shows sponsorship received by different sectors.

SECTOR	£ M
Sports	322
Broadcasting	111
Arts	96
Other	45
Total	574

TABLE 3.6 *UK Sponsorship of different sectors 1997*

Source: Sport England Fact Sheet 17, October 1999

However, sponsorship of sport does not come primarily from companies within the sports industry. In 1998 sports goods and clothing companies were only in fourth place when it came to the average number of sport sponsorship deals. This is represented in Table 3.7.

Table 3.7 shows the top eight sectors of the economy sponsoring sport based on the average number of deals in 1998:

SPONSORS BY SECTOR	NO. OF DEALS
Alcoholic Drinks	111
Cars/Allied Trades	87
Banks/Finance	79
Sports Goods Clothing	78
Insurance	63
Communications	58
Media	53
Soft Drinks/Water	38

TABLE 3.7 *Sport sponsorship for the top eight sectors*

Source: Sport England Fact Sheet 17

DISCUSSION

Why sponsor sport?

Why are alcohol companies so keen to sponsor sport?

Why did tobacco companies argue so strongly that they should be allowed to continue sponsoring sport?

Should tobacco companies be allowed to sponsor sports such as snooker and cricket?

ACTIVITY

Funding in sport

Consider the two sports you are investigating.

Look up the web site of those sports or contact the governing body and find out how the organisation is funded.

Can you see any evidence of sponsors' names anywhere? If so, what is the value of their input?

Funding of professional sport

At one time professional sport was almost totally dependent on gate receipts as its main source of income and gate receipts are still a vital source of income today. However there are now considerable opportunities (particularly for big and high profile clubs) for other forms of income such as sponsorship, catering and conferencing, merchandising and broadcasting money. Table 3.8 shows the turnover breakdown of three of the largest professional football clubs in the UK.

ARSENAL	£M
Gate Receipts	16.164
Broadcasting and other commercial activities	26.066
Retail Income	6.393
Total	**48.623**

GLASGOW RANGERS	£M
Ticket Sales, TV and related income	19.808
Advertising, sponsorship and related income	5.776
Retail	6.673
Publishing	1.332
Catering	2.775
Rent	0.162
Total	**36.526**

MANCHESTER UNITED	£M
Gate Receipts/Programme Sales	41.908
Television	22.503
Sponsorship, Royalties and Advertising	17.488
Merchandising and Other	21.586
Conference and Catering	7.189
Total	**110.674**

TABLE 3.8 *How football clubs get their income*

Source: Annual Reports MUFC, 1999, AFC, 1998–9, Glasgow Rangers FC, 1999

ACTIVITY

Do fans know where the money comes from?

Ask a sample of football fans how they think a professional football club earns its income.

How do their views compare with Table 3.8?

The organisation and funding of sport at international level

❝Sport is probably the most effective means of communication in the modern world, bypassing both verbal and written communication and reaching directly out to billions of people worldwide. There is no doubt that sport is a viable and legitimate way of building friendships between nations.❞
– Nelson Mandela

Source: UK Sport International Relations and Major Events

International Sports Federations (ISFs)

International sports federations such as FIBA (International Basketball Federation) or FIH (International Hockey Association) are the governing bodies of sport at international level. The structures of these organisations may vary from sport to sport, but generally their role is to administer their sport, implement policies on an international basis, make the rules and oversee the affiliated national governing bodies from each country. The ISFs also organise international championships in their sport such as the IAAF World Athletics Championships and the FIFA Football World Cup. Many sports also have international regional organisations that run competitions such as the EUFA Champions League.

CASE STUDY *The International Rugby Board*

The International Rugby Board, founded in 1896, has its headquarters in Dublin and is the international sports federation for Rugby Union. One of its major objectives, enshrined in its constitution is to 'promote, foster, develop, extend and govern the game of Rugby Union'.

The Board encompasses one regional association, Federation Inter-Europeen de Rugby Association (FIRA) based in Paris, and the national unions from 91 countries.

The Board comprises 12 unions and FIRA who all have representation on the executive committee (two representatives each from England, Scotland, Ireland, Wales, Australia, New Zealand, South Africa and France and one representative each from Italy, Japan, Argentina, Canada and FIRA).

Source: IRB web site (www.irfb.com/)

ACTIVITY

The structure of sport at international level

Identify the World Federations for the sports that you are investigating.

How are the sports organised, managed and funded at International level?

The Olympic family

6 Olympism is a philosophy of life, exalting and combining in a balanced whole the qualities of body, will and mind. Blending sport with culture and education, Olympism seeks to create a way of life based on the joy found in effort, the educational value of good example and respect for universal fundamental ethical principles. The goal of Olympism is to place everywhere sport at the service of the harmonious development of man. 9

– Olympic Charter, Fundamental Principles (www.olympic.org/)

The first modern Olympics were held in Athens in 1896 with just 311 athletes competing in six sports. Since that time the Olympics have flourished into a global international movement with an estimated 10,000 athletes competing in 296 events across 28 sports in Sydney 2000.

FIGURE 3.1 *The Olympic Family*
Source: International Olympic
Committee web site

The International Olympic Committee (IOC), based in Lausanne, Switzerland, is the global organisation responsible for the administration of the Olympic movement. It is responsible for selecting the host cities for both the summer and winter Olympics and running the movement's educational and commercial activities. The Olympic movement comprises the International Olympic Committee plus other organisations such as the International Sports Federations and The National Olympic Committees (NOCs) from each country (Figure 3.1(a)).

Each sport or event at the Olympics is run by its International Sports Federation. The IOC has 28 affiliated Summer Federations such as FIG (International Gymnastics Federation and IWF (International Weightlifting Federation) and seven affiliated Winter Federations such as FIS (International Ski Federation). In addition ARISF (Association of IOC Recognised International Sports Federations) contains non-Olympic sports such as the WSF (World Squash Federation) and the IFBB (International Federation of Body Builders).

The National Olympic Committees send teams and participants to compete in the Olympic games. They also undertake a preliminary selection process for cities bidding to host the games. There are currently 200 National Olympic Committees affiliated to the Olympic Movement. Only cities that win their domestic selection through their National Olympic Committee can be forwarded to the IOC for selection.

A successful bid for the staging of the Olympics requires the foundation of an Organising Committee who have the monumental task of staging the games and providing and arranging the facilities and accommodation for thousands of athletes. In 1998 ATHOC, the organising Committee for the 2004 Athens Games, was created to allow six years for planning and development.

Olympic funding

In 1984, Los Angeles hosted the Olympic Games. Many other interested cities were deterred by the enormous cost and commitment. However, there was immense competition to hold the 2004 Games, with Athens emerging as the winner. One might ask the question: 'What changed?'

Following the 1984 Games, with the future of the Olympic Games uncertain, the IOC decided to restructure its system of sponsorship. As a result TOP (The Olympic Partners) was created as a sponsorship scheme involving major multinational corporations to create a revenue base that was more diversified. These Olympic partners provide revenue and services in exchange for exclusive rights in their own areas and the global coverage and image that comes with being associated with the Olympic movement. With the globalisation of TV broadcasting these benefits are obviously even more attractive.

In its fourth cycle, 1997–2001, the Olympic movement had 11 partners, all of whom were major multinational companies such as Coca Cola, Kodak, Mcdonalds and IBM. All 200 National Olympic

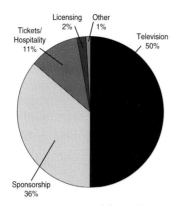

FIGURE 3.1 *Breakdown of Olympic funding*

Committees receive revenue through the programme while prior to its inception, less than ten NOCs received marketing revenue of any kind. The effect of this sponsorship arrangement has meant that whereas in 1980 broadcasting rights accounted for 95% of the income, sponsorship now accounts for 36% of the IOC Marketing Revenue (Figure 3.1). The income from broadcasting has also dramatically increased.

This Olympic Marketing Revenue is estimated to generate around US$3.5 billion between 1997 and 2001. The International Olympic Committee distributes over 93% of this to the 200 National Olympic Committees and their Olympic teams, the international sports federations and the organising committees for the Olympic Games (Source: IOC web site (www.olympic.org/)).

British Olympic Association

The British Olympic Association is our National Olympic Committee. It receives benefits through the TOP programme but also arranges its own fund raising activities. For the Sydney Olympics, British Airways and Adidas all supported the British Olympic team. The benefits to supporting companies include the value, prestige and positive image that comes with being associated with the Olympics and the public relations value of supporting a national effort. Despite this support, however, there is frequently the need for extra finance. For the Sydney Olympics the British Olympic Appeal was launched with the aim of raising £4 million.

The British Paralympic Association works in conjunction with the BOA and the Sports Councils and provides Britain's Paralympic Athletes with the organisational support to give them the best chance of winning medals at the Paralympic Games.

❝Representing your country is a fantastic feeling. Just look at the medals won and records broken by British athletes at the World Disability Athletics in Birmingham – 25 Gold, 22 Silver and 15 Bronze – a brilliant result.❞

– Tani Grey-Thomson MBE, Paralympic athlete from *UK Sport Annual Report*, 1998–9

The organisation and funding of sport at national level

The structure of sport in the UK has undergone profound changes in the last 20 years. It is dynamic, that is, it is constantly changing with new bodies being created and others changing. This section should help to give you a clear understanding of who the major organisations are, the role that they perform and how they are funded and organised at the beginning of the twenty-first century.

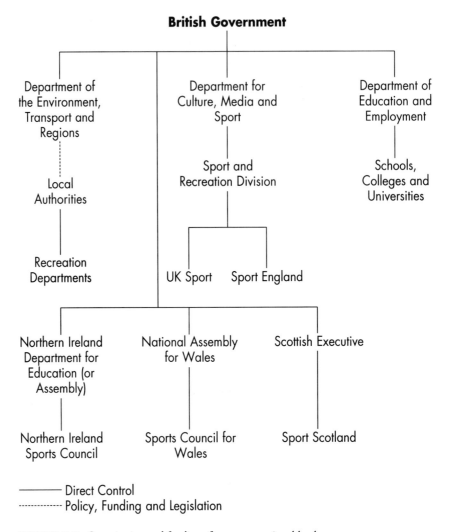

FIGURE 3.2 *Organisation and funding of sport at a national level*

Source: Sport England Information Fact Sheet 17

The main government department that is involved with sport is the Department for Culture, Media and Sport. However this must be qualified by recognising the enormous contribution that is made to sport by schools, colleges and universities and by local authorities. These bodies come under the remit of the Department for Education and Employment and the Department of the Environment, Transport and the Regions. Devolved government to Wales and Scotland means that their respective sports councils come under the auspices of the Welsh Assembly and the Scottish Executive. These parallels are represented in Figure 3.2.

The Sports Councils

In 1997, following many years of consultation, a radical reform was undertaken to restructure the roles of the sports councils. Following the government policy paper *Sport: Raising the Game*, the GB Sports Council was abolished and in its place two new organisations were created. The English Sports Council (or Sport England as it was renamed) was created to take over responsibility for the development of sport in England. (The sports councils in Wales, Scotland and Northern Ireland were already well established). The UK-wide responsibilities were taken over by a new organisation called UK Sport.

Although these reforms did not have as great an effect on the sports councils in Scotland, Wales and Northern Ireland, the advent of devolved government means that the sports councils in these nations are now responsible to their regional authorities. At the time of writing, the funding mechanism for the Northern Ireland Sports Council was dependent upon the future status of the Northern Ireland Assembly.

The precise objectives of the different Sports Councils may vary slightly but generally they include:

- improving facilities
- tackling exclusion and promoting equal opportunity to play or excel at sport
- widening participation
- promoting and developing sport
- disseminating information and advice
- supporting programmes of excellence

UK Sport

❝UK Sport was established in January 1997, to focus on high performance sport at the UK level, with the aim of achieving sporting excellence on the world stage. The work of UK Sport is all about building a framework for success – developing and supporting a system capable of producing a constant flow of world-class performers.❞

– UK Sport Annual Report, 1998–9

UK Sport is divided into three directorates:

1 Performance Services – responsible for distributing lottery funds to UK level sports with world-class performance plans and providing support through UK sports institutes.
2 Ethics and Anti-Doping Control.
3 International Relations and Major Events – responsible for assisting bids to bring major sports tournaments to the UK.

Sport England

Its aim is:

❝More places to play sport, more people playing sport, more medals.❞

It has responsibility for developing its network of eight regional hub sites for the UK sports institutes and runs six national sports centres at Crystal

DID YOU KNOW?

In 1998/99 UK Sport received approximately £11.5 million from the government and around £20 million to distribute as lottery grants.

Source: www.uksport.gov.uk

Palace, Lilleshall, Bisham Abbey, Plais-y Brenen, Holme Pierrepoint and the Manchester Cycling Centre. Sport England is funded through the Department for Culture, Media and Sport and is accountable to parliament through the Secretary of State for Culture, Media and Sport.

Sports Council for Wales

Its mission is:

❝Increasing participation, raising standards, improving facilities, providing information and advice.❞

The Council supports the Welsh Institute of Sport and the Plai Menai National Water Sports Centre. In the period 1999–2000 its income was over £9 million (of which around £6.7 million was granted in aid from the government) plus around £11 million of lottery money to distribute.

Source: *Sports Council for Wales Annual Report*, 1998–9 and www. uksport.gov.uk

The Northern Ireland Sports Council

Its aims:

❝Starting well, staying involved, striving for excellence.❞

The Council supports the Tollymore Mountain Centre and is involved with the development of the United Kingdom Sports Institute Northern Ireland. It also contributed £2.5 million towards a 200 m hydraulic athletics track, an activity floor and an international scale ice hockey pad at the Belfast Odyssey. In the period 1999–2000 it received government grants totalling £2.27 million and lottery money for distribution of around £7.5 million.

Source: *Northern Ireland SC Annual Report*, 1999

CASE STUDY *Sport Scotland – what does a sports council do?*

Sport Scotland has launched Sport 21 as its strategy for the new century. As well as lottery distribution its work to date has included:

1 Widening Participation

- £4.5 million pledged to offer every school in Scotland a sport coordinator
- 200,000 children have taken part in Team Sport Scotland Camps and activities
- Over £2000 million of new facility investment has been created by its lottery fund

2 Developing Potential

- 12,000 coaches and leaders have taken part in Team Sport Scotland activities and training courses
- Sport Scotland national training centres delivered over 50,000 student days of sports training in the period 1998–9 at the three national training centres

3 Achieving Excellence

- 50 coaches supported by the Performance Coach Development Programme and five Scottish Institute of Sport coaches appointed
- £2 million used to support 500 athletes from 40 different sports
- £1.6 million was awarded towards a hockey training and competition centre, and £242,450 towards a national performance centre for judo

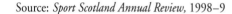

Source: *Sport Scotland Annual Review,* 1998–9

National Lottery

There have been radical alterations to the format of the lottery, due largely to the National Lottery Act of 1998.

These changes in the way that sports lottery monies are now distributed include:

- Funding of both revenue and capital projects rather than just capital projects.
- The ability of the sports councils to be proactive rather then just reacting to lottery applications as they come in.
- Setting up of the World Class Programmes to work at the elite level.
- Setting up of the New Opportunities Fund to distribute money to the sixth good cause concentrating on projects on or connected with health, education or the environment.

As the distributing bodies for sports lottery funding, the sports councils of the home nations have their own titles for schemes around the different areas of funding such as developing elite performance, developing potential talent, funding facilities and developing coaching. For example, to assist top national athletes, Wales has the Elite Cymru scheme whereas Scotland has the Talented Athlete Programme.

In addition, the World Class Events programme exists to help the national governing bodies to stage events or bid for sporting events to be held in the UK. This ranges from supporting large events, such as the FIFA World Cup, to less publicised events, such as Sport Scotland's £83,000 award to help stage the British Open Squash Championships in Aberdeen. (Source: Sport Scotland lottery fund report 1998/99)

CASE STUDY *Sport England, structure and funding of sports lottery from the year 2002*

The Sport England scheme has a two-fund approach.

1 The Community Projects Fund has three categories:

- Small Projects up to £5,000 supporting organisations such as clubs and schools. Priority is towards disadvantaged groups and poorer areas.

- Capital Awards, grants of over £5,000 going towards pitches, sports halls, major equipment, etc.

- Revenue Awards of over £5,000 particularly to tackle social exclusion. As such this will help fund School Sport Coordinators.

2 The World Class Fund is designed to help athletes win at international level and support stars of the future and it also has three categories:

- World Class Performance, funding elite sports people who have the potential to win medals or equivalent within six years.

- World Class Potential, aimed at up-and-coming professionals who have the potential to win medals within ten years.

- World Class Start Fund, identifying and nurturing the professional sports stars of the future.

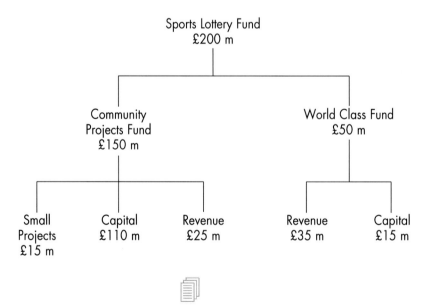

Source: ILAM Information Centre Fact Sheet 99/6

United Kingdom Sports Institutes (UKSI)

❛We can be winners, but winners need support every step of the way.❜

– Steve Redgrave, Rowing Olympic gold medallist from *UK Sport Annual Report 1998–9*

The sports institute aims to provide the facilities and support needed to give elite sportsmen and women the best chance of winning at international level. There are ten regional institutes in England, each with a coordinating focal point, and institutes in Scotland, Wales and Northern Ireland. Institutes utilise a wide variety of facilities and serve as the nucleus for a certain area by coordinating and supporting athletes and all the other people involved, such as their coaches, sport scientists and medical support.

CASE STUDY *A modern sports institute*

'The purpose of each institute is to provide specialist training facilities, but equally important, nationwide access to a range of services. In practice, the institute is a coordinating mechanism to harness the services in the local area. In the East Midlands for example, Holme Pierrepoint will provide facilities for canoeing and rowing, and some sports medicine and sports science, but it will also harness the services of the nearby Queens Medical Centre in Nottingham and the facilities, skills and services provided by Loughborough University.'

Source: Sport England Information Sheet 18, November 1999

The Scottish Institute of Sport was launched in 1998 with the initial aim of supporting athletics, badminton, curling, hockey, football, rugby and swimming. The Northern Ireland Sports Council is working in partnership with Ulster university to utilise an £18 million budget to develop the site and training facilities. The UKSI in Wales has already utilised some of its £22 million capital budget, on the £4 million national centre for cricket, opened in partnership with Glamorgan County Cricket Club.

Source: Sport England Information Sheet 18, November 1999

ACTIVITY

Sports funding

Revisit the web sites of the national governing bodies for the two sports you are investigating and the web sites of the national sports councils.

Can you find out if your sports have received lottery funding?

National Coaching Foundation (NCF)

The National Coaching Foundation's motto is:

❝Better coaching, better sport.❞

The National Coaching Foundation was originally the coaching wing of the Sports Council. Its purpose is to train, educate and develop coaches and to improve the quality of sports coaching within the UK at all levels. In 1989 the NCF became an independent charity and in 1993 it merged with the British Institute of Sports Coaches.

By 1998–9 the NCF had an annual turnover of around £3.4 million (excluding the Coachwise scheme) consisting of:

- Grant aid from UK Sport and Sport England   72.7%
- Earned Income   22.2%
- Subscriptions   5.1%

The NCF is organised into six teams:

1 Coach Education Services Standards and Structures.
2 Communications.
3 High Performance Coaching.
4 Local Coaching Development.
5 Management Services.
6 Research and Design.

DID YOU KNOW?

Each year 15,000 coaches and 12,000 school teachers participate in NCF programmes, and since its inception in 1983, the NCF has provided developmental and educational opportunities for some 130,000 coaches.

Source: Fact sheet from National Coaching Foundation (untitled)

Its network in the UK includes ten coaching development officers based at Sport England's Regional Training Units and partnerships with the coaching units of Northern Ireland, Scotland and Wales.

In 1999 the NCF had 110 Premier Coaching Centres in England, running coaching workshops covering a wide range of coaching themes. Workshops are also delivered by the Northern Ireland Institute of Coaches, the Scottish Coaching Unit and the Welsh National Coaching Centre. The NCF is also involved in the High Performance Coaching Programme which aims to improve the knowledge and skills of our top coaches.

The Foundation offers three qualifications: NCF Award in Coaching Studies, NCF Certificate in Coaching Studies and the NCF BSc (Hons) Degree in Applied Sports Coaching, which is validated by De Montfort University.

National governing bodies

Sports governing bodies like the Football Association, the Rugby Football Union, and the Lawn Tennis Association are names familiar to sports fans. Their main role is to administer their sport within their home country and to represent their sport abroad by affiliating to their International Sports Federation.

Many sports governing bodies emerged in the second half of the nineteenth century, mainly as a response to the need to harmonise rules, organise competition and coordinate the clubs or the local associations that had formed them. They were organised to a standard structure that was put into place in the late nineteenth century and which still exists in some governing bodies today.

Essentially clubs or players would affiliate to a County Association which would elect officers to a National Council. This Council would then elect a board or an executive to manage the affairs of the Association and appoint or elect specialist committees to undertake specific duties, such as disciplinary and appeals, finance, etc. Today governing bodies range in size from large organisations such as the Football Association, to smaller associations that rely on dedicated volunteers.

The 1990s saw many governing bodies change their structure in order to respond to the growing commercialism in sport and the need to develop elite performance plans. However, they continue to administer, nurture, serve and represent their clubs and the grass roots of their sport and to remain accountable to their members.

Central Council of Physical Recreation (CCPR)

The CCPR describes itself as the independent voice of British Sport.

It is divided into six divisions and each of the 285 governing or representative bodies are placed in a division that is most relevant to their activity. The six divisions are:

1 Games and Sports, for example, British Fencing Association.
2 Major Spectator Sport, for example, Professional Golfers Association.
3 Movement and Dance, for example, Keep Fit Association.
4 Outdoor Pursuits, for example, British Mountaineering Council.
5 Water Recreation, for example, Amateur Rowing Association.
6 Interested Organisations, for example, British Wheelchair Sports Foundation.

Each division elects a chairman and a supporting member who supervise the divisional meetings and are also members of the executive committee of the CCPR.

In 1989 the CCPR set up a charitable arm called the Sports Trust with the aim of providing administration and funds for the four leaders awards.

CASE STUDY *The CCPR and the sports councils*

Many of the institutions that you have studied in this section, such as the sports councils, the National Coaching Foundation, the sports institutes and the Lottery are all part of the same public sector strategy. The CCPR however has a different and much older story that has moulded the place it has today in the sports industry.

The Central Council of Physical Recreation was established in 1935. As its membership embraced sports governing bodies it was able to represent sporting interests in a far more powerful and cohesive way than any one governing body could. In 1957 the CCPR established the Wolfenden Committee to examine how voluntary and statutory bodies could best serve the cause of physical recreation. The Committee recommended the creation of a government funded sports development council and in 1972 the Great Britain Sports Council was established by Royal Charter. As much of the CCPR's role would now be undertaken by the new publicly funded Sports Council, the CCPR was forced to reconsider its future.

It was eventually decided that the CCPR had an important role to play as an independent organisation outside of the government funded and appointed sports councils. The division of duties between the new Sports Council and the CCPR was established. The CCPR transferred all its assets such as the National Sports Centres to the Sports Council and redefined its role, among other things, as an organisation where national governing and other representative bodies could be represented and collectively 'formulate and promote measures to improve and develop sport'.

Source: CCPR 'What it is, What it does, How it operates'

National Playing Fields Association (NPFA)

❝Healthy recreation opportunities for local people close to where they live is the NPFA's core purpose. It is that which drives its campaigns to protect recreation space from built development. In tune with the times, the NPFA is active in urban areas through its 'inner city village halls' project and its learning/recreation programme, Midnight Basketball, which appeals to young people.❞

– Elsa Davies, Chief Executive NPFA

The NPFA was founded in 1925. One of its most long lasting contributions has been the setting of the six-acre standard, which recommends six acres of playing field for every 1,000 of population.

The NPFA is a charitable trust, which has had a royal charter since 1933. It aims to stop built development on playing fields and gives advice and information to support campaigns aimed at preserving playing fields that are under threat. Today the NPFA owns 130 playing fields and has custodial responsibility for around 1,700 others. In 1999 there were over 900 sites under threat.

Sources: Interviews with NPFA and their web site (www.npfa.co.uk/)

ACTIVITY

What is happening in your region?

Look up the NPFA web site on www.npfa.co.uk/ and examine the lists of playing fields that are known by the NPFA to be under threat.

Is a playing field near you on a developer's drawing board?

Some other organisations

The Institute of Leisure and Amenity Management (ILAM) was formed in 1981 and has around 6,000 members involved in public and private sector leisure provision. The institute covers all sections of the leisure industry from sports and sports development to parks, open spaces, museums, tourism and leisure education. Its services include training courses, seminars, and conferences, a professional qualification scheme, a monthly magazine (*The Leisure Manager*), an information service, regular mailings to its members and a policy unit which campaigns on behalf of the leisure industry.

The Institute of Sports and Recreation Management (ISRM) is another institute that offers a wide range of services for its members and also offers a qualification scheme. The ISRM is a professional body covering sport and recreation facility management, but is known particularly for the emphasis it places on the technological side of sports facility management, particularly swimming pools.

The Sports and Recreation Industry Training Organisation (SPRITO) is the national training organisation for the sport and recreation industry and works on setting and implementing training standards. The organisation is prominent in the development and implementation of sport NVQs and covers sport, recreation, playwork, outdoor education and development, and fitness and exercise.

The organisation and funding of sport at regional and local levels

Local authority leisure departments

Leisure provision by local authorities is now a significant part of our everyday life. Few people have never strolled through their local park or swum in their local pool at some stage in their life. The range of local government services is vast, ranging from facilities such as sports centres and pools to sports development departments and summer play schemes.

The advent of Compulsory Competitive Tendering (CCT) radically altered the nature and structure of local authority leisure departments with a split emerging in leisure sections between contractor and client sections. The contractor section, usually the staff and management of the facilities, competed against private sector operators to see who would run the centres for the life of the contract. The winning bid normally received a management fee to manage the centres. Council sections that won were known as Direct Service Organisations (DSO) and had to manage the centre on the basis of the specification that had been laid down and the bid that they had placed. The client department was in reality what was left of the old leisure departments. They covered such duties as monitoring the contractor (either the private operator or the DSO) to ensure that the contract was being fulfilled and carrying out those duties that were often not in the contract, such as looking after the fabric and the structure of the buildings. Sports development departments and dual use centres that had a substantial school usage were exempt from CCT. As a result of CCT you will find that today some local authority centres are run by private operators and others by council staff.

Best Value has now replaced CCT. Under Best Value councils are not compelled to go through the tendering process but can select what system works best for them. They need to demonstrate that the system they have chosen for a certain service, such as leisure and recreation, exemplifies the three E's (efficient, effective and economic). They must also examine each area of service in terms of the four C's:

- Challenging the Purpose of the Service
- Consulting the Community
- Comparing with other providers
- Looking to Competition as a way of achieving the three E's.

ACTIVITY

Best value

You can take part in a small 'Best Value' exercise yourself.

Find out who runs the sports centres in your local authority and in two neighbouring authorities.

Make a list of things you are going to look at, such as cleanliness, customer service and services offered, among others. Visit the sport centres in each. How do the standards of service compare across the three?

Voluntary sector clubs

In Table 3.5 you were able to see the levels of club membership for different sports. Clubs obtain money primarily through membership fees, subscriptions and fund raising activities, sometimes backed up with financial grants. Clubs can also apply for lottery funding to build new facilities or to provide revenue under such schemes as the Community Projects Fund.

The organisation of clubs varies enormously according to their size and nature of the sport. For example, martial arts clubs tend to be led by one or two people who set up classes in leisure centres or community halls and affiliate to their governing body. On the other hand, organisations such as bowls and tennis clubs, and many team sports, often have a more democratic structure. This traditional organisational structure for voluntary sector sports clubs entails the election of officers to a club committee.

Normally the club members elect the committee to administer the club for a year at an annual general meeting. The committee usually consists of a chairman, a secretary and a treasurer plus other posts depending on the size and the nature of the club, such as a membership secretary, a fixtures secretary, a social secretary, team captains, etc. All the members of the committee are normally club members who volunteer to serve the club by standing for election to the committee for one year at a time.

The club would normally affiliate to the national governing body through the local county or regional association, depending on the structure of the governing body. Once affiliated to the governing body the club would be officially recognised and be able to enter leagues and tournaments and send delegates or representatives to local meetings of the governing body association.

Sport and the mass media

What is the sports media?

In simple terms the sports media comprises all the different ways that we are exposed to the world of sport apart from those occasions when we go to watch live sport ourselves or participate in sport. It therefore includes TV, newspapers, sports magazines, radio, Internet sports sites and fanzines.

The importance of sport to the mass media

❝If you look at the next time the live Premier League rights come up, they are going to go for something like £4–5 million a game. I don't think I can justify that. I think for £5 million we can make an extremely good and exciting drama series, quite a lot of innovative entertainment – and I have to say, is that worth one football match?❞

– Greg Dyke, Director General of the BBC – (Reported in *Metro* 31/1/00, as interviewed on *Breakfast with Frost*)

The sports media industry

Sport is a crucial part of the media and the advent of new technologies has radically altered the ways that the media portrays sport over recent years.

Newspapers were once the primary medium for sports coverage, now sport can just as easily be found as an entire colour supplement or as a centre page pull-out packed with photographs and sports news and containing endless rounds of sports topics ranging from in-depth analysis to tabloid gossip.

 **DID YOU KNOW?**

In 1999 Radio 5 Live broadcast 1,961 out of the total 2,516 hours that the BBC devoted to radio sports broadcasting.

Source: BBC Sport *Facts and Figures for Sport*

Radio was one of the traditional forms of the sports media and sports reporting was established by the BBC before the war. One of the flagship programmes, the *BBC Sports Report*, is still broadcast on a Saturday evening at its traditional time of five o'clock. The changes in the 1990s have been immense. To respond to the constant demand for sports coverage the BBC created Radio 5 Live, a whole new station dedicated solely to the coverage of news and sport.

Independent radio stations have also emerged that thrive on live commentaries, sports magazine programmes and fans phone-ins. These changes during the 1990s were partly due to the demand for sport being apparently insatiable and partly due to the increased opportunity for wider sports coverage brought about by the substantial increase in the number of radio stations.

The 1990s also saw the growth of magazines produced by sports fans themselves, usually known as fanzines. Their growth was made possible by the development of information technology which substantially opened up publishing opportunities at much reduced costs. Fanzines are often an alternative to the hype and 'official line' that are taken by sports clubs and can act as a focus for humour, praise or, more often than not, as a voice of the fans' discontentment at the club's progress.

The sports Internet grew in the second half of the 1990s both as a reporting medium for sports news and as an outlet for sports organisations and clubs to set up sites to communicate directly with their fans and the public. In February 1996 Sky Online set up its sports Internet news service. By the year 2000 it was common for most professional sports clubs and venues to have Internet sites although at the turn of the century they were frequently 'web brochures,' and not interactive sites for ticket bookings.

ACTIVITY

Media influences

Examine the media to see how the two sports you are studying differ in the amount of coverage they get. You can measure this in column inches.

Compare also the styles of reporting in the colour sports pages of a tabloid newspaper and the sports pages of a newspaper such as The Times or Guardian for the same day. In what ways is the coverage different?

DISCUSSION

How many hours of sport have you watched on TV in the last week? How many hours would you watch during Wimbledon or Euro 2000, for example? Is this figure more or less than that of your average week?

Sport and TV

Above all else it is television where the sport and media relationship is at its most powerful.

Television devotes a significant amount of time to sport and the demand to see live coverage of major sporting events is huge. It is not only the scale of the demand that is important, but also that people feel an attachment to major sports events, they are part of our national life and our national calendar. The month of May would not be the same without the FA Cup Final live on TV, nor June/July without Wimbledon. A balance has to be reached between protecting the coverage of these events so that everybody has the opportunity to see them and allowing sporting authorities to sell their broadcasting rights to the highest bidder so that they can maximise their income generating potential.

The complexities of this issue have led to the lists of protected events being redrafted on several occasions over recent years. The growth of satellite, cable and digital TV has made the matter even more intricate by increasing the number of stations that do not give access to the whole population.

The Broadcasting Act of 1996 ensures that the live coverage of certain listed major sporting events is made available to terrestrial TV for broadcast to the mass population. The act states that all listed events must be made available to Category A broadcasters (the terrestrial channels of BBC, the ITV network and Channel 4) on fair and reasonable terms. Category B broadcasters, such as Sky Sport and Euro Sport, are not allowed to show live coverage of these events unless they also make the live broadcasting rights available to Category A channels on fair and reasonable terms. Channel 5 is classed as a Category B broadcaster because it does not yet cover the whole population. This system is administered by the Independent Television Commission who must decide what constitutes a fair and reasonable price.

From June 1998 the listed events were divided into two groups as shown below. While full live coverage of Group A events remains protected as above, exclusive coverage of Category B events is allowed on a subscription channel, provided that adequate arrangements are also made for delayed coverage or edited highlights on a free to air terrestrial channel.

Group A Events (full live coverage protected)

- Olympic Games
- FIFA World Cup Finals Tournament
- European Football Championship Finals Tournament
- FA Cup Final
- Scottish FA Cup Final (in Scotland)
- Grand National
- Derby
- Wimbledon Tennis Championships
- Rugby League Challenge Cup Final
- Rugby World Cup Final

Group B (secondary coverage protected, that is edited highlights, delayed coverage and/or radio commentary)

- Cricket Test Matches played in England
- Non-Finals play in the Wimbledon Tournament
- All other matches in the Rugby World Cup Finals Tournament
- Five Nations (now six nations) Tournament Matches involving the Home Countries
- Commonwealth Games
- World Athletics Championships
- Cricket World Cup
- Final, Semi-finals and Matches involving Home Nations Teams
- Ryder Cup
- Open Golf Championship

Source: Department of Media Culture and Sport 'List of events Maintained under Broadcasting Act 1996'

ACTIVITY

Television coverage

Look at the list of events and decide how much you agree or disagree with it. If you were asked to add one event to the Category A list which event would it be?

Consider some of the most important competitions in the sports that you are investigating. Are they televised? What sort of coverage do they receive?

Television viewing

Football easily dominates television viewing figures, far exceeding the number of viewers for any other sport. While the 1999 Champions League Final topped the sports viewing ratings, the highest non-football event was the Grand National in seventh place. The figures in Table 3.9 show the extent of football's dominance in terms of viewing figures. All the other entries in the top 20 were football matches on terrestrial TV (mostly ITV).

POSITION	EVENT		AVERAGE VIEWING FIGURE (MILLIONS)
1st	Champions League Final	ITV	15.6
2nd	Euro 2000 Play off England v Scotland	ITV	14.6
7th	The Grand National	BBC 1	10.1
17th	The Brazilian Grand Prix	ITV	7.5
18th	World Athletics Champs (incl. 400 m men's semi final)	BBC 1	7.4
20th	The Grand National Repeat	BBC 1	7.0
20th	Wimbledon Men's Singles Final	BBC 1	7.0

TABLE 3.9 *Top 20 sport viewing figures 4 January–28 November 1999*
Source: Compiled from Statistics from BBC Sport Marketing and Communications

While major football matches are generally the most watched televised sport events, it is also the sport that absorbs most sports broadcasting time. Obviously these factors are interrelated as the mass exposure helps to stimulate high interest in football's big games. Table 3.10 shows sports coverage on TV in minutes.

	BBC 1	BBC 2	ITV	CH 4	EURO SPORT	SKY	CH 5
Football	4,800	650	7,475	2,930	29,725	102,765	2,815
Golf	1,485	3,548	0	60	2,160	83,900	90
Motorsports	390	1,680	5,620	0	26,065	31,945	645
Cricket	3042	9,327	135	0	0	44,970	0
Tennis	1,130	2,466	0	0	21,035	15,955	0
Motor Cycling	175	90	0	0	14,880	11,310	0
Horse Racing	2,581	1,161	60	7,635	0	13,460	0
Boxing	95	0	140	0	7,845	16,260	0
Rugby League	40	160	0	0	0	22,910	0

TABLE 3.10 *TV coverage of sport in minutes, 1998*

Source: Sport England Information Sheet 17 October 1999

ACTIVITY

Media coverage

Compare the coverage of the two sports that you are investigating across different forms of the media, that is, newspapers, terrestrial TV, subscription TV, and radio.

The ways the mass media can influence sport

❛Television is the engine that has fuelled the growth of the Olympic Movement.❜

– The International Olympic Committee

The 1990s were the age when television money flooded into sport. The major force behind this was clearly the media revolution that brought new media companies such as Sky TV into the bidding for sports events. These new companies did not only pay huge sums of money themselves, they also strengthened the negotiating position of the sports authorities so that terrestrial TV companies such as the BBC and ITV, were forced to offer higher bids to screen sports events. In some sporting competitions the terrestrial TV companies could not compete with the money being offered by subscription channels and have resorted to showing only highlights. It also forced some sports authorities to change the scheduling of their matches and in some cases, the very structure of their sport.

CASE STUDY *Sky TV and sport*

More than any other media organisation Sky has had the most effect on sport, both in terms of the money that it has invested and in the rescheduling of fixtures to suit the demands of subscription TV.

Football Premiership matches are now no longer played only on Saturdays but on Sunday afternoons and Monday evenings. Sky now has around seven million subscribers and 40,000 pubs and clubs. Clearly a large part of the attraction is Sky's live sports coverage.

The advent of digital broadcasting has allowed Sky to expand its broadcasting further with channels such as Sky Sports Extra and Sky Sports News. The contract that Sky signed with the Football Premier League to show exclusively live coverage between 1992 and 1997 was worth £191.5 million.

Compare this figure with the football deal done later in the decade to see how the sport broadcasting market changed in a short space of time:

- Football Premier League: 1997–2001 – four year contract to show exclusively live coverage £670 million
- Football Nationwide League: 1996–2001 – five-year contract with Football League worth £125 million
- Rugby League – Super League and World Club Championship: 1996–2001 – five-year contract, £87 million
- Domestic Cricket: 1999–2002 – joint deal with Channel 4 for four years, £103 million

Source: BSKYB Information

Olympic broadcasting rights

The globalisation of the media and the increased marketing power of sport are demonstrated by the change in fortune of the Olympics. You will have read in a previous section of this Unit that the Olympic movement has been transformed in recent years. The increase in broadcasting money to the Olympics (Figure 3.3) has helped to convert the movement from financial instability to a situation where the International Olympic Committee is able to distribute support throughout the Olympic movement.

DID YOU KNOW?

It is estimated that the Sydney Olympics will be watched in 220 countries by a *cumulative* television audience that is 3–4 times the size of the entire human race.

Source: Calculated from figures from web site www.olympic.org

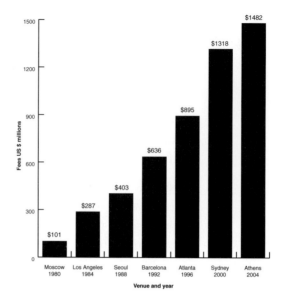

FIGURE 3.3 *Olympic Global TV Rights Fees*

Source: web site www.olympic.org/

The media, participation and awareness of sport

❝Tennis bookings rise steadily through May and June as the weather improves. In early July by the second week of Wimbledon demand soars way beyond capacity, it literally goes mad. Some customers emerge having spent a fortune on the latest gear, others turn up with wooden rackets or wanting to hire them. This is sustained for only a week or two after Wimbledon where lack of tennis on the TV leads to a steady decline throughout August.❞

– Sports Centre Manager in London

Sport needs the media in order to be able to communicate with the public. It stimulates us, turns us from viewers and readers into enthusiasts and inspires us to have a go. The Nigel Benn–Chris Eubank fights in the early 1990s were shown live on terrestrial TV and as a result became the talk of the work place, schools and colleges. The Lennox Lewis–Evander Holyfield World Heavyweight Title fight in 1999, on the other hand, was not available live on a terrestrial channel and aroused only passing public interest. Tennis courts around the country fill to the brim due to Wimbledon's coverage on terrestrial TV.

There is grave concern that any sport that is not covered by the media will lose public interest and the next generation of youngsters will fail to be inspired. Governing bodies are of course aware of this. In the 1980s the Squash Rackets Association ran a campaign for more televised squash. This failed to succeed in the long term, partly because squash is not as easy to televise effectively as other sports.

Major events such as the Olympics and the World Cup are watched worldwide by billions of people who are motivated, captivated and inspired. In developed and developing countries alike, people gather collectively around televisions in neighbours' houses, bars or cafés to see events like their country competing in the World Cup.

Without the media, events like the World Cup and the Olympics would have only passing significance and interest. The International Committee is mindful of this and sells its broadcasting rights to channels that will enable global mass viewing.

How sport is affected

The power of the media over sport is enormous and it can change the whole way a sport is structured. Small items of misbehaviour by superstars are now picked up by the press and turned into pages of news. The FA Cup Quarter Final once had all four ties kicking off at 3.00p.m. on a Saturday. At the start of the year 2000 only one tie kicks off at the traditional time.

CASE STUDY *The power of television in sport*

Rugby League

By the summer of 1995 professional Rugby League found itself trapped between the desire to impose higher standards upon itself and its players, and a gradually diminishing audience. The result was an increasingly difficult financial position and an internal survey revealed that the game was earning approximately £10 million each year but spending in the region of £30 million. The vast majority of the shortfall was being taken up by club directors funding teams from their own pockets, and an increasing dependence on banks and creditors.

One-third of the Rugby Football League member clubs had experienced some contact with insolvency during the first half of the 1990s so the very future of the game was being called into question.

In the summer of 1995 the Australian Rugby League's traditional administrators were challenged by the might of media baron Rupert Murdoch, who wanted to take over the best elements of the game to use as part of his satellite and 'pay-for-view' operations. Another media tycoon, Kerry Packer, backed the traditionalists and the domestic game was split.

To widen his range of interests in British sport and amid speculation that the move would seal off sources of new stars for the Australian Rugby League, Murdoch offered £87 million for the British game to sign an exclusive contract with his media group.

One major condition was that the British game forsook its traditional August to May playing season and aligned itself more closely with the Australian playing season. This saw the new calendar start in March and

DISCUSSION

When a national team is competing, such as England or Scotland, the sporting authorities have no right to sell the viewing rights to cable or satellite TV companies. The whole nation should always be able to see their national teams live, even if this means that the authorities have less money to plough back into their sport.

To what extent do you agree or disagree with this statement?

finish in October. It also saw the creation of a Super League, the elite clubs from the game whose players had to embrace full-time professionalism.

These revolutionary changes, to what had been a traditional part-time professional game since 1895, brought almost as many problems as benefits. While its stars became very highly paid performers and the top clubs were able to concentrate on expanding their marketing effort, the gap between the better-off clubs and their lesser colleagues began to grow at an alarming rate.

The sport's high-profile climax to the end of the season, the Silk Cut Challenge Cup Final at Wembley, suddenly found itself as a mainly pre-season competition that overlapped with the start of the Super League tournament. It also meant that the highly demanding Super League competition was very reluctant to become involved in international fixture planning during the season and this in turn forced the end of the extended two-month tours of the Southern Hemisphere countries and the popular reverse tours to this country.

Organisationally the game was changed too. While the Rugby Football League remains the Governing Body of the sport in Great Britain and Ireland, the marketing company Super League Europe Limited, has assumed virtually complete control over the top clubs and their financial muscle. The non-Super League professional clubs are grouped under the Association of Premiership Clubs but they are far more aligned with the RFL than Super League. The British Amateur Rugby League Association (BARLA) remains as the governing body for the amateur game with the exception of the clubs and competitions which are being nurtured by the Rugby Football League's Development Department.

In 1998 the Rugby League Policy Board was formed to oversee common areas of interest between the RFL and BARLA and discussions have started with a view to bringing all three bodies into closer alignment.

Although Super League is now exclusively broadcast on satellite television, the terrestrial services of BBC retain an important interest with their exclusive contract to cover the Silk Cut Challenge Cup. The Rugby Football League is concerned that the dependence on satellite broadcasters, who have substantially smaller audiences than the terrestrial stations, will mean that some of the 'star making' qualities have been lost for League players. In addition, because many games are played at times to suit the television contract, there has been a loss of coverage in national newspapers.

There are signs that the paying audiences are starting to return to the live games and that the spectators are coming to terms with the massive change undertaken by the game. Whether the national media will follow while Rugby League remains a largely north of England regional sport, remains to be seen.

Source: The Rugby Football League

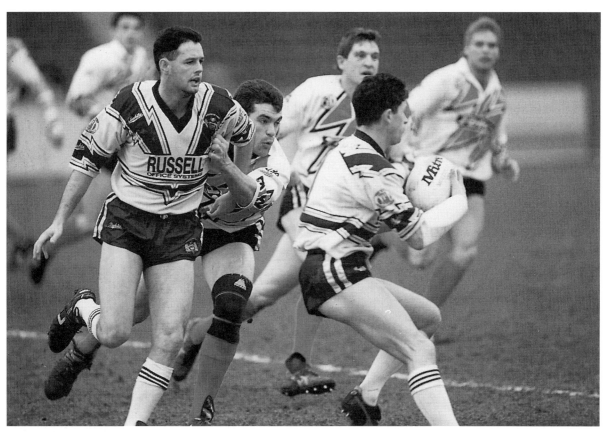

Rugby League match in play   *Source: © actionplus*

ACTIVITY

Does sport have a choice?

Read the Rugby League Case Study carefully. Do you agree that Rugby League should have made the choices that it did? Were there any other options for Rugby League?

If you want to know more, then why not investigate Rugby League as part of your assignment? There is plenty of information to get you started.

Trends in sport

New and emerging sports activities

In the last quarter of the twentieth century the health and fitness classes burst onto the scenes. From Legs, Bums and Tums to Body Pump, the variations on fitness training have been endless. In the twenty-first century the theme is continuing as more advanced types of fitness rooms emerge.

Another development for youth is the emergence of 'mini sports' games where children can perfect their techniques. These games (for example, mini soccer, short tennis and kwik cricket) are set to grow among the young in the years to come.

DISCUSSION

Until very recently, some sports (e.g. tennis until the 1960s) were against being paid any money at all, feeling that this would lead to money becoming more important than the sport itself. Do you agree with this view?

There has also been an emergence in street level games, that is, games that the young can easily contrive and play without going to a leisure centre. These range from two-a-side basketball in playgrounds to uni-hockey and skateboarding.

There is also a desire among the more adventurous to invent new adventure activities. The emergence of dangerous sports such as bungee jumping, has not stopped the process and new variations of dangerous sports are constantly being developed.

Commercialisation – Sport and Money

The connection between money and sport is not new. Athletes were sponsored in ancient Greece and in the 1920 Olympic Games in Antwerp, the programme was almost entirely filled with adverts. The arguments between professional and amateur sport have existed since the late nineteenth century.

The debate over commercialism revolves around how much money should be allowed to affect sport. It is one thing for sport and sports people to find ways of making money (although some people have reservations about how far this should go), but when money or commercial interests start influencing where and how sports are played and how they are organised, this is something quite different.

Throughout this chapter you will have read about the increasing commercialisation of sport, that is, the increasing role that money plays both within sport and the affect of powerful organisations outside sport, such as the media. This is one of the major trends of our time.

Sports participation increasing and decreasing

In total, the rise in sports participation that occurred in the 1980s was not sustained in the period 1990–6.

Figure 3.11 shows the trends in participation from 1987–96 based on people participating in the four weeks before being interviewed (excluding walking).

	1987	**1990**	**1993**	**1996**
Men (%)	57	58	57	54
Women (%)	34	39	39	38
Combined average (%)	45	48	48	46

FIGURE 3.4 *Trends in participation*

Source: *Living in Britain,* General Household Survey, 1996

The statistics in Table 3.12 demonstrate the sports with rising and decreasing participation. Most noticeably women's indoor swimming has risen steadily and women's keep fit also rose dramatically in the late 1980s, and this increased participation has been sustained without rising much further in the 1990s.

There has been a substantial increase in men's cycling and a steady rise in men's and women's weight training/lifting. Men's participation in snooker, pool and billiards has declined significantly over the period as did both men's and women's participation in squash.

ACTIVITY	MEN				WOMEN			
	1987	1990	1993	1996	1987	1990	1993	1996
Indoor Swimming	10	11	12	11	11	13	14	15
Keep Fit/Yoga	5	6	6	7	12	16	17	17
Snooker/Pool/Billiards	27	24	21	20	5	5	5	4
Cycling	10	12	14	15	7	7	7	8
Weight Training*	7	8	9	9	2	2	3	3
Weight Lifting*				2				1
Soccer	10	10	9	10	1%			
Running (Jogging, etc.)	8	8	7	7	3	2	2	2
Tennis	2	2	3	2	1	2	2	2
Squash	4	4	3	2	1	1	1	1%

*Surveyed together until 1996

TABLE 3.12 *Selected sports participation within four weeks of interview*   Source: *Living in Britain* General Household Survey, 1996

Women's rugby in action   Source: © actionplus

Changing expectations of participants and spectators

In the section on national facilities you will have read about the revolution that is taking place in our sports grounds. These higher standards are now being demanded and expected by more and more sports fans as part of the norm. In the 1980s inadequate toilet facilities at a major sports stadium would have brought a mild complaint, now it is often seen as intolerable.

Expectations have also changed with leisure participants demanding certain standards as a minimum. Leisure centres will not meet the basic expectations of customers unless they provide a good standard of service, are clean, with friendly and presentable staff in uniform and have up-to-date equipment. The increased professionalism of many sports and the influx of television money, has meant that professional sports people at the top are now expecting higher and higher rewards, although we should never forget that lower ranked sports people have a very short professional life without earning great deals of money. This gap between the rewards at the top and those lower down is growing.

Changing markets for sport

We have an ageing population that is becoming more and more aware of the benefits of an active lifestyle. This means that the modern leisure manager is expected to provide programmes and activities that do not cater just for the young and fit. The growth in low-impact fitness training and over 50s fitness classes is one manifestation of this. There is also the need for sports that do not involve the need to be super fit, such as short mat bowls, recreational badminton or tennis, and swimming where lanes can be provided for various speeds.

The other change has been the growth in demand for fitness and health products and services at the expense of traditional competitive sports. Closely linked to this was the growth over the last 20 years in the demand for active leisure among women.

Technological developments

Technology affects all our lives so it is not surprising that it affects sport as well. The fabrics used to make sports equipment have improved significantly. For example, tennis rackets have been transformed from the wooden frames of the 1970s to modern composite materials such as graphite. This has so increased the speed of the serve that sometimes there are calls for changes in the rules to reduce the advantage of the server, particularly on fast, grass court tournaments like Wimbledon.

DISCUSSION

Penalty or no penalty?

Should all sports embrace media technology by stopping the game and using video playback to help the referees make decisions?

Look at a video or a football nostalgia programme and see the mud-soaked pitches of 20 years ago. Modern turf technology means that pitches are staying greener for longer. The advent of astroturf pitches has also transformed the ability of local leisure centres to be able to offer year-round playing surfaces.

Video evidence is now used in disciplinary matters. For example, in cricket video playback is used by a third umpire to check for run-outs, etc. FIFA, which has rejected the idea of a third video playback official, is also interested in using technology in football to transmit signals to the referee to indicate whether the ball has crossed the goal line but is still not yet satisfied that the technology is of an adequate standard.

Technology can also have negative affects. One example is that performance enhancing drugs, or perhaps more accurately, training enhancing drugs, are becoming harder to detect through traditional drug testing methods. However the testing agencies have been forced to advance their technology and this has led to a kind of 'arms race' in drugs testing.

The influence of sport on fashion

You will have already read about the sports goods business in detail in an earlier section of this Chapter. You may well be reading this while wearing sports clothing, trainers, sweatshirt, tracksuit bottoms. This would have been very unlikely 20 years ago unless you had just come from playing or training.

A focus on selected sports

In this section you will examine three sports: athletics, tennis and horse-racing. This will enable you to gather background information to go towards your assignments, providing of course that these are among the sports that you select to study. If you choose to focus on other sports then these will act as a useful guide and reference base for you in terms of the type of information you should be looking to gather. You may select football as one of your sports, in which case, you should re-read this chapter, as it contains lots of useful information.

Focus on athletics

❝I could feel the tension ... all the people watching there ... how massive the event was ... and I thought, God, I have actually done that.❞

– Sally Gunnell, Olympic Gold Medallist, Barcelona 1992
(UK Sports *Major Events Blueprint For Success*)

Sally Gunnell   Source: © *actionplus*

Background

Traditionally athletics in the UK had six governing bodies, one each in Scotland, Ireland, Wales, the South of England, the Midlands Counties and North of England. Together these latter three associations formed the Amateur Athletic Association of England (commonly known as the 3A's) which had the responsibility for selecting the England team for the Commonwealth Games. In the absence of a UK-wide governing body, the British Amateur Athletic Board was formed in order to represent the nation at international level. By the 1980s it became apparent that the system required reform in order to cope with the demands of the modern sporting world. As a result the British Amateur Athletic Board disbanded and the British Athletic Federation (BAF) was formed as a new governing body in 1991. The 3A's, the home nation associations and the regional English associations remained in place.

In 1997, after six years, the British Athletic Federation (BAF) became insolvent and was wound up. It had not been well equipped and its structure was unable to handle the challenges and opportunities of the modern commercial world. Its organisation was in some ways like the systems that you read about in the section on national governing bodies with a large council of members at the core. Laudably, it tried to be both representative and accountable to the grass roots on the one hand and support and develop athletics at the elite professional level on the other.

Structure of UK Athletics

UK Athletics aims to be streamlined and effective by reducing the total number of positions (paid and unpaid) to 80 and the number on any decision-making group to a maximum of 10 (as opposed to the 250 positions in BAF which sometimes functioned in teams of 20–30 people

DID YOU KNOW?

Athletics is one of the UK's most successful major sports. Since the World Championships in 1991, Great Britain and Northern Ireland have fluctuated between fourth and fifth positions.

Source: UK Athletics

with 64 on the Council). The emphasis now is on the performance of the organisation, not on ensuring representation from the different groups within the sport.

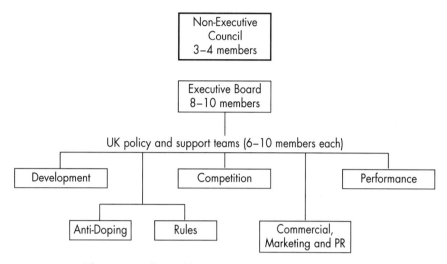

FIGURE 3.5 *The structure of UK athletics*

Source: UK Athletics

The most striking aspect about this structure (Figure 3.5) is that there is no line down to the 3A's, the home nation athletic associations, the counties or the athletic clubs. There is of course a relationship with these organisations who remain in place to run and administer the amateur and club level side of athletics. Clubs still must affiliate to their region and individuals are affiliated automatically to the governing body as members of a club. Clubs still send delegates to their county associations and the county, inter-County and regional championships are still organised in the traditional manner.

Such a structure would have indeed seemed outrageous 100 years ago but now governing bodies must be able to develop performance plans at the elite level, handle professionally the marketing and commercial aspects of the sport and deal with media and public relations pressures.

DID YOU KNOW?

There are estimated to be between 150,000 and 200,000 people affiliated to athletics clubs in the UK.

Source: UK Athletics

Funding of UK athletics

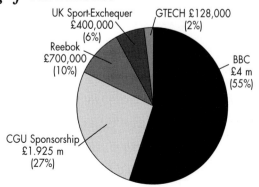

FIGURE 3.6 *UK Athletics Total Income, 1999*

Source: UK Athletics

Media and athletics

When athletics hits the screens during the big events such as the Olympics or the World Championships the nation is captivated. Outside of these events, however, athletics does not get mass coverage. Exceptions of course are the London Marathon and major indoor events, but generally the nation's awareness of athletics is focused around the big events.

Athletics gets a very short season in the public eye, normally around August or during the screening of the Olympics, the Commonwealth Games and the European or World Athletics Championships.

The bulk of UK Athletics' income comes from its five-year deal with the BBC.

International athletics

The international governing body of athletics is the IAAF which is based in Monaco and has 210 member nations. Executive control rests with the 26-strong IAAF Council backed up by numerous commissions and committees. There are also six regional federations including the European Athletic Association based in Germany.

Focus on tennis

❝As the governing body, the LTA exists to ensure the well-being and growth of British Tennis as a dynamic, healthy, year-round, competitive and enjoyable lifetime sport for all. ❞

— Lawn Tennis Association

DID YOU KNOW?

There has been a massive growth in the number of indoor courts due to the LTA's Indoor Tennis Initiative which offered financial support to the building of indoor tennis centres. Since the late 1980s the number of indoor tennis courts has increased tenfold.

Background

The Lawn Tennis Association, based at the Queens Club in London, is the governing body of tennis employing a staff of around 200. Tennis has not made the same radical alterations as athletics but has undergone some operational alterations in the mid-1990s.

Since 1995 there have been three main operating divisions:

● International and Professional (training of performance players and coaches and staging of professional tournaments)

● National Tennis Development (developing the game at county and club level, etc.)

● National Tennis Facilities (financial, technical, management support to improve and develop facilities in Britain)

The structure of the LTA is based along traditional governing body lines. The LTA Council is the main controlling body, consisting of elected representatives from the National Associations, the 36 English counties

and Island Associations. It is managed through a Board of Management. The 2,360 tennis clubs affiliate to their county association who until recently were concerned mainly with supporting tennis within the traditional county and club structure. The LTA explains:

❛As part of the National Development Strategy which included the appointment of County Development Officers, the role of the County Associations has broadened significantly to provide a coordinated approach for the development of the game in the club, education and local authorities. Each of the County Associations has produced its own county plan for the next five years.❜

– Background to LTA

Apart from LTA headquarters staff and County Development officers, people work in tennis at clubs, indoor tennis centres and as self-employed coaches, although most coaching is done part-time or voluntarily and almost all club administration is by volunteers.

Funding

The bulk of the LTA's income derives from the Championship at Wimbledon (Figure 3.7). Due to this almost guaranteed income from the Wimbledon Championships, the LTA has been able to resist the excesses of commercialism, and sponsorship income comprises only around 4.5% of total income.

Tennis at club level is mainly supported by the club members through subscriptions and other fund raising activities.

International tennis

The International Tennis Federation which has 200 member nations, organises the Davis Cup competition for men, the Federation Cup for

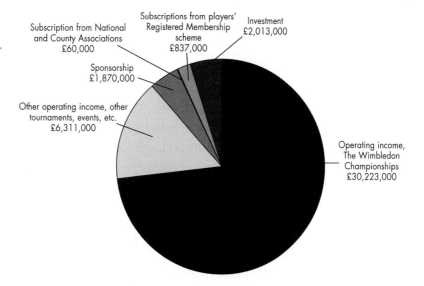

FIGURE 3.7 *Income of Lawn Tennis Association*

Source: *LTA Annual Report*, 1999

DISCUSSION

By the end of the millennium the last British men's champion at Wimbledon had been Fred Perry before the war and the last British women's champion had been Virginia Wade in 1977. Considering that we have the world's premier tennis tournament, why has Great Britain performed poorly at tennis for so long?

women and has involvement in other tournaments such as the Olympic games and the Grand Slams.

The leading male players affiliate to an organisation called the ATP Tour (Association of Tennis Professionals) an organisation of tournament directors and players who administer many of the major international tennis events. The organisation of tournaments by a players' association and not the international sports federation, is unusual in the world of sport. The women's equivalent is the WTA which administers 59 tournaments worldwide.

Tennis and the media

Although the ATP tour and the WTA tour operate for around 11 months of the year, the public perception of tennis in the UK focuses around mid-summer. The arrival of subscription channels has meant that tournaments such as the US Open or the Australian Open can be viewed by a minority of the population giving some stimulus to tennis outside of June and July.

Although tennis coverage on terrestrial television is substantial, this is largely because of the almost saturation broadcasting during the Wimbledon fortnight and some coverage of tournaments during the build up to Wimbledon. Despite tennis being one of the nation's favourite sports it does not get significant coverage and attention outside of Wimbledon, apart from special occasions such as the Great Britain team competing in the Davis Cup.

Focus on horse racing

Horse racing is a complex industry with organisations, associations and sections as diverse as the National Trainers Federation, British Equine Veterinary Association or the Horserace Totaliser Board.

Figure 3.8 gives a broad outline of the industry but does not show the entire industry.

Background

Traditionally the main governing authority in horse racing was the Jockey Club. In 1993 the British Horse Racing Board was formed as a new governing authority of racing in order to respond better to the commercial challenges facing racing in the modern era. Its directors come from different areas of the industry although the Jockey Club has strong representation on the Board.

The new organisation took on roles and objectives such as improving the financial position of racing, marketing and promoting racing, organising race planning and fixture lists and representing racing in dealings with the Government. The Jockey Club remained in existence to regulate the

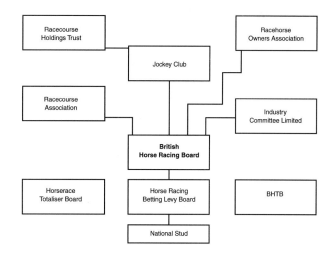

FIGURE 3.8 *Simplified Structure of the Horse Racing Industry*

Source: British Horse Racing Board

industry, dealing with areas such as licensing of trainers, doping control and appeals and disciplinary matters. It also continued to operate the 12 racecourses it owns through the Racecourse Holdings Trust and to operate its training facilities at Newmarket through Jockey Club Estates.

In 1961 the modern levy system was introduced whereby the betting industry would make contributions to the racing industry in return for the massive contribution that the sport makes to the gambling industry. To administer this system the British Horserace Levy Board was created with the responsibility of collecting the contributions from the bookmakers and the Horserace Totaliser Board and applying them to improve the breeds of horses, the improvement of horse racing and the encouragement of veterinary science or veterinary education. At the turn of the century the Horse Racing Board is pushing for an increase in the 1.2% of betting turnover that goes to racing.

The Racecourse Holdings Trust owns and operates 12 racecourses in the UK on behalf of the Jockey Club including Aintree, Cheltenham, Epsom, Haydock Park, Kempton Park, Newmarket and Sandown Park. There are a total of 59 racecourses in the UK managed by a variety of different organisations.

Mass media

Horse racing has its own media outlets, such as the *Racing Post,* largely aimed at providing information to those who bet on the sport. In addition, horse racing in many newspapers has its own section given to it where readers can look up form, runners, riders and betting odds. Horse racing is one of the more widely covered sports and its presence on TV and radio means that its gambling appeal and excitement is sustained, even for those who never visit a race track.

 **DID YOU KNOW?**

In 1999 there were licensed with the Jockey Club:

- **approximately 500 trainers**
- **411 jockeys**
- **588 amateur riders**
- **6,199 Stable Employees (of whom 3,992 were full-time and 333 self-employed)**

Source: *The Jockey Club 1998–9 Review*

In 1998 horse racing was the third most broadcast sport on BBC1 and the biggest single sport broadcast from Channel 4 (see Table 3.10 on page 180).

Trends

From 1994–8 the number of horses in training increased as did the total number of runners (Table 3.12). There was also an increase in the total number of fixtures, although the real trend was represented by an increase in flat racing (from 603 fixtures to 653) at the expense of jump fixtures (down from 499 to 486).

Total attendances at racing increased for both flat and jump racing, indicating that although the jump racing calendar declined, the average attendance at jump racing fixtures increased to compensate. Of the almost five million racing attendances in 1998, around 38% were at jump racing and 62% at flat meetings, a similar ratio to 1994. The levy from the betting industry increased from 37.5 million in 1990/91 to £52 million in 1998/99.

Funding

The horse racing industry contains a wide range of different organisations from diverse areas of the economy and there is no single funding mechanism. The following is therefore a simplified explanation:

In 1999 the British Horserace Levy Board raised £60 million of which £52.6 million was from the levy from the betting industry, £4.4 million from the Totaliser Board and the remainder from other sources. Of this £60 million almost £51 million went on improvements to horse racing. Table 3.13 details the main areas of expenditure.

The £29 million contribution from the Horserace Levy Board is the largest single contributor to prize money as shown in Figure 3.9.

It is this prize money that finances the running of large parts of the industry as the owners can use it to maintain their stables and training programmes. The Racecourse Holdings Trust finances the management

	1994	1995	1996	1997	1998
Horses in Training	11,366	11,785	12,423	12,281	12,594
Number of Fixtures	1,102	1,100	1,122	1,153	1,139
Number of Runners	71,217	68,565	73,352	73,367	76,219
Racecourse Attendances (millions)	4.67	4.71	4.73	5.00	4.98

TABLE 3.13 *Horse Racing Trends, 1994–8*

Source: British Horse Racing Board 1998 Report

Racecourse Prize Money	£29.4
Fixture Incentives	£4.9
Fixture Fees	£5.2
Horse Racing Forensic Laboratory	£2.6
RaceTech	£7.0

TABLE 3.14 *British Horserace Levy Board Expenditure*

Source: British Horse Racing Board 1998 Report

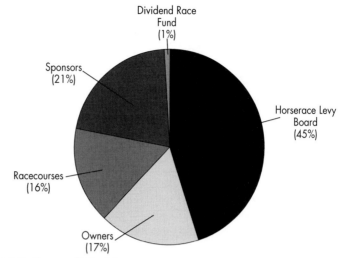

FIGURE 3.9 *Sources of Prize Money*

Source: Horserace Betting Levy Board 1998–9 Annual Report

and the improvements of its 12 racecourses and also donates 38% of the total prize money given out at these 12 courses.

Private sector companies also manage racecourses. Arena Leisure is such a company and runs several courses, including Lingfield Park, in accordance with Jockey Club's rules and standards.

Sport is more than just an industry

In this Chapter you have learnt about the sports industry, its organisation and structure and the growth of commercialism.

Sport is an industry, but it is also important to understand the bigger picture. Sport is also a part of our life that is based on values associated with healthy living, fun, fair play, self-sacrifice, loyalty to a team effort, self-fulfilment and being the best that you can be.

If the whole of the sports industry were to disappear tomorrow people would still play sport, and if they could not agree on rules they would form associations and governing bodies. That is how it all began before.

Sport is also about the people who give up time to play at the grass roots and amateur levels, who sacrifice time and gruelling training sessions and risk personal injury and time off work for a team cause or for their own self-fulfilment. It is about the commitment and unselfish sacrifice of thousands of volunteers who give up their time to support others in their sport through running clubs, administering leagues, coaching children, preparing food and playing fields or refereeing and officiating.

It is also about those sports spectators who only go along to support their local team not just because they are purchasing a value for money prod-

DISCUSSION

'The Revenue derived from television, sponsorship and general fund raising help to provide the Olympic movement with its independence. However in developing these programmes, we must always remember that it is sport that must control its destiny, not commercial interests.'

—Juan Antonio Samaranch, the President of International Olympic Committee

Do you agree? After reading through this Chapter find out how commercialism has affected the two sports you are investigating (e.g. replica kits, TV scheduling). Have these sports got the balance right?

uct but because of the desire to support and stay loyal to their hometown team, and in so doing to contribute something. The sports industry relies on this groundswell of enthusiasm and good will to survive. When commercialism goes too far, and sport loses sight of its traditions and values, it can cause problems, such as the frequent unannounced changes in Premier League replica kits in the late 1990s.

ASSESSMENT EVIDENCE

As part of the Sports Industry Unit you are required to produce a range of assessment evidence. The Unit specifications state that you need to produce the results of an investigation within the context of the sports industry in two sports of your choice.

Reviewing the structure and status of sport

You are working as part of a team at your National Sports Council dealing with issues surrounding governing bodies and the sports that they administer. Following a leading governing body getting into financial difficulties, your department has been asked to undertake a review of the structure and status of different sports to examine the current situation in each sport and how it is adapting to the demands of the new century.

What you have to do

Each member of the team has been asked to conduct research into two sports in order for the review to be compiled. Your investigation will need to make reference to:

- The scale and economic importance of each sport.
- The organisation and funding of each sport.
- The importance of each sport for the mass media.
- The ways in which the mass media have influenced each sport.
- Major trends in each sport.

Conducting your investigation

In conducting your investigation you must consider that:

- Your investigation should be well structured, designed and professionally conducted.
- Findings may be presented in either a report, written document or oral presentation.
- Findings must be objective and supported by valid evidence, data and statistics.
- You should refer to the unit assessment grid to see what you need to do in order to achieve different grades.

Key Skills

In completing the assessment for this unit, you can achieve the following key skills. These will be accredited at the discretion of your tutor on the basis of the quality of the work you submit.

APPLICATION OF NUMBER, LEVEL 3
N3.1 Plan, and interpret information from two different sources, including a large data set.

COMMUNICATION, LEVEL 3
C3.2 Read and synthesise information from two extended documents about a complex subject. One of these documents should include at least one image.
C3.1b Make a presentation about a complex subject, using at least one image to illustrate complex points. (If the results are produced in the form of a presentation).
C3.3 Write two different types of documents about complex subjects. One piece of writing should be an extended document and include at least one image. (If the results are produced in the form of a written/ word-processed report).

INFORMATION TECHNOLOGY, LEVEL 3
IT3.1 Plan, and use different sources to search for, and select, information required for two different purposes.
IT3.3 Present information from different sources for two different purposes and audiences. Your work must include at least one example of images and one example of numbers.

4

Marketing Leisure and Recreation

Aims and Objectives

Through the study of this unit you will have the opportunity to

- **define the nature of marketing**
- **understand the marketing process and the way in which it is used in leisure and recreation enterprises in order to achieve their objectives**
- **consider the role that marketing has to play in assisting organisations to identify customers' needs, and then supplying products and services to meet those needs**
- **gain an understanding of the role of research and development in attracting and retaining of customers**
- **identify the various marketing communications methods used by organisations to make customers aware of their products and services**

Introduction

Have you ever bought anything, gone to an organised event or activity, or been to a particular holiday destination because you were convinced that it was the right thing to buy or best place to go?

DID YOU KNOW?

It is estimated that most people in the industrialised West see between 2,000 and 3,000 commercial messages a day!

If you have answered yes, you can be sure of two things. The first is that someone has thought very carefully about the message, and the format, needed to persuade you to choose that particular product, facility or service, rather than another one. The second is that you were a beneficiary (or victim) of someone else's marketing activities.

In every industry and across all sectors, businesses and organisations are using a variety of marketing techniques to help them achieve their particular objectives. Some will have departments or specialists dedicated to marketing, some will incorporate marketing into other, more general, managerial functions, and others will approach it on an ad hoc basis.

Ad hoc: something done for one particular occasion or use.

The leisure and recreation industry is no exception. Organisations within the industry, particularly commercial organisations, are constantly questioning and identifying new ways in which they can best tell others what it is they have to offer and why they should be chosen in preference to other providers of the same product/service: a leisure centre trying to maximise usage of all its facilities, a theatre working out what shows, plays and films to put on over the next 12 months, or a local photography club looking for ways to increase membership – all are looking for the best way to market themselves.

Marketing, both as an approach and as a set of techniques and activities, is highly relevant to the leisure and recreation industry. The purpose of this Unit, therefore, is to introduce you to some of the key concepts of marketing and demonstrate how these are applied by leisure and recreation organisations from the private, public and voluntary sectors.

Throughout this chapter, you will encounter a number of case studies which focus on the work and experience of two organisations. These are:

The Winning Performance – A design and marketing consultancy, specialising in the leisure industry. One of their main responsibilities is to provide their clients, principally in private health and fitness clubs and local authority leisure centres, with a full range of services for promoting their facilities to new members. As such, their services include advertising, PR, brochure design and production, sales promotion campaigns and marketing and sales advice. The Winning Performance also assist their clients with corporate identity development, pre-sell campaigns (i.e. attracting new members before a club opens), membership drives and programmes to increase business through internal mechanisms. Sarah Hitching, a marketing consultant with The Winning Performance describes their main role as 'through creative design and marketing strategies to enhance our clients profiles and help them maximise the potential of their business'.

Lee Valley Regional Park Authority – Occupying a designated area of some 10,000 acres of the Lee Valley, the Park stretches 25 miles from East India Dock Basin (opposite the Millennium Dome) up to Ware in Hertfordshire. The Authority embraces every aspect of leisure and conservation covering games, amusements and entertainment, nature reserves, Sites of Scientific Interest, and sport and recreation. Simon Gardner, principal sports development officer at the Park, explains that 'among the numerous facilities and activities available, the Park has two sports and leisure centres as well as centres catering for ice-skating, horse riding, sailing, windsurfing and waterskiing. There is also a purpose-built cycle circuit and a leisure pool. In addition, the Park also provides informal leisure pursuits including camping, boat hire, boating marinas, holiday chalets, a show farm, angling facilities, guided walks, practical conservation tasks and a schools programme'.

Marketing leisure and recreation
So what exactly is marketing?

DISCUSSION

Before considering the textbook definitions of marketing, write down in a single sentence what you understand the term marketing to mean.

How would you define it? Can you include any examples to illustrate your thinking?

Marketing is both a term and a function that is frequently misunderstood. For example, if you were to try and find out what other people think the term marketing means, or what it is that marketers do, you would end up with a number of different answers. Some might say *selling*, some *advertising*, and others that it is *packaging*. In each case they would be right but what they would be describing are marketing activities, not definitions of marketing as a whole.

So, to begin with it may be useful to refer to one of the most widely accepted definitions of marketing.

The Chartered Institute of Marketing suggests that marketing is:

❝The management process responsible for matching resources with opportunities, at a profit, by identifying, anticipating and satisfying customers' requirements demand.❞

By understanding and using these definitions you should realise that marketing has a number of key characteristics. Chiefly, these are:

- Marketing is a management process and business philosophy that puts the customer at the centre of everything the business does.
- Marketing involves identifying and anticipating customer requirements.
- Marketing involves offer and exchange.
- Marketing meets customer requirements in a way that is mutually profitable.
- Marketing is not just selling, advertising or packaging, but rather a collection of different business activities working together to identify and satisfy customer needs.
- Marketing is not just the responsibility of a few, but of everyone in the organisation.
- Marketing is the reason for the business's existence.

Leading authorities on marketing theory and practice suggest that these characteristics can be grouped into three distinct elements, namely:

1 Customer satisfaction.
2 Profit.
3 Marketing function.

Each of these is reviewed briefly below, but will be explored in greater detail later in the chapter.

Customer satisfaction

It is essential that leisure and recreation businesses identify, anticipate and satisfy customer requirements. After all, marketing is about attracting and keeping customers by providing them with the product and/or service they want. Any business, whether it is profit or non-profit orientated, that failed to live up to customer expectations would soon find itself with a diminishing customer base, or even worse, out of business. Customer satisfaction is reviewed in more detail in Chapter 5.

Profit

If profit is an organisation's primary objective. then that organisation needs to determine which customer needs can be satisfied profitably or cost-effectively, by matching customer needs and wants with appropriate products or services. However, profit and financial reward do not motivate some organisations. In these situations an alternative objective will need to be identified and used instead. For example, a publicly owned leisure centre may have as its primary objective or target, a percentage increase in specific usage, over a specified time period, while maintaining (or even reducing) current running costs.

Marketing function

If a business is to attract and then retain its customers, it must find out in plenty of time what its customers want and then make arrangements for meeting or exceeding those needs and wants. This process is known as the marketing function.

One of the key marketing functions is to anticipate changes that might affect customers' wants and needs and to develop organisation-wide strategies and plans to ensure that the organisation is well placed to respond to such changes. Marketing strategies are a fundamental business activity for leisure and recreation organisations, involving analysis, planning, monitoring and evaluation as part of a marketing plan.

A marketing plan encourages an organisation to ask itself a number of questions, namely:

- What business are we in?
- Where are we now?
- Where are we going?
- How do we get there?
- How are we doing?

This in turn enables it to:

- evaluate market opportunities before production
- assess potential demand for the good/service
- determine product/service characteristics – as identified by the customer
- establish the value and method of exchange
- supply goods/services corresponding to customer needs more effectively than other providers.

KEY TERMS

Marketing plan: A statement identifying an organisation's objectives, together with the strategies and specific courses of action it will need to pursue when, or if, certain events occur.

DISCUSSION

Choose two or three organisations and then identify their products and the various groups of customers that they target. For example, SAGA sells holidays and excursions specifically for the 50+ age group.

Thus, we can see that marketing is concerned with trying to get and keep customers. It can be defined as 'the anticipation and satisfaction of demand through an exchange process' – businesses produce goods and provide services in order to satisfy customers' needs. At the broadest level, therefore, we can see that the function of marketing activities is to bring buyers and sellers together.

For example, on a hot summer's day at the park, a visitor will probably seek out some form of refreshment. The park's resident ice-cream seller could meet this demand. It is the result of the ice-cream seller's marketing activities, not chance, that brings the visitor and the ice cream together. He or she will have carried out:

- Market research – resulting in pitch location, product range, and pricing strategies.
- Advertising – in the form of a brightly coloured van, music and the price list.

ACTIVITY

Marketing philosophies within the different sectors

Choose one organisation from each of the private, public and voluntary sectors. Identify and compare what 'marketing' means to each.

Compare your findings with the information given to you. What does this tell you about the way in which marketing as a term, and therefore a strategy, is employed from one organisation to another?

Is there a difference in people's perception and understanding of the term? Why?

Does being profit-making or non-profit-making make a difference to an organisation's marketing philosophy?

The marketing environment

Have you ever planned an activity or event, only to see your plans amount to nothing because something happened that was beyond your control? A trip to the seaside or a picnic perhaps, washed away by unseasonal weather or 15-mile long traffic jam? Many aspects of our lives are unpredictable and beyond our control. These uncontrollable elements can affect individuals and organisations alike.

KEY TERMS

Marketing environment: The world in which an organisation and its customers (both existing and potential) exist, within the context of which marketing decisions need to be made.

Uncontrollable elements, as far as leisure and recreation organisations are concerned, include things like the economy, the introduction of new laws, technological developments, changing social patterns, new competition and even the weather! The broad context in which organisations exist and operate, is commonly known as the 'marketing environment'.

While organisations might not be able to alter or influence the uncontrollable elements, they can prepare for them. In order to do this successfully, organisations need to keep a close eye on what is happening in the marketing environment and also attempt to identify what effect, if any, these changes or developments are likely to have on business. Such developments could represent a new business opportunity. For example, growing public concern over the use, and escalating costs, of fossil fuels in cars coupled with growing road congestion, could be all that is required for an electronic scooter company to try and persuade people to look at its product as a serious alternative.

On the other hand, developments can also represent a threat to an organisation's business. For example, the development of 'supermarkets' and 'retail parks' has led to the decline in the smaller family business corner shop!

There are, generally, two planning tools that can be used by leisure and recreation organisations to help them analyse the environment in which they operate and to develop appropriate strategies. These are the SWOT analysis and STEP analysis.

Before we look at each of these two methods of analysis we should remind ourselves that marketing is not a function that operates independently of any other function within an organisation. Indeed the role of marketing is one of actually supporting and guiding the organisation by making sure that not only are the right products and services made available to the right customer, but that all of the organisation's resources are also used effectively and appropriately. Above all else, therefore, the fundamental purpose behind the following analysis methods is to help the organisation understand where it is, where it is (or at least should be) going, and how it can make best use of its resources.

SWOT analysis

SWOT stands for 'strengths, weaknesses, opportunities and threats'. It is, essentially, an exercise, which should be carried out by any organisation that has a desire to improve its overall performance. The elements of a SWOT analysis are normally separated so that:

- Strengths and weaknesses examine **internal** factors
- Opportunities and threats examine **external** factors

This approach has the distinct advantage of ensuring that strengths and weaknesses are not viewed in isolation. For example a strength is only a strength if it can be matched to an emerging opportunity in the external environment.

Consider, for instance, the SWOT analysis of a local photography club given on the next page.

KEY TERMS

SWOT: An acronym for internal strengths and weaknesses and external opportunities and threats.

DISCUSSION

In small groups, discuss how each of the four elements of the SWOT analysis apply to an organisation of your choice.

STRENGTHS	WEAKNESSES	OPPORTUNITIES	THREATS
• Good well equipped facilities • Knowledgeable and friendly members • Consistently good results in local and regional competitions	• Lack of junior members • Cost of membership fees • No access via public transport	• New photography course starting at the local college • Lottery funding available	• Increase in local authority rates • New club recently established

TABLE 4.1 *SWOT analysis of a local photography club*

As you can see, the club's strengths can clearly be matched to the opportunities, that is, the well-equipped facilities and friendly and knowledgeable members should enable the club to forge good links with the local college and as a result, could even lead to an increase in membership.

STEP analysis

STEP stands for 'social, technological, economic and political', and is sometimes presented as PEST. This is mainly a tool used to analyse the external environment. Indeed, given the points made above about SWOT, many organisations find it beneficial to carry out a STEP analysis followed by a SWOT analysis. The individual factors are discussed below:

Social factors – a review of the last 30 years will show that there have been a number of significant changes related to employment patterns, lifestyles and the structure of the household. These changes have had, and will continue to have, clear effects on the buying patterns of markets for many goods and services. Consider, for example, the effects on leisure service provision in an area where there is a marked increase in the number of nuclear families locally as a result of employment and housing developments.

Technological factors – have had a profound impact on organisations and consumers. For example, the impact of new materials used in the manufacture of sports equipment and facilities, developments in the media (satellite television) and improvements in IT are clearly evident. For example, the introduction of CDs back in the early 1980s caused a dramatic fall in the sale of LPs. The question now is will mini-discs do the same to CDs?

Economic factors – changes in local and national employment patterns, areas of new business development, retail spending patterns and the state of the national economy, have all impacted on people's spending ability and, therefore, their ability to satisfy personal wants and needs through

KEY TERMS

STEP: An acronym for the four broad categories of influences that create the marketing environment, namely: social, technological, economic and political.

the purchase of goods and services. In a recession, for example, people will still want to buy goods of a particular standard or visit the theatre as often as usual, but are likely to find themselves unable to afford to do so.

Political – central and local government policy and legislation, European Directives, and health and safety legislation all influence how organisations operate. For example, Best Value, due to come into effect from April 2000, will have had a profound influence on how local authorities provide their services.

ACTIVITY

Conducting a STEP analysis

Working in small groups of three or four, identify any leisure and recreation organisation, local or national and carry out a STEP analysis. Can you perceive any changes to the external environment and if so, how might these changes affect or influence the products and services of your chosen organisation? Consider both the benefits and problems!

Report your results to your classmates and justify your findings.

In addition to the factors mentioned above, organisations (where applicable), must also be aware of their competition. This is a key consideration which, while falling outside the boundaries of the STEP analysis, has clear and obvious links to the threat element of SWOT, and as such is of vital importance to any organisation making decisions based on the analysis of its environment.

CASE STUDY *SWOT Analysis*

The Winning Performance

DISCUSSION

Think of a number of different leisure and recreation organisations locally. What are their relevant strengths and weaknesses? What opportunities and threats exist?

We use the **SWOT** analysis to:

1 Achieve a general overview of a new or potential client for our own purposes to enable us to understand the client better.

2 To provide a client with a 'helicopter view' of their business and identify clear areas in which we can assist them.

We also use the **STEP** analysis in conjunction with the **SWOT** to indicate to clients that they are not operating in a vacuum, and that their business is affected by external forces that they must be aware of (and need to prepare for) so that they are proactive and not reactive.

We generally include both the SWOT and the STEP (or some variation of this) at the beginning of a comprehensive marketing report. Businesses often do not clearly understand what marketing is and how it can assist their business and so these analyses start this process and help us to demonstrate our worth to them.

Marketing goals and objectives

Marketing objectives:
What the organisation is trying to achieve through its marketing activities.

Having completed a SWOT and STEP analysis, an organisation is more able to establish its marketing goals and objectives. These will of course vary depending on the type of organisation and the sector in which it operates. However, there are a number of similar broad aims. These are likely to include

- Increase product awareness among the target audience.
- Inform target audience about features and benefits of products and services.
- Decrease or remove potential customers' resistance to buying product.
- Increase customers/membership.

While identifying objectives it is important that most, if not all, organisations break each objective down into smaller, more precise goals. For example, if a local authority leisure centre had identified an increase in membership as one of its marketing objectives, this could be presented as:

- Increased usage by target specific groups, that is, women, young people, ethnic minorities by a specific percentage and by a set date, that is a 5% increase by each target group by March 2001.
- Within the next six months, annual, quarterly and monthly memberships of the fitness suite to be increased by 2%, 4%, and 6%, respectively.
- Introduce a concessionary membership scheme for use by disadvantaged groups during off-peak hours, and set a target of 500 memberships by the end of the current financial year.

The process of breaking objectives down into more precise goals means that an organisation is capable of setting and working towards what is fashionably called SMART goals.

Let's look at our objective again, which was to increase membership at the local leisure centre. By breaking this down into more specific aims, i.e. introducing a concessionary membership scheme for use by disadvantaged groups during off-peak hours and setting a target of 500 memberships by the end of the current financial year, you should be able to see that the aim is:

- **S**pecific – that is, introducing a concessionary membership scheme for the disadvantaged.
- **M**easurable – that is a target number has been set, e.g. 500.
- **A**greed – that is, by all those who will be involved and/or responsible.
- **R**ealistic – that is, the target is not set too high but at the same time is sufficiently challenging.
- **T**imed – that is, a time has been set to achieve the aim, e.g. by the end of the current financial year.

Identify one organisation from within the industry and a product that it 'sells'? Who are their target customers and what do you suppose these customers want in return?

Market research

Earlier we identified that marketing is, among other things, about being customer-focused. Organisations that adopt a marketing orientation are required to ask themselves '*Who are our customers*' (both existing and potential) and '*what do they want?*'

You will also recall that our examination of the 'marketing environment' introduced you to the fact that organisations *need to know* about their competition in the marketplace, together with how all, or any, of the STEP factors might affect business overall.

The gathering, analysis and use of information, then, is an important and integral component of the marketing process. If organisations don't know enough about the needs and wants of existing and/or potential customers, then it is unlikely that they will be able to come up with effective strategies that will enable them to meet those needs. On the other hand, having the right amount and type of information will help them to recognise and respond appropriately to market opportunities and thus, develop suitable products and services that meet their market's needs.

The more relevant, accurate, up-to-date and reliable the information that an organisation has about its marketplace, the better its marketing decisions will be. This is not only because *fact* and *solid evidence* replace guesswork and estimation, but also because the information is current. For example, Marks and Spencer have recently undergone a period where they have lost some of their dominance in the high street. Many critics have put this down to losing touch with their core market, accusing them of no longer knowing what it is their customers *actually* want. By contrast, Sega and Nintendo continue their longstanding dominance of the computer games market. One of the reasons for this is because they constantly update their information and modify products accordingly.

The process of gathering, analysing and using information is commonly known as **market research**. The findings generated by market research help organisations to:

KEY TERMS

Functions of Marketing Research: To generate information for use in marketing decision-making

- Analyse the needs of people who use the product and decide if consumers want more or different products.
- Predict what types of product different users will want and identify which of these people the organisation will try to satisfy.
- Estimate how many of these people will be using the product over a given time period and how many products they will be likely to buy.
- Predict when the users will want to buy the product.
- Determine where these users are/will be and how to get the organisation's product to them.

DISCUSSION

Have you ever completed a questionnaire, been stopped on the street and asked for your views, or been part of a market research investigation? Who was it for? What was its purpose?

- Estimate what price(s) they are willing to pay for the product(s) and if the organisation can make a profit selling at that price.

- Decide which kinds of promotion should be used to tell potential customers about the firm's products.

- Estimate how many competing companies will be making similar products, how many they will produce, what kind, and at what price, etc.

The function of market research, therefore, is to provide an organisation with information that enables it to respond to market opportunities, and to develop suitable products and services that meet market needs.

The information gained can be used in:

- identifying the root cause of a problem
- comparing alternative courses of action
- testing alternatives in the marketplace
- testing a hypothesis
- assessing the effectiveness of various activities.

Identifying the root cause of a problem

A local authority sports development team is keen to support local sports clubs through the provision of a 'coach education' programme. However, despite their best efforts, take-up has been poor.

Is the reason for the poor response because there is something wrong with the promotion of the product, that is, the message is not reaching the intended target audience? Or, is there something wrong with the product itself, perhaps the courses on offer are not what the clubs or coaches want? Maybe the distribution is wrong, that is, the venue is not easy to access and/or the time (Sunday mornings) is not suitable because many of intended the target audience have other commitments at this time? Or is it because some other organisation is also providing the same product, and, as a result, is competing for the same target group? Or have they simply developed a product that nobody wants and which no amount of promotion will sell?

Whatever the reason(s), market research could help the organisation to establish the answer(s). The organisation would then be in a better position to make an informed decision regarding what corrective action it needs to take.

Comparing alternative courses of action

A local authority leisure services department is assessing whether to permanently host its summer holiday playschemes at three key sites in the district for the duration of the holidays, or to rotate the schemes across a number of sites around the district throughout the holidays.

In this situation, market research could help the local authority find out how the customers would feel about either option and simultaneously give some indication of their response. This information would allow the local authority to plan and provide a summer holiday playscheme that meets the needs of the majority.

Testing alternatives in the marketplace

A chain of private leisure centres is considering some fundamental changes to the range of activities and services it offers at each of its various centres, that is, it is thinking of separating some sessions into male or female only, along with introducing early morning swims, shiatsu massage and a coffee shop.

It has decided to test each of these alternatives simultaneously and, to this end, has scheduled for a different alternative to be introduced at each centre. This method will allow the company to test customer reaction to each of the proposed changes quickly and efficiently.

Testing a hypothesis

Returning to our local authority sports development team for a moment, we find that one of the team believes that there is the possibility of establishing a junior basketball league within the district. However, rather than just investing all the necessary resources required for this sort of venture on the strength of a 'hunch', the principal sports development officer decides to test the hypothesis (or supposition) with some market research. He/she explores how much demand there is, where the activities can take place, who needs to be involved and their availability, etc.

The findings from the market research ultimately provide the sports development team with the feedback and information that they need in order to make the right decision about what course of action they need to follow, what resources are required and who to involve.

Assessing the effectiveness of various activities

Leisure and recreation organisations frequently need to review and assess their customers' reactions to the current offer. A restaurant, for example, might want to identify what is, or is not, popular on its menu, what new 'dishes' the customers would like to see included in future and how satisfied they are with the overall service.

Once again, through market research, the organisation gains access to the information that it needs to make informed decisions.

As you can see from the above examples, the benefits of marketing research are that it provides an organisation with the ability to identify opportunities and gaps, reveal weaknesses and provides the basis for effective planning on where it should be going and a means of evaluating whether or not the right methods are being used to get there.

ACTIVITY

The role of market research

List three aspects of a product/service and its potential market that an organisation will need to consider for any two of the above examples.

Compare these with others in your class. What did you find out? And what does this tell you about the role and function of market research?

KEY TERMS

Market: A group of actual or potential customers for a particular product and/or service.

DISCUSSION

List four or five examples where the customer is not the consumer and where the customer is also the consumer.

Are there any differences in the way that organisations market themselves in each case? Can you also identify what the benefits might be to a customer who does not consume the product?

DISCUSSION

What do organisations, such as restaurants and cafés, etc, do to make you want to eat their product or eat at their establishment?

Which are the most effective marketing techniques?

Customers

In marketing orientated organisations objectives are best achieved:

- When the customer has been properly identified
- When the organisation has an understanding of the customers' wants and needs and is aware of how it can meet these needs

Customers and consumers

We have already defined what a market is, but let's remind ourselves of the definition. A market is a group of individuals or organisations that may want the good or service or benefit being offered for sale.

The terms 'customer' and 'consumer', refer to different roles that people take in the buying process. For example, when young children plague their parents with requests for the latest team strip, the latest 'craze', for example, Beanie Babies, Furbies and Power Rangers or some trendy new clothes, they rarely come up with the money themselves. In this situation, the children are taking the role of consumers and their parents customers.

What this simple example tells you is that, in essence, a customer is someone who does the buying, or at least guarantees payment for the product or service on offer. A consumer, on the other hand, is someone who actually consumes or uses the product or service.

If organisations are to be successful in reaching the markets they want to meet, then they must have an understanding about the needs associated with each of these roles. The main reason for this is to adapt the 'total offer' so that it appeals to both the customer and the consumer. (You will be exploring what is meant by the 'total offer' in the next section).

Wants and needs

Reference was made above to customers' needs and wants. The question is what are the differences between the two? One way of distinguishing between them is to define needs as basic physical and psychological drives arising from being human (for example, the need for food, water, security, and self-esteem) and to define wants as specific desires directed towards fulfilling the basic needs.

Abraham Maslow, an eminent psychologist, believed that although each individual is unique, everyone has certain needs in common. He created a hierarchy of needs, where all human needs were put into a specific order (Figure 4.1), and ranged from the most basic to the highest.

Customer: Someone who does the buying, or at least guarantees payment.

Consumer: Someone who consumes or uses the product or service.

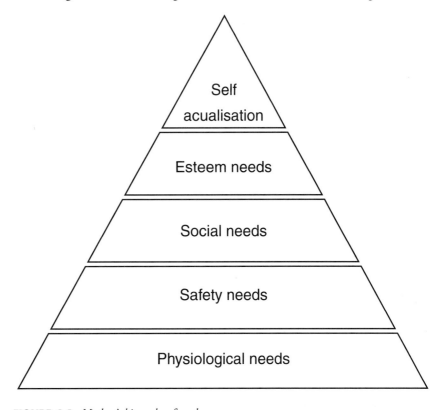

FIGURE 4.1 *Maslow's hierarchy of needs*

As you can see the five levels identified by Maslow are:

1 Physiological needs – water, air, food, sleep.
2 Safety needs – security, protection from harm.
3 Social needs – acceptance, belonging, friendship, affection.
4 Self-esteem needs – achievement, respect, feelings of self-worth.
5 Self-actualisation needs – becoming all that one is capable of being.

Think about a band, group or singer that you would really like to see in concert? How much would you be prepared to pay? How far would you be prepared to travel?

A need for food could be transformed into a specific desire (want) for a McDonald's burger, a piece of fruit, a low-fat yoghurt, or countless other variations of food. Not surprisingly, therefore, most marketing efforts concentrate predominantly on satisfying people's wants. The fact that numerous potential customers are likely to share a basic need or want does not mean, however, that they are all the same and can be treated in the same way.

Economists often give the impression that all customers are alike. They make no distinction between who buys the product or service; they are only concerned with the fact that the customer has the ability (that is, the money) and the willingness, to buy. This may be fine for the economist, but it is not enough for the market-orientated organisation, which

understands that in many cases buyers differ from one another even though they may be buying the same product.

For example, people participating in sport and physical recreation share a number of common needs when purchasing goods, these include: clothing, footwear and equipment. However, when it comes to satisfying their needs, different customers will not only be influenced by their particular 'wants', they will also be subject to factors such as the amount of disposable income that they have. Even where 'needs' are similar, 'wants' can be different.

Let us look at disposable income and value perception and show how these affect the final purchase of four customers, A–D, with the same need for ski wear.

CUSTOMER	CAN AFFORD TO BUY C&A	CAN AFFORD TO BUY NEVICA	CAN AFFORD TO HIRE	PERCEIVES C&A AS BEST	PERCEIVES NEVICA AS BEST	FINAL PURCHASE CHOICE
A	YES	YES	YES	YES	NO	Buys C&A
B	YES	YES	YES	NO	YES	Buys Nevica
C	YES	NO	YES	NO	YES	Buys C&A
D	NO	NO	YES	N/A	N/A	Hires

TABLE 4.2 *How income and perception can influence choice of purchase*

DISCUSSION

If you are not familiar with either C&A or Nevica ski wear then perform the same exercise using two 'same' products that you are familiar with. It does not have to be ski wear.

Conduct this study among your class mates. What are your findings?

Now incorporate into your study somebody in full-time employment who earns a salary? Are your results any different?

Table 4.2 illustrates how a number of variables can influence who the organisations' (in this case C&A, Nevica and the hire company) customers are. To maximise the marketing effort it is vital that the organisation learns and understands the key variables – in this case disposable income and value perception. It can then decide whom to 'aim' at and how, thus reducing wasted resources in the promotion effort. For example, it is more cost effective to promote Nevica to customers B, A and C in that order. It is least cost effective to promote Nevica to D, C and A in that order.

One of the most useful benefits that organisations can gain from market research is the identification of a realistic target to aim at. For instance, if potential customers can be narrowed down to a hard core of suitable prospects, by eliminating those who are unlikely to buy the product or use the service, then wastage of resources will be greatly reduced. Thus marketers, unlike economists, endeavour to identify groups and subgroups within total markets so that the organisation can:

● Direct attention towards those customers whose needs can be met by the organisation's resources and skills. For example, in New Delhi, India, you will find the only McDonalds in the world with no beef on the menu. This is because the majority of Indians are Hindu and it is

DISCUSSION

How do each of the above illustrations relate to Maslow's hierarchy of needs? Can you think of other wants that can be satisfied in this example?

against their religion to eat beef. So instead of the Big Mac that you and I know of, the Indian menu features the Maharaja Mac, which is made with mutton!

● Put together sales packages that are capable of meeting customers' needs more closely. Take sports shops, for example, most will stock a wide range of running shoes to cater for the needs of the casual and committed runner. Their stock will also cater for different 'budgets', and they usually offer the customer a choice of in-store and/or mail order shopping.

Market orientated organisations know that if target marketing is to be effective then it must be done systematically.

The process of target marketing goes through three distinct stages:

1 market segmentation
2 market targeting
3 product positioning

Market segmentation

KEY TERMS

Market segment A group of customers that can be clearly seen to share particular wants and needs. For example, middle-income couples with children may be Tesco's main target segment, whereas higher income couples and singles may be Waitrose's main target segment.

Market segmentation is the process of dividing the total market available to the organisation into segments, which can be targeted with specifically developed and marketed products.

The four most common segmentation methods used by leisure and recreation industries are:

● demographic
● socio-economic
● lifestyle (psychographics)
● geodemographic

Demographic

The term 'demographics' refers to the analysis of population profiles. Populations are traditionally broken down by age, gender, ethnicity, marital status, etc. Demographic data provides a major source of information for organisations attempting to analyse their markets. The data is easily attainable from institutions such as the Central Statistical Office (CSO) which provides information on UK population demographics.

Most organisations undertaking surveys will include categories that identify age, gender and ethnicity.

As a means of providing information about distinct market segments, demographics can be made more effective if additional criteria are applied, for example, the stage of life that a person has reached and the circumstances in which they live.

DISCUSSION

For each of the life cycle stages identify two or three leisure and recreation providers together with the product/services that they offer to people at that particular stage?

What does this tell you about how organisations view their customers?

Wells and Guber (marketing specialists) devised a series of life-cycle stages, based on people's household and marital status. Some of the key stages include:

1 Bachelor stage – young single people not living at home.
2 Newly married couples without children.
3 Full nest 1 – youngest child under six.
4 Full nest 2– youngest child six or older.
5 Full nest 3 – older married couple with no dependent children.
6 Empty nest 1 – no children living at home, head of family in work.
7 Empty nest 2 – head of family retired.
8 Solitary survivor in work.
9 Solitary survivor retired.

Further criteria can be added, or the list amended to satisfy the needs of the organisation doing the research. That is, the life stages can be selected by establishing criteria that are appropriate to the product/service being offered in that particular market segmentation. For example, much of Club 18–30 target group are 'bachelors', but others are young singles living with their parents which would be a different category to any of those on our list. It may also be prudent to include single-parent families, divorced or unmarried single people living on their own. Oasis Forest Holiday Villages are an organisation who have assessed the value in targeting specific groups of people, one example being the 'empty nesters' who are referred to directly in their marketing brochure.

Socio-economic

The social class of a person is likely to influence their buying behaviour. Although it is quite difficult to define social class, because of the number of factors involved, (such as income, status, education, etc.) it is, nevertheless, one of the most commonly used methods of dividing the market. It is a particular favourite of the leisure and recreation industries. The National Readership Survey (NRS) scale, based upon the occupation of the main wage earner of the household, uses the following classifications:

DISCUSSION

How does this method of segmentation, i.e. dividing the market, compare with the Wells and Guber example? Do the segments have comparable characteristics? Would the product have to differ?

A   Upper middle class – higher managerial, administrative or professional people
B   Middle class – intermediate managerial, administrative or professional people
C1 Lower middle class – supervising, clerical and lower managerial administrative or professional people
C2 Skilled working class – skilled manual workers
D   Working class – service and unskilled manual workers
E   Subsistence level – pensioners, unemployed, casual or low-grade workers

Lifestyle

Psychographics is a very modern method that classifies individuals by their personality, attitudes and lifestyle. To obtain psychographic data an organisation needs to carry out detailed research into the behaviour and beliefs of consumers. The research is usually conducted with individuals, or in focus groups and attempts are made to classify individuals on the basis of statements that they make about themselves or on how they perceive a product/service.

For example, in the UK, Access, the credit card company, came up with six lifestyle segments, built up from profiles of its 10 million cardholders. They are:

YAKS 'young, adventurous, keen and single' – These are the 18–24 year-olds, who have no heavy financial burdens yet, since they either live at home with their parents or rent cheaply, and can afford to ski in the winter and seek the sun in the summer. They are status seekers who like, fashion, flash cars and eating out.

EWES 'experts with expensive style' – Aged between 25–34, they have two incomes, a mortgage, but no children. They are high-flying, trendy and enjoy a busy and extensive social life. They can still afford two to three holidays a year, despite heavy spending on the home.

BATS 'babies add the sparkle' – These couples are similar in age to the EWES, but in addition to the mortgage, they also have the responsibility of children. Their holidays will be more restricted and modest, since most of the spending is home or children orientated.

CLAMS 'carefully look at most spending' – These are 34–44 year-olds with heavy financial burdens, such as mortgages and school fees. Their car is likely to be a second-hand estate. Since cash is so tight, they will be high borrowers and will restrict their social life to things like dinner parties with other CLAMS of their acquaintance.

MICE 'money is coming easier' – At 45–55, MICE are at the peak of their earning and, because the children are in the process of leaving home and the end of the mortgage is at least in sight, they have more disposable income to enjoy for themselves. They can, therefore, enjoy regular holidays.

OWLS 'older with less stress' – These are the over-55s who have paid off most of their long-term debt. Their children are now independent, so they have more disposable income for themselves, and may have even moved into a smaller house that is cheaper to run and maintain. They have plenty of leisure time and are determined to enjoy it, particularly as they are generally healthy and like travel.

(Source: *Daily Mail* 1991, from *Principles of Marketing* p 179, Pitman Publishing, 1977)

You can see how this classification system can give a company or organisation insights into the needs and wants of different groups of customers. By understanding the customer's cash flow pressures and spending profiles, an organisation can better tailor its service and marketing mix to appeal to each group, thereby forging closer bonds with them. For example, a holiday company might target YAKS with their one-week ski holidays in Europe, and OWLS with their Mediterranean cruises.

CASE STUDY *Lifestyle (psychographics)*

The Winning Performance

'We have recently used this method to highly target a membership drive for a Golf Club.

An untargeted promotion through general advertising/leaflet distribution in the local media would have been too risky as there are so many golf facilities in the locale. We have, therefore, used the following criteria to select a database and target our promotional activities on:

People who –

(i) are interested in golf

(ii) live within a 30 minute drive (postcode areas)

(iii) have an income level of £25,000+ per annum

The advantage of using such a database of people is that we can guarantee that our offer will be reaching the right people, who have an interest in our service/product.'

Lee Valley Regional Park

'When the Lee Valley Regional Park Authority was reviewing the customer base of its Water-Sports Centre, before writing a new strategic business plan, the team writing the report did desk research, using purchased (external) data, looking at lifestyle and attitude of the population within a 30 minute drive of the centre. This data was used to discover the needs and perceived requirements of people living close to the facility. The marketing of the new Centre was designed around and targeted the psychographics of the local population.

Geodemographic

The final consumer market technique to be described in this section is geodemographics. This classification system was developed in 1978 by CACI who linked geographic and demographic data to create a classification of residential neighbourhoods, generally referred to by its acronym 'ACORN' (Table 4.3).

This method is based on the assumption that the neighbourhood areas in which people live will reflect their professional status, income, life stage and behaviour.

CATEGORY	GROUP	POPULATION (%)	CORRESPONDING SOCIAL GRADE
A Thriving	1. Wealthy achievers, suburban areas	15.1	A, B, C1
	2. Affluent greys, rural communities	2.3	A, B, C2, D
	3. Prosperous pensioners, retirement areas	2.3	A, B, C1
B Expanding	4. Affluent executives, family areas	3.7	A, B, C1
	5. Well-off workers, family areas	7.8	A, B, C1, C2
C Raising	6. Affluent urbanites, town and city areas	2.2	A, B, C1
	7. Prosperous professionals, metropolitan areas	2.1	A, B, C1
	8. Better-off executives, inner city areas	3.2	A, B, C1
D Settling	9. Comfortable middle-agers, mature home-owning areas	13.4	A, B, C1
	10. Skilled workers, home-owning areas	10.7	C1, C2, D, E
E Aspiring	11. New home owners	9.8	C2, D, E
	12. White-collar workers, better-off multi-ethnic areas	4.0	C1
F Striving	13. Older people, less prosperous areas	3.6	C2, D, E
	14. Council estate residents, better-off homes	11.6	C2, D, E
	15. Council estate residents, high unemployment	2.7	C2, D, E
	16. Council estate residents, greatest hardship	2.8	D, E
	17. People in multi-ethnic, low-income areas	2.1	D, E

TABLE 4.3 *ACORN Geodemographic Classification*

Source: CACI Information Services, London – The ACORN user guide

ACTIVITY

Using segmentation to identify customers

Arrange to visit at least three different and diverse leisure and recreation organisations, for example, a theme park, a leisure centre and a high street retailer, dealing predominantly in leisure and recreation goods.

Interview a representative of the 'marketing' team and establish what marketing segmentation each organisation uses and why? How does their approach help the organisation to deliver appropriate goods/ services?

Target market: A particular group of homogeneous customers for whom an organisation creates and maintains a specific marketing mix that has been designed specifically to meet and satisfy that particular group's wants and needs. For example, a tour operator will present a different 'package' to the 18–30 and over 50s markets.

Market targeting

Once segmentation is complete, organisations decide which segments will provide them with the best opportunities for meeting their specific goals and objectives. Essentially, there are three strategies open to all organisations. These are:

1 **Undifferentiated/blanket marketing** – this approach sees the organisation target the market as a whole rather than in segments:

For example, *Yellow Pages*. The same product is offered to the whole market. There is no *Yellow Pages* especially for young fashionable customers, there is no Yellow Pages especially for retired couples. Even though the product can be accessed in hard copy, via the Internet, or over the phone, it remains the same product for everyone. That is to say, the market is treated as one homogeneous group.

2 **Differentiated marketing** – here the organisation aims it products and/or services at a number of segments with different offers for each.

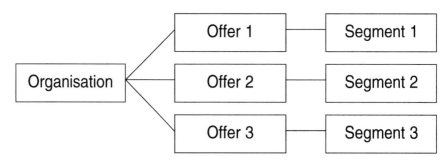

For example, a magazine publisher who publishes a range of magazines aimed at different target markets: a fashion magazine aimed at single women under 30, a home focused magazine aimed at married women over 25, and a fashion and fitness magazine aimed at men under 35.

3 **Concentrated (or Niche) marketing** – in this instance the organisation attempts to achieve a large share in one or a few segments

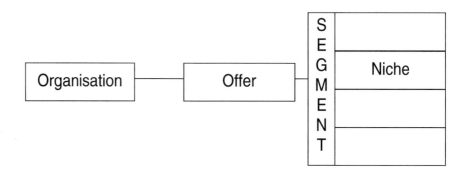

For example, both Sock Shop and Tie Rack are companies that concentrate their efforts on a particular niche market segment within the clothing industry.

Product positioning

Product positioning is the process of distinguishing a brand from its competitors so that it becomes the preferred brand in defined segments of the market. To position a product or service, organisations must select the differences it wishes to appeal most strongly to its target audience and then communicate these differences clearly. For example, Coca-Cola charges much more for its cola than, say, Virgin Cola. It has always emphasised its superior taste ('Just for the taste of it') as well as its history (being the first big brand cola and dating back over a hundred years).

KEY TERMS

Brand: An identifying feature that distinguishes one product from another, sets it apart from its competitors, and establishes it in the market place.

A C T I V I T Y

Mickey Mouse marketing

How does Walt Disney World (www.disney.com) cater for diverse visitor groups? You will need to consider factors such as the attractions, rides, special events, facilities, services, etc.

What do each of these tell you about the importance of not only classifying customers into sub-markets, but also about market targeting and product positioning in general?

DISCUSSION

Coca-Cola is one of the most influential market leaders in its field. In the 'fizzy-pop wars' who are their closest rivals?

Consider the role that organisations play in marketing and sponsorship? You may wish to refer to the Atlanta 1996 Olympics for examples.

Methods of market research

In this section you will come across the terms 'information' and 'data'. It is important for you to understand what each term means and how they are used to give the organisation the information it needs to make effective decisions.

Market research can be broken down into two distinct categories, namely secondary research and primary research. These two categories are discussed further below.

Secondary (desk) research

Involves the collection and analysis of data already in existence. There are two sources of this data:

1 *Internal* – data is available within the organisation.
2 *External* – data has been published and is available for others to use.

KEY TERMS

Data: is statistical information (i.e. facts, figures, etc.), which is in its raw state or unprocessed.

Information: is data that has been converted or processed into a format relevant to the end-users purpose.

Desk research is usually the first type of research undertaken. There are three reasons for this:

1 It is generally much less time-consuming and cheaper than field research.
2 It may provide the organisation with information that it would not otherwise have the time and/or resources to collect.
3 It may be sufficient in its own right.

A weakness of this method of research is that the data might not be totally relevant to the task in hand because the data were not originally produced for this specific task, and this type of data has quite a short shelf-life. For example, an organisation using information from a previous survey about customer satisfaction might find the information questionable if their customer base has changed significantly and/or there have been substantial changes to the organisation's offer.

It would be impractical to list all potential sources of internal data. However, the most common examples include:

- **Sales figures** – These can be used to identify how many of a particular product have been sold, or what the usage rates for a particular service are and can be broken down by market segment to illustrate market profiles
- **Financial information** – Used to identify overall sales, average spend per head per visit, etc.
- **Customer complaints and/or enquiries** – These are a useful way of establishing what customers are dissatisfied with and why, and also what new products or services they want
- **Customer details** – Illustrates where customers live, how far they travel, their age, sex, income and preferred activities, etc.

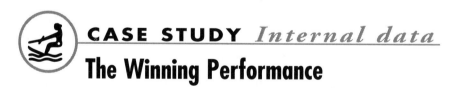

CASE STUDY *Internal data*
The Winning Performance

DISCUSSION

Looking at the examples opposite, how many categories of internal data sources can you identify? What do you think were the reasons for choosing these methods?

'We use internal data to monitor the effectiveness of our marketing activities for clients. In the health and fitness clubs that we market, we use the following methods on a daily basis:

- the number of (sales) pitches made to prospects
- the number of pitches closed (i.e. number of new memberships sold)
- the number of walk-ins
- the number of appointments made (from making scripted telephone calls to prospects)
- member traffic (number of people using the club).

The advantage of gathering internal data such as this is that it gives us an immediate indication of any problem areas, e.g. if the number of pitches made is high but the number of pitches closed is low then we know that we have to do some sales training with the staff.'

Lee Valley Regional Park

'When the Lee Valley Regional Park's Efficiency Team were conducting desk research regarding its Sports Centre, it used internal data about the customers to discover that only a local population was using the facility. Marketing activities were changed to target geographical areas further from the centre.

The data was collected from a membership computer summary of post-code details that when analysed, showed that the majority of customers travelled for less than 15 minutes from their homes to the centre. The advantage of this method for the team was that there was no cost involved, the data was easily accessed and the interpretation of the data was uncomplicated.'

Examples of external data include:

- Market and consumer **surveys** – provided by organisations such as Mintel (Marketing Intelligence) and the Henley Centre for Forecasting, etc.
- Government **publications** – *The British Household Survey*, *Social Trends*, HMSO reports, etc.
- The **Internet**.
- Industrial **reviews**.
- Trade **journals** – *Institute of Leisure and Amenity Management* (ILAM), *Institute of Sport and Recreation Management* (ISRM).
- **Government-funded organisations** – Sport England's information service.
- National, regional and local **newspapers**.
- Opinion **polls**.
- Reference **libraries**.

CASE STUDY *External data*
The Winning Performance

'We use external data in reports to indicate to a client why we are proposing to carry out certain marketing activities and to add credibility/credence to a statement. Two examples follow:

External data used to demonstrate the market for a ladies-only health club franchise in the UK.

Extract from the franchise prospectus that we have produced for our client

The Health and Fitness Market has altered considerably over the past five years and is now one of the most rapidly expanding and developing industries in the UK. There is a greater awareness of the importance of being fit and healthy and the number of leisure facilities of all types has risen in direct proportion to this.

The British have traditionally tended to leave gyms and fitness fads to the Americans. But the growth in the US industry (where there has been a 50% increase in health club membership over the past ten years) is now being mirrored in the UK, particularly amongst women.

National high profile health and fitness campaigns are now being actively encouraged by the government after official figures revealed that over half the UK population is believed to be overweight.

The search for a healthy lifestyle is not new. But where multi-gyms, miracle diet books, jogging and home videos were in fashion; they are now being supplanted by hi-tech, well-designed fitness clubs.

According to Mintel, one in three adults in the UK would like to join a fitness club. Spending on health and fitness in the UK has increased by 58% in the past five years, from £615 million in 1993 to almost £1 billion in 1998 and has continued to grow. Fitness membership has increased by 25% over the same period to 2 million, with the majority of these being women. (Sources of data: MINTEL Leisure Intelligence/Keynote Marketing Review – UK Leisure & Recreation).

Whilst the UK health and fitness industry continues to expand and follows the American trends, the ladies-only sector of the market remains remarkably unexploited.

External data used to demonstrate why a leisure centre should break into the corporate membership market and why companies should take advantage of what the leisure centre is offering.

Extract: Fit staff are good for business

A growing number of companies are encouraging staff to forego an ice cream in the park, a cake in the canteen or a pint in the pub and opt for an aerobic class, a weights workout or a few lengths in the pool instead. They are realising that a healthy workforce can have a dramatic impact on the amount of time staff take off sick. According to the Fitness Industry Association (FIA), an estimated 127 million working days are lost each year in the UK due to illness and a further 40 million days due to stress. This literally costs UK industry billions of pounds.

Why exercise?

Some of the most important benefits of activity and fitness, supported by a wealth of scientific evidence includes:

- reduced risk of heart disease
- better control of blood pressure in cases of mild hypertension
- increased stamina
- management of body weight
- reduced stress, enhanced mood and self-esteem
- prevention of brittle bone disease (osteoporosis)
- maintenance of muscle strength and joint flexibility.

Source: Allied Dunbar National Fitness Survey

When you use information provided by a recognised national body or organisation it adds weight to your argument.

Lee Valley Regional Park

'External data was purchased from a specialist market research company (Mintel) by the Lee Valley Regional Park, when it was decided that it needed to know about the national data regarding people interested in sailing, windsurfing, water-skiing and power-boating. Data included average age, average income, gender, sports specific interests, car ownership and the number of children. This method of research has an initially high purchase price but saves time and expense in gathering detailed information that in most cases is unobtainable by the park.'

ACTIVITY

Using data

Contact a number of organisations from the private, public and voluntary sectors and establish what internal and external sources of data they use and why?

- Ask them if they use any market research agencies.
- Ask them if they use information or data supplied to them by local or national government.
- Do they collect their own data on customers?
- How do they use it?

Primary (field) research

This is undertaken, or commissioned, by an organisation for a specific purpose. The required information does not already exist, or is not available in any suitable format, therefore research has to be undertaken from scratch. It is generally obtained by asking people questions or by observing their behaviour. There are two main sources of this data:

1 **Surveys** – This is data that is collected both directly and indirectly from people through the use of questionnaires.
2 **Observation** – This is data that is collected by means of witnessing or recording events taking place.

There are a number of different **survey methods** used in market research. The most common include:

- surveys
- sampling
- attitude scaling

Surveys

A survey is any research method in which data are gathered systematically from a sample of people by means of a questionnaire. Surveys are conducted through face-to-face interviews, telephone interviews, mailed questionnaires, and focus groups. We will now look at these methods in greater detail.

Face-to-face interviews

Many people consider this to be the most comprehensive method of carrying out field research. It is the most natural kind of communication as it allows the respondent time to consider the questions being asked, and also gives the interviewer the opportunity to ask additional questions or clarify particular answers.

Advantages include:

- It can have a higher response-rate than by mail.
- It is direct and enables two-way communication.

Disadvantages include:

- It is expensive, labour intensive and time-consuming.
- The interviewer could accidently influence the respondent.
- Finding the right person to talk to and the right time to call can be time-consuming.

Telephone interviews

As the term implies this method involves the interviewer using a telephone to contact respondents. The method is useful for collecting both qualitative and quantitative data and can be used in a number of different ways, including:

- As a means of initial contact – that is, when market researchers choose to interview people with whom they have had no previous contact (this is often referred to as 'cold calling').
- As a means of follow-up contact – that is, when respondents have previously taken part in some form of market research and have consented to taking part in further research over the phone.
- As a means of following-up a sale – that is, when market researchers endeavour to establish why someone has chosen a particular product or service.

Advantages include:

- Most households have a phone.
- It is a very fast survey technique, i.e. results can be available in a short period of time.
- It is relatively cheap, compared with face-to-face interviewing.
- It is direct and enables two-way communication.

Disadvantages include:

- The interview can only last for a short time and, as a result, questions are limited.
- The interviewer cannot visually check that the questions have been understood.
- Finding the right person to talk to, and the right time to call, can be time-consuming.

Mailed questionnaires

This is a popular method of research and normally involves sending a questionnaire through the post to the respondent for self-completion and return. Distribution can also involve handing questionnaires out at the point of sale, or including them in product packaging, for the buyer to fill in at their own convenience before posting back.

Advantages include:

- It is the cheapest of all the methods.

- Large samples can be used.
- It is a good method for getting qualitative and quantitative data.

Disadvantages include:

- It is a one-way flow of information, i.e. it is not possible to clarify unclear responses.
- Response rates are often low.

Focus groups

This is the most popular form of face-to-face interviewing. It consists of selecting a small group of people, normally between 6 and 10 that share a number of common characteristics that are relative to the requirements of the research being carried out. During the session the interviewer will encourage participants to discuss the topic(s) being investigated. This process often leads to insights that fail to materialise in other survey methods.

Advantages include:

- It is a cheaper and faster alternative to full-scale research.
- It can generate proportionately more feedback than one-to-one face-to-face interviews.
- It is direct and enables two-way communication.

Disadvantages include:

- The interviewer could accidentally influence the group's responses.
- Finding the right people to talk to and the right time to call can be time consuming.

Sampling

The basic principle behind sampling is that organisations can obtain a representative picture of the whole (that is, the total group of people being investigated) by looking at a small sample. There are two main types of sampling, Random and Quota.

Random sampling

This consists of selecting respondents on a speculative basis. The interviewer, for example, will choose every nth person until someone agrees to be interviewed. So if a cinema wanted to do a survey to establish visitor satisfaction levels, they might decide to interview every fifteenth customer during the research period. On completion, the cinema would have a fairly accurate idea of the satisfaction levels for the whole of the market using the cinema.

Quota sampling

This is a widely used method where the respondents are selected from a particular market segment. Once the size of the sample has been established, the respondents that conform to certain characteristics are selected and the interviewers are given their quota, i.e. the number of respondents they must interview. For example, an interviewer may be required to find and then interview a certain number of respondents that are CLAMS, or MICE, or BATS, etc.

Attitude scaling

As well as measuring behaviour, that is, what consumers actually do, market research also attempts to assess attitudes towards products and/or services. Consumer attitudes are an important consideration when assessing the impact of a new product/service or for identifying reasons for the success or failure of existing products/services.

To measure attitudes it is necessary to have a scale. The most frequently used scales are:

Thurstone's comparative judgement technique – a selection of consumers are presented with a number of statements and asked to select the one most in line with their attitude. A score is given to each statement to produce an overall summary.

Likert scales – a selection of consumers is asked to indicate levels of agreement or disagreement with each one of a series of statements. Respondents are usually offered five categories: strongly agree, agree, uncertain, disagree, and strongly disagree. A sample question could be: Would you consider your visit to be value for money?

DISCUSSION

Look at the example questionnaire. Have you ever completed a form like this? Where was it and who was it for? What information were they trying to find? What do you think of this approach? Do you feel the questions enabled you to give sufficient detail?

	V. good	Good	Fair	Bad	V. bad
Friendliness/ Helpfulness of staff	☐	☐	☐	☐	☐
Cleanliness of Centre	☐	☐	☐	☐	☐
Fitness Gym	☐	☐	☐	☐	☐
Swimming Pool	☐	☐	☐	☐	☐
Prices of Facilities	☐	☐	☐	☐	☐
Health Suite	☐	☐	☐	☐	☐
Squash Courts	☐	☐	☐	☐	☐
Aerobic Classes	☐	☐	☐	☐	☐
Opening Times	☐	☐	☐	☐	☐
Reception	☐	☐	☐	☐	☐

FIGURE 4.2 *Attitude questionnaire based on the Likert scales*

The semantic differential technique – a selection of consumers is presented with a concept about a brand or product and asked to rate it by means of ticking an entry on a five-point scale. Pairs of adjectives, i.e. strong – weak, heavy – light, good – bad, etc., define the end point on each scale. For example:

How would you describe your visit?   Exciting __:__:__:__:__Boring

CASE STUDY *Surveys*
The Winning Performance

DISCUSSION

It is clear that both the organisations opposite benefited from doing surveys. Why do you think they chose different methods? Do you think the results would have been different if they had used each other's method instead? Why?

'A Health Club's falling membership rate for January was very high and in order to take the correct action to reduce/address it, they needed to know why it was so high – why were people cancelling their memberships? They carried a very simple survey of the members by asking them a few questions as they left the club. The survey revealed that their customer service was questionable and that the changing rooms were often dirty because of the high usage.

As a result of the survey they:

a) Employed a 'front of house manager' to meet and greet members and deal with any queries.

b) Put a member of staff in the changing rooms on a permanent basis.'

Lee Valley Regional Park

The Lee Valley Regional Park recently introduced a limited period evaluation questionnaire at its farms. Over a two-week period, staff approached customers, ranging from schools and youth groups to families and individuals, to ask them to evaluate different aspects of their visit. Questions were asked on various criteria, including the likelihood of a repeat visit and the customers' opinion of the quality of the visitor attraction. The information gained was used to improve customer service delivery, marketing of the facility and quality of attractions. A Likert scale questionnaire was used and the advantages of this were twofold: analysis of the results was relatively simple and secondly, it allowed for an objective assessment of the questions by the customer.'

Observation

In addition to formally requesting information from respondents, some organisations use observations to help them collect primary research data. Observational research involves the systematic recording of behaviour or events as they are witnessed. For example, companies that place adverts outdoors will be interested to identify traffic patterns (that is, the number of people on foot or in cars, etc. that pass a particular point each day), this enables them to consider the suitability of sites when placing adverts. Theme parks, on the other hand, will most likely want to get information regarding visitor patterns to the park and/or any particular attraction. In both cases, either mechanical counters or human observers could record the information.

Other observation methods include researchers disguised as customers (that is, mystery shoppers) who are used to check on staff courtesy and/or their product knowledge. Electronic Point of Sale (EPOS) data collecting allows organisations like shops, and even leisure centres, to track who is buying (or using) what and when and is also a form of observation.

CASE STUDY *Observations*
The Winning Performance

'Some of our clubs have electronic membership swipe cards that enable members to gain entry to the Club. This system enables us to accurately monitor many things – here are just a few:

- Number of members using the club.
- Certain members who have not visited the club for a while (so we can write to them and hopefully keep family membership rates low) and also members who have attended regularly (so we can reward or congratulate them – retention).
- Peak times and, therefore, quiet times.'

Lee Valley Regional Park

'The Lee Valley Centre based in Edmonton, North London, uses data from its bookings and sales computer to observe the patterns of customer attendance during a day, week and year so that the Centre manager can staff the Centre based on historical data. The computer that tracks the sale details can provide a detailed break down of all activities from aerobics to gym attendance, this allows managers to know when peak attendance is anticipated and plan the delivery of quality services, while being able to control costs by not having the Centre overstaffed.'

Types of data

There are two types of data, both of which are important to leisure and recreation organisations. Each can provide the researcher with a different perspective of what is being investigated.

- **Quantitative** data is derived from structured responses that can be qualified in numerical form rather than general open-ended information. For example, how often do you use the fitness suite?
- **Qualitative** data provides in-depth, open-ended and unquantifiable information describing opinions and value, etc. rather than sizes or amounts in numerical form. For example, what do you like best about the fitness suite?

While each has its own particular characteristics and benefits, it is normal for organisations to collect both types as this allows each method to complement and augment the other.

Quantitative data

Quantitative data, as the term suggests, is data that is expressed in numbers. Quantitative data:

- is easy to collect
- generates a large amount of reliable and valid information
- statistically much easier to analyse than qualitative data
- less subject to ambiguity and misinterpretation
- is collected largely by questionnaire or observation.

Questions are normally 'closed' because the respondent is restricted in the choice of answer that she or he can give. Typical examples include:

Choose the answer that best represents you from the listed alternatives:

I take part in sport or exercise

To have fun	[ ]
To compete	[ ]
To improve/learn skills	[ ]
To socialise	[ ]
To keep fit	[ ]
To lose weight	[ ]

Select one or more answers from a selection of alternatives:

Put a mark against any of the facilities which you use

Gosling Sports Park	[ ]
Hatfield Leisure Centre	[ ]
Hatfield Swim Centre	[ ]
Roller-City	[ ]

Stanborough Park   [ ]
Panshanger Golf Complex   [ ]

Rank a series of alternative answers in a specific order of priority:

Identify in order of preference what new facilities/services you would like to see introduced at the leisure centre

Crèche   [ ]
Members' Bar   [ ]
Fitness Testing   [ ]
Physiotherapy   [ ]
Beauty Salon   [ ]
Sauna/Steam Room   [ ]
Jacuzzi   [ ]
Members' Newsletter   [ ]

Quantitative methods are useful for illustrating consumer behavioural patterns and purchasing trends.

CASE STUDY *Quantitative data*

The Winning Performance

Examples of quantitative data that is useful:

- The number of tennis courts/sun beds/football pitches/(or any service that is intangible), for example, sold at certain times of the day for a particular time period (e.g. May).
- This number compared to the number sold during the same time period the previous year.

Example:

We have an optician as a client whom we get to monitor the number of appointments made compared to the number available. If there were, for example, 100 appointments available in one week period (the daily number fluctuates according to what staff are available), and only 20 appointments were made, then clearly some action is needed to fill up the appointment times.

The 80 appointments from that week that were not booked are now 'missed opportunities'. We could not allow this to happen again because if they are not seeing patients they cannot sell spectacles and turnover drops.'

The methods we use to gather quantitative data include:

- Daily Sales Summary sheets.
- Membership swipe cards used in conjunction with computerised sales system (e.g. Microcache and ACT).
- Computer booking sheets.

Lee Valley Regional Park

'Quantitative data is used by the Lee Valley Regional Park to analyse attendance at every facility on an annual basis. Data is used to track performance indicators. These indicators are annual targets set for the number of visits in a year. This data is recorded and used by managers to see how they are performing on a regular basis, in most cases monthly. The Lee Valley Cycle Circuit counts the number of regional events it runs against a set target. If the manager is not achieving the target, action is taken by the manager to achieve the target. Data is collected at the point of sale in this particular case.'

Qualitative data

This data arises from group discussions or interviews and the results are based on content rather than numerical analysis. It is more subjective than quantitative methods, and is generally used when:

- markets need to be explored
- products and services are being developed
- quantitative methods produce unexpected results.

Questions are 'open' and can generate a wide and varied response to a particular question. For example, respondents could be asked:

- What sporting activities do you enjoy and why?
- How might our service be improved?

CASE STUDY *qualitative data*

The Winning Performance

'Methods we have used include:

1 Focus groups: to gather information and opinions from existing members and non-members about a Café Bar situated within a Country Club.
2 Questionnaires: to gather data at Gosling from members about certain services/facilities.

We also use questionnaires in some of the health and fitness clubs that we work with not only to gather their details (name and address, etc.), but to get to know a little more about them, so that the sales consultants can tailor their sales "pitch" to suit the person (i.e. do not heavily sell the crèche if they do not have children, or, fully explain the weight loss programme if they have told you on the questionnaire they want to lose weight.'

Lee Valley Regional Park

'The Lee Valley Water-Sports Centre has set annual targets for its performance. A qualitative measure that the Centre uses is to ask customers at the end of a course how the course content and delivery could be improved. This allows customers' subjective opinions to be considered by the Centre staff for improving the services.'

Gathering and analysing data is, therefore, an essential and permanent feature for any marketing orientated organisation. This process is known as 'market research'.

Once data has been collected it must be transformed into information that can be used. However, in order to be relevant and therefore useful, information must be appropriate for its purpose. It is the combination of information purpose and appropriateness to the task that gives an organisation the 'intelligence' it needs.

If you refer back to our definition of marketing, you will recall that we identified that marketing involves a number of different activities which, when combined, facilitate the satisfaction of customer demand through an exchange process.

Choosing the right kind of research

You will recall, from the above that is important that organisations establish what sort of information they want from their market research, for example, information about their customers, their operating environment, their markets and competitors, or current social and economic trends. Regardless of the type of information sought, organisations should be mindful that too much information or information of the wrong sort would work against, rather than for, effective decision making.

While working through this section you might find the following Internet sites useful:

Central Statistical Office	*www.ons.gov.uk*
Department of Trade and Industry	*www.dti.gov.uk*
Office for National Statistics	*www.ons.gov.uk*
Mintel	*www.mintel.co.uk*
CACI Information – ACORN	*www.caci.co.uk/products/market/*
	acorn.htm
MOSAIC	*www.kormoran.com/mosaic.htm*
Financial Times	*www.ft.com*
UK Government Information	*www.open.gov.uk*
The Stationery Office	*www.the-stationery-office.co.uk*
The Economist	*www.economist.com*
The Times	*www.the-times.co.uk*
ICC Information Sources	*www.icc.co.uk*

The Marketing Mix

Once an organisation has identified its customers and established what their wants and needs are, it must begin to act on that information. This is where the marketing mix comes into play.

If you take another look at our earlier definitions of marketing, together with the resulting key characteristics, you will recall that marketing requires an organisation to combine numerous interrelated and interdependent activities if it is to be successful in achieving its organisational goals and objectives.

Because marketing involves so many business functions organisations find it necessary to apply all these activities in a planned and systematic way. A convenient method is one that groups all the activities into four basic categories:

1 Product
2 Price
3 Place (distribution)
4 Promotion

These are commonly referred to as the **4P's,** and together they make up the **Marketing Mix**. Because just about every conceivable marketing activity can be placed in one of these categories, the 4P's

KEY TERMS

The Marketing Mix: The term used to describe the combination of four variable controllables – Product, Price, Place and Promotion – open to an organisation, and which aid the process of selling a product.

provide a framework upon which marketing efforts can be planned and developed.

Just as a baker mixes various ingredients in differing quantities to make different types of bread, cake and/or biscuit, etc., leisure and recreation organisations vary the emphasis that they place on each of the four elements in the marketing mix when trying to meet their customers' different needs? For example:

- **Product** – A leading sportswear manufacturer might switch production from swimwear to clothing for aerobics to cater for a sudden increase in demand in this product.
- **Price** – A fast food restaurant, having just found out that its main rivals have reduced their prices, may restructure its own prices to remain competitive.
- **Place** – A city centre sight-seeing tour bus company might relocate some of their pick-up points following changes in visitor patterns to some of the city's attractions.
- **Promotion** – A newly opened facility will spend a lot on promotion to inform and attract potential customers, whereas an established one will be spending less to maintain its profile.

While the above examples reinforce the fact that the emphasis on each of the various elements within the marketing mix will vary between organisations, you should also be aware that time is a key factor. In short, if the market situation changes, as in the case of most of the above, then the mix will need to be adapted to the challenges presented by the new marketing environment.

Together the 4P's create a *total offer* to the customer in that they enable an organisation to:

- get the right **product** and/or **service**
- at the right **price**
- delivered in the right **place** and at the right **time**
- supported by appropriate **promotion**

We shall now look at each of the 4P's in turn and in more detail.

Product

This is the most important single element in the marketing mix. The term 'product' refers to what is being offered to the market for its use or consumption. A product is best described as anything and everything one receives in exchange. It can be an idea, a service, a good or any combination of these three. For example, the offering may be a tangible good – such as a personal CD player, a service – such as a private tennis lesson, or an intangible idea – such as the benefits of regular exercise.

However, there are distinct differences between the marketing of goods and services. Goods, for example:

● Are **tangible** – they can be felt, heard, tasted, smelt, seen.

● Are **manufactured** – they are created separately from the point of sale.

● Are **capable of being stocked** – they can be held in stock and sold at a future date/time.

● Can be **delivered** to places that are convenient to the customer.

● On completion of the sale, become the **property of the owner** and can be used whenever the owner likes.

Whereas, services:

● Are **intangible** – they cannot be touched, heard, tasted, smelt or seen. Services have to be experienced.

● Are **performed** – they can only be created with the customer's involvement.

● Are **perishable** – they cannot be stocked. An unsold cinema seat cannot be resold at a future date or time.

● **Remain the property of the producer** – purchase only confers a temporary right for use by the purchaser at a specific time and place.

● Carry a **perceived risk** – customers are less easily convinced of reliability with an intangible product than they are with a tangible one.

● **Quality is viewed as variable** – customers tend to use price as an indicator of quality.

The range of products offered by an organisation is called the **product mix**. The product mix for a small sports centre, for example, could include:

● 25 m swimming pool and jacuzzi

● squash courts

● aerobics studio

● sauna and steam suite

● fitness gym

● hairdressing salon

● projectile hall

Within most of the above product groups it would be possible to provide a number of different product services and/or combinations. For example, in the swimming pool an extensive pools programme would make it possible for the sports centre to offer early morning sessions, club training, school swimming, late swim, swimming lessons and canoeing, among others, and/or combine the sale of a ticket for swimming with the use of the sauna and steam suite.

DISCUSSION

Working in small groups, identify the product mix for three different leisure and recreation organisations with which you are familiar and develop this to include options for each product line.

How extensive is the product mix for each organisation? How do they compare with each other?

DISCUSSION

Choose three different leisure and recreation organisations or providers.

Identify a product or service offered by each organisation and identify whether it is innovative, adaptive or imitative.

What reasons can you give for their use of these categories?

KEY TERMS

Branding: The process of assigning specific characteristics to a product or service which consumers can identify and which influence their buying patterns.

Product types

Products fall into three distinct categories:

1 **Innovative** – These are completely new products resulting from market research and development. As such, they help to keep an organisation at the forefront of the market.
2 **Adaptive** – These are existing products that are modified to extend their life cycle. Modifications are generally undertaken in relation to a number of the marketing mix elements, e.g. a change in pricing or distribution.
3 **Imitative** – These are products that are developed along similar lines to other products already on the market. These other products are usually ones with proven sales attraction, but here the organisation is a follower rather than a leader!

Benefits

Although we have talked about the buying and selling of products and services, it is important to realise that customers *don't actually buy 'products'*. What they buy are '*benefits*'. What this really means is that whenever anyone wants to buy something, what they really want are the benefits that the product confers, rather than its features. For example, where the product is an aerobics studio, the product features are the equipment, the classes, the instructor, and so on. However, the benefits conferred are health improvement, self-esteem, companionship, a sense of well-being, skill development, weight loss, fun etc.

Some of the benefits, however, could also be derived from the purchase of different products, for example, plastic surgery, drugs, or even new clothes. Understanding what 'benefits' rather than what 'products' your customers are buying, will help you to understand what a diverse group your competitors might actually be.

ACTIVITY

Benefits of purchases

Choose five contrasting products and/or services from across the leisure and recreation spectrum. Identify as many benefits as you can that are associated with each purchase.

Ask other people, such as family and friends, to do the same. Do they list the same benefits as you? What differences are there? What does this tell you about benefits?

Branding

Legend has it that branding began when an ancient king decreed that products should bear some sort of symbol or mark, so that if something should go wrong, then both buyers and the authorities would know who to blame. By being made to associate themselves with their products, and being fearful of the king's wrath, the producers began to take greater pride in their work and to make better products than those of their competitors. Whether there is any truth in this tale or not, it still makes the point that branding serves a purpose for both the buyer and the seller in that it makes it easier to buy and sell products.

Some of the benefits of branding for the buyer are that it:

- helps to establish which manufacturer's products are to be sought and which are to be avoided
- reduces risk in purchasing, i.e. without branding a buyer would have difficulty in recognising products and producers that have proved satisfactory in the past
- creates a quick and easy link to the buyer's past, favourable, experiences of that brand, making the purchase decision-making process quicker and easier. For example, someone who has had a good experience of Pizza Express is more likely to eat there when faced with a choice between it and a brand unknown to them

And for the seller, branding:

- helps to create and develop loyal customers
- defends against competition
- facilitates the pricing strategy, e.g. premium pricing
- helps when introducing a new product within an existing brand, for example, when Nike, Reebok or Adidas extended their running product range into other sports
- enables organisations to develop different brands to help penetrate different market segments with the same, or similar, product. For example, Cadbury sells the same chocolate to different market segments through their Dairy Milk and Freddo brands.

KEY TERMS

Competition: Other companies or organisations marketing similar products or services to the same target market.

DISCUSSION

Look at the following brands. Which companies do they represent and what products do they sell?

Product life cycle

It has been suggested that products, just like the people who use them, go through a life cycle. Products are born, grow to maturity, enjoy their prime, grow older and weaker and, eventually die. The gramophone for example, was considered to be cutting edge technology when it was first introduced, and it wasn't long before most households had a gramophone. Popular for many years the gramophone went through a number of subtle changes until the hi-fi replaced it – superior technology in a new product that provided similar benefits, only better.

The length of the life cycle for all products will be dependent on the nature of the market. This includes the product's relevance to meeting customer wants and needs, its adaptability to STEP factors (you may wish to refer back to the section on the marketing environment on page 204 of this text) and whether it is the focus of short-term or long-term trends. For example, basic foodstuffs will have a long life cycle whereas products that depend on fashions or trends, such as certain toys (for example, the yoyo), will not. Although, as in the case of the yoyo, they may come around again at some stage in the future!

There are five main phases in the product life cycle:

1 **Introduction** – The product is launched and supported by a strong promotional campaign. At this stage few customers are likely to know about the product and those that do need to be persuaded to buy. Product costs are high and sales and profit will be low. The emphasis for the organisation is to make potential customers aware. The launch of the 'Planet Hollywood' restaurant chain, for instance, was accompanied by high profile media coverage that included 'celebrity endorsement'.

2 **Growth** – If the product is successful, then sales will begin to grow steadily and profits will increase as a result. At this stage, the price of the products is normally reduced slightly as competition grows. The emphasis for the organisation is on developing a total offer that will persuade the customer to buy its goods and services rather than those of a competitor. For example, the cost for digital TV receivers has seen a marked reduction in cost compared with the launch price, and both SKY and Ondigital now include various incentives to tempt customers to buy into their service.

3 **Maturity** – Sales continue to rise, but more slowly. Most new customers who wanted to buy will have done so already. Profits level off. Competition becomes fiercer as organisations battle it out for gains in market share. The emphasis for the organisation is to decide whether it will let the product die, increase marketing support to generate more sales, or to remodel it altogether. In the case of 'Aerobics' this was given a renewed lease of life by remodelling it as a new product and calling it 'step aerobics'.

4 **Saturation** – Sales begin to decline, profits shrink and the market begins to evaporate. For example, when everyone who might ever buy a particular CD has done so, the remaining stock is relegated and offered at sale prices or as part of multiple buy offers. As competition tends to focus on price at this stage, the emphasis will be on creating an offer, which sets it apart from its competitors.

5 **Decline** – Sales are rapidly falling as superior products or substitutes overtake the product. Profits, if any, are low. Some organisations will withdraw the product from the market, whereas others will endeavour to milk it to the last. For example, Subbuteo has recently announced that it is to cease production, one of the reasons being that it cannot compete with the electronic games market.

Regardless of how successful a product or service is going to be it will require support in the early stages. Therefore, it makes financial sense for an organisation to have a suite of products that are all at different stages of their respective life cycles, as shown in Table 4.4.

 **DISCUSSION**

Choose five or six products offered by various leisure and recreation organisations, and then identify where each of these falls within the product life cycle.

Can you explain the reasons for their position in the product life cycle? Are they replacing or being replaced by other products? If so, what are the reasons for this?

Introduction	Growth	Maturity	Saturation	Decline
Product/offer E	Product/offer D	Product/offer C	Product/offer B	Product/offer A

TABLE 4.4　*The product life cycle*

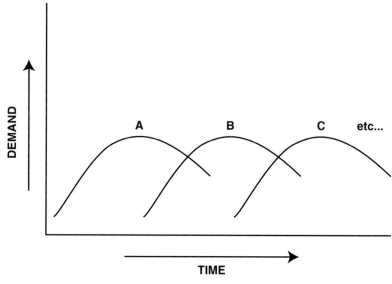

The product life cycle

The Boston Matrix

The Boston Matrix is a tool that provides a simple yet effective way for organisations to assess where their products are within the product life cycle.

Market share indicates how the product/service compares against competitors, while market growth indicates the growth of the market. The matrix is divided into four quadrants as follows:

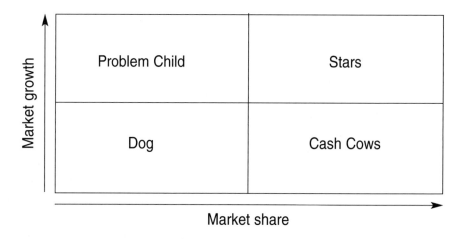

1 *Dog* – This represents a low market share product in a low-growth market and indicates that the product is weak and, ultimately, is a

drain on resources, e.g. local governments continued to build skateboard parks well into the 1980s, by which time the skateboard craze had died down. These 'products' cost a lot to maintain and did not 'pay' for themselves in terms of usage rates – they had become dogs. Luckily they were saved somewhat by the growth in BMX and in-line-skating.

2   *Cash Cow* – This represents a high market share product in a low-growth market and usually refers to yesterday's star, e.g. McDonald's hamburgers.

3   *Problem Child* – This represents a low market share product in a high-growth market and normally refers to new products recently launched, e.g. when sports centres first offered step aerobics they had to make initial investment in promotion, equipment, instructor qualification and tuition. This was risky as they could not be sure the product would eventually pay for itself.

4   *Star* – This represents a high market share product in a high-growth market and suggests that the product is probably a market leader, which is a good source of revenue for the organisation, e.g. Sony's Walkman started out as a star and later became a cash cow for them.

ACTIVITY

The Boston Matrix

In small groups identify a leisure and recreation organisation and list its entire product mix. When you have done this use the Boston Matrix to plot where each product is in the matrix.

What does this tell you about each of the products? How should the organisation react to this information?

Price

As you have already seen, marketing revolves around the process of exchanging things of value. 'Value' is the balance between the customer's desire for a product and the price that the customer is willing to pay. In other words, the amount of money, time, and so on that he or she is willing to exchange for the product is its 'price' range.

Price is the second element of the marketing mix, and is unique in that it is the only element of the mix that can generate profit. All the others represent costs. Getting the price right, therefore, is crucial.

Price determination

Getting the price right in the leisure and recreation industry, however, is not easy. This is because a large part of the industry revolves around the provision of services which are intangible products. When attempting to establish what the 'right' price is, organisations begin by asking themselves a number of key questions. These can be placed into one of two categories, internal or external. Internal questions are to do with the organisation itself and external questions are concerned with the wider market-place, i.e. customers and competitors.

Typical internal questions include:

- How much will it cost to produce and develop the product/service? *(cost).*
- How much will the organisation need to charge in order to generate sufficient revenue and/or profits? *(cost).*
- Which price will help the organisation gain market share? *(objectives).*

Typical external questions include:

- How much are customers willing to pay? That is, what range of prices would they consider to be value for money. This is an important consideration for the organisation when identifying target groups or segmenting the market *(demand).*
- What are the prices being charged by the competition for similar products and services? *(competition).*

Pricing strategies

Having asked their questions, leisure and recreation organisations will use the answers to establish their pricing strategies. In the leisure and recreation industry some of the most common strategies adopted by organisations with regard to pricing, include:

Gaining the desired market position through price

One of the main ways that potential and existing customers assess the value of an organisation's product offer is in its relation to other products in the market-place. Two examples that illustrate this point are value for money and status. The former is concerned with comparing the benefits of various products with each other, e.g. if three TVs each cost the same what, if any, additional benefits do they offer that would help sway judgement in favour of one over the others? The latter point, status, is concerned with offering both quality and exclusiveness, i.e. in order to give the appropriate impression the organisation will need to set a premium price. For example, designer label clothes cost virtually the same to produce as those of a high street store.

Achieving or improving upon the desired market-share

Increasing a product's share of the market is often achieved by setting a lower than desired price and accepting a lower level of profitability over

DISCUSSION

Compare two organisations which 'sell' like products, for example, a pizza in a restaurant, a trip to the cinema or a swim at a pool. What are the prices associated with each? Is there any difference in the price of each? Can you account for the differences?

DISCUSSION

What other questions might an organisation ask when trying to establish the right price?

List your answers under the headings internal and external.

Can you identify differences between the private, public and voluntary sectors? If so, what does this tell you about organisations in each of those sectors?

a given time period. For example, when the *Times* newspaper wanted to increase its market share it had a period where the cost was 10p instead of the normal price of 35p, the idea being to entice new customers who would stay loyal once the normal price was reinstated.

Maximising profit in the short- to mid-term

In this instance prices are set as high as the market will bear – this is easiest to do when your product is scarce in relation to market demand. Prices are maintained at this high level until demand falls and/or competitors enter the market and begin to undercut them.

Survival

As the term implies, organisations set the lowest possible price to ensure that their products sell. It is, for obvious reasons, an approach that can only be maintained for a short period of time.

Pricing policies

Pricing policies are used to help an organisation achieve the various objectives of its pricing strategy. A number of strategies are available:

Standard cost pricing

In this method the standard variable cost per unit is calculated by adding all the production and development variables together, i.e. materials, labour, etc. Added to this are the fixed costs per unit, i.e. running expenses, administration, etc. And finally, the profit per unit is determined. These three factors are then combined to give a provisional price per unit. Provisional prices can be adjusted, if necessary, to take market price levels into account.

Standard cost pricing fits into a pricing strategy that aims to cover current costs and short-term planned investment.

Cost-plus profit pricing

This approach requires a standard mark-up to be applied to the total cost of the product. For example, if a retailer pays a supplier £20 for a product and then marks it up to sell at £30, there is a 50% mark-up and the retailer's gross profit is £10. If the operating costs of the store are £7 per unit sold, the retailer's profit will be £3 or 15%.

Cost-plus pricing can also be part of a strategy to simply cover current costs and short-term planned investment.

Penetration pricing

This is used by organisations wanting to get into a new market (for them) where there are existing providers. The price will be set low in an effort to persuade customers to switch their allegiance. This approach is commonly referred to as a 'loss leader'. Penetration pricing then, fits within a pricing strategy used to gain market penetration.

Competition pricing

This approach involves pricing the product or service in relation to both the competition and the customer's perception of value for money. As such, consideration must be given to whether or not the organisation feels that it can provide 'added value'. For example, if an organisation believes it has more to offer (and believes the customer will recognise this) it is likely to keep its prices just above those of its nearest competitor, if not, it will price just below.

You should also note that the pricing objectives for profit and not-for-profit organisations differ. For example, in the private sector the aim is solely to maximise revenue and prices are set to help achieve this objective – although it is not always necessary to charge high prices as a lower price maintained over a longer time period is usually more effective. Public sector and voluntary organisations, however, can benefit from the receipt of subsidies, which enable them to use concessionary pricing to help them achieve their social aims.

ACTIVITY

Pricing

Examine the pricing structure of a local leisure and recreation facility with which you are familiar. Analyse the factors that have influenced the prices being charged.

Do any of these reflect the product's position within its life cycle? Can you identify any other reasons for the organisation's pricing structure?

Place

KEY TERMS

Place: The specific element of the marketing mix concerned with all aspects of getting products to the right customer, in the right place and at the right time.

Earlier in the text we said that at the broadest level, the function of marketing was to bring buyers and sellers together. Place, the third element in the mix, is concerned with just that. For example, most customers expect products to be available where and when they want them. They put a premium on convenience and availability. They are not concerned with how the organisation plans to meet their needs; they just want their needs met.

Place, in the context of the marketing mix is, therefore, concerned with how the organisation delivers the product or service to the customer as and when it is required. The extent to which this is achieved depends on **location** of the product or service, the **availability** of the product or service, and the method in which it is **distributed**.

With these three points in mind organisations have to make sure that it is easy and convenient for customers to:

● buy the product and/or service – *the trading transaction*
● have the product and/or service available for use – *the physical distribution.*

On some occasions both the trading transaction and the physical distribution take place simultaneously. For example, when you go to a coffee house, you expect to hand over your money and either leave with your purchase or consume it on the premises. You expect the proprietor or staff to accept responsibility for the quality and standard of your drink. On other occasions the transaction involves an intermediary. For example, when you buy a ticket for a show or a concert from a booking agent, you don't expect the booking agent to be responsible for the condition, that is the services, facilities and cleanliness, etc., of the venue. In this example the trading transaction is organised separately from the physical distribution.

DISCUSSION

How far would you be prepared to travel to obtain a particular good or engage in a particular activity? What factors would have a positive or negative impact on your decision?

Location

Decisions regarding location need to take into account the convenience for customers in the buying and/or using equation. For example, leisure and recreation consumer goods, that is, TVs, videos, hi-fis, books, cameras, sports clothing and equipment are all, generally, available through retailers who are tied to the development of shopping precincts and out-of-town shopping centres.

In addition, many of the larger shopping precincts and out-of-town shopping centres, have recently seen developments that include leisure and recreation facilities being made available on the same site, that is multi-plex cinemas, bowling rinks, bingo halls and restaurants. This means that many consumers will not only be able to buy products from one point, which satisfies a wide range of needs, but they will also be able to participate in a variety of activities, which increases the potential number of needs satisfied. Another key consideration in location is access. Whether it's a leisure centre, a theatre, a cinema, library or retail park, customers have to be able to get there. An adequate transportation infrastructure supported by adequate parking, etc. is, therefore, an important consideration.

DISCUSSION

Think about the sales process. Identify a product, service or activity and state the means or mediums through which your product is distributed to you.

Distribution

The term 'channels of distribution' refers to the system of marketing institutions through which goods or services are transferred from the original producers to the ultimate users or consumers. There are a number of channels by which a product or service is transferred and each involves a mix of different intermediaries. The most common include:

● producer direct to consumer
● producer to consumer via a retailer

- producer to consumer via a wholesaler and retailer
- producer to consumer via an agent, wholesaler and retailer.

For example, if you want to buy a train ticket you have the option of buying in person at the station, or through an intermediary such as a travel agent, teletext or the Internet.

Ultimately, the role of distribution is to ensure that the 'right product is available in the right place and at the right time'. Organisations need to consider how this is best achieved with regard to the route of exchange and its administrative and financial control.

ACTIVITY

Distribution channels

Choose three diverse leisure and recreation organisations and establish what 'distribution channels' each employs.

You will need to identify whether they use different channels for different products and what benefits each has?

In addition, what factors does each organisation have to consider in choosing the most appropriate channels, or are these factors beyond the organisation's control?

Promotion

Some elements of the marketing mix deserve special attention. Promotion is one. As such, it will be dealt with in detail in the next section, but you should consider the following introductory points at this stage.

KEY TERMS

Promotion: The element of the marketing mix associated with all forms of marketing communication.

Promotion, the fourth P, is primarily about communication. After all, there is little, if any point in creating a product if you don't tell people about it. Merely having the best product or service is not enough. People need to be made aware that the product exists, where it is and what benefits it provides. In other words, the organisation must convince both existing and potential customers that what it produces matches what they want.

Promotion is used by organisations to **inform**, **persuade,** or **remind** existing and/or potential buyers. In relation to the product life cycle, inform is used at the introduction stage, persuade during the growth and maturity stages and remind during saturation and decline.

Like the other elements of the marketing mix promotion also has its own unique mix. The major ingredients being advertising, personal selling, publicity and sales promotion, all of which are discussed further.

Advertising

This involves the use of any non-personal media to convey information or a persuasive message. Media include:

- television
- national newspapers
- commercial radio
- specialist journals
- local newspapers
- poster campaigns
- promotional leaflets

Personal selling

This approach covers all the processes involved in informing customers and persuading them to buy products or services by communicating with them orally or visually on a personal basis.

Publicity

This is a form of promotion that has a distinct benefit over other types in that it is free. Examples are: articles in newspapers and items on radio and television. One of the most effective methods an organisation can use to raise its profile is by working closely with the media. However, unlike the other methods at its disposal, an organisation will have little, if any, control over what is actually published.

Sales promotion

Essentially this is about using discount and special offers as a means of encouraging customers to use an organisation's products or services. It can be applied equally to first-time users as a means of introduction, or to existing ones as a means of encouraging greater frequency. Typical examples include:

- Two for the price of one offers.
- Taster sessions, i.e. 'Come and try it' – these can be either free or offered at a special introductory price.
- Discounted membership, i.e. 3, 6 or 12-month memberships each offering greater savings pro rata on the normal price.
- Member discounts, i.e. a member is invited to use other facilities or services (not included in their membership) at less than the normal price.
- Samples given free through magazines, the post or even at point of sale.
- Coupons, as samples but also included in packaging – these generally offer money off future purchases.

KEY TERMS

Sales Promotion:
Promotional activity involving incentives or offers designed to add value to a product or service in order to boost its sales.

DISCUSSION

Think of all the incentives and concessions offered by organisations to induce the customer to buy.

Which are you most impressed by? Why?

Analysing the 4P's

Consider some of your most recent purchases (the last five).

For each of these, what was the relevant importance of each of the 4P's? Was it the product itself, its price, the place where you bought it, or the manner in which it was promoted?

Rank your answers on a sliding scale from 1 (not important at all), to 5 (very important).

What does this tell you about your different purchases and what does it say about the 4P's?

The service and public sectors often extend the marketing mix to include other elements that are less tangible but nevertheless critical to success. It is often considered necessary to have **three additional P's,** these are:

People

Services often depend on people to perform them, creating and delivering a product that the customer wants. A customer's satisfaction with a restaurant, a theatre or a leisure centre has as much to do with the quality and nature of the interaction between the customer and service provider as with the end result. For example, if customers feels welcomed and valued by a service provider, they are more likely to return. On the other hand, if their experience is the opposite then they are likely to look elsewhere in the future.

In the service organisation, the distinction between selling and service delivery is blurred. From the perspective of the customer the service is also the product, and all visible functions connected with delivering the service are part of the service offering – the perceived product.

As the personal qualities of staff can be a critical factor in adding value to the service process, especially in high contact service operations, organisations should be mindful of their commitment to employee selection, staff training, motivation and control.

Physical evidence

Décor and ambience are very much part of the product offer. Physical evidence covers all aspects of the physical environment in which the service occurs. How the environment is designed, decorated and maintained will impact upon customer's perceptions. For example, if you went to a restaurant and, despite the fact that the food was first class, you found the premises, crockery and cutlery to be dirty, you would think twice before returning.

Process

The behaviour of people in service organisations is important. So too is the process, the 'how' element of service delivery. Happy, friendly and caring staff can help alleviate the effect of having to queue for a service or deflect the impact of a breakdown that halts service delivery, e.g. when a ride breaks down at a theme park. However, they cannot fully compensate for such problems.

The process element is, therefore, concerned with how the overall system of an organisation operates. It includes:

- the organisation's policies and procedures
- the amount of mechanisation used in the service delivery
- the extent to which customers are involved in the service experience
- capacity levels and waiting/queuing systems
- the flow of information.

ACTIVITY

The service process

Go to any of the following and observe the service process:

- train station
- coach/bus station
- airport
- bank or post office

What stages can you see? What affects the success of the process? How do staff add value? What role do they play?

Marketing communications

Previously you saw how market research is used to *listen* to consumers. In this section you will be examining the other half of that dialogue, that of *talking* to the consumer. The promotional element of the marketing mix is the recognisable method by which an organisation attempts to *tell* its target market that what it produces matches what they want.

Promotion is also, without doubt, the most recognisable and visible aspect of marketing, including as it does the business of advertising, direct marketing, public relations, sales promotion and sponsorship.

In essence, promotion is the process of making a product/service familiar in the minds of the consumer. As such, it is used by organisations to

inform, **persuade,** or **remind** existing and/or potential buyers, by creating favourable attitudes and a willingness to buy. This process is also one of *pulling* consumers to the product/service by using a variety of media to present an image that is attractive, or even compelling.

The overall aims of promotion (or 'persuasive communication', as it is otherwise called) can be summarised thus:

- Stage 1 – create an **awareness** of the organisation and its products/services.
- Stage 2 – create an **interest** in the organisation's products/services.
- Stage 3 – create a **desire** to purchase the organisation's products/ services.
- Stage 4 – prompt the **action** of buying.

In marketing speak this four-stage process is commonly referred to as **AIDA**. The AIDA technique, in relation to sales and selling, is addressed in Chapter 5.

The five promotional methods mentioned (advertising, direct marketing, public relations, sales promotion and sponsorship) above are applied, where appropriate, to each of the stages in the AIDA process. For example, advertising and public relations tend to draw customers in by arousing attention and interest, while sales promotion and selling methods tend to induce desire and prompt action to buy.

It is rare in the leisure and recreation industry for an organisation to be able to use any one of the promotional methods consecutively throughout the AIDA process. More often than not, organisations have to blend different promotional methods to achieve each of the aims in the AIDA process. Take, for example, a tour operator promoting summer holidays to the 18–30 age group. The tour operator will probably begin with a press campaign designed to arrest the attention of the identified target market, and encourage them to think about the benefits of this particular type of holiday.

The press campaign will also probably include a mechanism that enables the target market to contact the tour operator directly, or an agent working on their behalf, for promotional literature and information detailing the benefits of the tour operator's products. The next stage normally involves an interview with a salesperson whose job it is to get the necessary information required to design a tailor-made proposal for the customer.

Both the promotional literature and interview are designed to encourage interest. Furthermore, the interview, through the method of personal selling, enables the tour operator to lead the customer into the final two stages of the process. The first involves the salesperson eliciting, and then responding to, the specific needs of the customer, and then showing how the tour operator's products meet that particular customer's needs. This would, hopefully, result in the creation of a desire to purchase, at which point, the salesperson would move on to the final stage – prompting the action of buying.

Before we move on to describing each of the promotional methods in detail, you should realise that just as an appropriate marketing mix has to be developed for the marketing effort overall, so an appropriate 'promotional mix' has to be created for an organisation's communication with its market. This requires an organisation to identify what, exactly, the promotional effort is going to achieve.

Typical marketing objectives in leisure and recreation industries include:

DISCUSSION

In small groups identify as many other communication objectives as you can. Link these to specific products and/or services where possible.

When you have done this add them to the list and sort them according to inform, persuade and remind. What does this tell you about promotion?

- Telling consumers and other end users of the organisation's products/services.
- Reminding consumers and other end users of the organisation's products/services.
- Announcing new products/services or changes to existing products/services.
- Informing consumers and other end users of the positive differences between the organisation and its competitors.
- Influencing consumers' and other end users' attitudes.
- Advising consumers and other end users of changes to prices, activity schedules and facility opening and closing times, etc.

The communication process

Before you look at the main promotional methods used by leisure and recreation organisations in their promotional effort, you need to ensure that you understand that they are only communication tools. It is important, therefore, to remind yourselves of the key elements of communication.

The communication process is easier to explain with a diagram. The following model illustrates the key elements involved:

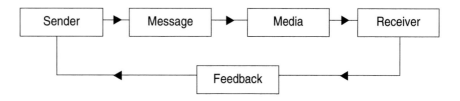

Let's take a brief look at what each of these five stages involves.

1 Sender – quite simply, this is the organisation or person who has something to say.

2 Message – this refers to what is being said. In the case of promotion, for example, the message would have to relate to the promotional objectives. So, if a leisure centre wanted to inform existing and potential customers that it has recently opened a new fitness suite, that is exactly what it would do. Of course the message would not simply be 'we have recently opened a new fitness suite', but would be related more specifically to the perceived benefits that this new facility could offer. For example: 'Come to our new fitness suite. Improve your health and fitness using the latest equipment. Our qualified instructors will be happy to tailor a programme to meet your needs.'

3 Media – this covers the various communication options open to the organisation. These might include press advertisements, radio commercials, roadside banners, direct mail and so on.

4 Receiver – this is whoever the sender intended the message to go to. If the sender is at all unclear as to whom the target audience is, then it is unlikely that the message will be effective. In marketing communications the receiver, generally, represents a market segment. Organisations must, therefore, make every effort to ensure that the content and media of the message appeals to the selected target.

5 Feedback – whatever the response to its actions, the organisation will want feedback so that it can ascertain that the message has been received, understood and acted upon. Satisfactory feedback normally closes a particular communication loop, whereas unsatisfactory feedback causes the sender to go around the loop again. This process continues until satisfactory feedback is achieved.

ACTIVITY

Communication strategies

Go to a local travel agent and obtain a number of brochures that concentrate on holidays in the sun. For each of the following groups: single 18–30, married couples with two children, and retired couple, evaluate the style, format and content of the various brochures with regard to how they are communicating with each respective target group. Are there any differences? What are they? What does this tell you about communication?

Promotional methods

Remember promotion is communication used by organisations to inform, persuade and remind both existing and potential customers. Advertising, personal selling, sales promotions, direct marketing, public relations, publicity and sponsorship are all communication methods that an organisation can use to promote a message. Each, however, has its advantages and disadvantages and needs to be considered in relation to a number of factors, these include:

● The size and type of organisation – large or small, public, private or voluntary.

- The organisation's resources – how much money the organisation can afford to spend on its promotional efforts. Whether it has in-house specialists or is it dependent on external agencies.
- Cost of the various promotional methods – is the method chosen the most cost-effective, and is it within the organisation's budget capabilities?
- Timescale – how much time does the organisation have to prepare the promotional effort and are any of the methods inhibitive or likely to be affected by time constraints?
- Target market – is the target market local, regional or national? Is it subject to any particular demographic characteristics such as age, gender, race, etc.?
- Stage of the product/service in the product life cycle – is the product/service new or in decline? Is the organisation trying to inform, persuade or remind?

DISCUSSION

Which media do you think the following organisations are likely to use for advertising?
- **British Airways**
- **Nike, Reebok or Adidas**
- **Your local leisure centre**
- **A local amateur dramatic society**
- **Alton Towers**
- **A school fête**

Whatever the organisation is trying achieve through its promotional efforts, it must ensure that the promotional mix accomplishes the following:

- Reaches and is suitable for the target market.
- Uses the most appropriate and effective communication method.
- Achieves the organisation's marketing objectives.

A large national organisation with abundant resources wishing to reach a large and diverse target market would most likely use television. For example, whenever Alton Towers introduces a new ride or major attraction it uses a mixture of TV and high profile magazine adverts to communicate this fact. Both methods convey the information but are also supported by the use of images, which add impact and serve as an inducement. On the other hand, a local sports centre with limited resources would most likely be restricted to using the local paper to place an advert or carry an article.

In reality, and as you will probably have realised from the above discussion, many organisations, irrespective of their size and purpose, will select a variety of media when promoting their products/services. This ensures that the market is adequately covered. You can get details about sources of advertising media, classified by area, price and potential audience from the British Rate and Data (BRAD) directory. We will now look at the main promotional methods used by leisure and recreation organisations.

Advertising

Advertising is a costed form of communication used by an organisation to promote itself, its products and its services. Organisations can use any of the following media to get their message across to the public.

DISCUSSION

What types of leisure and recreation activities would benefit from being advertised in the national, regional or local press? Can you find actual examples of adverts in the press?

What benefits are there to the newspapers in carrying adverts? And why would this affect the sort of advert that they would be happy to carry?

Newspapers

There are three basic types of newspaper publications that leisure and recreation organisations can advertise in:

- national (e.g. *The Times*, the *Sun* and the *Financial Times*)
- regional (e.g. the *Wessex Gazette*)
- local (e.g. the *Croydon Advertiser*).

ADVANTAGES	DISADVANTAGES
• Can access a large number of prospective customers • Can use pictures as well as words • Can help you target particular geographic areas • Much cheaper than TV	• Can be very expensive • Is blanket advertising, so it goes to lots of people you are not targeting • Short message life of daily papers – a prospective customer who does not get a paper on the day you place the advert will not hear about you

Magazines and journals

Although similar to newspapers both magazines and journals appeal to readers with specific interests. They also tend to have a longer shelf-life, e.g. many magazines are weekly or monthly, rather than daily.

ADVANTAGES	DISADVANTAGES
• Magazines tend to be targeted more than newspapers. An example would be trade press (e.g *Leisure News*) – advertising in it can help an organisation reach a very specific target audience • Longer message life than papers – a prospective customer has a whole month to buy the issue you advertised in, also magazines tend to be re-read • Can access a large number of prospective customers • Can use pictures as well as words • Much cheaper than TV	• Low frequency means you can't change your advert quickly in response to, say, running out of stock • Long 'closing dates' mean you have to send your advert to the magazine at least a month before publication

Television

Advertising on television is a very effective method of reaching a large audience, after all, most households in the UK have a television. It is however, very costly and is generally only undertaken by large organisations with a regional or national remit, normally the latter.

ADVANTAGES	DISADVANTAGES
● Can access the largest possible number of people ● Is the best way of showing how things work, e.g. a new washing powder	● You cannot say as much in 30 seconds of TV as you can in a one-page newspaper advert ● Air time and production costs are high

Radio

There is an increasing number of national, regional and local radio stations. Although radio advertising is cheaper than television it does have smaller audiences.

ADVANTAGES	DISADVANTAGES
● Can access a large number of prospective customers ● Can help you target particular geographic areas and demographic groups ● Cheaper than TV	● Is blanket advertising, so it can go to lots of people you are not targeting ● No visual capability

Leaflets/fliers and brochures

Leaflets are probably the most effective form of advertising open to leisure and recreation. The medium can be used in a number of different ways. For example, leaflets can be:

● given away or collected from the point of sale
● inserted into newspapers or magazines
● dropped through people's doors
● handed out on the street
● posted on noticeboards, or in shop windows.

Brochures can be used in a similar way, but allow the organisation to include more information, e.g. showing its products. They are best suited to those who have already decided to buy the type of product/service the organisation is offering.

Brochures can be used in a similar way, but allow the organisation to include more information, e.g. showing its products. They are best suited to those who have already decided to buy the type of product/ service the organisation is offering.

ADVANTAGES	DISADVANTAGES
• The organisation has complete control over the production process, e.g. it can guarantee colours are true, etc. • Fliers in magazines and papers stand apart from the adverts on the pages	• Brochures are more expensive to produce than fliers, leaflets or newspaper adverts

Posters

You will have seen many examples of posters on billboards, the sides of buses, in shop windows, at train stations, or at bus stops. They are similar to adverts, but tend to be bigger, with a 'honed down' message, and less detail.

ADVANTAGES	DISADVANTAGES
• Relatively cheap • Can be made in-house or professionally • Long message life – adverts are seen many times and are re-read by many • Can access a large number of prospective customers • Can use pictures as well as words • Much cheaper than TV • Can be used all around the facility	• It can be hard to work out the best site for a particular poster • In-house can look amateurish • The new poster must contrast with the previous one displayed, otherwise people will not notice it

ACTIVITY

Advertising techniques

Consider a range of organisations operating at local, regional or national level from the public, private and voluntary sectors. Use actual examples to complete this activity:

● Identify which media type is most likely to be available to each.

● What techniques might each of your chosen organisations employ to reach their target markets? What are the practical factors that they would need to consider in making their choice.

DISCUSSION

Think about examples of direct and indirect marketing. Can you identify specific organisations and products that employ these methods?

How effective do you think they are?

KEY TERMS

Direct Marketing: A method of marketing wherehy the prdducer supplies direct to the consumer – using advertising, telephone sales, or other communication media – to elicit a direct response, i.e. an order by mail or phone.

Direct Mail: Advertisements, leaflets, letters, brochures and other forms of literature sent to existing and potential customers through the post.

Advertising can be direct or indirect:

● **Direct advertising** aims to influence a customer to make a specific purchase, for example, a billboard poster showing a car and its price is designed to convince you to buy the car.

● **Indirect advertising** aims to subtly increase awareness, for example, a billboard poster just showing a company logo is designed to ensure the brand is in the customer's mind next time they make a purchase decision.

Direct marketing

Direct marketing is any form of communication between the organisation and the end customer directly. It includes direct mail and personal selling.

Direct mail

When most people think of direct mail they generally think of 'junk mail'. But junk mail is just badly targeted direct marketing. Rather than going to people who are known to be interested in the organisation's offering, they go to all sorts of people who have no interest whatsoever in the organisation's products or services. Ideally direct marketing should be supported by a useful database of customers' preferences, behaviour and other profiling information such as age, sex, income bracket, etc. Promotional information can then be sent to those who are most likely to respond to it. This increases the success rate and reduces the costs.

The leisure industry is a service industry and, as such, is in a position to use personal selling to great effect. If you have ever formed a good opinion of an organisation after dealing with one of its employees you will appreciate the value of personal selling. Personal selling is any communication between an employee of the organisation and the customer, where the customer sees that employee as representing the organisation itself. It can be done in two ways:

1 Face-to-face, for example, across the counter of a coffee bar, or via a presentation at a trade conference.

2 By phone, for example, when calling a customer to check on satisfaction with a purchase.

Public relations

Public relations (PR) is about reputation. As it says in the name, it is about the organisation's relationship with the public. It has many different names:

- corporate communications
- publicity
- customer relations
- public/community affairs
- crisis management
- media relations

But whatever its name, its purpose is to promote the organisation as a whole, rather than to promote a particular product or service. The idea being that if customers, and prospective customers, view the organisation positively they will be more inclined to buy their products/services. Likewise, if others who may be able to influence the success of the organisation (such a local government), feel well disposed towards it they will be more likely to allow the organisation to pursue its goals.

PR functions often get involved in organising:

- roadshows, which allow the organisation to meet groups of its customers (and prospective customers) face-to-face
- exhibitions of the organisation's offer at fairs and conferences.

Sponsorship

Sponsorship and the role that it plays within the sports sector of the industry was addressed in detail in Chapter 3.

Sponsorship is a type of public relations focused on associating the sponsor with appropriate events and/or individuals. For instance, in return for supplying an athlete with kit, emblazoned with the company logo, the sponsoring company hopes to attract sales from customers who admire or identify with the athlete. In return for contributing towards the refurbishment of a theatre and having its name up on the wall, the organisation hopes its name will be recognised when theatregoers next shop for its product.

DISCUSSION

Observe carefully the next professional sporting event you watch on TV. How many different hoardings can you see around the playing area? To which organisations do they belong?

In the leisure and recreation industries examples of sponsorship can be found at both national and local levels, such as:

- **Direct advertising** –for example, where advertising space at an event is given to a sponsoring organisation. You only have to look at the hoardings surrounding a football pitch to see this in operation.
- **Indirect promotion** – for example, press coverage of the organisation's sponsorship of, say, a new hospital wing.

Sales promotions

Sales promotion is anything an organisation does to give its customers an added value incentive to purchase its products/services. They are usually used to achieve a specific, short-term purpose, such as clearing surplus stock or attracting new customers. Promotional techniques include:

- Reduced or discounted prices – usually offered via a coupon and valid only for a set time period.
- Free samples – normally used to introduce the customer to a company's products and designed to give a favourable impression leading to a purchase.
- Multiple purchase offers – where the customer gets a discount for repeat or multiple purchases. The most well known example is 'buy one get one free', known as 'BOGOF' in the trade.
- Free premiums – these are additional goods or services acquired when buying a product/service, for example, getting your membership card stamped every time you attend the gym entitles you to a free sunbed session when your card is full.

DISCUSSION

Visit your local sports store or other favourite shop, even the local pub or bar. What sales promotions are currently on offer?

- Cross-sampling – this is very similar to free samples in that a complimentary product comes with the one being purchased, however, in this instance the free gift is linked in some way to the main purchase, for instance receiving an 'energy drink' sachet when buying a cycling magazine.
- Competitions, including 'sweepstakes' where no skill is required to enter.

DISCUSSION

Consider the promotional techniques employed. Link each of these with the methods employed by actual organisations in 'selling' their products and services.

How successful are the methods they employ?

As mentioned previously, promotions must fit in with an organisation's overall marketing strategy. They must be well thought out, serve their purpose in the short-term and add to the longer-term success of the organisation.

In promoting an offer organisations should always:

- Make sure they have clear objectives, for example, what will they be achieving by running a money offer promotion?
- Check that the objective fits within the overall marketing strategy, for example, reducing the price of a premium product could result in its no longer being perceived as a premium offer.

- Budget for every part of the promotion, for example, don't make the price lower than the organisation can afford.
- Research and review success of promotions, for example, have free samples been more successful than competitions in the past?

Keeping on the right side of the law

Legal and regulatory requirements for safe working practices that bind organisations have been outlined in more detail in Chapter 2.

There are several laws, which seek to govern the communication activities of organisations as well as protecting the consumer. Those involved in the promotional effort *must* make themselves aware of the legislation affecting their work.

Trade Descriptions Act 1968

This Act makes it illegal to give a false description of a good. This covers descriptions in writing, in advertisements or in anything that the seller says when discussing the good with the customer. The act also makes provision regarding the pricing of goods. For example, an organisation cannot charge a higher price than the one marked on the good, nor can it claim the price of the good has been reduced unless the same good was offered for sale at a higher price for a period of at least 28 days.

Consumer Protection Act 1987

Makes it an offence to supply any consumer goods that do not meet with general safety requirements. Organisations have a general duty to trade safely and meet certain standards. For example, furniture and toy manufacturers are governed by standards relating to fire hazards and choking respectively.

Data Protection Act 1984

In today's technological climate, numerous leisure and recreation organisations are reliant on computers and other automated information systems. Membership lists and databases for marketing and promotional services are among the many examples of the systems organisations use that require the collection and storage of personal data on individuals. Staff and management of those organisations using computers and/or other automated information systems, need to be aware of the principles of the Data Protection Act and the extent to which it affects their operational practices. This topic was covered in detail in Chapter 2.

ACTIVITY

Visit a local leisure and recreation facility that uses computers and/or other automated information systems and establish how this organisation deals, in practice, with the Data Protection Act.

Regulation of marketing practice

Within the UK there are a number of regulatory bodies involved in the regulation of marketing practice. Among them you will find the Advertising Standards Authority (ASA). One of the roles of the ASA is to oversee the British Code of Advertising Practice, which covers a wide variety of advertising media including:

- print
- cinema
- video
- posters
- leaflets
- teletext

The ASA also supervises the British Code of Sales Promotion Practice, which lays down guidelines for good practice in sales promotions, including the principles that advertising should be:

- legal, honest and truthful
- prepared with a sense of responsibility to consumers and society
- within the generally accepted principles of fair competition in business.

The Independent Television Commission (ITC) has responsibility for terrestrial and cable television advertising, and the Radio Authority (RA) supervises radio advertising.

ASSESSMENT EVIDENCE

This Unit is assessed by external assessment. For the assessment you are required to demonstrate your understanding of how UK leisure and recreation organisations use marketing, specifically how they identify:

- missions and objectives
- internal and external business environments, using SWOT and STEP analyses
- analysis of marketing research techniques and how they influence marketing mixes and other segments
- analysis of the marketing mix, covering product, price, place and promotion

The following Case Study provides a sample assignment, based on the external assessment procedures used by the Edexcel Awarding Body. Tutors could use this as a practice or mock exam during January if the centre is entering the June Test series.

A period of 2 hours 30 minutes is recommended for the assessment question, reflecting the time allocation used in the external assessments.

Hadfield College Sports Centre

Hadfield College Sports Centre provides health, fitness and leisure facilities to staff, students and the local community. Facilities include:

- 25 m swimming pool and jacuzzi
- four squash courts
- sauna and steam suite
- fitness gym
- aerobics studio

The Centre is open seven days a week:

- Monday–Friday 7.00 a.m.–10.00 p.m.
- Saturday and Sunday 8.00 a.m.–6.00 p.m.

Swimming pool and jacuzzi

The 25 m pool is maintained at a temperature of 28°C (82°F) and is an excellent lap training pool with slow, medium and fast lanes. The pool is complemented by a jacuzzi, which provides visitors with the opportunity to relax after their swim.

Pool programme

Provides a timetable which includes:

- early morning sessions
- club training
- late swim
- swimming lessons

Changing rooms

Separate men's and women's changing rooms are available. Poolside cubicles complement these. Each changing room has showers, toilet facilities and clothing storage lockers, operated by a returnable 50p coin. Under 5's swim free. An adult must accompany children under 10 years wishing to use the pool or jacuzzi.

Sauna and steam suite

An eight-seat sauna and steam cabin is available in a self-contained area within the Centre. The suite includes two showers, one of which is a cold needle shower.

- Monday–Friday 7.00 a.m.–10.00 p.m.
- Saturday and Sunday 8.00 a.m.–6.00 p.m.

All sessions are mixed except:
- Tuesday: women only
- Thursday: men only

A member's only restriction is operated from 4 p.m. on Thursdays.

Fitness gym

The fitness gym is a fully air-conditioned facility. It is **compact** but offers a full range of exercise equipment to tone and develop all major muscle groups. Equipment includes: Treadmills, Concept II Rowers, Aero-cycles, Step machines, Gravitron, Cable column, Seated fly, Chest press, Lat pulldown, Shoulder press, Leg extension, Leg curl, Multi-hop machine, Leg Press, Abdominal bench and abdominal trainer, Warm up, Cool down matted area.

Only persons aged 16+ are permitted to use the gym.

A one hour and 15 minute time limit is operated during peak hours. Capacity 30.

Aerobics studio

The studio is air-conditioned, with a sprung floor providing a comfortable and safe environment for aerobic classes. The diverse schedule offered by the centre includes Step, Body Sculpt, Yoga, Dance, Tone Up Stress Down and many more.

Squash

The Centre provides four squash courts. Group courses and individual tuition are available for all levels, from beginners to advanced.

Refreshments

Four vending machines provide hot and cold drinks, sweets and soup.

Booking

Members can book up to seven days in advance. Non-members can make bookings in person up to three days in advance. Fees are payable at the time of booking.

Membership

Membership fees:

- Adult 13 weeks: £35.00
- Adult 6 months: £55.00
- Adult annual: £80.00
- Family 13 weeks: £50.00
- Family 6 months: £85.00
- Family annual: £130.00

Membership entitles members to a 25% discount. College staff and students get free membership and are entitled to a 50% discount.

Usage

Analysis of internal data shows that:

- The fitness suite is the most popular facility and is fully booked on weekdays between 4.00 p.m. and 8.00 p.m.
- The swimming pool is next and is used mostly in the early morning and late evening.
- The aerobics studio has an acceptable level of use Monday to Thursday evenings.
- The squash courts are hardly ever used.
- Sauna, solarium and jacuzzi have a moderate level of usage throughout the week, but pick up quite considerably at weekends.
- There is a significant drop in attendances in all activities during college closure periods.

Environment

Hadfield College Leisure Centre is situated near to the centre of the town and is within five minutes walk of both the bus and train stations. The population of the town is 28,000 (although during term time this swells to 33,000) and within a five mile radius 42,000. Unemployment is below the national average at 3%. Car ownership is high (76% of households own a car). The town has five junior mixed infant schools and two secondary schools.

Socio-economic profile

A: 12%
B: 23%
C1: 21%
C2: 14%
D: 15%
E: 15%

Competition

Two hotels in the area have recently added leisure facilities. Both hotels have similar facilities, including small swimming pool, sauna, jacuzzi and beauty treatment rooms.

There are two local authority leisure centres within a five-mile radius. The first is a 'dry' facility and has a 5-court sports hall, squash courts, fitness suite (with good free-standing equipment), fitness testing and sports injury clinic, aerobics and dance studio, lounge bar, and 8-rink indoor bowling green. The second is an outdoor 'wet' facility comprising a 30 m swimming pool and a 5 m learner pool. The local authority has decided to permanently enclose the pool. Work will begin in the autumn and is expected to last for six to eight months.

Hadfield College Sports Centre – case study question paper

1 Suggest suitable corporate objectives for the leisure centre and give an example of a SMART goal for each.
2 Describe the Strengths, Weaknesses, Opportunities and Threats that exist for Hadfield College Sports Centre.
3 How might the leisure centre make use of such information? Give examples to illustrate your answer.
4 Drawing on your knowledge of the leisure and recreation industry, indentify which STEP factors are most likely to have an influence on the leisure centre and explain the reason for your answer(s).
5 Write a brief marketing research plan with the aim of increasing usage of the centre's facilities. Justify your proposed methodology and give examples of how this could be applied.
6 Outline a promotional plan to communicate with the leisure centre's target market, both existing and potential, with a budgeted spend of only £5,000.
7 Show how the leisure centre can use the marketing mix to meet the needs of both existing and potential customers.
8 Give one advantage and one disadvantage to Hadfield leisure centre of each of the following:
   - internal data
   - external data
   - quantitative data
   - qualititative data
   - face-to-face interviews
   - newspaper advertising
   - brochures and leaflets
   - personal selling

Key Skills

In completing the assessment for this unit, you can achieve the following key skills. These will be accredited at the discretion of your tutor on the basis of the quality of the work you submit.

COMMUNICATION, LEVEL 3

C3.1b Make a presentation about a complex subject, using at least one image to illustrate complex points.

C3.2 Read and synthesise information from two extended documents about a complex subject. One of these documents should include at least one image.

INFORMATION TECHNOLOGY, LEVEL 3

IT3.1 Plan, and use different sources to search for, and select, information required for two different purposes.

CHAPTER **5**

Customer Service in Leisure and Recreation

....

Aims and Objectives

Through the study of this unit you will have the opportunity to:

- **consider the range, type and quality of service offered by organisations to consolidate the products, services and activities they 'sell' to customers**

- **analyse the role(s) played by the employee in the delivery of customer service**

- **realise the emphasis placed by organisations on the delivery of good quality customer service in terms of retaining and increasing customer numbers**

- **understand the significance of personal presentation skills and communication in dealing successfully with customers**

- **appreciate that all customers are different and that each has specific and individual needs**

- **learn how to handle complaints**

- **measure, monitor and evaluate customer service procedures and practices**

Introduction

Think about the last time you took part in a leisure and recreation activity away from the home. What was it? Where did it take place? Which organisation or facility was your host? During the course of that activity you would have had some sort of contact with an employee from that organisation. Who were they?

For example, the employee might have sold you a ticket for a performance, or might have been your step aerobics teacher, fitness instructor or your sports coach. He/she could have served you a drink, been the resident DJ at a nightclub, or your tour guide or holiday representative during your last holiday. Think about the contact you had with those employees. What did they do for you? What type of service did you receive from them? Would you make a repeat visit to that organisation?

You may even work within an aspect of the leisure industry. Think about the type of contact that you have had with different customers. As an employee you would have had to provide a service to customers. What quality of service did they receive from you?

The customer

It is the customer who is responsible for the constantly changing and evolving (dynamic) nature of the industry. Most organisations (particularly the multinational companies) have so-called 'watchdogs' that are responsible for monitoring products, activities and services in relation to recent initiatives or new fashions and trends. They will pay detailed attention to participation rates so that they can anticipate the needs and wants of the customer and cater for them accordingly.

It is the customers' needs, wants, their interests and desires that drive the industry forward and the customer is often the catalyst for new change. For example, more attention to people's own individual levels of fitness resulted in the prolific growth of the hi-tech individual exercise facilities in the 1990s. The fitness industry alone in this country is worth an estimated £1 billion.

Change has also occurred in the pub industry, and some sectors have been redefined. In recent years there has been significant diversity and sustained growth within the pub industry in terms of catering for children. Some pubs, such as The Wackey Warehouse Chain and the now established Playbarns at Tom Cobleigh's pubs, have designated child play areas with appropriately trained staff.

Customer service situations

In any sales-orientated, people-based industry there will inevitably be a starkly contrasting range of situations in which both the customer and employee find themselves. It is important to remember that not all of these situations, meetings or confrontations will be about selling.

Role plays

Throughout this chapter there are a number of role plays and scenarios, each of which presents a different type of situation. You are encouraged to play out these roles in order to understand the immense variety of encounters that occur. By taking on these various roles you will begin to understand the emphasis organisations place on dealing with customers in an efficient, effective and courteous manner. These role plays will help improve your ability to deal with customers and give you the valuable practice you need before you are assessed more formally on your ability to deal with customers.

Situations between an employee and a customer will vary. You will need to be able to:

- provide information, assistance and give advice
- make sales
- take and relay messages
- keep records
- deal with problems and handle complaints.

As part of the assessment evidence for this Unit you will have to show evidence of your involvement with different customers in a range of customer service and selling situations. Customers have different needs and wants and it is your responsibility to recognise these needs and respond accordingly. For each situation you should consider the following:

What type of customer am I dealing with?

- internal or external
- age group
- cultural background
- specific needs
- individual or group

What does the customer need?

- information
- help with a problem
- sales and purchasing advice
- to complain

What are the priorities for this customer?

- health and safety
- price
- value for money
- reliability
- staffing levels, quality of staff or service levels
- timing of service
- enjoyment of experience
- provision for individual needs

What is the best way to communicate in this situation?

- verbal or non-verbal
- telephone
- written
- positive personal image

How will I best record the information?

- booking or order form
- register
- statement of account or bill
- memo
- e-mail
- complaints form
- refer the customer to someone else

The information included in this Chapter will help you answer some of those questions.

DID YOU KNOW?

Organisations selling services depend on existing customers for 85–95% of their business.

Why excellent customer service is important

The late Sam Walton, the once Chairman of the American trading giant Wal-Mart said:

❝A customer can fire everyone from the chairman on down simply by spending his money somewhere else.❞

The collective power of the customer cannot be underestimated. In essence, the customer is the one that purchases an organisation's products and services; customers generate income. In order to secure their custom, patronage and loyalty, customers need to be regarded as infinitely more than the faceless, nameless many that come through an organisation's doors.

Customers should be central to an organisation's planning, management and philosophy; quite simply, the customer should be an organisation's 'number one' priority.

What is customer service?

DISCUSSION

What does customer service mean to you?

Within your working group can you come up with a definition of 'customer service'?

The emphasis in the increasingly competitive marketplace of the leisure and recreation industry is on a quality customer service. But what exactly do we mean by 'service'?

From the customer's point of view, the term service has many different interpretations and meanings. Is it the way in which your questions and queries are answered? Is it the way the product, service or activity is delivered? Is it the way in which you are welcomed and treated? Is it the behaviour and attitude of the employees? Is it the way a complaint is registered and resolved? The concept of customer service can be separated into the following distinct areas:

- The product itself.
- The employee as part of that product.
- The quality and service associated with the sales process.

You will investigate these aspects throughout this chapter.

Who are the customers?

Within the industry there are a range of different products, services and activities that are 'sold' by organisations. The type, range and quality of the goods bought will vary from one organisation to another, yet they all have one element in common – the 'customer'.

The industry as a whole relies heavily on the frequent use of its facilities, its products, services and activities by customers. Customers are a very precious commodity, and without them, organisations could not exist in what has become a very competitive marketplace.

There are two types of customer, the internal and the external customer. You must be aware that the difference between the two is a significant one.

Internal and external customers

Internal customers are people who work within an organisation, who may need information, technical support and other internal services to do their job. They may be an integral part of the delivery of a quality service to the external customers although they may have no actual or real contact with them. External customers are people outside the organisation who use or buy the organisation's products and services.

The delivery of a quality customer service must, therefore, extend to the internal as well as the external customer if an organisation is to achieve its aims and objectives.

The customer may be referred to by a number of different terms which include client, consumer, guest, user, purchaser, buyer and so forth. All of these terms imply that some sort of sale has been agreed between the organisation or vendor and the customer. The sale might range from a hamburger in a fast-food restaurant, a bottle of beer in a bar, the entrance fee to a night club, a video that you have rented to the use of aerobic fitness equipment in a gymnasium or an aromatherapy massage.

Who is responsible for delivering customer service?

Effective and successful customer service depends on the unity and good working relationship of *all* the employees or staff within the organisation and is not only the responsibility of the employee designated as the first point of direct contact.

Staff roles in providing customer service can be placed into two distinct categories:

1 front of house staff
2 back of house and support staff

Front of house staff

These are the staff that come into contact with the customer at any time. It is part of their designated job role to always be ready to meet, greet, help and advise customers in any way they can.

Such staff include receptionists, customer advisors, sales assistants, waiters, hosts, bar staff, porters, recreation assistants, instructors and coaches, tour guides, air stewards and others.

Backroom staff

These staff have indirect or irregular contact with the customer, but they still play an integral role in the provision of a quality service. As a customer you would be aware of their existence but you would not necessarily have any interaction or contact with them, for example, housekeepers, chambermaids, chefs and kitchen assistants, possibly even the manager, unless you were unhappy with the standard and quality of service you were receiving and asked to see him.

DISCUSSION

Choose one role from each type, preferably within the same organisation. Whose role is the most significant?

Support staff are those people that work in marketing, accounts, the technical department and administrative services have little or no contact with the customer but their role is still essential.

What can an organisation achieve?

The marketplace of the leisure and recreation industry is increasingly competitive with many organisations offering 'like for like' products, services and activities. How can an organisation sustain the commercial viability of its business with such immense competition?

How do you decide which cinema complex to view a film at when such a variety of options are available to you, the customer? Competing organisations include Warner Bros, UCI, Showcase and the Odeon, which offer the same movies, at virtually the same prices, at similar show times.

Much of your decision will be swayed by its location and proximity to your residence, ease of access and the availability of transport to and from the venue (public transport will be particularly important to those of you who do not have access to a car). However, if the facilities were equidistant which would you choose? One significant factor that may influence your choice of venue may well lie in the quality of the service that you receive from staff members.

Successful organisations in the industry have made the concept and practise of customer service one of their highest priorities. These organisations realise that without the customer there would be no organisation. An outstanding and effective quality service ultimately enhances the commercial status of the organisation and can bring a number of benefits. These are discussed next.

Satisfied customers

Customer service means more than just a token smile and being polite when a customer approaches. Effective customer service is about caring for the customer and working to meet their needs, wants and expectations. It is also about satisfying them, their requests and more.

DISCUSSION

What other examples of cross-selling can you think of?

Customers who feel they are treated well are more likely to return to an organisation. If a customer returns, the organisation can assume that they have secured repeat business. There is the distinct possibility that satisfied customers may tell their friends, family and colleagues about the organisation, how well received and well attended to they were and what value for money they enjoyed.

DID YOU KNOW?

If you resolve a complaint on the spot, 95% of complaining customers will do business with you again.

Retaining existing customers however, is not enough. Even the best and most satisfied of customers can become ex-customers for all kinds of reasons. The dividing line between old and new customers is not clear. The best new customers for your product may well be the ones who already buy from you. For instance, cross-selling to customers from different departments or branches of business can often prove lucrative. For example, the regular morning swimmer who would like to take up squash at your centre. Or the businessman who attends a conference at a holiday village and takes advantage of the incentives and discounts offered by the organisation by booking a week's summer holiday for his family.

If customer service at an organisation is of a continually poor standard the organisation could stand to lose a considerable amount of revenue and goodwill through the loss of its customers.

ACTIVITY

Satisfied customers

Read the following scenario:

'An airline passenger on return from the United States was on a connecting flight home to Glasgow, while her bags were on the original flight bound for Manchester. This was only discovered at the airport when her bags failed to arrive and a phone call established their location. The passenger expressed her annoyance at the airline's inefficiency as she needed her bags for an important meeting the following day.

In responding to the complaint the airline ensured her bags arrived by express delivery the following morning in time for her appointment. They also gave her a £200 travel voucher which she could redeem against further travel with the airline.'

Questions to consider

Would the customer have been satisfied that the situation had been thoroughly resolved?

What if it had been 48 hours before her bags were returned and there was no travel voucher in lieu of an apology?

WE PROMISE

Excellent care for the National Collections.
We are working to bring the management of our collections to the highest standards.

Displays and events that are accurate, stimulating and enjoyable.
We improve them continually in response to your comments.

High quality educational and research facilities.
We provide a comprehensive service to schools. Our Educational Bookings Office is open for enquiries on 01904 621261 between 09.00 and 17.30 Monday to Thursday and 09.00–17.00 on Friday. A curator is available to answer questions about the Collections between 09.00 and 17.00 Monday to Friday. Please ring 01904 621261, or write to Curatorial Enquiries at the National Railway Museum, Leeman Road, York YO2 4XJ. We aim to acknowledge enquiries within five working days.

Up-to-date information about the Museum.
Staff at the Ticket Points and Information Desk are there to help you. We produce a 'What's on' Leaflet twice a year. Copies are available from the Information Desks. If you would like us to send you 'What's on' Leaflets, please ask at our Information Desks. Summarised guide books are available in five languages. Please listen for announcements about today's programmes on the public address system, and read about them at both entrances.

A prompt and helpful response to enquiries.
We aim to respond promptly to all enquiries. Our switchboard (01904 621261) is open between 08.30 and 17.30 Monday to Thursday and 08.30 and 16.30 on Fridays. At all other times calls are directed to our control room. Our address, telephone and fax numbers are given at the end of this leaflet. Whether you write or telephone, all staff will give their name and either help you immediately or agree a response time with you.

A warm and courteous welcome.
All our staff wear name badges, and will be pleased to help you.

A safe, clean and comfortable museum.
We meet all official health and safety standards and exceed them wherever we can.

FIGURE 5.1 *National Railway Museum customer charter*

Most organisations will identify in writing how they intend to achieve high standards of customer service. Examples of promises and expressions of duty towards the customer may include the following:

- *'You can be sure that, 'like for like', our prices won't be beaten.'*
- *'Our aim is 100% customer satisfaction.'*
- *'We will be polite and helpful.'*
- *'We measure our performance against standards, targets and competitor services.'*
- *'If we don't get it right, we will admit to it and put things right quickly.'*
- *'We will do everything reasonably possible to make our services available to everyone, including people with special needs.'*

DISCUSSION

What other promises have you seen organisations give to a customer? List them.

Most organisations in their Customer Charter will state officially in writing what their aims and objectives are with regard to the customer. An example of one type of expression of duty within a charter is given in the National Railway Museum's literature (Figure 5.1).

Customer loyalty

Good customer service can produce customer loyalty. Customers have long memories and will remember how they were treated by an organisation. Significantly, examples of when they were treated poorly will be most vivid in their memory.

ACTIVITY

Customer loyalty

Read the following scenario:

'A couple hailed a taxi having just left the train station. The taxi ride taken from the station to the hotel was not within a realistic walking distance for the couple with their luggage. On getting into the taxi they were met with a filthy glare and a torrent of abuse from the disgruntled taxi driver. He informed the couple that he had been waiting in the queue for almost an hour and a half and would have to do so again on his return. He also said that he was not happy to be driving less than three miles for a fee of less than £4. He made no apologies for his behaviour, even refusing to help the couple out with their bags.

The couple needed to book a return taxi from a wedding reception later that evening. They used another taxi firm.'

Questions to consider

What could the taxi driver have done differently to secure the couple's loyalty? Did the taxi driver lose any further potential for work with the couple?

An organisation cannot take a customer's loyalty for granted, it must give the customer a reason to stay loyal. Not just by selling a good product or service, but by initiating a relationship, by taking the trouble to communicate and by finding out what that customer wants and then offering it. By extending consistently high standards of cour-

teous and quality service to the customer, an organisation is likely to ensure repeat business. Often organisations will invite loyalty by offering incentives to the customer to ensure repeat business. Examples include, the local swimming pool's 'pay for 10, get 12 swimming sessions', the season pass into the sports ground, or the nightclub membership card which reduces the cover charge to £8 from £15.

Having once received a quality service or experience with an organisation or brand, customers are likely (albeit subconsciously), to be loyal to that brand. For example, if a hockey player has always played with a stick made by the same manufacturer and has been pleased with its performance, then he or she is more likely to continue using sticks by that manufacturer. The same loyalty is evident with organisations. People have a general preference for certain organisations for any number of reasons, not necessarily related to the service they receive but to how the organisation makes them feel. For instance:

- John prefers the intimacy of the old, Victorian swimming pool as opposed to the new leisure centre because it is quieter and he can get an uninterrupted swim there.
- Judith likes to spend time in Harry's Bar at the 'happy doubles hour' before going on to the Majestic Nightclub, because that is where all her friends meet to go out, and drinks are cheaper than anywhere else.

Increased customer numbers and increased sales

The main aim of organisations within the industry is to increase customer numbers and ultimately profitability. Organisations should realise that:

- Satisfied customers not only mean repeat business themselves, but are more likely to bring new customers with them.
- The size of the market of the 'potential customer' is inevitably larger than the number of current users and should be the focus of marketing and advertising initiatives.

An effective customer service strategy or policy must be in place in order to ensure repeat business. Increased numbers and profitability cannot be achieved if the customer is not satisfied with the service received from the organisation.

Airtours, 'the holiday makers', in their winter brochure, make a promise to skiers and suggest that:

❝Our chances of sorting out any problems ... are much better if we do it on the spot.... We want you to have the holiday you have looked forward to so please talk to our team in the resort – they can and will help.❞

DISCUSSION

In your local area have you ever been to a facility or organisation just once? Why have you not been back?

How many times have you been to a new facility with another individual because they have 'raved' about it? How many times have you been to watch a film on the strength that your friends have seen it and it is a 'must see'?

DISCUSSION

Has David Beckham's endorsement of Adidas football boots helped increase sales of the shoes?

In terms of the organisation and its ability to serve people, recommendations from existing to potential customers can have a profound influence on the organisation's standing in the market-place. Word-of-mouth is unique among all other promotion methods. Not only is it a dynamic method of communicating with consumers but is also the enviable sign of success in a competitive market-place. Organisations can feel a sense of pride in knowing that some of their business comes by referral from satisfied customers.

An improved and enhanced public image and reputation

In order to establish themselves and earn a positive reputation, organisations need to present a good image. Image refers to the staff in terms of their physical appearance, attitude and body language. These concepts will be discussed later in the Chapter when we consider the importance of personal presentation.

The way in which customers are treated is a direct reflection of this image. The time, effort, energy, training and money invested in producing a good image would be shattered instantly were customers not to receive a service as professional as the image promised.

In advertising the facility and its services, an organisation will often use direct quotes from satisfied customers or visual images of customers enjoying themselves on site to project a positive image and influence sales and retention figures. These affirmations are referred to as 'endorsements' and help build up the trust of existing customers and the expectations of potential customers.

An edge over the competitors

In catering for the needs of customers, an organisation must remember that there will always be other organisations trying to do it better. If, however, you can secure both repeat and new business as a direct result of the quality of service that you extend towards all your customers, then you will be achieving some of your objectives.

Questions that you should consider when analysing competitor organisations include:

● What are the participation rates at the different organisations?
● How big is the market-place and how much room is there for similar ventures?
● What is the single most significant factor in determining which venture has the lion's share of the market and therefore the edge over their competitors?

ACTIVITY

What is the difference?

It has already been suggested that the market-place is overwhelmed by 'like-for-like' facilities, activities, products and services.

Examples include:

- Theme parks, such as Alton Towers, Thorpe Park, Blackpool Pleasure Beach
- Theme and dance bars, for example, The Firkin Brewery chain, nightclubs
- Cinema complexes, for example UCI, Warner Bros, The Odeon
- Retail and shopping, for example, Warehouse, Principles, River Island, the Metro Centre
- Fast food restaurants such as McDonald's, Burger King, Pizza Hut and Pizza Express
- Fitness centres, leisure pools and sports centres
- Video stores
- Home-based leisure equipment, such as stereos and televisions

Questions to consider

Choose two organisations that offer a similar product to each other. What is the difference?

Consider factors such as location, access, price, timings, opening hours, session times and availability and an organisation's existing reputation.

You will realise that personal preference is possibly the single most important factor in the decision making process. Ask friends, family, colleagues and peers what factors influence their choices when making a purchase.

A happy and efficient workforce

Employees are also customers of an organisation – they are *internal* customers. Any member of staff should expect the same service afforded to them as is invested in the customer. Internal customers should be made to feel that they are a valued and significant asset of the organisation.

They should be:

- Treated with respect by peers and superior colleagues alike.
- Kept abreast of current initiatives within the organisation including new developments, technical, construction and otherwise.
- Informed of forthcoming job vacancies and receive appropriate training.

By treating employees as they would like any customer to be treated, an organisation can encourage employees to take an interest and pride in their work. Every member of staff within the organisation has a responsibility for creating the customer service product that is so significant in this unique sales industry.

Some organisations offer incentives, such as 'Employee of the Month' and 'Most sales award'. Photographs of employee of the month often appear on the wall of the facility or in the monthly magazine. Often financial rewards are attached to these bonuses as a further incentive.

Richard Branson in Virgin's in-flight magazine encourages passengers to vote for their favourite air steward. Every month the steward receiving the most votes is rewarded with an all-expenses-paid Virgin Holiday. By contrast McDonald's restaurants have a star system in operation. When a member of staff has gained all five stars they can assume increased levels of responsibility and an increase in salary.

Personal presentation and communication

An organisation's image and reputation can take months, even years, of hard work, staff training, energy, effort and dedication to establish. All of this can be undone and an organisation's reputation tarnished in significantly less time if it does not present a consistently high standard of customer service.

The way in which an organisation, and by definition its staff, present themselves to you, the customer, on your arrival to the venue, facility or activity is a significant factor in the moulding and maintenance of this reputation.

First impressions

DID YOU KNOW?

Organisations do not get a second chance to create a first impression.

An organisation's image is often measured against how it meets up to the standards it sets itself and the expectations of its customers. Creating a positive first impression and maintaining set standards is the key to success.

ACTIVITY

First impressions

If you have ever been on an aeroplane you will have been used to being greeted and welcomed aboard the flight at the entrance to the plane by a number of immaculately dressed, smiling stewards, anxious to see your boarding card and show you to your seat. You will probably have accepted this behaviour as 'normal' and moved along to your seat. What would your impression have been if they had stood in the galley, chatting with each other and bemoaning the early hour of the morning?

What would be your impression if you were attending a step aerobics session at your local fitness centre for the first time, and your instructor arrived late? She eventually turned up five minutes after the class was due to start, apologising that she had overslept and couldn't find a parking space.

A first impression is the best opportunity that an organisation has to shape an individual's ideas, thoughts, feelings and bias towards the organisation, its facilities, services and staff. First impressions, perceptions and therefore attitude, are significant in that they are enduring, vivid and often difficult to change.

Physical facilities

A customer's impressions are formulated from the moment he or she enters the car park, grounds, premises or doors. Do not forget that the state of these physical areas will be the first contact a customer has with the organisation and may influence decision and impression making.

At a hotel the first point of contact for a new customer or guest will be with the reception staff at the front desk. However, a customer's impressions of an organisation can be influenced by a number of factors other than the quality of their reception. These include:

- Accessibility of the hotel and clarity of signposting
- Location of the car park in relation to the hotel and whether it is safe and well lit
- How well the grounds are kept and whether there is any litter lying around
- How well presented the lobby area is. Are complimentary newspapers and coffee cups strewn on the tables or are they neatly stacked?
- Whether the staff are seen to be industrious or just lolling around chatting
- Whether the booking has been received and their arrival has been anticipated
- Whether the bedroom is in immaculate condition or if the bed is unmade, with wet towels thrown around the bathroom floor and hairs in the bath?

Obviously the responsibilities for completing these tasks do not fall with the reception staff but with other team members, the groundsmen, bookings and administrative services team and the domestic services team (waiting staff). These staff do not necessarily have any direct customer contact but their role behind the scenes is just as significant and important. The scenario suggests that every employee within an organisation contributes to providing customer service, not just those who deal with the customer directly.

Personal presentation

An integral part of the customer service philosophy is the personal presentation of staff. Customers make value judgements about the quality of service they receive on the basis of what they observe in the overall

DISCUSSION

Think of an organisation within the industry, perhaps a theme park or a sports centre. Now think of the physical facilities, including the toilet, changing and waiting areas and the work done behind the scenes by the staff members that you do not not meet? How important, in the scheme of things is their role in the organisation?

dress and demeanour of staff. This means that the personal presentation of staff takes on added significance, in terms of delivering customer service.

Personal presentation refers to an employee's dress, personal hygiene, personality and attitude.

Dress

The leisure and recreation industry is a customer orientated industry, where much emphasis is placed on the job done by, and the nature of, the service extended by staff towards customers.

Many organisations are aware of the significance and importance of smartly turned-out staff. Some issue uniforms, others set out guidelines or dress codes for appropriate clothing. Lauda Airlines have a casual dress code for air cabin staff. Their dress code mimics that of the dress style sported by its owner Niki Lauda. Staff wear red baseball hats, a smart blouse and the obligatory black jeans.

Clothing that might be considered appropriate for the pool lifeguard may not be appropriate for the chef, the trainee manager at a bowling alley, the tour guide at the local heritage site or the receptionist at the hotel. Kitchen staff have uniforms that are standard across the sector and these are dictated by health and safety guidelines.

Uniforms should be properly fitted. Staff who are uncomfortable in their uniform or self-conscious, will be distracted and this will impact on their ability to deliver a quality customer service.

ACTIVITY

Appropriate clothing

Identify clothing that would be both appropriate and smart enough for an employee in the following situations:

- Assistant manager of a cinema complex
- Step aerobics instructor
- Coach tour party guide
- Kitchen assistant
- Bar tender

In stipulating dress codes in the workplace, organisations and employers must ensure that they are not contravening any laws or regulations and are complying with equal opportunities policies.

DISCUSSION

List all of the jobs that you can think of within the leisure and recreation industry that require staff to wear uniforms.

Find photos of staff wearing uniforms and think about uniforms which you have seen staff wearing. Did they wear it well? Did it fit? Was it clean and neatly pressed?

Now think of the image that was portrayed. Discuss it with your group.

CASE STUDY *Judy Owen versus the PGA*

In January 2000, the Professional Golfers Union (The PGA) lost their battle against former employee, training manager Judy Owen. She took up legal proceedings for sexual discrimination when she was asked to leave the office to return home and change into a skirt from her trouser suit. She won her case. The PGA however, still operates a dress code in its Belfry office, which stipulates that women are not allowed to wear trousers.

Organisations expect front line staff, and even those who have intermittent contact with customers, to look smart every day and check their appearance throughout the day. Air stewards are expected to look as fresh, smart and tidy at the end of the journey as they did at the beginning, regardless of the length of the journey.

Personal hygiene

There are three main aspects of personal hygiene to bear in mind, for an employer and employee. These are hair, personal freshness and hands and fingernails.

Hair
Hair should be clean, tidy and attractive. When dealing with customers it should be kept off the face, so that customers can see and be seen, especially when you are engaging in conversation with them. The same principles can be applied to beards and moustaches.

In a restaurant, long hair should be tied back and in the kitchen it should be tucked inside a chef's hat or hair net.

Personal freshness
In close proximity, say across a counter, teaching area or table, bad breath and body odour (underarms and feet) can be distinctive and off-putting.

Hands and fingernails
During face-to-face contact these are continually on display and should be kept clean, especially if you have used the toilet, if they are dirty or if they have nicotine stains.

All kitchens should by law have a wash hand basin with soap and a scrubbing brush just inside the door. Most establishments have notices reminding staff to wash their hands before returning to work.

McDonalds insists that crew members report to work on time, neat and clean. They also suggest that with regard to personal hygiene, the most important thing crew members do to ensure customers receive safe food is wash their hands often and dry them thoroughly using disposable paper towels.

 ACTIVITY

ROLE PLAYS: PERSONAL HYGIENE

In terms of customer service, proper personal hygiene is essential.

As a manager or supervisor you have to be responsible for ensuring that minimum standards are maintained. How would you deal with these scenarios as both a manager and employee?

1   You are working in The Academy Health and Fitness club. You are informed on more than one occasion that Dan, one of your fitness instructors, has a quite distinct and offensive body odour. You noticed this when you were working as an instructor yourself but were too polite to say anything. As a manager, current colleagues have asked you to do something about it.

2   You are the manager at the busy 'Pizza Italia' restaurant. You have been informed that Jim, one of your waiters, does not wash his hands after going to the toilet.

3   Charlotte, your front of house receptionist at the Travel Inn Hotel, has long hair. You have noticed that it has become increasingly greasy and unkempt.

Questions to consider

Do you follow the tactful approach or do you adopt the 'straight talking and no-nonsense' approach? How do you avoid hurting their feelings?

What are your priorities?

Personal habits can be just as frustrating as poor levels of personal hygiene, for example, habits such as picking noses, scratching ears and biting nails. Equally if staff have allergies or a cough and cold they should be considerate of others, particularly customers, and excuse themselves.

Personality

 **KEY TERMS**

Personality: Set of behavioural or personal characteristics, by which an individual is recognisable.

It is important to let your personality show through in a thoughtful and controlled way when you are dealing with customers, for a number of reasons:

- They know they are dealing with a real person as opposed to a robot.
- They know you see them as a real person and not just another customer.
- You have the opportunity to make them feel a valued and necessary part of the organisation.

Anybody involved in contact with people as part of their job, will realise that customers can be demanding, awkward and difficult, and therefore need your time, energy, commitment and tireless enthusiasm. In order to be all of these things and more, you need to be a 'people-person' with good social skills, endless patience, humility and the ability to keep smiling.

DISCUSSION

Most, if not all, young people will have been in a fast food restaurant at some stage, some of you may even work in one. The pace is frantic and on a busy Saturday afternoon everybody looks rushed off their feet. You are aware of McDonalds' expectations of their staff, do you think you have the right personal skills and qualities to work in that sort of environment?

If not, why not? What personal skills do you not possess that are required by the position?

CASE STUDY *McDonalds restaurants*

McDonald's Independent Franchisees and company-owned restaurants serve over 22 million customers every day worldwide and in order to retain and even increase that number they have a number of expectations of their staff. They have laid down standard operational procedures for crew members to follow so that customers will always receive exceptional quality and service.

McDonalds insists that each and every one of those customers deserves good service, from the moment they approach the counter or drive-through window until they leave the restaurant, even if they arrive as you are coming to the end of an exhausting eight-hour shift.

They depend on their employees to provide a fast, friendly and courteous experience to all guests so they will visit again and again. In terms of the type of people they employ they are seeking individuals who like to have fun while delivering a fast, accurate and friendly service, with a smile. Their job is to make each customer feel unique.

In advertising for cabin crew British Airways stipulate specifically what their expectations are of new staff members (Figure 5.2). Could you live up to their expectations?

Cabin Crew
Heathrow & Gatwick

When it comes to delivering the very best in customer service, British Airways Cabin Crew stand apart. They have the blend of skills and experience to understand and respond to customer needs and, equally importantly, they have the freedom to take those spontaneous decisions that create a special in-flight atmosphere.

Our approach is challenging the traditional view of the cabin crew role. Those who join us can look forward to using their initiative and people skills to the full, doing that extra something that makes the difference. It could be as simple as helping to comfort a "first time flyer" or talking to a customer in their own language … whatever it is, it demonstrates our fundamental belief that every one of the 35 million people who fly with us each year deserves individual attention – a service that goes above and beyond their expectations.

As our global network grows, we are looking for more people who can provide the essential personal touch. You must have the right to live and work in the UK indefinitely, be aged 20–49 or above, standing 5′2″–6′2″ with weight in proportion and conversational abilities in at least one of the following second languages:

FRENCH, GERMAN, ITALIAN, SPANISH, PORTUGUESE, GREEK, DUTCH, RUSSIAN, TURKISH, HEBREW, ARABIC, JAPANESE, MANDARIN, CANTONESE, THAI, KOREAN, URDU, HINDI, GUJARATI, PUNJABI, SWAHILI, ANY SCANDINAVIAN LANGUAGE, ANY EASTERN EUROPEAN LANGUAGE AND EXISTING CERTIFICATE HOLDERS OF SIGN LANGUAGE.

FIGURE 5.2 *Job advert for British Airways cabin crew*

DISCUSSION

Using the list of adjectives think about an employee within the industry, for example a receptionist, a sales assistant at the new sports store or a coach. What qualities do they need to be able do their job? Are there any words that have been missed out from the list?

KEY TERMS

Attitude: 'Disposition, posture ... a posture of the body ... implying some action or mental state ... behaviour or manner of acting, as representative of feeling or opinion'

Behaviour: 'Manner of conducting oneself ... conduct; course of action towards or to others ... handling (of anything)'

Source: *Shorter Oxford English Dictionary*, Volume II

ACTIVITY

Your own personal skills and qualities

What sort of person do you think you are? If you had to describe yourself or your personality with a number of adjectives, what would they be?

Have a look at the list below. Which words best fit a description of you?

- Outgoing
- Confident
- Loud
- Extrovert
- Humorous
- Cheerful
- Lively

- Chatty
- Motivator
- Leader
- Shy
- Introvert
- Sensitive
- Listener

- Patient
- Calm
- Well organised
- Thorough
- Industrious
- Polite
- Honest

Questions to consider

What do these words tell you about yourself? Do you think that you currently have the necessary skills to deliver a quality customer service?

Now ask your friends, your tutor, colleagues or parents to look at these words and choose words to describe your personality? Compare the two lists. Do other people see you as you see yourself?

Do you actually project the image and attitude you think you are projecting? Is your personality consistent from one situation to the next?

Attitude and behaviour

The way that staff appear before their customers usually says something about their attitude, not only towards the customers but towards their job, their colleagues, the organisation itself and themselves.

Attitude is a state of mind, influenced by thoughts and feelings. The attitude that is displayed towards customers is usually the attitude that is received back.

ACTIVITY

ROLE PLAYS: ATTITUDE AND BEHAVIOUR

As a customer, play out the following role with a rather indifferent member of staff:

'You approach a recreation assistant in the changing rooms of a sports centre to ask for instructions on how to work the new lockers, but you get no response. They are mopping the floor. When you ask for the second time and tap them on the shoulder to get their attention, you realise that they are wearing a personal stereo. They do not attempt to turn the stereo off, but merely pull the headphones to one side and say 'What?'

Questions to consider

What do you do next? Should you report the employee to the manager for his hostility and rudeness? Should you reprimand them yourself?

DISCUSSION

What aspects of your behaviour could you change to improve and influence your customer service skills?

Your attitude can be reflected in a number of ways, although your mannerisms are probably the most telling. Other examples include your appearance, body language, posture, tone and gestures.

Your attitude and behaviour towards customers will vary according to the situation you find yourself in. For example, you may address a child by the their first name, but an individual of pensionable age as either Sir or Madam. We will consider the different ways of dealing with customers later in this Chapter.

ACTIVITY

ROLE PLAYS: ATTITUDE AND BEHAVIOUR

Play out the scenario with someone else, change roles if you have to.

'You have just five minutes left before the end of your shift on the reception desk at the leisure centre. It has been a very busy day, you are tired and ready to go home for the day. A new customer approaches the desk and having thoroughly enjoyed their gym induction would now like to join as a member. The enrolment process, however, takes 15 minutes. You know that if you stay to complete the enrolment you will miss your bus and the next one is not for another 40 minutes.

You can see that the customer is in a rush. You know that the next shift does not start for at least another five minutes and you are aware that if you ask them to wait they may well not bother joining. There is no one else currently on the reception desk.'

Questions to consider

What would be the consequences of leaving at the end of your shift to catch your bus and leaving the client unattended?

Would you feel 'duty bound' to stay and attend to the client?

Remember, you can change your feelings by changing your behaviour. For example, it is very difficult to be sad while smiling. Simply by standing up during a phone conversation you can perform with more energy and confidence.

ACTIVITY

ROLE PLAYS: ATTITUDE AND BEHAVIOUR

'Your receptionist, Janice, has just received a telephone call from her boyfriend Simon during which they had a huge row and Janice was reduced to tears. It is now 9.45 a.m., and Janice is due on at main reception at 10 a.m. to greet the all-day business convention taking place in your hotel. Even though Janice has stopped crying and reapplied her make up, she still looks upset and depressed.'

Questions to consider

What is your short-term solution? How do you persuade Janice to go out into main reception and play the role of the organised, capable and friendly receptionist?

What is your long-term solution? How do you deal with Janice, to avoid a recurrence of the situation?

KEY TERMS

Customer: 'One who customarily purchases anywhere; a buyer, purchaser ... a person with whom one has dealings.'

Source: *Shorter Oxford English Dictionary, Volume II*

Types of customers

Customers are people who exercise their choice to 'buy' products, services and activities from within the market place and at specific organisations. Organisations rely on customers for their continued existence and prosperity in the market-place.

The industry relies on external customers and so does the commercial world, in order to achieve financial stability and profit. Public services that are free or subsidised still rely on the patronage and continued use of their services and products by customers. For example, if the local village library was not regularly used questions might be asked as to the viability and need for such a service.

In order to be able to cater appropriately for the customer's needs it is important to understand who the customer is. Customer definition will vary from one organisation to another and according to the type of products, services and activities they offer. Organisations will refer to customers differently. For example, a golf club will refer to its customers as members whereas a tourist attraction will call them visitors.

ACTIVITY

The customer

Consider the definitions below and identify to what type of organisation these 'customers' might belong. Where possible identify an actual organisation.

- Spectators
- Members
- Non-members
- Guests
- Consumers

- Players
- Users
- Visitors
- Clients
- Holiday makers

Target groups

Before entering the market-place an organisation will already have focused on, or decided who, their 'target market' is. For example, SAGA, are a holiday firm that have focused specifically on meeting the holiday needs and requirements of people in the 50+ age range. In their advertising literature Oasis Forest Holiday Villages actually names 'empty nesters' as one of their target groups. That is, people whose children are grown, have left home and who now have their own space and time to pursue new leisure interests.

If you imagine that the 'market' is all of the public, then organisations will target specific sections or groups of people within the market who will be interested in their services. Usually these groups are structured into 'like types' based on the fact that they may have certain qualities or characteristics in common.

DISCUSSION

Consider a range of sessions at different organisations within your local area. You may well have to look at their advertising literature to help you.

Are they focusing on specific groups? On what basis are the people placed into these groups?

For example, a sports centre advertising a learn-to-swim session may focus on pre-school children as their target group. A nightclub may have an 80s theme for the evening and target the over 25s as their focus group. A hotel offering a Valentine's weekend break is quite obviously targeting couples.

Some organisations are more discreet in targeting specific groups of people. For example, by advertising ski holidays in the US and Canada the company is indirectly targeting individuals with a large disposable income.

Age groups

Different age groups have different interests, needs and wants. Some organisations cater for a range of groups, some target particular groups. Cinema complexes are bound to target specific and different age groups as films are given ratings according to their suitability for certain ages. Pubs, clubs and restaurants in terms of alcohol sales are obliged by law to target only those individuals above the age of 18.

Young people

Young people are often distinguished into specific age groups that relate to their level of schooling, for example:

- Pre-school or nursery
- Infant and juniors
- Secondary
- College age, (18–24)

Organisations will need to be aware that young people have specific needs, for example, their stage of development and height will mean that they have specific requirements. Sports facilities will adapt activities and equipment to enable a child to participate and succeed; short tennis and Kwik cricket are just two examples of modified sports. Many sports have adapted their equipment for 'juniors', for example, mini rugby balls, lightweight volleyballs and shorter, lighter golf clubs. Leisure centres, in their changing facilities, may dedicate a shower cubicle where the push button is lower and restaurants may provide cushions or raised seats to ensure comfort at table height.

Drayton Manor Park, is a 250-acre theme park which boasts a range of rides and attractions. Their entrance fees have tariffs based on height. If an individual is below a certain height then their entrance is free, if they are below a second height then their fee is a percentage of the full fee. This tariff is a refection of the amount of access they can get to rides in the park, some of which have height restrictions.

Safety is a major concern for all people working with children. The Children's Act, 1989, places clear responsibilities on all staff who manage, provide and supervise activities for children. These include providing and maintaining services for children with disabilities and providing information on services. The implications of the Children's Act were most profoundly felt in the outdoor activities sector, these are discussed in more detail in Chapter 2. Staff also have to be aware of issues relating to child protection and know how and where to seek advice.

Senior citizens

The most significant age group statistic for the leisure industry has been the increase in the population above retirement age, most noticeably in the 75+ group. The 65+ (or retired) age group, like the unemployed and mums and toddlers, are a user or target group in their own right. Sport England have for a number of years targeted the 50+ age group in their campaigns to increase participation and so promote a healthy lifestyle.

Groups

Many services and products within the industry are intended solely for the use of individuals, for example, a sun bed in a solarium. Others are aimed at groups. Organisations will group people together based on their relationship to and with each other, their interests and needs. Examples of these user groups include:

- Families
- Clubs
- School groups
- Office parties

Catering for groups is more often cost effective than for individuals. For this reason organisations may offer incentives and concessions such as group discounts, family tickets, or free places for children (usually under a certain age). When buying a product or service as a group the customer might have more bargaining power with the organisation because, as a group, they equate to more sales and more money, therefore the organisation might be more willing to be flexible.

Different cultural backgrounds

Many organisations, particularly those within major towns (Leeds, Birmingham and Manchester to name but three), where there are increasing numbers of ethnic groupings, will have to be aware of the range of cultural needs of the community, for example:

- Language
- Religious affiliations and significant dates in their religious calendar, for example, the festival of Ramadan in the Moslem calendar stipulates that individuals should neither eat nor drink during the hours of daylight
- Diet
- Dress codes
- Social gatherings

Non-purpose-built facilities have a responsibility to be sensitive to the requirements of the different cultural groupings. For staff that are ignorant of the needs and requirements of distinct groups, management has a responsibility to deliver in-house training and information to increase awareness.

Understanding the beliefs and significance of the major religions will provide greater understanding and empathy when analysing customer behaviour. Cultural differences are often just as significant as religious differences. Cultural differences refer to inherited ideas, beliefs, values and knowledge and these differences are often reflected in their social behaviour. Staff therefore should be taught to respect the values and beliefs of others.

Non-English-speakers

The UK has long been a destination place for tourists and business people from non-English-speaking countries. Increased access opportunities, in terms of international links such as the Channel Tunnel, local and regional airports whose routes now encompass international destinations and competitive, reasonably priced airfares, has served to increase the number of visitors to the UK.

Many of these visitors have little or no English language skills, so staff should be given specific training in dealing with these customers. That is, conversing either through their language, visual aids or accepted diagrams. Some staff are recruited to an organisation specifically for their language skills.

 **DID YOU KNOW?**

There are approximately six million adults with one or more disabilities in Britain and around 350,000 children under 16 with a disability.

Specific needs

The opportunities available within your organisation must be accessible to everyone. However, not all individuals are the same and some have specific physical requirements. Therefore, an organisation should have mechanisms and procedures in place to ensure that all people, regardless of their physical capacity, have the same opportunities.

Catering for special needs can be as simple as the provision of signs with pictures and words, arm bands for non-swimmers and left-handed golf clubs, or the use of a hoist in a swimming pool (a mechanical device whereby wheelchair bound individuals can be moved safely and comfortably into the pool).

Make a list of the different types of disabilities under the category headings, mental, physical and sensory disabilities.

DISCUSSION

What other stipulations does the Disability Discrimination Act of 1994 make?

Are those individuals who have specific needs sufficiently well catered for? Is an equal opportunities policy actively promoted?

Have a look at a range of facilities and ask yourself whether they are user friendly for those individuals with disabilities.

Organisations should be aware that some individuals have specific disabilities, such as:

- Restricted mobility and trouble getting around. Some individuals may be independent but confined to a wheelchair, others may require the constant support and attention of another individual.
- Sight, visual impairments.
- Hearing impairments.
- Problems with literacy or numeracy (reading and writing).

The Disability Discrimination Act of 1995 only applies to businesses employing 20 or more people. The Act applies to all people who have or have had a physical, sensory or mental disability.

In essence the Act makes it unlawful for organisations to discriminate against people with disabilities or special needs. All people with disabilities have to be treated with and given the same priority as able bodied people.

By the year 2000, it is likely that all providers will have to change their policies so as to provide accessible information and appropriate auxiliary aids. By the year 2005, providers are likely to have to remove physical barriers or to provide service by another means.

It is easy to identify the needs of customers who are physically incapacitated. They may have a leg in a cast, or they may be using crutches or a wheelchair to enhance their mobility.

An organisation may need to give information on access facilities such as lifts, escalators, special needs toilets and hand rails. Some staff may feel self-conscious when giving instruction or dealing with customers. When dealing with individuals with special needs staff should ensure that the attitude they adopt is not a patronising one.

Some customers have learning difficulties. Their needs may not be as visually apparent as those of an individual confined to a wheelchair, but are nevertheless just as significant.

In order to address the needs of such individuals organisations may be required to present information in unique ways. For example, physical demonstrations may be preferable and more effective than verbal instructions, as will speaking slowly and clearly in words with short syllables. Designated members of staff will require thorough and comprehensive training in a range of different scenarios.

ACTIVITY

ROLE PLAYS: DEALING WITH SPECIAL NEEDS

The following role plays will test your ability to identify a variety of special needs and will present you with the opportunity of analysing those needs and responding to them.

Some of these requests will not be verbal requests and you should respond to them without offending the customer, drawing attention to them, or losing their business custom.

Play out the scenario with someone else, change roles if you have to.

1 You are working behind the till at Burger King. You very quickly realise that your next customer has a severe speech impediment and you find it difficult to understand his request.

2 You are at the front desk in the reception area at The Olympia sports centre. The carer of a young person confined to a wheelchair asks you for directions to the changing rooms for the swimming pool. They ask if you can accompany them both to the changing rooms and provide assistance as the carer has recently injured her back and cannot lift.

3 You are a hotel porter and have been warned by management to expect a party of holiday makers. Four members of the party are confined to wheelchairs and will need some assistance. However, the main lift is out of order and the only one currently available is the service elevator.

4 You are expecting a contingent of foreign visitors, however, the signs that your manager asked you to have ready to be displayed in the lobby, restaurant and bedrooms are not yet ready. What do you do in order to ensure that the information they need is relayed to them without confusion or error?

Questions to consider

Some of the requests you may not be able to cope with, how then do you accommodate these individuals?

Caring for customers with specific or special needs is one of the most important aspects of any service industry. The editor of *Leisure Management* suggests that:

❝The real point to customer care is to create a service which speaks for itself in terms of excellence, attention to detail and customer needs, and then to enhance it with attention from staff who have been trained to treat customers with warmth and a personal touch. ❞

Why target specific groups?

It is has been suggested that 20% of something is often responsible for 80% of something else. For example, 20% of motorists cause 80% of accidents, 20% of a carpet suffers 80% of the wear and tear, and on holiday you only wear 20% of the clothes that you take with you.

In business, this 80:20 ratio also applies, and in two key areas:

1 20% of products generate 80% of all sales
2 20% of customers generate 80% of all profits

The implications of the 80:20 rule means that when looking for new customers, organisations should not target every potential customer in the market, only those that will contribute most to the success of the business.

ACTIVITY

Using the 80:20 rule

The following organisations are trying to identify to which target group the majority of their customers belong. You are required to identify specifically who those groups are.

You may wish to refer to the list in this text to identifty the range of target groups, or by observation and questionning at the venue, establish the type of target groups that frequent:

- your local McDonalds restaurant
- your local sports centre on a Saturday morning
- the most popular nightclub in your town or city on a Thursday night
- a premier league football match
- your local pub on a Friday night
- the town's shopping centre or retail outlet on a Saturday afternoon
- a tenpin bowling alley on a Sunday afternoon.

From your findings do the majority of customers or users belong to one target group, or are they from a range of target groups? Do you think that the type of users will vary according to the time of day or day of the week?

Dealing with customers

In any service industry contact with customers is regular and inevitable. It is the nature of this contact that will determine how successful one organisation is in comparison with another.

Communication

In dealing with customers, staff have first to identify the customer's needs and then offer a service which meets and exceeds their expectations. The ability to communicate is an integral part of this service and delivery.

Communication is essentially of two types, _verbal_ and _non-verbal_. The first type refers to the use of words, whether these are spoken or written and is regardless of the type of medium used to relay the information. The second type relies on the use of visual communication, that is signs, images, pictures or photographs to relay a message. Effective communi-

KEY TERMS

Communicate: 'To put into words ... to make known ... to give expression to, as by gesture, facial aspect or bodily posture.'

Communication: 'Exchange of ideas by writing, speech or signal ... something communicated as information ... situation allowing exchange of ideas.'

cation means giving the correct information to the relevant people at the proper time in the most appropriate way.

Customer contact

As a customer you will have different types of contact with staff members.

If you have had direct contact, through tuition, instruction, guidance, a sale or transaction with an employee or staff member then you would have had some degree of **formal** contact with that organisation.

If during your visit you saw or overheard someone who was employed by the organisation, for example, an announcer, chambermaid or resort manager, then your contact would have been **casual**.

There are individuals you will not see but whose contribution towards the provision of your service or activity is essential, for example, a chef, the cleaning staff, the plant room operator at a swimming pool. Your contact with these individuals is **indirect**.

Contact with the customer can be:

- face-to-face
- on the telephone
- in writing

Face to face

In a service industry like the leisure and recreation industry the majority of contact between the employee or staff member and the customer is both personal and direct. The attitude, professionalism and the way in which staff assess and deal with customer requests has a significant bearing on whether customers will enjoy their experience enough to return.

Face-to-face contact has many advantages, for both the staff member and customer:

- The communication is two-way.
- Needs and wants can be communicated and assessed immediately as there is no time delay as there is with written communication, telephone or e-mail.
- Staff can check on the spot that they have understood a customer's request.
- Staff can assess customer reaction and customers can assess the manner in which they are being dealt with. Over the telephone a customer is blind to the expressions and gestures being made towards them.

When dealing with customers staff need to be aware of their body language, alongside verbal conversation this is a language of its own and can communicate a very different message to the one that is being spoken. Body language refers to your:

- Facial expression – whether you are smiling, frowning, concentrating or daydreaming.
- Eye contact – whether you are engaging the customer by looking at them, whether you are looking into their eyes to establish contact or avoiding them.
- Body position – whether you are sitting, standing or propped and where this is in relation to the customer. The amount of space in between you and the customer is important. Some people like their personal space – about an arm's length, any closer and some people find it disconcerting and off putting.
- Body posture – the way that you stand, sit and move all have an effect on the impression that you are trying to create and that customers receive.

A tidy (neat, smart and well-dressed) posture implies that the staff member is in control. An untidy or dishevelled posture can imply that you tend to fidget and fuss. A friendly posture is welcoming. The customer can feel unwanted or unwelcomed if the posture is not orientated towards or facing them, similarly an employee with hands folded across the chest may be interpreted as defensive and hostile.

DISCUSSION

What would you assume about a staff member whose gestures were nervous and restless? What impression does a staff member who is constantly looking at the clock or watch create?

Some gestures indicate that the staff member may be nervous, bored and restless. What effect would this have on the customer? As a manager how would you address the staff member who gave this impression? Would you warn them about their behaviour?

ACTIVITY

Body language

Body language has been identified as a field of research in its own right.

Identify and gather as much information as you can about body language, particularly images, for the 'picture paints a thousand words'. Now order this information into negative and positive gestures and behaviour.

Your task is to design a code or guide for use by customer service employees in the leisure and recreation industry.

The presentation of your information should be based around the theme 'achieving customer satisfaction through appropriate and effective body language'.

DISCUSSION

Make a point of listening to the way in which telephones are answered, particularly when calling an organisation within the industry.

How many give you their name and ask what they can do for you?

What different types of 'welcomes' do you receive? How many answered with just a 'hello'?

On the telephone

The telephone is very often the first point of contact a customer will have with an organisation and as such, the impression that can be made is significant. Most hotels have a policy to answer the phone within three or a maximum of five rings. The first welcome any customer receives should

DISCUSSION

Next time you are on the phone, either at home or at work, try smiling and mean it. Is there a difference to your tone, energy and enthusiasm towards the caller?

be polite and courteous, for example, 'Good morning/evening, you have reached the Aldwark Hotel and Golf Club, how we can help you'.

It is often easy to establish a good rapport with a customer when you are in face-to-face contact with them, it is more difficult to achieve this through another medium such as the telephone. In these situations all of the information that you need to analyse their request must be taken and interpreted verbally and where possible recorded on paper.

There are occasions where you may well receive phone calls from customers with speech impediments or unfamiliar accents that are often difficult to interpret. For example, a Geordie, Brummie, Liverpudlian or Glaswegian accent can be difficult to decipher. You will, at some stage, have to ask the customer to stop, slow down or repeat themselves; this is a difficult skill to master.

Equally, customers will need to be able to understand you and your voice, therefore you must remember to speak clearly and be able to portray a bright, friendly and efficient service.

ACTIVITY

ROLE PLAYS: USING THE TELEPHONE

You are ringing a cinema box office to find out some information about this weekend's performances. That is, what performances are on at the minute and at what time. You also want to find out about credit card bookings and you need directions to the cinema.

Play out the following scenarios with someone else, change roles if you have to:

1 The first call is answered by an efficient and informative employee, who unfortunately is busy. She is the only staff member available to give information and eager to attend to the seven callers on hold. The caller does not feel that his/her questions have been answered and is still not aware of the prices nor if there are any concessions available.

How does the employee respond to all of the customer's requests without sounding rude, impatient and abrupt?

2 Another call is answered by a trainee who has been left alone for a ten-minute period while his/her mentor attends to another customer. The customer has a barrage of questions, none of which the trainee seems able to cope with.

How does the employee attend to the caller without sounding ignorant, unhelpful and incompetent?

Written communication

Written communication can take a variety of forms, some of which are used to promote two-way communication between the organisation and customer (both internal and external):

- letters
- e-mails
- reports and forms (including customer complaint forms)
- memos, reminders and confirmations

Some written communication is used for information purposes, such as staff handbooks, instruction manuals, signs and notices. Other forms are used for advertising purposes and marketing initiatives, such as posters, leaflets and brochures.

Whatever the format, there are some simple rules that should be followed:

- It should be clearly laid out, well structured and logically presented.
- It should use accurate language, grammar and spelling and should be proofread. There is nothing more unprofessional than a glaring error in your communication.
- Always ask yourself if the reader will be able to understand it? Information, particularly when geared towards external customers should be clear, concise, to the point and easy to understand.
- Give details of who to contact for queries or further information.

ACTIVITY

Producing written materials

You have been asked by the fire and emergency services team to prepare for an emergency drill at your organisation. You have not been told when it will happen but your staff have to be notified and informed how to respond in case of an emergency.

They need to be aware of the following information:
- What the fire alarm sounds like
- Procedure for evacuation of all people from the building
- Protocol, in terms of quiet and orderly exit from the building
- Responsibilities for checking the building
- Outdoor meeting or assembly point
- Procedure for re-entry.

You have decided to have a preliminary practice. If so you will need to inform staff members of when and what time.

Your task is to write a memo explaining what is about to happen following your brief from the fire services. It will be circulated to all employees, that is, from management to cleaning staff. You will only be writing one memo, and the language you use must be clear and concisely written. It must include all the necessary information and cater for all reading ages and abilities without patronising staff members.

Observing, listening and questioning

Understanding a customer's needs and wants, particularly one with specific or special needs, requires the undivided attention of the staff member. They have to observe the customer, listen to the customer and ask questions to obtain a clear understanding of that customer's requirements.

By observing a customer's mannerisms, actions, body language and tone, staff can gather evidence about mood, patience, and whether the customer is in a hurry or not. For example, if a customer stands at a reception desk fidgeting, and constantly checking the time, one might assume that that person is short on time, impatient or running late. A staff member will, therefore, need to realise this and deal with the customer efficiently, effectively and quickly.

By really listening to a customer a staff member can quickly establish what that customer's needs are. Some staff will even note down some of the more important details of their requests in order to make sure that they have it absolutely right.

 ACTIVITY

ROLE PLAYS: OBSERVING, LISTENING AND QUESTIONING

Try this with a group member. Change the roles to ensure that you both practise your listening skills:

'You are a customer in a busy restaurant ordering food for a group of six people. Having ordered two bottles of house red, you then give the food order to the waiter ...'

In this role play the customer who is ordering the food should use an actual menu where possible. The customer should then order a portion from it, but then change their mind about one of the dishes. Having then given the full order, a member of the party should change their mind about their choice. There have been three steaks ordered, all of which are to be cooked to different requirements.

Questions to consider

Has your waiter got the order right? Has he or she matched starters, main courses, side dishes and cooking instructions? Has the order been confirmed with you?

This process of listening and questioning is often referred to as the 'feedback loop'. The significance of understanding the customer and identifying their needs and wants correctly cannot be overstated. In order to ensure that this has been achieved, check that:

- The customer's needs have been identified correctly by asking and confirming with them their request
- The correct product is being produced. If the product they request is not available you may well have to offer them an alternative. For example, the customer who wants to book a squash court at 8 p.m. on Monday evening and finds that this booking is not available, must be offered an alternative without being offended or given an unequivocal 'no' in response to their request

Selling skills

Leisure and recreation products and services are not essential items, we do not need them to exist and they do not meet crucial physiological needs. Selling is a skill, it is an art form, it relies on your ability to persuade the customer to buy something that they don't actually need but that they think they want.

There are countless examples and instances of purchases made within the leisure and recreation industry. For example, customers buy tickets for a performance, tee times at a golf club, a step in a step aerobics class, an airline ticket to a destination, a bed for the evening, a meal in a restaurant and a beer in a bar.

Many of the sales in the industry result in the temporary ownership of some space, seat or part of an area or facility. Customers will also purchase *tangible* goods, that is goods they can touch and feel, such as CDs, stereos, clothes, toys, PCs, etc.

 **DISCUSSION**

Think of the last leisure related purchase you made. What was it? How much did you pay?

More importantly, when you made the purchase did you know what you wanted or did you seek the advice of a sales assistant? How significant a role did the staff member play in your decision to buy?

The objectives of selling

In any sales process there are a number of objectives that the seller, vendor or organisation is trying to achieve. In the short term they are looking to:

- Create and raise customer awareness of their product, service or activity.
- Achieve customer satisfaction by delivering a quality customer service.

By achieving these immediate goals, an organisation can look to its more long-term future and work towards achieving more distant aims such as:

- Securing an edge over competitors in terms of the quality of service, sale and aftercare.
- Achieving customer satisfaction.
- Securing repeat business.
- Increasing sales in terms of both existing and potential customers.
- Ultimately increasing profitability.

The achievement of these goals does not happen overnight and an organisation has to be patient in realising these aims.

The functions of selling

In order to achieve these objectives in both the immediate and long term, there are a number of functions that an organisation has to be aware of.

In practice, organisations have to:

- Provide customers with accurate and reliable information about the product, the price, the package, that is, what they actually get for their money and the service associated with the purchase.
- Deal with customer queries.
- Deal with customer complaints.

In some instances, for example, when purchasing or making travel arrangements, customers need to be informed of their responsibilities. In the case of an overseas flight for instance, it is the customer's responsibility to ensure that they arrive at the airport at the check-in time as opposed to the departure time. When purchasing tangible goods there are often guarantees and disclaimers which the customer should read as they identify the limits of the organisation's responsibilities. For example, after the sale of a wide-screen television the organisation would not be responsible for the set after a child has spilt a glass of milk down the back of it.

Handling customer queries and complaints is something we will address later in this Chapter.

Selling skills and techniques

Before identifying the range of techniques and strategies that people adopt when 'selling', organisations must consider the reasons why people buy. Once the reason why the customer is making the 'purchase' has been identified then staff can determine which strategy they will adopt as part of their sales pitch. For example, it is much easier to sell a room in a four-star hotel to a businessman than to a holiday maker, because inevitably the businessman's company will be paying and he can cover the cost through his expense account. On the other hand, when the purchase is being made out of the customer's own pocket then the approach used needs to be much more personal and persuasive.

Reasons why people buy

People buy because they perceive that they have needs. Such needs may range from a haircut because their hair is too unmanageable and untidy, new shoes because theirs are worn out, or new golf clubs because their old ones have been technically superseded.

An organisation can find out what a customer's need are by recognising the motive behind the purchase. Motives are either emotional or rational.

Emotional motives relate to the customer's feelings and include:

● Fashion – 'It's all the rage' or 'Everybody's got one, I haven't.'
● Pride – 'If Simon bought tickets for the Manchester United game then so can I' or 'Graham used to take me out for dinner, you never do.'
● Desire – 'I really want the new Playstation game' or 'I can't play without a new racket'.
● Fear – 'If we don't stop here we might not find another hotel for hours' or 'If we don't go now we'll never get a taxi.'

DISCUSSION

Look at some of the comments listed here and reasons for purchase. Do you recognise any of these?

When was the last time you made such comment? Think about the situation and reason for it? Did you make the purchase? If not why not?

Rational motives relate to a customer's logic and their thinking:

- Need – 'I really need a holiday … a break … a beer.'
- Pleasure – 'Let's go out for dinner, go on we deserve it' or 'Let's spoil ourselves and go abroad for two weeks.'
- Comfort – 'I need a room with en-suite facilities' or 'Flying business class gives me more leg room and personal attention.'
- Value for money – 'You can get two meals for under £10 here' or 'It's happy hour at Scruffy Murphy's, doubles for the price of singles.'
- Convenience – 'Lets have a curry, it on the way home' or 'We might as well while we're here.'
- Service and efficiency – 'They're always so polite here, nothing's too much trouble for them.'

The AIDA technique

The AIDA technique is commonly recognised as the most effective means by which sales and business can be secured. The AIDA technique is simply a guideline or strategy that is designed to be implemented or used by those in sales:

- Attention
- Interest
- Desire
- Action

Attention

Any prospective meeting should seek to gain the customer's attention. In order to gain their attention, as a staff member you will have to prepare for the 'sales interview'. This interview is a meeting between between two people, the sales person and the customer. It does not have to be formal, complex or time consuming. Remember the customer's motives, as these will dictate the nature, tone and context of the conversation.

Interest

In order to develop interest in a product or service some sort of approach, whether formal (arrangements, appointments or meetings to discuss potential sales) or informal (random, chance meetings, ad hoc, on the spur of the moment), will have to be made between the vendor and customer.

Within the industry there are a number of different mediums through which customers are approached. The approach adopted depends on the type of product or service on offer. More often than not, it is staff members who are approached by the customer. For example the travel agent approached by prospective holiday makers. This method is easy for the vendor to respond to as they can take comfort in the knowledge that the customers already have some level of interest, awareness and intention to buy.

DISCUSSION

Can you think of any instances in which the customer would be approached by the vendor?

How successful are these approaches? Are they more or less effective than the customer approaching the vendor?

Desire

In order to decide whether the customer has any real intention or desire to make a purchase, the vendor must first establish the customer's needs and wants.

Action

Once the needs and wants of the customer have been established, it is time to take action. When the customer agrees to buy then it's up to you to 'close the sale'

In understanding and implementing the AIDA technique, you will need to be aware of specific issues, roles and responsibilities that occur. During the sales process you will need to:

- raise customer awareness and establish a rapport
- investigate customer needs
- negotiate a sale
- close the sale
- deliver after-sales service.

These are discussed in further detail below.

Raise customer awareness and establish a rapport

The purpose of the meeting is to provide sufficient accurate information to allow the customer to make an informed decision. For example, in buying a household leisure item, such as a computer or stereo system, the customer may simply wish to find out prices, capacities, deals and will be comparing packages from one organisation with another.

In any contact between the customer and employee both will have their own agendas, aims and anticipated outcomes. Preparing well for a sales interview by identifying the customer's motives, needs and wants, can help employees meet these aims. Remember, when making a big purchase the customer cannot be rushed into a decision. Your patience may be rewarded with a sale.

Investigate customer needs

A customer's needs and wants are inevitably matched with what the organisation can provide. Market research can help organisations to identify a range of products, services and activities that they can realistically offer within the confines and constraints of their budgets, facilities, resources and staffing skills.

These activities are then tailored by sales staff to meet the needs, wants and desires of the customer. Being able to tailor a sale to suit the customer involves asking questions to establish specific needs. Such questions may be closed and require a simple yes or no answer, for example, 'May I take your coat, madam?' or 'Are you a beginner level skier?'.

In order to establish choice, preference or opinion other questions may be more complex, for example, 'How many ski lessons will you need during your weeks holiday?' or 'How would you like your steak?'.

ACTIVITY

INVESTIGATING CUSTOMER NEEDS

'You are working at the front desk of The Station Hotel (a luxury hotel in the town centre) when you are approached by a young man. He tells you that he is due to get married in three months' time and would like to stay at your hotel with his bride before they fly off for their honeymoon.

He is making enquiries and hopefully a reservation based on the recommendation of a friend. He does not know what the prices, or facilities include but has suggested that money is no object.'

Questions to consider

How do you establish specifically what he wants and ensure that he walks away having made a reservation?

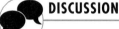
DISCUSSION

If as an organisation you could not meet your customers' requests, say a particular seat at a pop concert, would you consider offering them a 'same quality alternative' for a reduced price to avoid losing their custom?

Negotiate a sale

Some sales, in terms of prices and what is included in the sale, are not set in tablets of stone and are open to negotiation. For example, an individual who goes into a city centre hotel on a quiet Sunday evening would have more chance of getting a reduction in the price of a room than he would on a Monday morning. His grounds for negotiation might be that it's late and quiet and no one would want it anyway.

Not all purchases are easy. There are occasions when the product that a customer requests or demands is not available. You may have to ask if they would be prepared to wait the delivery time or encourage them to consider alternatives in the same price range.

Close the sale

In closing a sale you need to observe, listen and question the customer.

Their body language, whether it is positive, open, eager or enthusiastic, will give you some clue about their intention to purchase. Look at their face. Are they smiling, pensive, frowning and what do these facial expressions mean? Listen to the comments they make and the conversations they are having with either their partner or friend. Some may even need to leave you for a second while they make a phone call. What might you conclude? Ask them questions and answer their concerns with confidence, trust and reassurance. Attempt to allay their fears by informing them that they can return goods if they are unhappy or that there is a money back guarantee. Do not be seen to want to take their money and run.

Customers are a strange breed. Even if you think that you have identified, assessed and confirmed that you can meet all of their needs and wants they still may decide to delay the purchase, particularly if the purchase involves significant financial expenditure, such as a car or computer. That is their prerogative. At this stage you must simply smile, be patient, and above all, respect their decision.

Deliver after-sales service

Explain what the purchase entitles them to, for example, a gold membership at the golf club entitles them to play at any time whereas the silver and bronze memberships are restricted use. Before agreeing a purchase, identify the different payment plans or methods available to them and how they can pay.

You will need to ensure that the customer is aware that the organisation's role does not end just because a sale has been agreed and the money accepted, but that its interest is genuine and that support for the customer, be it technical, or more simply, advice and guidance about other products and services, will always be available.

Handling complaints

DID YOU KNOW?

A 1997 UK National Consumer Council survey found that in 1992, 25% of people surveyed had made at least one complaint.

DID YOU KNOW?

Studies show that customers tell twice as many people about a bad experience as they tell about a good one.

DID YOU KNOW?

A typical dissatisfied customer will tell 8–10 people about their problem.

Organisations with incidences of poor customer service will lose custom. Statistics suggest that most organisations only hear from 4% of dissatisfied customers. If the statistic is turned on its head the implications are that they do *not* hear from 96% of customers who are unhappy. In terms of actual numbers, only one out of every 25 dissatisfied customers complains.

There are two major problems with this silent majority. First, most of them (90% of the 24, or about 22) simply won't come back, so an organisation may never find out what the problem was. Second and more importantly, each of these 22 people will tell an average of ten of their friends. The net effect is that an organisation may not only lose their business, but potentially that of people they know. In the worst case scenario, if these 22 ex-customers are persuasive enough, they can scare off up to a total of 220 (10 × 22) more prospective customers. Even if an organisation can afford to lose the 22, can they afford to lose the other 220 potential customers?

It is not the case that organisations with good customer service never make mistakes – they do. What is important, is their ability to handle these complaints, by bending over backwards, and going the extra mile to correct the mistakes they *do* make. It makes good business sense for them to do this.

DISCUSSION

Think of all your encounters with employees and staff members. Have you ever been difficult?

Have you ever been with someone who was difficult? Have you ever overheard or seen a customer being particularly difficult with an employee?

What was the nature of these situations? In what way were they difficult? Discuss this with your group.

Dealing with awkward customers

These customers are different from the dissatisfied customers in that they are not necessarily unhappy with the service or the product, but they can be equally, if not more, demanding on your customer service skills, patience and tolerance. They are also referred to as the difficult customer.

Difficult customers come in many forms:

- the rude customer
- the obnoxious customer
- the over demanding customer
- the angry customer
- the seething but silent individual
- the 'nothing's ever going to be right for this person' customer
- the constant critic
- the non-stop talker
- the weirdo
- the indecisive customer
- the drunk
- the argumentative customer

Staff members are encouraged to see the attitude and the behaviour that is being presented to them rather than the individual. They are encouraged to view the situation as challenging as opposed to seeing the customer as tiresome, irritating and/or a pain.

There are a number of guidelines for dealing with difficult customers. Staff are encouraged to:

- keep calm
- not to take any aspect of the situation, its conversation or accusations, personally
- ignore rudeness
- not to laugh at or put down the customer
- explain to a customer what they can and cannot do and why
- know what the organisation can do
- not show that they are annoyed or bored
- be polite but firm
- know the company's products and policies
- not make promises which they cannot keep
- not argue
- apologise where appropriate

ACTIVITY

ROLE PLAYS: DEALING WITH DIFFICULT CUSTOMERS

Using the advice given above, deal with the following difficult customers. Play out the scenario, change roles if you have to.

1 You are working behind the bar in McMillans and have just finished serving a large drinks order when a gentlemen who has been waiting calls over to you quite aggressively and says, 'Do you work here or do I have to come round and serve myself?'.

2 You are waiting on tables in a restaurant and the specials board promises a meal which has run out. The board has not been wiped clean and the young businessman you are serving requests that meal. When told it is not available he says, somewhat sarcastically in a deliberate attempt to belittle you, 'Honestly what sort of place is this? You promise something and then you say you don't have it. Do you know what you have got on your menu or not?'

3 You are working at the City Pool sports and leisure centre on a Saturday morning, when you are approached by an elderly customer who has just arrived at the front of a long queue the majority of whom are increasingly impatient families with small children. The elderly individual is enquiring about a series of 'fitness for all' sessions which start on Monday. It becomes apparent to you after two or three minutes that this individual is a chatterbox and enjoying the conversation and will not be moved on quickly.

4 You receive a telephone call at the reception desk of the Clairemount Hotel, from a guest in Room 204 enquiring about the evening's entertainment. The guest is foreign and has poor English. You have trouble understanding the accent and therefore the questions being asked. The guest is becoming increasingly frustrated because you are not providing the information that is needed.

5 You are working at Nitespots nightclub when you are approached by a guest who appears to be a little inebriated, starts making advances towards you and asks you for a kiss.

Questions to consider

There are a number of different ways in which you could have dealt with the customer. Did you choose the most appropriate?

If you could replay the scenario again would you still deal with them in the same manner?

Dissatisfied customers

Dissatisfied customers are a 'gold mine' of opportunity. Their grievances should be pursued actively because a customer with a complaint is at serious risk of becoming an ex-customer and of driving away would-be customers too.

As an employee you will receive complaints in various ways: in writing, over the telephone or in person. Regardless of the mode of presentation you should be able to deal with that complaint. You should be familiar with the procedures and protocol laid down by your employer in order to deal with that complaint. If you are not familiar with them, you should at least know who to refer the complaint to without sounding evasive or unhelpful to the customer. Your most difficult challenge lies with dealing with the customer in an attempt to rectify their dissatisfaction.

DID YOU KNOW?

Those companies who actively encourage customers to complain can increase customer retention by 10%. Actually responding to complaints can boost retention by up to 75%. If the customer is very satisfied, retention increases to 95%.

Source: Strategic Planning Institute

 **DISCUSSION**

Are any of these situations familiar to you? What was that situation? Who was involved, was it you, a family member, a friend, did you overhear or see it happen? Were you the employee on the receiving end?

Discuss this among your group, stating how the situation was resolved. Was the customer satisfied with the outcome?

Customers can be dissatisfied for any number of reasons, which may include the following:

- A member of staff has failed to do something properly or forgotten to do something.
- Information, messages and requests have not been passed on or attended to.
- A customer may have been kept waiting.
- Equipment or supplies may have been broken, damaged or missing.
- A member of staff has misunderstood or misinterpreted a customer's requests.
- A customer has been led to expect something that the organisation cannot provide.
- A customer feels that they have not had value for money.

There are organisations within the industry that have specific guidelines for dealing with dissatisfied customers. If you receive a complaint then there are general guidelines laid down and steps to take, which identify how the customer should be dealt with. These steps are listed below.

1. Keep calm

It will not help the customer or resolve the issue if you become flustered, aggressive, angry or abusive either verbally or physically.

Customers who have a complaint will often become angry. You must remember that it is the situation and not you that is the problem. Even if you are responsible for the situation, do not panic. Follow the organisational policies.

2. Listen

Your job is to try and put things right, not to shift the blame or responsibility to another colleague or department. You need to pay careful attention to the customer and listen to everything that they are telling you. Do not interrupt or jump to the wrong conclusions.

You may be required by your employer to document the complaint. It is essential that you record all of the details and ask the customer to verify that you have accurately recorded the complaint. If it is possible, then you should move out of other customers' hearing or viewpoint. If they will not be budged, do not manhandle them but try to steer them diplomatically to a quiet corner.

3. Apologise

Apologising to the customer can usually take the heat out of a confrontation, it may take them aback or remove the 'wind from their sails'. It may make the discussion easier. You might say something like, 'I am sorry that this has caused you such upset, please tell me everything ...'

or 'I do see your point of view, please do accept our apologies'. By empathising with the customer you may be able to defuse the situation. Do not, however, patronise or belittle them. Equally, be careful not to admit liability or responsibility for a situation – it may be grounds for a law suit against the organisation.

4. Find a solution

You must decide as soon as is practically possible, who is capable of dealing with the situation. Is it your job? You may have to refer it to somebody more senior within the organisation who has the capacity to take the appropriate action to remedy or rectify the situation and placate the customer.

The extent to which you need to involve senior colleagues or management will depend on the nature and severity of the complaint and the circumstances involved. For example, a double booking on a squash court may be resolved by the receptionist, whereas allegations of theft, abuse or assault will have to involve management and possibly external organisations, such as the police.

Once you have identified who should be dealing with the complaint you need to agree a course of action. If it is not within your capacity to deal with this issue then make it clear who you are going to involve, giving their name and position if necessary – do not just leave the customer unattended while you go off and search for somebody to deal with them.

Do not make promises you cannot keep. For example, if the gym is closed due to essential maintenance work and some clients have not been informed and turn up to use the facility, then you could possibly offer them another free session at their convenience. Offering them a month's free membership by way of apologising for their inconvenience is promising possibly too much.

Do not break or deviate from standard practices and procedures.

5. Follow up

In offering or identifying a solution it is essential that this is agreed with the customer. Customers need to be satisfied that you have acknowledged their complaint, that you will actively deal with it as opposed to 'shelving it' as soon as they are gone and above all, by the end of the encounter or situation, they must be satisfied. Ask them if they are content and if you have addressed their complaints to their satisfaction? If you have not, then the encounter must continue until they feel that you have dealt with them to their satisfaction.

Where possible, steps should be taken to ensure that the problem does not occur again. If your organisation has a records book, or complaints form then the complaint and response must be logged accurately.

DID YOU KNOW?

95% of customers prefer a letter to a phone call when you are dealing with their complaints. A letter is more personal, demonstrates a greater commitment on behalf of the company and its tangibility suggests that the complaint has been taken seriously and is concrete evidence that something will be done.

Source: Strategic Planning Institute

ACTIVITY

ROLE PLAYS: HANDLING COMPLAINTS

Using the advice and steps laid out, deal with the following complaints. You may wish to change roles with a partner to understand both positions.

1   You are waiting on tables in a restaurant when you are called over by an anxious diner. He says somewhat aggressively, that he has been waiting for over 20 minutes for his steak and that he has an urgent appointment to get to and does not now have the time to finish his meal. He says that he does not want the meal and will not pay for any of the meal because he is appalled by the slow and apparently non-existent service in your restaurant. He has, however, had half a caraffe of red wine.

2   You are working at the reception of the Lyndon swimming pool, when a swimmer wearing only a swimsuit rushes out to main reception on the verge of tears stating that her locker has been broken into and all of her belongings, apart from her shoes, have been stolen.

3   You are working at the Seegar Art Gallery when an elderly gentleman, holding a young boy aged about 10 by his collar approaches you. He says that he found this young mongrel writing his name on the corner of one of the exhibits.

4   You are working in Harry's Nightclub when one of your guests approaches you in a very agitated state. She reports that one of the bouncers has hit her boyfriend and they won't allow him in and that she thinks his nose is broken and she is going to call the police.

5   You are working in a cinema complex when one of the viewers approaches you and is disgusted to have found that the tickets they booked in advance are not now available and the film is already full. He says that there is nothing else they would like to watch and that it has cost them £4 each on the bus to get to the cinema.

6   It is Saturday afternoon at the local school's dual-use sports facility and you are working at reception. You fail to notice that the astro-turf has been double booked and it is not unitl four team captains arrive at the counter to question the booking that you realise.

7   A young couple are on their way to Dublin for a weekend break and are staying at the Apollo Hotel, next door to the airport. They arrive at main reception in the morning furious that the alarm call they ordered never materialised and as a result have missed their flight.

There are endless other scenarios that you can think of or may have actually been involved in. Try these out as well. They must, however, be realistic and could conceivably occur within the industry.

Questions to consider

Do you think the customer had grounds for complaint?

Have you resolved the complaint or did you have to refer it to somebody in a more senior position?

How do you think you handled the complaint? Would you handle it differently next time?

Assessing the quality and effectiveness of customer service

Even though an organisation claims to have an effective and efficient quality customer service in place, how can they substantiate this claim and check that their system does actually work? How can they prove that their customer service policy is effective and that the customer is satisfied? Does the organisation have hard evidence to prove their claims? The Rank Group plc, in its 1998 Review has highlighted its commitment to developing its employees' relationship with customers:

❝ We believe that improved customer satisfaction can only be achieved through a commitment to training and developing our people. Many of our business have made great improvements during the last two years in employee development and training. We are monitoring how this is being translated into improving customer satisfaction levels. These processes are well advanced in some of our brands. ❞

Oasis Forest Holiday Villages employs a number of procedures that allow them to measure customer satisfaction, one method being a customer survey. Through this survey they can measure whether customer needs, wants and expectations have been met. At the year end of 1998, Oasis achieved satisfaction ratings of 96%, with the majority of those questioned suggesting that their expectations had been met or closely exceeded.

DISCUSSION

Investigate the ISO 9000? What does it cover exactly?

How can it help leisure and recreation organisations assess the quality of customer service it delivers?

In today's competitive marketplace, quality improvement has now become a key international business strategy. There is massive interest in the establishment of quality systems as one method of assuring the consistent conformity of products or services to a defined set of standards.

More and more organisations are now required to achieve levels of performance based on national, European and international standards. For example, a growing number of organisations are assessed to ISO 9000 – the quality systems standard. In order to reach this standard an organisation must set down how all its systems operate and prove that it is running according to these prescribed systems at all times.

Most organisations, particularly the commercial organisations who are financially accountable to boards, trustees and shareholders, have procedures in place that allow them to continually assess and monitor the quality of the customer service they provide. Many organisation are striving for recognised industry awards such as the Investor in People Award and, the Hospitality Assured Award. Centre Parcs was one of the first organisations to receive this.

Benchmarking

Some leisure and recreation organisations set themselves standards of customer service quality which they aim to achieve. This process is referred to as benchmarking and has only recently begun to be used in the industry. Within this process an organisation's actual performance can be assessed against or compared with their own quality standards and those of competitors.

Benchmarking as defined by Xerox is,

❝the continuing process of measuring products, services and practices against the toughest competition of those recognised as leaders❞.

The Benefits
Benchmarking allows the organisation to:

- identify its own strengths and weaknesses
- help identify 'best practice'
- establish from the customer's point of view what makes the difference between an ordinary service and an exceptional one
- find 'best practice' examples for those differences and set themselves realistic and sustainable goals to achieve them
- find out how 'best organisations' achieve those goals
- adapt and apply lessons learned from those organisations to achieve their own goals and even exceed them
- search for industry 'best practice' which leads to superior performance
- demonstrate achievement through year on year improvement against benchmarks.

Standards and quality criteria

Some organisations are compared directly with an external set of standards and criteria. The most notable example of external standardisation and comparison has been laid down by the English Tourism Council. It has in place a star ratings system that was developed on the basis of a benchmarking exercise conducted by the old Department of National Heritage and was called 'Competing With The Best'.

The star ratings system informs guests of the type of service they are likely to receive and the value they will get for their money. The new scheme puts greater emphasis on quality in hotels, particularly in areas of cleanliness and guest care. Any hotel sporting a star will have been visited overnight anonymously by a qualified assessor. The new standards and accommodation ratings highlighted in the extract below are from the English Tourism Council web site – www.englishtourism.org.uk/quality/england.htm.

CASE STUDY *English Tourism Council Hotels – star ratings*

The system of star ratings symbolises the level of service, range of facilities and quality of care, guests can expect.

At a one-star hotel you will find:

Practical accommodation with a limited range of facilities and services, 75% of bedrooms will have en-suite or private facilities and there will be a high standard of cleanliness throughout. Friendly and courteous staff on hand to give you the help and information you need to enjoy your stay. Restaurant/eating area open to you and your guests for breakfast and dinner. Alcoholic drinks served in a bar or lounge.

At a two-star hotel you will find (in addition to what is provided at a one-star)

Good overnight accommodation with more comfortable bedrooms, better equipped – all with en-suite or private facilities and colour TV. A relatively straightforward range of services, including food and drink and a personal style of service. A restaurant/dining room for breakfast and dinner. A lift is normally available.

At a three-star hotel you will find (in addition to what is provided at a one- and two-star)

Possibly larger establishments, but all offering significantly greater quality and range of facilities and services, and usually more spacious public areas and bedrooms. Room service of continental breakfast. A wide selection of drinks, light lunch and snacks served in a bar or lounge.

A more formal style of service with a receptionist on duty and staff responding well to your needs and requests. Laundry service available.

At a four-star hotel you will find (in addition to what is provided at a one-, two-, and three-star)

Accommodation offering superior comfort and quality; all bedrooms with en-suite bath, fitted overhead shower and WC.

The hotel will have spacious and very well appointed public areas and will put a strong emphasis on food and drink. Room service of all meals and 24-hour drinks, refreshments and snacks.

Staff will have very good technical and social skills, anticipating and responding to your needs and requests. Dry cleaning service available.

At a five-star hotel you will find (in addition to what is provided at a one-, two-, three- and four-star)

A spacious, luxurious establishment offering you the highest international quality of accommodation, facilities, services and cuisine. It will have striking accommodation throughout, with a range of extra facilities.

You will feel very well cared for by professional, attentive staff providing flawless guest services. A hotel that fits the highest international standards for the industry, with an air of luxury, exceptional comfort and a sophisticated ambience.

ACTIVITY

Quality standards and criteria

Look at the Case Study on star ratings.

Identify, perhaps in your local area, hotels with different star ratings. Where possible obtain any information or advertising literature about the establishment that identifies the range of facilities and services that it promises to customers.

Make an enquiry at that facility. Pretend that you are a potential guest and establish whether they can meet your needs. Before you make contact with them identify what you want from them, whether it is an enquiry about the possiblity of an overnight stay for your parents on their anniversary or whether it is a personal gym membership. You may decide to make a telephone enquiry instead of a personal enquiry; this is equally acceptable.

The organisation will also have some sort of customer feedback form. Ask for a copy of this form in order that you can identify which aspects of customer service are important to them in their analysis of a customer's views on their stay. Identify what information the organisation needs to find out from the customer about their stay in order that they can assess their customer service delivery.

Identify from the information you gather in this activity whether you think the hotel deserves its star rating.

Internal standards and quality criteria

Organisations set their own standards and have their own procedures in place that allow them to continually assess and monitor the quality of the customer service they provide.

These monitoring procedures relate to a number of different quality criteria, some of which relate specifically to the organisation and include:

- Staffing levels, mix and quality of service delivery.
- Consistency of service.
- Reliability of staff in terms of work commitments and fulfilling job roles and requirements.

Other quality criteria relate to the organisation and its ability to serve the customer in terms of anticipating their needs and wants. These are:

- Cleanliness and hygiene of the facility.
- Customer enjoyment of experience.
- Price/value for money.
- Health and safety of employee and customer and security of themselves and their belongings.
- Accessibility and availability of advertised products, services and actvities.
- Provision for individual needs, particularly for specific needs, such as wheelchair access.

NATIONAL RAILWAY MUSEUM
COMMENTS, SUGGESTIONS AND ENQUIRIES

We welcome any comments and suggestions which will help us to improve our services. Alternatively, you may have an enquiry which you would like us to answer. In either case please use this form. We will reply as quickly as possible. If you do not require a reply, or wish to comment anonymously, there is no need to give your name and address.

Name _____

_____

_____

_____

Address _____

_____

_____

_____

_____

_____

Telephone number _____

_____

Date of visit _____

_____

FIGURE 5.3 *Customer comments form*

Feedback

It is worth remembering that feedback from staff and employees is often just as significant and as valuable for the purposes of self-analysis as feedback from the external client base.

In order to analyse these factors, it is important to gather not just statistical evidence in the form of raw data but also feedback from customers. The National Railway Museum has in place a strategy by which they can analyse their provision. Their customer comments form (Figure 5.3) enables them to collect both raw and subjective data.

Raw data and statistical analysis results can be very useful to an organisation in terms of analysing its financial position, year-end targets and comparison with competitor organisations. For example an organisation can:

- Identify customer numbers over a period of time.
- Identify a breakdown of specific user groups.
- Analyse ticket sales, receipts and other income against net expenditure.
- Compare statistics against competitor organisations as part of a benchmarking exercise.

Feedback from customers, however, can prove to be just as valuable because it presents the organisation with subjective thoughts and feelings that relate to how the organisation works, its staff and service delivery. Even if these comments are not stated in sentence format, but inferred in a scaled answer on a questionnaire, they are still useful because the findings, and therefore operational practices, can still be analysed.

Leisure and recreation organisations use a range of techniques to find out if customers are happy with the standards of customer service they receive. These include informal feedback, surveys, suggestion boxes, focus groups, mystery shoppers and observation, and are discussed further below.

Informal feedback and information may be obtained from customers, staff, management and non-users through conversation both face-to-face and via the telephone, or on the basis of written comments or messages received, or it may even be a comment overheard and relayed third hand.

DID YOU KNOW?

80% of successful new product and service ideas originate from customers.

DID YOU KNOW?

43% of companies surveyed were unable to identify why they lose customers. Of the remaining 57%, one-fifth were unable to explain how.

12% were unable to even say how many customers they actually have.

Source: KPMG Consulting Report

FORTE
Posthouse

Guest
Questionnaire

FORTE
Posthouse

A warm welcome to Forte Posthouse, whether it is your first visit or one of many. We all aim to be friendly, prompt and helpful at all times. Our style is informal, relaxed and professional. However, should we get it wrong, please tell us straight away and we will put it right.

Please spare a few moments to ask yourself whether you feel that we have delivered our promise as above, and then fill in this questionnaire. The information you give us will be carefully analysed so that we will be able to take action where necessary to make sure that the high standards we set ourselves are maintained.

Free prize draw. Your name will be entered into a monthly draw to win a night away for two at the Posthouse of your choice. Full terms and conditions of the draw can be requested from reception.

Thank you for choosing Forte Posthouse. We look forward to seeing you again.

FIGURE 5.4 *Forte Posthouse guest questionnaire*

 **DISCUSSION**

How many times on leaving an organisation such as a hotel or restaurant have you been asked to fill in a questionnaire? Did you complete it? What information was it trying to find out?

Surveys may be conducted of customers, staff, management and non- or potential users. Organisations must consider that if surveys are written questionnaires distributed through either a mail drop or completed by customers in-house, there will be a substantial amount of returned forms which will have been destroyed and will not be able to be included in the findings.

An excellent way of pre-empting complaints and identifying areas of weakness is by sending out questionnaires. As long as questions are posed in customer-friendly language, that is jargon-free and straightforward, and cover areas recognisably of benefit to them, an organisation can ask customers' opinions on any number of areas. For example, how do your customers rate you for service, staff friendliness, efficiency and delivery times? Are there any areas where they feel you could improve?

Club World Travel
26 William Street, Lurgan ★★★★★

A VERY eye-catching and attractive shop and the agency had a nicely furnished interior.

The brochure racks were well stocked. Three sales consultants were on duty and I was served immediately by a polite girl who listened to my enquiry and was happy to suggest a number of options.

She gave me her opinions on Majorca from her personal experiences and chatted about the various resorts. She gave me printouts of costs and flights for Thomson Summer Sun, Falcon Hot Choices and Aspro deals and gave details of discounts available and the best departure times.

Among the options suggested were packages featuring the Jardin De Playa in Santa Ponsa which she said was near a good beach. She also mentioned the Magamar apartments in Magaluf and the Ferrera Blanca apartments in Cala DOr. She did a printout of the options and in all cases pointed out to me what discounts were available.

She drew my attention to the properties with air conditioning and suggested I book as soon as possible. She gave me her business card and told me to call back. This was definitely the best sales technique of them all and her helpful attitude was impressive.

★ Agency appearance
★ Staff attitude
★ Brochure racking
★ Product knowledge
★ Sales technique

FIGURE 5.5 *Feature on Club World Travel*

Questionnaires

Questionnaires are also an excellent source of information for any organisation (see example in Figure 5.4). They make customers feel they are in a two-way relationship and that their views count. Some organisations, such as Forte Posthouse (Figure 5.4) offer incentives to customers to complete their questionnaire, such as entry into a free prize draw.

Suggestion boxes, where used, are placed in a central location and usually have customer feedback cards or forms next to them. Organisations are always looking for ways in which they can improve, be it the facility or venue, their scheduling or the service they provide and they normally encourage customer comments and feedback.

Mystery shoppers

Focus groups are often brought in by the organisation to attend informal meetings or seminars and to share thoughts, feelings, views or opinions. They may be led by a senior manager and the findings of the forum are often recorded and analysed.

Mystery shoppers are often employed by the organisation to visit a facility as a mystery customer and to report back to the management on their findings. Some of the larger pub chains, like Yates Wine Bar, employ this strategy, where staff within the bar being 'inspected' will have no clue as to the reason behind that 'customer's' visit. The English Tourist Board employs qualified assessors to visit their hotels anonymously and verify that the hotel has been awarded the appropriate star rating.

The Travel Weekly, an industry trade magazine, has a mystery shopper feature (Figure 5.5). Each week visits are made to different agents and stars are awarded to those that score for the appearance of the facility, product knowledge, staff attitude, brochure racking and sales technique. The top scoring agency each week receives a certificate of commendation.

Observation

Observation can sometimes be done informally from an office window, across a reception area or it can be more formal in the form of an appraisal, test, interview, presentation or practical situation. For example, prospective sports coaches are often observed delivering a practical session to a group and are rated on their ability to communicate, inform, lead, demonstrate and organise.

ACTIVITY

Obtaining Feedback

For each of the feedback methods outlined in the text, identify an organisation within the industry that employs that method of compiling feedback.

Where possible obtain a copy of the procedure, policy, comments or feedback form. If this is not available, then make time to chat with somebody at the organisation about which methods they employ to assess customer feedback.

Find out specifically what information they are trying to obtain. Identify whether they have chosen the best method of collecting customer feedback or whether there is another method they could have employed? How effective are these methods?

How does the organisation employ or use the information once they have compiled it?

It is through the collation and analysis of evidence that organisations can identify weaknesses in their customer service delivery. Feedback, when analysed properly, can help an organisation to adapt its practices, products and services to suit the constantly changing needs of its customer base.

ASSESSMENT EVIDENCE

As part of the Customer Service Unit you are required to produce a range of assessment evidence.

The Unit specifications state that you need to produce the following:

1 Evidence of your involvement in a variety of customer service and selling situations with at least four different types of customers
2 An investigation into the effectiveness of customer service delivery in two lesiure and recreation organisations

In order to compile this assessment evidence you must take part in both the delivery and evaluation of customer service.

1 Customer service and selling

You must show evidence of your involvement in at least four customer service situations. These situations may be ones that arise naturally in your work place or as part of your work placement. Or equally they may be simulated by your tutor, that is, simulated situations to assess your ability to deal with the customer in a range of situations. Where possible, usually in the simulated situations, these interactions should be videotaped and subsequently used for the purposes of analysis and feedback.

Have a look back at page 270 of this Chapter to remind yourself of the different types of situations that may arise and questions or prompts that you should be thinking about when dealing with customers. By answering these questions and responding to the different prompts you should be able to deal competently and thoroughly with each customer.

For each situation you must produce a record or testimony of that interaction. You may gather witness statements from your work place to testify that the situation has actually occurred, or video evidence compiled at your school or college.

Your tutor at your school or college may give you a standard proforma to use as your customer service record, or you may be asked to design a record sheet yourself. It must, however, include the information given in Figure 5.6.

CUSTOMER SERVICE SITUATION:
Identify the type of customer and describe the customer service situation
Describe the needs and priorities of that customer
Describe the different communication methods and at what stage they were used during the situation
Describe the objectives of the approach you adopted
Note any other additional information pertaining to the situation

EVALUATION
Were the customer's requests satisfied and their needs met? How successfully?
How well do you think you handled the situation. What is your evaluation of your own performance?
What, if anything, would you do differently if exactly the same encounter were to occur?

WITNESS STATEMENT/OBSERVATION REPORT
Supervisor's or tutor's evaluation of your performance

SUPERVISOR/TUTOR SIGNATURE	DATE

FIGURE 5.6 *Customer Service Assessment and Evaluation Report*

2 The effectiveness of customer service delivery in the industry

You have been employed by the Customer Service 'Watchdog' Group and asked to conduct an investigation into the 'effectiveness of customer service delivery' at two contrasting leisure and recreation organisations. You may concentrate on two organisations of your choice.

To analyse the effectiveness of an organisation's customer service delivery you will have to consider the way in which they employ key quality criteria. Standard quality criteria include the following:

- price/value for money
- consistency/accuracy
- reliability
- staffing levels/qualities
- enjoyment of experience
- health and safety
- cleanliness/hygiene
- accessibility and availability
- provision for individual needs

You will need to identify the quality criteria used at your organisation and identify the way in which that organisation relates those criteria to the customer, via its service and selling strategies. Depending on the type of organisation, and the provision they specialise in, you will find that quality criteria may vary from one organisation to another. For example, the quality criteria employed by an outdoor activities centre will differ vastly from those employed by a wine bar or a museum. Most organisations have a customer charter which outlines its promises and commitments to the customer, you should try and obtain a copy of this for your investigation.

One of the most effective ways of analysing customer service provision is to be their customer. For the purposes of this investigation, you may wish to act as an anonymous 'mystery shopper' in order to assess whether what the organisations promise the customer is actually what they deliver. Organisations produce advertising or promotional literature for their customers, this too will be useful for you to analyse in your evaluation of their provision.

Alternatively or in conjuction with your evaluation exercise as the customer, you may consider formally interviewing staff at the site who have varying degrees of responsibility for the customer. Within these interviews you should question the practices and procedures laid down by the organisation and implemented by staff. Some of these procedures are critical, both in the delivery (standard working practices) and self analysis (benchmarking) of their customer service strategies. The information gleaned from these interviews and from the literature they produce, such as customer comments cards or feedback questionnaires, will help you establish a view on the nature of provision from 'both sides of the fence' as it were.

Conducting your investigation

In conducting your investigation, you should consider the following:

- It may be conducted in pairs or small groups.
- It must be well structured, designed and professionally conducted.
- Findings may be presented in either a report, written document or oral presentation.
- Findings must be objective, supported by valid evidence and confidential.
- It must give accurate details of the key customer service quality criteria implemented by each organisation.
- It must justify the methods you have used to measure, monitor and appraise the effectiveness of customer service at the two sites.
- It must compare the differences and evaluate the effectiveness of customer service delivery.
- It must suggest and justify methods or actions both sites could take up in order to improve their customer service delivery.

Key Skills

In completing the assessment for this unit, you can achieve the following key skills. These will be accredited at the discretion of your tutor on the basis of the quality of the work you submit.

COMMUNICATION, LEVEL 3
C3.1a Contribute to a group discussion about a complex subject.
C3.1b Make a presentation about a complex subject, using at least one image to illustrate complex points.
C3.2 Read and synthesise information from two extended documents about a complex subject. One of these documents should include at least one image.

6

Leisure and Recreation in Action

. . . .

Aims and Objectives

Through the study of this unit you will have the opportunity to:

- **consider a range of events or business projects across the leisure and recreation spectrum, that you and others, working as a team, could realistically organise**

- **consider the feasibility of an event or business project and consider how realistic and viable it would be for you to organise**

- **having considered a range of choices, produce a business plan and feasibility study for a specific event or business project of your own choice**

- **understand how important teamwork is, as part of the management and organisation of your event or business project. You will be able to identify where and how you fit into a team and the role you will undertake within that structure**

- **be part of a successful team and to take the credit that you can earn from taking responsibilities and achieving your initial objectives, one of which might include raising money for a charity of your choice**

- **evaluate your team's performance, the success of your event or business project and, with the benefit of hindsight, make recommendations for any similar future events**

Introduction

The leisure and recreation industry by definition is centred around the customer. Organisations, providers and groups of people organise, manage and run activities for individuals to take part in. These activities vary widely in type, some of which require direct participation and energy expenditure, such as sport and recreational activities. Others allow the customer to take a passive role and simply view the proceedings as spectators.

Activities within the industry are not confined to those offered by professional and commercial institutions, but are often localised events such

KEY TERMS

Project: There are a number of meanings to this term:

- Method for making or doing something
- Something undertaken requiring extensive work or planning
- To form a strategy
- To have in mind as a goal, or purpose

as jumble or car-boot sales, an Amateur Dramatics Society's presentation of *Romeo and Juliet*, a soccer activity day during the half-term, or beginners' golf at the local driving range.

Remember that the bigger the scale of the project the more work it will involve, but there is also more satisfaction to be had from its successful completion!

You have spent a considerable amount of time during this course confined to the classroom, considering the theoretical side of the leisure and recreation industry. It is now time to stop talking and put much of what you have learnt and know about the industry into practice.

ACTIVITY

Looking at Events

Think about all the events and activities that you have either participated in, spectated at, or heard about. You may have been in a few swimming galas, taken part in a fun-run, or perhaps been involved as a participant or a helper in a sponsored event. You may feel that you are an accomplished athlete, swimmer or mountain biker and may well be able to prove this by your results from various competitions and events.

Start to compile a list of those events, activities and projects that you have been involved with, write some of them down now.

Compare your list with those compiled by others. Do they have anything in common?

Have you ever considered who is responsible for organising an event? Could you begin to imagine what the time and energy commitment involved really is? In this Chapter you will consider what goes on behind the scenes, that is, you will look beyond the competitors' and spectators' viewpoints and identify who is working and what their roles and responsibilities are in order to make the event happen.

As part of this unit you will also have the opportunity to work as part of a team in organising, managing and running an event of your own. Throughout this text are statements or practical reminders of what you should be doing, or thinking about doing, with regard to planning and organising your own event or project.

KEY TERMS

Unit specification: refers to you (the student) organising an event or business project. This chapter refers to both as an event.

Types of events and business projects

Start by looking at the list you have already made, add any that your friends suggested that interest you. Now, be honest and ask yourself, is there anything here that would interest me enough for me to want to get involved in organising?

If you are not the sporty or outdoor type why not consider a business project. Perhaps you could set up a small company and look at the feasibility of a business idea or proposition, or maybe put on an exhibition?

You should by now:

● Be discussing with your friends some interesting event/project ideas. Are they as keen as you?

If you have not organised an event or project before then you will naturally be apprehensive. In terms of organising your own event or business project then you will have to be realistic. Your attentions may focus on small, localised projects which you know are manageable and realistic given the timescale you are working within, and the limited access you will have to resources, particularly financial resources. However, you should not be discouraged in looking at a major project if you feel you are able, capable and confident. If in doubt discuss the scale and size of your event at an early stage with your tutors or teachers.

Events can range from organising a primary school sports tournament through to staging your college Open Day and from putting on a concert in your local town hall to organising a triathlon competition. The choice of event to organise, ultimately, is yours and your team's.

You should by now:

● Be starting to think about the people that you work 'best' with. You will be organising this event as part of a team. You will have to select your team very carefully!

The scale of events and business projects

The leisure and recreation industry may be seen as a 'calendar of events', for example, the soccer season, the cricket season, winter sporting events and the bi-annual winter Olympics with the various ski disciplines of downhill, slalom, giant slalom, the bobsleigh events, the ice skating, the shoot and ski biathlon and the cross-country ski events. Consider that alongside the organising and planning that is required to stage these events, there are the travel and accommodation arrangements for thousands of competitors and hundreds of thousands of spectators to relatively remote and mountainous regions.

Wimbledon, the Six Nations Championships and events such as Net Aid in Wembley in 1999 are other examples of events. Some events are regular features, others are unique, they are one-offs; the likelihood that the band 'Take That' will perform together again is unlikely.

ACTIVITY

Possible events for you to organise

The list below may give you some ideas, it is not exhaustive and they have all been done before. This list may also give you some ideas of your own. Get a blank piece of paper and start brainstorming these now.

Organising an Orienteering Event
for a local schools competition

- Primary school's 5-a-side soccer tournament
- Secondary school's/college's 3-on-3 basketball tournament
- Triathlon competition
- Fun run
- Fitness campaign
- Musical event
- Barbecue
- Orienteering event
- School/college open day
- Cub/Brownie outdoor activity programme including an overnight camp
- Auction

What about adding two or three smaller events together, for example, at your college open day organise the secondary school's 3-on-3 basketball tournament and maybe an evening barbecue.

The ability to plan and organise, or at least assist in the planning and organising of event and business project management, is a valuable skill in the industry. Be aware that these skills, like any skilful movements, are learnt and acquired. The development of these skills takes time and practise and above all they demand a total commitment to 'team work'.

ACTIVITY

Deciding on an event or business project to look at in more detail

Why not look at some that you have attended? Brainstorm these now and start to make a list. You may wish to compare this list with the one already compiled. Compare the two lists and you will see that the range of events and projects organised within the industry is both vast and varied.

Using the following criteria as sub-headings to order the list of events you have compiled, group the examples according to:

- cost – very expensive or relatively cheap?
- numbers – huge numbers of people or relatively few?
- sporting or wider leisure type event?
- enthusiast attended or mostly inquisitivenes, for example, a railway exhibition will attract only those individuals with an interest in the railways, whereas a summer fete will attract a variety of people.

Identify whether any of these events has sponsors, prize monies or personalities associated with them. In applying these criteria to three or four you are considering, decide which ones are realistic for you to organise and run.

In order to start to understand the complexities of event you may wish to visit or take part in an event yourself. Personal involvement will be useful for you as you will be able to use your experience as a source of reference and comparison when organising and planning your own event.

ACTIVITY

Organising a study visit

Is there any possibility of making a group visit to an event?

Could you arrange a visit to a local event venue and get the events manager/coordinator to give a presentation?

Your tutor may well have contacts, ask him or her to help you organise a visit. In reality you could well be organising your first event for your own group/class!

Before committing time, money and other resources to a specific idea it is advisable to consider how feasible or realistic that event or project is. The assessment of the viability of an event is referred to as a 'feasibility study'. Although this concept is not confined to events and projects, it is often associated with them. The basis for conducting a feasibility study requires you to complete a business plan.

Good managers and teams regularly produce business plans. It is usually quite a large document and is used to plan and propose, ultimately, the financial short- and long-term goals for a business or organisation.

Completing a business plan

To consider the feasibility of planning and organising an event and in planning the event itself, a business plan allows you to consider a number of points.

As part of your assessment, you will be required to complete a business plan for your project. Within that plan you will need to address:

- the aims and objectives of the project
- your customers, their needs and how they will be met
- how the project will be marketed
- physical resources needed, (for example, equipment, venue/premises, materials)
- financial aspects of the project, (budgeting, start-up costs, income, handling cash)
- staffing for the project
- administration systems, (bookings, record keeping, paper-based, electronic)
- project timescales
- legal aspects of the project (health and safety, security, insurance)

- contingency plans
- how the project will be reviewed and evaluated

Working as a team member

It has already been suggested in this introduction that in order to organise your event or business project you will have to work as part of a team.

You should start to consider the different people that you want to work with. For this scale and type of project, groups of four and five are big enough. Remember, you are required to work closely with the people you choose as team mates for a considerable period of time. As a team you will have to be able to trust and rely on each other that work is being done, and that deadlines are being met. You need to be confident in the team mates you choose. Are you?

You should by now have:

- Started to consider different people that you could work with on a project that is constrained by time and one that will require commitment and involves a great deal of work for all team members.

 ACTIVITY

Analysing your team mates

Use the following table to 'check-out' your team mates' strengths. Do the words describe your team mates? Answer with a simple yes or no.

ACCEPTABLE APPEARANCE	EXTROVERT	POLITE
ACTIVE	GOOD TIMEKEEPING	POSITIVE THINKER
AMBITIOUS	HARD-WORKING	PUNCTUAL
BELIEVABLE	IMAGINATIVE	QUICK-THINKER
CAPABLE	INDEPENDENT	RELIABLE
CONSCIENTIOUS	INTELLIGENT	RESPONSIBLE
COURTEOUS	KIND	SELF-DISCIPLINED
CREATIVE	LISTENER	SENSITIVE
DEDICATED	MOTIVATED	THOUGHTFUL
DETERMINED	ORGANISED	TRUSTWORTHY
EFFICIENT	PATIENT	UNDERSTANDING
ENTHUSIASTIC	PLANNER	WILLING

Are you still sure that you want to work with them?

Learning to work as part of a team involves working with and for each other, supporting others and taking responsibility. Some of these responsibilities will be financial in terms of handling and accounting for money. Can you trust your team members, are they responsible and trustworthy enough? Your team will establish a number of specific objectives, one of which might be to get your picture in your local newspaper, or to hand over a cheque for a well-deserving charity. During the course of your organisation you will make many friends (organisations and groups) who may wish to be associated with your event. Some of them may well sponsor your event or project and even wish to share in your success!

Can your team mates achieve such aims and objectives? Are they sufficiently hard working, enthusiastic and determined to achieve what they set out to do?

Think about these questions and the responsibilities associated with planning and organising and ask yourself the question: Are you in the right team?

Using the work done by others, to help you

In order to help you with your own planning and organisation, examples of the work done by other groups during their planning stages have been included in this text for you. You will consider the work done by them and will look at case studies of their events. Being able to refer to work done by another team may well be useful for you, to compare yourselves with, or to act as a source of inspiration for you.

The feasibility of an event or project

You should work through this next section step-by-step. It will give you the information you need to start thinking about the feasibility of a range of events or projects, from which you will choose just one to focus your planning efforts on. In terms of how feasible an event is, you will have to think about the planning and organising that is required from start to finish.

Aims and objectives of an event

It is important to be clear as to the aim and purpose of the event. What do you want it to achieve and why are you organising it? By being clear as to the objectives of the event, you have a base against which to plan activities and decide on strategies for evaluating the event. The key here is to be realistic and the SMART approach is well proven and well used within the industry in management and event organisation. Objectives

KEY TERMS

Aim: What one aims to do or achieve

Objective: Short-term realistic aims

should be:

- **S**pecific – accurately target groups and be accountable.
- **M**easurable in order that progress may be accurately monitored.
- **A**greed by all team members and minuted/recorded.
- **R**ealistic for all the team to believe in.
- **T**imed – targets need to be set and stuck to.

Event objectives

Groups or organisations involved in staging events usually have broad aims (either educational, charitable, competitive or social). Setting the objectives (short-term, realistic, attainable goals or aims) for an event in order to achieve the original aim is the starting point of the whole event planning process.

In organising the event, you do not have to restrict yourself to just one objective, but set yourself a range of targets or goals. Would you consider any of the objectives below as the basis for your event?

- To increase profitablity – you could raise money for a charitable purpose or as a fundraising activity. You will have to balance the books and be accountable for all financial transactions.
- To increase take-up (numbers) – increased numbers bring other rewards such as increased income, bigger crowds and a better atmosphere. How many people will you hope to attract?
- To increase customer interests – staging events can raise awareness of products and services. Some events attract sponsors, who see these events as excellent vehicles for promoting their products and services. Will you be able to attract a sponsor?
- To create a favourable image – to create repeat business and customer loyalty. Are you looking to create a favourable image for yourselves or on behalf of another organisation?
- To bring the team together – it is a well known fact that if people come together, have a good time and achieve some degree of success they usually feel better about themselves, their colleagues and hopefully, their organisation (feel good factor).

There are common goals in many events; the majority of localised events aim to raise money for an organisation, cause or charity. Events which are organised on behalf of an organisation or charity are often well supported and the event is able to attract increased publicity.

ACTIVITY

Looking at sponsored events

Look at the events below, why is it that they are so popular? Do any of them interest you?

- BBC Children in Need
- Blue Peter Appeals
- Sponsored Famine for World Aids Day
- Parachute Jump for Cancer Relief
- Cycle Across Africa for Famine Victims

Visit the relevant web sites for these organisations. What information can you find out?

Look at different foundations and charities, such as leukaemia or cancer research. Obtain a contact name and number. What information can they give you about organising fundraising events?

Many people have a charity that is special to them, perhaps their favourite grandparent died from cancer and they were moved and impressed by the care of the Macmillan Nurses. If you have an interest in a particular charity, then you should write explaining why and how you would like to raise money.

Most major charities will send you a fund-raiser's pack, which will help you to understand where the money goes. If you are happy with this then you will have to convince the other members of your team that it is indeed a worthy cause.

In order to stage some events a certain amount of money is required, so as well as raising money from your event you may well have to raise money to put your event on. This can be difficult and you may be tempted to quit before you even make a start! If you find yourself in this situation you should consider what you can realistically do to fund the event or project. You may have to seek expert advice and guidance.

The people who offer advice and guidance may well wish to be associated with your event and may even become sponsors. In raising money for a good cause you will also have the opportunity of raising your profile and perhaps that of your school or college. This is often called public relations, or PR for short. Major businesses have specialised PR departments who keep the media informed of their activities supplying them with mailshots and regular updates on progress.

KEY TERMS

Public relations: Building an image and raising the profile with all interested groups, of an event team that are dynamic, ethical and professional.

Mailshot: Telling all remotely interested parties of your plans, proposals, event or project with a well written and even better prepared e-mail, fax or letter, that they will find impossible to ignore!

Networking: Building up a database of useful specialist contacts in order to be able to get help with any situations that may arise.

ACTIVITY

Producing a mailshot

Find out the name of the editors of your local newspapers and when ready send them a mailshot. The purpose of the mailshot will be to publicise and advertise your event. Do not send it until you know specific details about the event.

This will be the first of many contacts you will make and is known in the industry as 'networking', you can make some quite influential friends in high places in this way.

In order to establish how feasible your event is you may need to conduct some form of market research. Most market research takes the form of a simple questionnaire to which a yes or no is answered to a selection of short questions.

When researching your own project you will have to consider the information you are trying to find out before designing the questions to be asked, for example, if you want to find out how accessible a certain venue is you will ask the subject in which area they live and how far they would be prepared to travel for a certain type of event. It can also be great fun and provide an opportunity to practise your communication skills on the general public.

Having agreed the aim, purpose and objectives it is important to identify the distinct characteristics that the event may have, for example:

- a start and finish time
- the date of the event
- the target group for the event

All of these will need to be considered when planning for the event.

You should by now:

- Be considering a range of events or projects that you and your team would like to organise. You should also be thinking about narrowing that choice down to one.

Meeting your customers' needs

In Chapter 5, Customer Service in Leisure and Recreation, you will have discovered that the customer is your priority, your main concern and the focus of an organisation's objectives, attentions and intentions. You will have come to realise that customers can sometimes be very demanding. Just because you are 'amateurs' and your event may not be of regional or national significance does not mean that for one minute your customers will not have high expectations of you, your organisation and the event or project itself. Never underestimate the power of your customers and good customer service as these may well determine the overall success of your event.

Marketing: This is the process of identifying customer needs, wants and wishes and satisfying them (profitably?)

Advertorial: This is a clever way of making your event or project into a news item. The report appears as editorial but advertises your event at the same time. It is also much cheaper than paying for advertising space!

During the feasibility stage of your planning and organisation you will have to consider who your customers or target group are, and make every effort to ensure the event is special for them.

Realise that with any event or project, things can and inevitably do go wrong. You will have to give much thought and consideration to what might go wrong, and what you can and will do if things do not go to plan.

Marketing the event or project

In Chapter 4, Marketing in Leisure and Recreation, you will have realised that marketing is something that we need and use all the time in our industry. This is never more true than when organising an event.

Major companies in the event and project management business use specialist companies whose sole job may well be the marketing of events. These organisations have to be good, and some are paid the major part of their fee according to the degree of success of the event.

Effective marketing will bring the public to your event but this will cost you time and money. Between 10–20% of your total budget is the average amount you should be thinking of committing to advertising.

There is a school of thought that states that the best marketing is done unobtrusively and very cheaply. One way of achieving this is through advertorial coverage, you will need to contact local newspapers and convince them of your intentions and causes. They may then offer to write about your event, thus offering support and some sort of sponsorship and may even wish to lend their name to your event. When other organisations see that you are gaining credibility this can have the effect of prompting a variety of sometimes unexpected offers!

Press releases are a good starting point so various media sources should be circulated including television, radio, newspapers and local journals. These will provide the first hint of your event and so it is very important to get these right.

You should know by now the name of your local newspaper editor. Local newspapers, in particular, are often keen to be associated with local colleges, people and events.

Figure 6.1 shows an example of a successful press release.

PRESS RELEASE PRESS RELEASE PRESS RELEASE PRESS RELEASE PRESS RELEASE

TO:

- WEST COUNTRY TV
- PIRATE FM
- PLYMOUTH SOUND
- BBC RADIO DEVON
- WESTERN MORNING NEWS
- CORNISH TIMES

Duchy College Fun Run supports local special needs outdoor activity centre

A group of five students from the college are organising a 'fun run' in order to raise public awareness of special needs participation in Outdoor Adventure Activities.

They are all studying an ADVANCED VOCATIONAL A LEVEL QUALIFICATION IN LEISURE AND RECREATION and, having recently visited the Churchtown Farm, are intending to raise money through this fun sponsored event to enable more 'special needs' activities to be run at the centre.

The run will be open to all and it is hoped that there will also be some special needs athletes taking part. The date is yet to be confirmed, but will be sometime in June.

If you know of any organisation or individuals that may wish to be associated with this event then you should contact the college ASAP.

FIGURE 6.1 *Duchy College Fun Run*

Identifying essential physical resources

Depending on the choice of event, these may be many, large and expensive or few, small and sometimes free. An important indoor resource will be the building and subsequent costs.

ACTIVITY

Identifying resources that you will require

Using one of the event or project examples that you have decided may be feasible, make a list of the resources that will be required.

During the summer months there are many events that are far more enjoyable in the open air, for instance an orienteering event or a schools soccer tournament, and being outdoors means that you can add a barbecue, open air disco, some fireworks or real rain! In the UK you can never rely on the weather, therefore you must have a contingency plan. Contingency plans will be discussed later in the Chapter.

Financial implications

All of you will be familiar with how important money is, whether your parents give you a weekly allowance or whether you have a part-time job. Being a student is hard enough, but when some of your friends have chosen to start full-time jobs while you study then suddenly money becomes very important.

One of the criteria you must meet is to show that you can handle money, and obviously keep careful and accurate records of your transactions. You will almost certainly have to spend some money before you can even think about making any. This is often the first hurdle where many events fail. One way of getting started is to share the cost with another interested party, for example, a sponsor or a charity. This will have the added advantage of providing credibility right from the outset for your event.

Charitable organisations are used to handling money and will offer all sorts of advice, especially if you are raising money for them. They may even produce income and expenditure and cash flow and running balance sheets to help you with your event. However, it is possible to raise some money in advance with, for example, advanced ticket sales, raffle tickets, entry fees and donations.

You should by now:

● If you are organising your event on behalf of, or in conjunction with, an organisation or charity have you made contact with them? Why not invite a representative in to meet your team.

Human resources and staffing

The leisure industry is people led and people orientated and for this reason you will have to look at what qualities make up a good event team. Individuals will already be known to you as effective leaders, good motivators, enthusiastic, practical and methodical, amongst other things.

Many individuals have become famous as the result of a great team effort, historically they are the ones credited with the glory, but in real terms, it is very difficult to achieve success without the support of a good

DISCUSSION

John Adair was an army captain who decided to look at styles of leadership and has successfully written books for the civilian world. One of his theories revolves around the issue of whether leaders are born or made.

Look up his work and then debate this theory. Conclude your discussions with an individual skills audit and list your personal strengths and weaknesses.

team. This is not to say that there will not be opportunities for individuals, a strong leader, an enthusiastic ideas person a flamboyant marketer or a studious financial spreadsheet wizard!

For the majority of your team members this will be the first time that they have been involved with and been required to take responsibility for something of this size. They will be accountable for all to see, but they will also, hopefully, be able to share in the success of the whole team's effort.

Event administration

This is an important area that, if conducted properly, will make your event run smoothly.

Throughout the planning and organisation stage you will almost always need to produce records of meetings, cash received and cash spent, timescales and deadlines. This will be easier to read and update if recorded in an appropriate manner. This may be by using a computer and a software programme, or by using a cheaper method of recording. It will probably be the responsibility of one or two team members and you must be prepared to put your trust in them and supply them with all the information they require. You must keep a back-up copy of all your administration procedures. This is not only good practice but a method of ensuring that, in the event of a technical hitch, you do not lose all of your work.

You will also be producing a business plan and it is here that you must initially attempt to balance your outgoings or expenditure against your projected income. You should be honest and realistic with your projections and aim to stay well within any targets.

Any additional income you generate will benefit your worthy cause, however why not promise yourselves some sort of reward if you should meet some great target! Maybe a celebratory party where you invite the media to witness you handing over your hard-earned cheque, and who knows, you may even get some major supermarket to sponsor the refreshments, after all won't they want to be associated with your local success and share in any good publicity.

ACTIVITY

Seeking financial advice

Visit a high street bank and pick up information on starting a small business. There will be much useful information available ranging from writing a business plan, to raising funds. There will also be a list of useful names and contacts.

Discuss with your tutor or teacher the possibility of inviting one of the bank's specialists to make a presentation to your group. Where appropriate, enquire about the possibility of sponsorship.

Timescales

Remember, 'there is no time like the present'.

Major events just like minor ones, take some serious planning, in fact the Olympic Games are now planned four to six years in advance. When you consider that many countries build completely new stadiums and villages for the Olympics, you will understand the need for careful planning and high-level sponsorship deals.

Your event will be planned over a relatively short period of time which has many implications for you. In terms of the concept of time your event will be characterised by:

● a specific start and finishing point

● a series of fixed deadlines, before, during and after the event

● schedules and actions needed to meet the priorities and deadlines.

As a team you will need to get started right away on making crucial decisions like setting dates and ensuring that they do not clash with other local events that may compete with you for the same customers. You will then need to make sure that you extensively publicise your date so that other organisations do not put their events on the same date as you. After all, you want as many people at your event as possible and sharing them with someone else is not a good idea.

You should by now:

● Have fixed a provisional date for your event(s).

A sense of urgency is never a bad thing, although this may go against some of your team mates' usual traits! You may well have to convince them of the importance of a number of issues such as punctuality, committment, attitude and general appearance.

Legal and regulatory requirements

It is important that as organisers you are aware of your legal duties from the outset, otherwise this may produce serious problems.

Obtaining permission to run an event can involve seeking approval from external organisations to cover legal requirements. If you are using an indoor facility you will have to adhere to the Occupiers Liability Acts which state that those responsible for staging special events have a 'common duty of care' to ensure that in all cases: 'the visitor, user or participant will be reasonably safe in all circumstances concerned with the event or its activities. Also, the organisers must ensure that there are no hidden dangers, that equipment is fit for its purpose, that there is adequate supervision and that routine safety checks are undertaken'. The

Act goes on to highlight the liability for injury, loss and damage, which may fall upon the event organisers where negligence or poor standards are found.

There are other legal duties that you will have to be aware of and you will need to be familiar with the various Health and Safety Regulations (outlined in Chapter 2). Just because you are representing your college or school does not mean that you do not have to give due consideration to the enforcement of these regulations.

Do not be discouraged, you will discover that there are many sources of information and many friends to be found in the world of health and safety, some are even government funded agencies, for example, The Health and Safety Executive (HSE) and the Environmental Health Department. Your college or school will have approached these organisations before for their own events and you may find that an interview with your Vice Principal or Bursar will provide you with most of the information and contacts you require.

ACTIVITY

Health and Safety

Arrange for a formal meeting with your school or college Health and Safety Officer.

Explain what you are thinking of doing and ask for his or her comments, support and help. Keep a record of this meeting to use as evidence in your assignment.

Contingency plans

Having back-up plans in place can take some of the worry out of the planning and organisation of an event. Unforeseen circumstances can be limited and situations that initially could prove horrendous can and should be anticipated. The aim of contingency planning is to anticipate unforeseen circumstances. For example, consider the college group who had organised a European ski trip, they did not anticipate that the company they had booked with would go into liquidation the day before departure.

Genuine emergencies may occur and should be dealt with by following the correct procedures as instructed by the emergency services. These should be discussed at your meeting with the health and safety representative of your school or college. The weather can spoil outdoor events, but if an indoor space can be reserved or some other solution or arrangement made, then this is preferable to cancelling the event altogether.

The following Case Study emphasises the need for thorough organisation and well-planned, workable contingencies.

CASE STUDY *Millennium Party on Plymouth Hoe*

Q How did the New Year's Eve celebrations go?

A As good as they could have done on the Hoe, all things considered. Because of the unprecedented weather, we were left in a very, very difficult position. The Thursday night should have been a dress rehearsal but because of the weather we weren't able to do anything. We didn't even have the surface of the screen up. We went home believing we might not be able to have a celebration the next day. It was a bit of a miracle that it went on.

Q This is Plymouth – you have to expect gales and rain in December. What about contingency plans?

A We had contingency plans but we ran out of them. We've done the Soundwaves (summer concerts) up there, so we know what it can be like and we prepared for the worst weather, but it was worse than anybody imagined. We had about one-and-a-half days without wind and rain out of two weeks of gales.

Q The problems started on Christmas Day when the stage was wrecked.

A The gales had been building up for days. We weighed the stage down with extra sandbags and cut the sheeting to allow the wind to get through and it survived a Force 10 on Christmas Eve. Early on Christmas Day the whole thing lifted up and moved 18 inches – four or five tonnes picked up and moved – and was wrecked. The wind then must have been off the scale. We worked all Christmas Day and then, on the Monday after Christmas, started from scratch clearing the wreckage.

Q What about the specific complaints about the things that went wrong – the countdown for example? Do you blame the BBC link on the screen for that?

A I don't blame the BBC. The BBC went to Big Ben but then cut to inside the Dome. We didn't get the full 20 seconds of "bongs", which threw us. We were running slightly late because one of the bands went on a little too long and there was a breakdown in communication between myself and the other 10 people who were co-ordinating things in Plymouth – that was due to the lack of a rehearsal the night before, a casualty of the bad weather.

Q And the piper? People were expecting him on Smeaton's Tower.

A Because the forecast was for Force 8 or 9 gales – which didn't materialise in the end – we had to make a last-minute decision to switch him to the stage for safety reasons.

Q And the fireworks?

A I did not have anything to do with that but again, because of the change in wind direction and the cloud cover, they could not fire the big shells – they could not be certain where the remains would land. They were only able to fire half the fireworks they planned to use.

Q The stage and screen were halfway down the grassy slope, a long way from the crowd. Many people could only see the top of the screen and couldn't hear the stage. Some people were unaware that there was even a compere.

A The plan was to have had people on the grass, giving a perfect view. But the grass was so boggy it wasn't safe for a crowd and had to be fenced off.

Q Why not have everything on the top on the tarmac?

A That was taken out of our hands once the BBC wanted to have the hardstanding clear for the sunset ceremony. I'm not complaining about that – the ceremony was broadcast around the world and gave Plymouth superb publicity – but that decision dictated where the stage and screen would have to be.

Q Some people complained that their view of the fireworks was blocked by the control platform.

A Again, the platform had to be in that position.

Q So all the problems were caused by the weather which made the ground too boggy and prevented a dress rehearsal? And the layout was mainly dictated by the BBC?

A Yes. We fulfilled a contract set by the city council and the Millennium Experience Company, the people who provided the vast amount of money for the evening and who had a lot of say. Had we had decent weather, people would have been completely bowled over. The fireworks alone would have been incredible.

Q Will you tell me how much Pyramid was paid for this?

A No! I will tell you that it wasn't enough. I reckon we all, the entire crew, earned our money twice over.

Q Would you do it again?

A Never. Ah, well – I suppose I would do it again. It's just you can't plan for weather like that. It's madness to try to do out-door events at this time of year. Even in the summer here it can be terrible.

Q What message would you give to everybody who has complained about the events on the Hoe?

A I am really, really pleased that they were able to go to the Hoe on the night. We came so close to having to scrap the whole thing. At 6pm the night before that's how it looked. In the end the majority of the night went very well.

Q What are you doing now and what will you do next?

A We're doing all the paperwork. There are people still working on the Hoe, taking stuff down. I'm busy writing thank you letters. People have worked incredibly hard on this. We've already started on planning for summer events for the National Trust and English Heritage. We're doing screens and a camera for Rick Stein's new restaurant in Padstow and lighting improvements for Plymouth Pannier Market.

Q Do you agree that we start counting at the number one, so decades end after 10, centuries end after 100 and millennia end after 1,000?

A Yes. I saw the astronomer Patrick Moore at Plymouth Pavilion a few years ago and I agreed with what he said – that the Millennium starts after midnight on December 31, 2000. The whole celebration was a worldwide farce – but that's the time the world chose to celebrate.

FIGURE 6.5 *Millennium party on Plymouth Hoe. Organiser answers critics after severe weather halts celebrations.*

DISCUSSION

Family pride

Ask your parents and grandparents about their feelings. Start with their earliest memories of the birth of their children, including you! Discuss with them how they felt when they took you to school for your first day, and in particular when they left you with this relatively strange person who was to be your first teacher. Ask them how they felt when they came to watch you at your primary school's sports day or attended your school's prize day when your name was called as one of the recipients.

Have you ever been a part of a team which included another family member, brother, sister, mum or dad? How did that feel to you? Could you never imagine being part of a team with another member of your family? Having the discussion above may enable you all to work better together.

After the event – review and evaluation

Performance can be measured in many ways and doubtless you will feel good about a successful event. Were you interviewed by your local newspaper or radio reporter? Did your picture appear in the local newspaper? How did you feel when you handed over the cheque to charity? What did your friends and family think about your success? Would you do it all over again?

It is important that you try to understand these feelings both as an event organiser and as a participant. For example, you will doubtless have experienced a feeling of elation when holding on to a one–nil lead for thirty-five minutes until the final whistle blows in an important hockey game, or leading the field in a cross-country event from start to finish, never quite knowing when you might be overtaken, until you cross the finishing line as the winner. You may have felt happy, sad, excited, tearful, or emotional, among other things. These are personal feelings and are often hard to define and describe.

 ACTIVITY

Propose options and select a feasible event.

As part of the requirements of this Unit you have to conduct a feasibility study.

To identify an event that you wish to plan, organise and then run you will have to consider at least two options. You may have a preferred event but you should consider other options in case your original choice is deemed unrealistic by others.

You will have to present the following information to gauge the viability of staging each event in terms of:

- why is the event being proposed, list its aims and objectives
- dates and contingency dates

- assets (resources – human, physical, financial)
- support (help in terms of advice, guidance)
- cost (in terms of money, effort and time)
- problems that could occur at any time
- will the effort reflect the aims of the event?

You must believe in this event, and be prepared to follow it through to fruition – it is not merely a paper exercise. You will be assessed on the accuracy of your research and the real possibilities of success for your event or project.

You should by now:

- Have completed your feasibility study and decided on one event to organise.

ACTIVITY

Completing your business plan

As part of the requirements of this Unit you have to complete a business plan for your chosen event.

On the basis of the findings of your feasibility study you and your team should have decided on an event or project that you want to stage.

In order to complete a business plan you will have to:
- explain the distinctive characteristics of your chosen event
- explain the objectives of your event; what is its purpose?
- give/make realistic estimates of the resources required to run your event, including costs and benefits
- explain any constraints or problems that could/may affect your event
- justify your event with facts and figures
- be prepared to put your event forward as a feasible option at a formal meeting
- research a similar event and produce/include promotional material from this similar event

This activity will form the basis of your knowledge required to plan and run your event, which will be the next stage of this Unit.

Team: A group of people organised for a particular purpose.

Teamwork

This Unit is based on your team's ability to organise a successful event. You should start by defining the meaning of the two key words, that is, 'successful' and 'event'. Without teamwork your event or project will inevitably fail. You should look carefully at the strengths and weaknesses of your team members. Look critically at your proposed projects, before deciding as a team on one.

You should by now:

- Have decided on the team members.
- Have debated your choice of event or project, decided on the most viable or feasible and be ready to hold your first planning meeting for your chosen project.

The following piece is a case study of a group coming together and starting the planning process in order to stage a successful event. You might find it useful to refer to this when planning and running your first meeting.

CASE STUDY *'A Fun Run for charity'*

The group's first task is to organise and conduct a planning meeting.

The following is a checklist of items that need to be addressed:

- appoint a chairperson for the meeting
- set objectives for the meeting
- set the date and time of the meeting
- set the agenda
- choose a suitable venue
- appoint somebody to take the minutes
- let everybody know as soon as possible about the meeting
- send an agenda detailing date, time, venue, a list of attendees and, of course, your agenda items.

The group then staged their meeting, this is a copy of their agenda:

MEETING OF THE 'FUN RUN' COMMITTEE

Date: Monday 25 September, 2000

Time: 10.30–11.30 a.m.

Venue: Room P8

To: Phillip, Grace, Timothy, John, Mark and Kylie

Chairperson: Stewart

AGENDA

1. This is our first planning meeting so we need to get some **ideas** down in writing to develop for next time. Please bring any information you feel may be relevant.
2. Set our aims and objectives for the event.
3. List resources needed.

- human
- financial
- equipment and facilities

4. Consider the possibility of supporting a local charity.

5. List possible sponsors.

6. Allocate responsibilities for all of the above.

7. Date of next meeting.

The group then produced a copy of the minutes of the meeting:

MINUTES

Date: Monday 25 September, 2000

Time: 10.30–11.30 a.m.

Venue: Room P8

Present: Timothy, Grace, John, Mark

Apologies: Kylie

Chairperson: Stewart

Item 1 – Team has decided to look at the feasibility of planning, organising and running a **Fun Run**. It is not a new idea, we have wanted to do something like this for a while.

The Chairperson brought details of a fun run he took part in in Plymouth, including a poster, newspaper article and an application form.

Item 2 – Aims and objectives were discussed but **Grace** felt that the team should look at raising money for a local charity. It was decided to make the event open to any and everybody and may be try to include other subsidiary activities. Some other organisations might like to get involved in some way.

Item 3 – Resources

Human: **Tim** was very positive about us as a group being capable of running the event, and he has helped to organise similar things through his Scout Troop. **Mark** was nervous and felt that we may need the tutor's help for much of the organisation. **Stewart** (chair) pointed out that this was what teamwork was all about and that we would all work together, calling on external experts as and when necessary.

Financial: **John** pointed out that we would need to find some money initially to pay for posters and other forms of advertising. **Grace** mentioned that her friend's mum works on the local newspaper and so we might be able to get some editorial coverage. Grace also volunteered to produce a 'mock-up' poster for our next meeting.

Equipment and facilities: **Stewart**, (chair) said that he would speak to the college Principal about using the campus and grounds as the starting and finishing point for the run, **John** will accompany him. They will report back to us at our next meeting. **Mark** said that he would ask **Kylie** to help him look at a possible route.

Item 4 – A Local Charity: The team agreed that we should be supporting 'The Churchtown Farm Outdoor Education Centre', after our visit there for our Outdoor Adventure Activities module when we had a talk from their director on their work with special needs clients. We will always remember the look of satisfaction on the young people's faces when they completed what, for us, were relatively simple tasks, like balancing on the planks and barrels. All of us were agreed on this worthy cause.

Tim offered to write to the director and ask him if this was acceptable, **Stewart** suggested he also ask him if he would be interested in being our official starter? **Grace** asked if special needs competitors were to be encouraged. It was suggested that **Tim** also ask the Centre director about this.

Item 5 – Sponsors: It was felt that there would be quite a lot of local businesses interested in supporting our event and that we should send letters as soon as possible. **Mark** will draft one out for our next meeting.

It was agreed that we would start with the big companies first and check if any already had links with the Centre and/or special needs groups. **Stewart and John** will produce a list for our next meeting of possible sponsors.

Item 6 – To confirm responsibilities and action plan for our next meeting

Grace to speak to her friend's mum about advertising and produce a mock-up of a poster.

Stewart and John will arrange a meeting with the Principal and discuss the use of the campus (and ask for any other advice).

Tim will write to the Director of Churchtown Farm asking if they would be prepared to be our charity for the event. He will also ask if the Director would like to officially start the race and whether he feels that we could have special needs runners taking part as well.

Mark will inform **Kylie** that they are going to plan the route and it was felt that between 2 and 4 kilometres was about the right distance.

All of the above tasks are to be reported on at our next meeting.

Item 7 – Date of next meeting

Monday 9th October (same time and place)

The Chairperson thanked everyone for attending. The meeting closed at 11.35 a.m.

You should by now:

- Have conducted your first planning meeting.
- You should already have made the following key decisions, which should have been confirmed at the planning meeting:
  - What the event is
  - When
  - Where
  - Who in terms of roles and responsibilities
  - Who in terms of target groups
  - Identification of required resources
- You should have written up and circulated a copy of the Minutes of your first meeting.
- You should also have started to think about allocating roles and responsibilities.

Allocating roles and responsibilities

During this next part of the Unit you will have the opportunity to look at some of the theory behind teamwork, and in particular, individual team roles. R Meredith Belbin defined teamwork as:

❝A group of people supporting each other in their strengths, (e.g. building on suggestions) helping members with problems and improving communications between members, and promoting a team spirit.❞

You will quickly understand the expression that, 'a chain is only as strong as its weakest link'. So be warned, and don't let it be you!

A successful team is the ideal starting point for any project or event. You will have been a member of many different types of teams during your life. For example, being in a school sports team, being in a concert, play or other production and simply being part of your own family.

 **ACTIVITY**

Teams and you

Make a list of all the teams you have been involved with. List the roles that you had within those teams. Did you have a preferred role or one you were most successful in?

What qualities have enabled you to take on these roles? Typical qualities identified as being valuable for a team member include good organiser, natural leader, enthusiastic approach, good listener, total commitment and never wanting to give up.

Can you list other qualities? Why are there certain undesirable qualities for a team member?

You will find that there are many different aspects to teamwork and that once you start considering them, the whole nature of teams and how they function starts to make sense. You will find that you are best suited to some types of or particular roles and that you are most comfortable when operating within these roles and responsibilities.

The purpose of your team

Always remember that a group of individuals who are not prepared to work together as a team are only fooling themselves. They will, however, be able to blame each other when their event inevitably fails! How do you deal with failure?

A team is a group of people that can work together in an effective and efficient way to complete a given task. When you are working together you should feel valued, respected included and confident. For example, when you make a point or raise an issue the rest of your team should show their respect by listening to you. Remember, this has to be the case for all of your team members. In the words of Barry Neil Kaufman:

❝A loud voice cannot compete with a clear voice, even if it's a whisper.❞

If you do not feel included as part of the team then you should arrange a meeting with the others and discuss your role. It would be a good idea to include your teacher or tutor at this stage. It may be quite simply that you have been given the wrong role, chosen the wrong role, or perhaps have realised that the role you took on was not quite what you were expecting.

Either way, once you have explained your predicament then the rest of the team should rally round to assess and change the situation accordingly. For example, if you found it difficult talking to your local newspaper reporter then you should ask another team member to help you, or even take over your role.

Team structures

R Meredith Belbin grouped people according to their personality types. Think about the people in your team and try to guess which type they will be.

You will look at Belbin's Team Types Model. These questions will together form an exercise which will give you a good indication of your suitability for certain specific roles within the team.

Belbin's Theory

R M Belbin made a long study of teams and teamwork. He concluded that a fully effective group or team requires the following roles:

Coordinator

The coordinator is the person who coordinates the team's efforts towards the final objectives. The coordinator should question and listen rather than dictate. This person requires good judgement and must be respected for this by the whole team.

Shaper

The shaper is the person who is enthusiastic and has passion for the task. This person shapes the group's efforts, making the whole thing feasible. The shaper is often outgoing and dominant, and can be impatient.

Plant

The plant comes up with original ideas, and is often the most intelligent and imaginative member of the team, however, this person can miss out on detail and can be sensitive to criticism.

Monitor-Evaluator

The monitor-evaluator is also intelligent but in a different way. This person carefully analyses things and is often not interested in the creative side of things. He or she can carefully examine ideas and proposals and come up with arguments for and against. This person may be a loner choosing to be left out, but with a superior attitude.

Resource-Investigator

This person is often a popular and relaxed member of the team. They like meeting people and making contacts and so bringing new ideas and developments to the team. They will often encourage others, but not always have the personal drive to follow things through.

Implementer

This person is the practical organiser who can turn decisions and ideas into a workable action plan. The implementer will enjoy drawing up plans, rotas, flow charts and the like. This person doesn't give up easily and sees little value in creative ideas.

Team-Worker

The team-worker holds the team together by supporting others when the going gets tough. He or she is not competitive but is a good listener and communicator and tries to keep the whole team focused and on course.

Finisher

The team needs the finisher to ensure that deadlines are met, details are checked and promises kept. This person isn't always popular with other team members as he or she is continually nagging and pushing in an attempt to complete the task.

There is a real case for an expert in some teams and you may find that you include your teacher or tutor in your team to fulfil this role. They may have specialist information, but will not be a permanent member of your team, and as such, should not be involved in its decision making.

ACTIVITY

Personality types and teamwork

In order to assess your personality type and so allocate you to a role or position within your team, it would be useful for all of your team to complete the following test. This will give the opportunity to find out where you all fit into Belbin's team model.

You will need between 20 and 30 minutes of full concentration to complete the following exercise effectively.

INSTRUCTIONS

Produce tables similar to the ones below. For each section of the exercise, tick in the far left-hand column the one, two or three sentences that most apply to you.

Then in the column on the right, allocate 10 points across those sentences you have ticked which will indicate to what extent each applies to you. For example, you might feel that there are only two sentences that apply to you; one of which, you feel, sums you up well while the other only applies some of the time. In this case you could give your first choice seven points and the remaining three points to your second choice. In some cases you might decide that there are two sentences which apply to you equally – if this is the case award five points to each.

You must allocate all ten points in each section.

SECTION A: *When involved in a project with other people:*		
TICK		**POINTS**
	1. I can be relied upon to see that work that needs to be done is organised	
	2. I notice when other people make mistakes, or forget things	
	3. I react strongly when meetings look like going off the point and away from the main objectives	
	4. I come up with original suggestions and ideas	
	5. I analyse other people's ideas, and can see the relevant strengths and weaknesses	
	6. I am keen to find out about the latest ideas and developments	
	7. I am good at organising other people	
	8. I am always ready to support good suggestions and help to resolve problems	

SECTION B: In seeking satisfaction through my work:		
TICK		**POINTS**
	1. I like to have a strong influence on decision making	
	2. I really enjoy work that requires a lot of concentration and attention	
	3. I am willing to help other team members with their problems	
	4. I enjoy looking at all the alternatives available	
	5. I tend to have a creative approach to solving problems	
	6. I enjoy listening to and bringing together different points of view	
	7. I am happier working in a proven way than experimenting with new ideas	
	8. I particularly enjoy listening to different views and trying different techniques	

SECTION C: When the team is trying to solve a particularly tricky problem:		
TICK		**POINTS**
	1. I look out for areas where difficulties may arise	
	2. I look at the whole project and see where this particular problem fits in with the overall action plan	
	3. I like to go through all the options before making up my mind	
	4. I can listen to and bring together other people's skills and talents	
	5. I stick to my steady approach, and don't really feel the pressure	
	6. I often come up with a new idea to solve a long-term problem	
	7. I am ready to make my personal views known in a forceful way if necessary	
	8. I am ready to help whenever I can	

SECTION D: *In carrying out my day-to-day work:*		
TICK		**POINTS**
	1. I am happiest when my tasks and objectives are quite clear	
	2. I am happy to emphasise my own point of view in meetings and make my views and ideas known	
	3. I can work with anybody, as long as they have got something worthwhile to contribute and say	
	4. I make a point of following up interesting ideas and people	
	5. I can usually find the argument to prove when unworkable proposals are not worth pursuing	
	6. I can see how things fit together when other people often can't	
	7. I get real satisfaction from being busy	
	8. I have a quiet interest in getting to know people better	

SECTION E: *If I am suddenly given a difficult task with limited time and unfamiliar people:*		
TICK		**POINTS**
	1. I would prefer to work on my own as I find myself frustrated in these situations	
	2. I find my personal skills with others can have the effect of the whole team reaching agreement	
	3. I find that my judgement isn't affected by my feelings and I just get on with the task accepting the challenge	
	4. I try to build up an effective team structure within the given constraints	
	5. I can work with most people regardless of their personal qualities and views	
	6. I don't mind being a little unpopular if it means that I get my views across to the rest of the team	
	7. I can usually find someone with specialist knowledge and skills to help out	
	8. I seem to develop a natural sense of urgency	

SECTION F: *When suddenly asked to consider a new project:*		
TICK		**POINTS**
	1. I immediately start to look around for possible ideas	
	2. Before I start I feel I must finish my current work or project	
	3. I carefully analyse the project in a careful way	
	4. If necessary I can assert myself to get other people involved	
	5. I can give a personal, and often different, view of most projects	
	6. I am happy to take the lead, if that is what is required	
	7. I can work well with the rest of my team and am happy to work on any of their ideas	
	8. I need to know clearly the aims and objectives of a project if I am to give it 100% effort	

SECTION G: *In contributing to group projects in general:*		
TICK		**POINTS**
	1. I feel happy to produce an action plan once I have been given an overview of the project	
	2. I may not make the fastest decisions but I feel they are worth waiting for	
	3. I use a lot of personal contacts and friends to get the project completed	
	4. I have an eye for getting the details just right	
	5. I try to make my mark in group meetings and am never short of something to say	
	6. I can see how new ideas can develop new relationships in building a successful team	
	7. I see both sides of a problem and then try to take a decision that is acceptable to all	
	8. I get on well with others and work hard for the benefit of the whole team	

When you have completed each of the seven sections you should transfer your scores to this blank matrix. For example, if in section A you ticked statements 3 and 6, and gave six points to statement 3 and four points to statement 4 then you should put a 6 on the dotted line next to the 3 statement and put a 4 next to the 6 statement, see the example below in italics.

Ensure your column totals equal 70 then you will know you answered all the sections.

TEAM TYPE-> SECTION	CO	SH	PL	ME	RI	IM	TW	F
A	7...	3.(6)	4...	5...	6.(4)	1...	8...	2...
B	6...	1...	5...	4...	8...	7...	3...	2...
C	4...	7...	6...	3...	2...	5...	8...	1...
D	3...	2...	6...	5...	4...	1...	8...	7...
E	5...	6...	1...	3...	7...	4...	2...	8...
F	4...	6...	5...	3...	1...	8...	7...	2...
G	7...	5...	6...	2...	3...	1...	8...	4...
TOTALS								

(Sum of columns must equal 70)

Analysing your statistics

So just how useful a person are you to have in a team? Are you surprised at your findings and are you happy to take on this role within your event or project team?

Table 6.1 summarises the features, qualities and weaknesses of the individual team roles.

Roles and responsibilities

There will often be a scramble for key positions and group members will try to assert their authority on roles *they* feel suited for. In deciding on roles, you might like to ask your tutor or teacher to give advice and guidance. One possibility might be that team members could apply for a particular role expressing their suitability and previous experience.

As you can see from the *Team Forming Model* below, there are distinct stages to building a successful team. Initially it is important to remember that team roles should come about as part of a democratic decision, this in fact is the first decision to be made by any team.

TYPE	TYPICAL FEATURES	POSITIVE QUALITIES	ALLOWABLE WEAKNESSES
COORDINATOR	Calm, self-controlled and self-confident	Welcomes all positive contributions and considers them on their merits. Feels strongly about meeting objectives	No major weaknesses
SHAPER	Enthusiastic, outgoing and dynamic	Lots of drive and a readiness to 'have a go'	Can be impatient and irritable
PLANT	An individual, often serious and sometimes a little different	Genius, imagination and a good knowledge	'Up in the clouds', doesn't think about practicalities
MONITOR EVALUATOR	Careful, unemotional and sometimes bland	Judgement, discretion and occasional stubbornness	Lacks personal inspiration or the ability to motivate others
RESOURCE INVESTIGATOR	Extrovert, enthusiastic, a good communicator	Good with people (networking) An ability to respond to a challenge	Loses interest once the initial fascination has passed
IMPLEMENTER	Predictable, well-meaning	Practical commonsense, hard working, has good self-discipline	Can be very inflexible and hard to convince of new ideas
TEAM WORKER	Team player, sensitive and patient	Good for team spirit, ability to respond to people and situations	Indecisiveness when put under pressure
FINISHER	Always prepared, checks everything, very conscientious	A perfectionist, right to the end	A tendency to worry about nothing. Sometimes finds it hard to actually trust others

TABLE 6.1 *Features, qualities and weaknesses of individual team roles*

When you start at a new college or school you will find that there are people that you like and wish to be associated with and they may become your friends. Initially you will go through a *forming* stage where you all agree to work together in the class situation.

As your confidence develops you will start to speak out and make your own views known, some of your class will associate with your ideas and you will share ideas within these interest groups. This is known as the *storming* stage.

Other groups within the larger class will agree in part or even disagree with your views, this is healthy and you should remain open-minded, fair and polite when debating various issues. You will reach a mutually agreeable position from which you can work together and still appreciate each other's differences. This is a sure sign of maturity and is known as *norming*.

When you have reached this stage you will be ready to take on most challenges and work to the best of your ability in the *performing* stage.

TEAM FORMING MODEL

Forming	The team accepts its challenge or purpose and agrees to work together in principle
Storming	Individuals state their interests and specific qualities, their own goals and those they desire for the team
Norming	An agreement is reached and standards and goals are realistically accepted for all concerned
Performing	If all has gone according to plan, then the end result will be a successful event led by an effective team
Mourning	With success may come great friendships and a sense of real togetherness. Some individuals may find the reality of 'the final curtain' quite traumatic! How do you say 'goodbye'

TABLE 6.2 *Team forming model*

As a team member, you are likely to find that a large proportion of problems are caused by other team members taking on roles to which they are not naturally suited, or because certain personalities in your team seem to clash.

Team building

In the words of William Feather:

'We always admire the other person more after we have tried to do their job.'

Having completed Belbin's test you should now have a better idea of the sort of role that you are best suited for. Is it as a specialist, completer, implementer, teamworker, monitor evaluator, shaper, coordinator, resource investigator or plant? If your interests and skills have been identified as being in a particular area and you are happy taking on that role then you should identify that role and agree to take on the responsibilities associated with it.

You should by now have:

- Started to allocate roles and responsibilities based on individual abilities, requests and perhaps based on the findings of Belbin's test.

Resources

There are three major resource areas, often referred to as human, financial and physical, that is:

- Human: you, and your team members without doubt the most important resource of all
- Financial: money, finance, funding and sponsorship
- Physical: buildings, venues, equipment, maintenance, repairing, adapting and sourcing

How and where each of these resources fits into your event/project will affect your role, for example, if you have been identified as being good with numbers and computers then you may well choose to handle the financial management of your event. One advantage of this role is that there are usually not too many takers!

You should by now:

- Have compiled a list of the resources that you will need in order to plan, organise, stage and run your project.

One of the aims for your team will undoubtedly be to organise and manage your allocated and acquired resources, for example, if you have chosen to be responsible for financial resources then you must make sure you manage them wisely and do not over spend! You will also need to be financially accountable for every penny.

You will see from the statements above that there may be some overlap between the three areas and as a result, there may well be some conflict in terms of the management of these resource areas. As part of your role and the responsibilities within it, you will be expected to be working on your chosen event to an agreed standard and by a specified deadline. You may well have a limited budget and this may make the difference between completing the task on time or not.

You will be dealing with your team and most of its members, but also depending on outsiders, who may not be as reliable as you hope, for example, a newspaper reporter who may rearrange a meeting with you or even cancel it indefinitely.

Your team must have faith in its abilities to complete the task they have set themselves. In the words of Michael Korda:

❝In order to succeed we must first believe that we can.❞

Whether you like it or not, you will have to take on some level of responsibility and here you may surprise yourself, your friends and even your family. During your event planning stage you will be requested, or may offer to take on various commitments and you will be expected to fulfil them.

For example, if you have offered to arrange a meeting with a local newspaper reporter or get some prices for supplying drinks for an event then you must do all you can to complete your task. Records of meetings, (or minutes) will be kept and you will become accountable for your actions. You will probably discover how annoying it is to be let down by others and even end up doing someone else's work if it is holding you up. Remember this when you contemplate procrastination.

Other factors that influence team work

There are a number of factors that may well affect a team's ability to do work. In some instances they will enhance the unity of the group and foster a positive working environment. For example, the financial backing or support of an external agency will promote team spirit.

However, there are some factors that will have a detrimental effect on the group's work rate and might well cause instability within the group, and causing planning and progress to be severely hampered. These factors are discussed in more detail below.

Leadership

DISCUSSION

Are leaders born or are they made?

John Adair had a distinguished military career and after observing the army's leadership development process published his thoughts and ideas for general management in the modern world of work. His findings have been accepted by many great institutions, he believes that leadership is a learned skill, rather than a natural phenomenon.

Do you agree with this, or do you have a view on natural leaders?

There will undoubtedly be members of your group who will want to lead and 'be in charge'; they may be sports team captains, prefects or simply loud individuals. Many experts have written about leadership and it is now accepted that leadership skills can most certainly be learnt. There is great responsibility involved in being a leader and you should think carefully before offering. In fact, if you have to offer, then perhaps you are not the right choice.

There are many definitions of leadership. Leadership is the relationship through which one person influences the behavior of other people. Leadership is often associated with motivation, personalities, communication and delegation. It is also often associated with the willingness and enthusiasm of the other team members.

Leadership can be measured in terms of how inspired the team feels. If you do not feel inspired then your event or project is going to suffer.

If you want to have a go at leading your group, fronting your event, or simply taking charge of a particular aspect, then you should not be put off by the fact that you have not done anything like this before. It will not be easy, but you may find some of John Adair's writings inspire you and maybe give you the confidence to change things. Have a look at his work in the *Action Centred Leader* by John Adair published by the Industrial Society.

Personality clashes

You may encounter some hostility to your attempts at leadership. If there are members of your group that have been used to having their own way then they may need convincing of your skills, motives and intentions. Personality clashes can seriously affect the overall team performance and so need to be dealt with as early as possible. A good team will spot this sort of problem early on and deal with it in a mature and sensible way.

Communication

Possibly the single most significant factor in most event failures is the breakdown in group communication. Again, you should consider the result of your actions if you should fail to communicate with the rest of your group, always allowing for a variety of eventualities.

What if you are sick or injured and cannot attend your group's planning meetings, can your notes and role be covered by someone else, does anybody else know the name of the local newspaper reporter that you have been dealing with? If you are keeping up-to-the-minute notes of your work, and this is minuted in the meetings, then there should be no problems. You will find that when you return to your group they will not only be grateful to you, but will also not mind you simply slotting back into your old role.

The working environment

In terms of staging an event you should realise that you are responsible for the health, safety and security of your customers. You will have to consider the working environment in which the event is to be staged. You may have to discuss security issues with your local police and fire service representatives and they will be looking for a responsible and mature approach if they are going to trust you with the public's safety.

For example, if you are planning to organise an indoor sporting event like a three-on-three basketball tournament, and you have 40 teams entered, then you will be expecting a large number of spectators. Your local sports hall will have a maximum limit on numbers and you should discuss this with the manager. He will advise you on health and safety legislation and may recommend that the local fire officer make an inspection to agree on a maximum number. He may also advise you about the security of personal belongings.

You should consider yourself as an employee of your team and as such, be proud to be associated with your event. You should agree a dress code for the event, but also if you are to appear in any photographs prior to the event then you should be prepared to look professional and well organised. Maybe you could agree on some kind of corporate image.

ACTIVITY

Team Identity

It is important to have a team identity, discus within your group the reasons for this.

A sponsor may wish to be seen to be supporting your event, what better way than by having their name on your tee-shirts? If that sponsor is a printer or tee-shirt manufacturer, or both, then you might just be lucky!

As a group consider a tee-shirt design for your event.

Could these tee-shirts be sold as promotional items? A word of warning – before placing an order collect money in advance.

Access to resources

You will not have access to the resources of a large organisation specialising in major events, so do accept that, to be realistic may seem rather defeatist. If you are comparing yourselves to a professionally organised event, such as a large music concert or a sporting event, then you could be somewhat disappointed.

Nowadays, so many people have the opportunity to attend large, well organised events that they pay little or no attention or fail to acknowledge just how much effort goes into the organisation of even a small event or project like yours. The acquisition of resources will be a challenge in itself and with a limited budget, you will have to beg and borrow for all you are worth.

ACTIVITY

Sponsorship challenge, how persuasive can you be?

Make a list of possible sponsors for your event.

List your needs and look at your sponsor's list and identify what you think they can all afford to donate. Make realistic requests.

For example, if you are going to need to buy refreshments and food for your event then ask a local supplier for sponsorship. They may offer to give goods at cost price in order to be associated with your event/charity or just to be involved with the local community. Some sponsors may even approach you, as they may not want to be overlooked or left out in favour of the opposition. You might mention this to selected prospective sponsors and indicate that an early reply to your letter will ensure that they are associated with your event and that they will not be overlooked.

In obtaining what you want and need in order to resource the event you will require the charm of a salesman, the patience of a saint, the hands of an artist, the negotiating skills of a highjacker and the business sense of Richard Branson.

In the words of Jim Goodwin:

❛The impossible is often the untried.❜

Event planning checklist

You should by now:

- Have compiled a list of things that you and your team need to do in order that the project or event will happen.

The success of your event or project depends on the effectiveness of your team and their ability to complete the many tasks involved in putting on the event. Knowing what those tasks are, when they need to be completed, and which team member has responsibility for the management of each task is a crucial feature of teamwork. You may wish to make reference to Table 6.2, below, to help you compile your own list of things to do. This list has been adapted from George Torkildsen's *Guide to Leisure Management*.

EVENT PLANNING CHECKLIST

FACILITIES FOR EVENTS		TICK	INITIAL BY WHOM	DATE BY WHEN
1	Main area, sports hall, arena, playing field/pitch, etc.			
2	Alternative areas, contingency plan, etc.			
3	Car parks			
4	Changing rooms			
5	Disabled access			
6	First aid points			
7	Toilet facilities			
8	Power points			
9	Safety provision, fire extinguishers, throw lines, smoke alarms, etc.			
10	Seating			
11	Signposting			
12	Special restrictions, overhead cables, etc.			
13	Warm-up/practise area for competitors			
STAFFING		**TICK**	**INITIAL BY WHOM**	**DATE BY WHEN**
14	Announcer			
15	Barman			
16	Car park attendants			
17	Caterers			

STAFFING		TICK	INITIAL BY WHOM	DATE BY WHEN
18	Cleaners			
19	Medical cover, e.g. St Johns			
20	Interpretation officers			
21	Maintenance staff			
22	Responsible for guests			
23	Lifeguards			
24	Security guards			
25	Technicians			
26	Volunteer helpers			
ADMINISTRATION AND FINANCE		TICK	INITIAL BY WHOM	DATE BY WHEN
27	Accounting			
28	Admissions			
29	Fund raising			
30	Donations			
31	Insurance cover			
32	Invitations			
33	Licensing			
34	Postage and printing			
35	Programmes, printing and sales			
36	Sales			
37	Signs			
38	Tickets/invites			
EQUIPMENT		TICK	INITIAL BY WHOM	DATE BY WHEN
39	Chairs and tables			
40	Communications, radios, etc			
41	Decorations, flowers, etc			
42	Disco			
43	Display boards			
44	Barriers			
45	Lighting			

EQUIPMENT		TICK	INITIAL BY WHOM	DATE BY WHEN
46	Litter bins			
47	Marquees and tents			
48	Sound system, PA and music, etc			
49	Scoreboards			
50	Staging			
51	Timing equipment			
52	Uniforms			
PRESENTATION AND MEDIA		**TICK**	**INITIAL BY WHOM**	**DATE BY WHEN**
53	Advertising and artwork			
54	Badges and banners, (tee-shirts)			
55	Announcer			
56	Video and photography			
57	Corporate logo			
58	Marketing, press releases			
59	Newsletter, posters leaflets			
60	Presentation of awards, medals, cups and engraving			
61	Publicity and public relations			
62	Radio and television			
63	VIPs			
SUPPORT SERVICES		**TICK**	**INITIAL BY WHOM**	**DATE BY WHEN**
64	Accommodation			
65	Bar and catering			
66	Childminding/crèche			
67	Disabled support services			
68	Emergency support, fire, police, ambulance			
69	Health and safety			
70	Lost property and lost children			
71	Photocopier			
72	Security of people and property			
73	Tourist information, local maps, etc.			

TABLE 6.2 *Example planning checklist*

ACTIVITY

Planning for your event or project

In order to plan for your event you will need to compile your own planning checklist.

The items on your checklist should be specific to your event; maybe you could identify why they are needed.

Do not forget to identify whose responsibility each task is and, where possible, identify deadlines for the completion of each task.

You should complete your checklist as soon as possible.

Carrying out the project

You should by now have:

- Allocated roles and responsibilities, be hitting targets and deadlines and actively working towards the day of the event and the event itself.

Having investigated the feasibility of your chosen project or event and decided upon how realistic and viable it is to manage and run, you are now ready to carry out the project. It is a good idea at this stage, to consider a 'dress rehearsal'. You can still make some major changes at this stage and if advice from your tutors or teachers, friends or family is acceptable, then don't be afraid to rethink a few things!

In planning, organising and staging your event you should consider the assessment evidence that the Unit specifications suggest that you are required to produce.

ACTIVITY

Planning an event as a team

As part of the requirements of this Unit you have to plan, organise and run an event.

The first stage of your assessment required you to conduct a feasibility study to assess the viability of a range of events or business projects. Having decided to focus on one of these choices you were asked to produce a business plan. You should have formed a small team, (between 3 and 6) to develop such a proposal, and take it forward to fruition.

Remember that any team is only as strong, or successful, as its weakest individual. You will be assessed on your total planning, contingency planning, financial planning and final success of the event.

Remember that you and your team will be directly responsible for your event's success. However, do aim high, raise your profile and that of the college, possibly through the involvement of a major charity or cause that is special to you.

You will need to complete all of the following tasks.

1 Set targets for your event or project.

2 Identify key factors, for example, promotion, resources, providers of services, health and safety, etc. and incorporate them into your event or project plan.

3 Devise with your team, a planning flow chart and use it while preparing the event or project. Date key meetings, deadlines and targets.

4 Draw up a contingency plan with your team, allowing for emergencies and foreseeable non-emergency situations.

5 You should agree and allocate roles, listing responsibilities, lines of authority and any other relevant functions.

6 You must contribute to producing a Team Plan for your event which must show targets, key factors, planning flow charts, resources, contingency plans, role allocations, briefings, evaluation process, etc.

This assignment will involve you actually running your own event where you will be assessed on your participation in the event. Therefore, careful and thorough planning is absolutely essential.

Completing the task

This is the most dynamic part of your project, it is the doing part, and potentially the most interesting part. Undoubtedly it will present you with much hard work and place demands on your time, energy, spirit, determination and enthusiasm. Do not succumb to this pressure otherwise you and your team will be beset by self-doubt and negative energy.

A successful event or project is often characterised by a sense of routine calmness where everything appears well rehearsed and running like clockwork. This is rarely the case with first attempts! In the words of Beverly Sills:

❛You may be disappointed if you fail, but you are doomed if you don't try.❜

When thinking about your planning, remember the seven P's

- **P**rior
- **P**lanning and
- **P**reparation
- **P**revent
- **P**retty
- **P**oor
- **P**erformance

All the work, questioning, talking and decision making that you have done during the planning stage is now coming to fruition. You will realise that there are lots of 'ifs and buts' and a considerable amount of luck required to pull off a successful event. Hopefully you will not need to activate your contingency plan and team members will do all that is expected of them and more. With the guidance of your tutors and teachers you should feel confident, positive and in control – failure should not be an option!

Your personal contribution

You will have to keep a diary or logbook of your own contribution in relation to the whole project. You may include copies of the Minutes from your team's meetings, highlighting your particular involvement.

ACTIVITY

A checklist of your contribution

In terms of monitoring your own contribution to the organisation and management of the project, you can record your contribution in a variety of forms. You must, however, make sure that these records are true and not in any way fabricated.

The list below should give you some ideas for collecting this evidence.

- Personal diary
- Logbook
- Video footage
- Computer software
- Audio Cassette
- Photographs, 35 mm or digital
- Personal correspondence

Are you doing enough?

Just how much and how far you support your event or project, will ultimately be down to you, but it will not just be you who suffers if you do not pull your weight, remember this is what teamwork is all about. No one will really be able to motivate you if your heart is not in it. It is very important that you immediately tell the rest of your team if you have any doubts about your ability to contribute fully and complete the roles that have been allocated to you.

DISCUSSION

Although it is the team effort that is being assessed, your tutor or teacher needs to know what your personal contribution is.

Why do you think this is important?

Your team will then have to consider two options. The first one is to reallocate your work load and find you another role that you feel better suited to and the second one is simply to ask you to leave the team. No one will want you in their team if you are not going to pull your weight.

If you are asked by your team to leave, then you must ask yourself the following questions:

- Is it just me, or are there other team members that are not fulfilling their roles?
- Why have I lost my enthusiasm for the project?
- Could I take on a different role within the team?
- Will any other team want me to join them if I leave my current team?

On a positive note, it may be better to quit if you can see that you are hindering, rather than helping your group to achieve its aims. This in itself could be seen as a constructive decision but should, in the first instance, be discussed fully with your teacher or tutor. In the words of Lao Tzu:

6 He who knows others is clever, he who knows himself is enlightened. 9

Maintaining records of team meetings and keeping minutes

It is important to minute meetings, in terms of charting progress, tracking input, workload and achievement. It is also a valuable document to refer back to in case any questions, arguments or points are raised. It is a historical document and must be kept in a safe place. Minute taking is not a difficult skill to learn and once you realise the value of keeping clear, accurate records of what your group has decided, then you will wonder how you could survive without them. It is a good idea to appoint one of your team to this administrative role.

The Minutes should be written in a note pad and then as soon as possible, word processed and distributed among the group with a copy being retained for historical purposes. Individual team members then know exactly what is expected of them, and each other. At the next meeting the Minutes can be read out and progress recorded for the following meeting and so on. Once you have decided on your team and your project, you should start thinking about dates and timings for your meetings. Once a week, or certainly every ten days, is a realistic timescale to meet, particularly if time is constrained and roles, responsibilities, workloads and deadlines need to be monitored.

In order to find out how to structure the agendas and minutes of meetings, refer back to page 344 of this Chapter and have a look at the records maintained by the Fun Run team.

Your weekly, minuted meetings must be structured and fit in with your long-term plan. The Minutes must clearly show individual's roles and commitments. They should clearly cross-reference with your personal logbook and you are strongly advised to highlight your involvement at all key stages.

Customer care

A good starting point is to know your customers. That is, to identify who your target group is.

You should by now:

- Have identified who your target group is.

If you are planning an event or project for a similar audience to yourself then ask yourself and other members of your team three simple questions:

● Would I genuinely be interested in supporting an event or project organised by my colleagues, classmates or buddies?
● What sort of event would it have to be for me to attend?
● How much would I be prepared to pay to attend?

ACTIVITY

Just an idea: the clothes show!

Which shops and designer clothes labels would you like to wear?

Make a list of your favourites and then discus how you might convince them to let you model their stock.

You may be surprised to know that most high street stores have a regular stock of clothes specifically for events like yours and quite often they will offer to help you put on a show. They will have access to lights, sound and music systems and lots of previous experience. They will expect you to be able to attract a sizeable audience and will also expect to be highlighted on your programme and linked to any charitable cause that you may be supporting.

You will have to make it quite clear to them what you intend to get out of the event, your involvement and your team's commitment.

DISCUSSION

Compare your answers with others within your tutor group. What do you notice? Are your tastes and interest different? If so how different? You might even decide that your peers will not be the best or easiest audience to cater for.

Ask your parents the same questions and you may well be pleasantly surprised. Experience has shown that fashion and music themes are often attractive and that by utilising these, you can attract quite an audience.

DISCUSSION

Are you happy in your role?

Belbin's Test may have identified you as a particular team player, but it is only based on a number of prescribed questions, and as such, can only come up with a recommendation.

You should discuss with your team whether you feel happy in your suggested role.

Much of what you learnt in Chapter 5 about customer service will be immensely useful. Try not to forget that 'the customer is *always* right'!

Supporting your work team

Being supportive and being able to ask for and accept support from others within the team is a crucial quality. Vision in these situations is key, and being able to see and acknowledge when you or another team member has, for example, taken on too much and require help is often an issue within teams. Some individuals do not know how to ask for help, some are too proud to ask for your help and support, others are simply too shy.

You need to be able to recognise when team members need help and support and then identify what you can do to help them. This is an area that may make the difference between you enjoying your event or project or simply wishing that it was all over and quickly forgotten. Your tutor or teacher is probably the best person to speak to if you get in this situation, although the sooner you admit to your failings, the easier it will be to put right. However, if you are part of a team then you should be able to accept democratic decision making and go along with the group's ideas, feelings and ultimately its decisions.

Trouble-shooting

Things **will** go wrong and someone will have to make decisions. If time permits, then the whole team can be consulted, but should this not be possible then you may have to make a decision on behalf of your team. You will have to be able to justify your decision, and if necessary, argue your case or point. If this really worries you then you need to think about your involvement and commitment to your team's overall objectives.

An example of this would be knowing when, and how, to activate your contingency plan. Just how much rain has to fall before you decide that the school's football tournament becomes an indoor five-a-side event? Will the rest of your team find your decision acceptable?

Who will decide, and when, to implement your contingency plan? If you have chosen a leader will you all support his or her decision unquestionably or should you nominate a troubleshooter whose role it could be to be prepared for 'anything'?

ACTIVITY

Contingency plans

Earlier in the Unit we referred to the contingency plan. You should have considered yours.

Ask yourself, and team, a number of questions:

- Is your contingency plan in place?
- Is it acknowledged?
- Will it work?
- Can it be implemented given the timescale you are working to?

If these questions cannot be answered then you and your team have some work to do in order to put a contingency plan in place.

Many people like the idea of a troubleshooting role and see it as quite a glamorous one; that is until they actually have to make a big decision! If you decide to take on this role then can you guarantee the support of the rest of your team? Aggressive individuals often feel that they are well suited to these kinds of roles but then discover that their popularity isn't strong enough for them to be able to rely on the support of others!

ACTIVITY

Troubleshooting

List famous people who have been cast in this type of role. Think about the worlds of politics and entertainment, for example, Bruce Willis in *Die Hard*.

Make suggestions and nominations from your group and identify who would take on this role if required.

Do you think that the troubleshooter should also be the team leader?

370 ADVANCED LEISURE AND RECREATION

Try to anticipate how you would individually, and as a group, react to and support each other in a crisis situation? Would you stand and support, or simply run and hide? You may not like some of your findings but by talking about them you will be better prepared for any crisis that may occur.

Are those deadlines being achieved? If not, why not?

Whose responsibility is it to ensure that deadlines are kept? How will your team deal with missed deadlines?

Have you built in a time cushion to allow for time delays?

Deadlines and time management

In the words of Ted Blake:

❛If you can't manage your own time, then you certainly can't manage anybody else's.❜

You will more than likely have had much discussion on this subject. There is a brilliant word that you should try to remember as it sums up all that we mean when we discuss time management. It is *procrastination*, and it means putting off till later what you can do now. Your parents, teachers or tutors often use the word tomorrow, but why wait until then if you can do it now. 'Fail to prepare, prepare to fail!'

You should by now:

● Have identified deadlines by which various planning stages and tasks should be completed. These deadline dates can be reflected on your list of things to do.

Points to remember

The following points are offered to you as words of wisdom, motivational tools and generally, good, sound advice, which you should consider applying during the planning, organisation and management of your project or event.

You may have come across many of the following points in other units of your Vocational A Level. You may also have experience of them from a part-time job, or even have heard them uttered during situations in your family home:

● Plan very carefully and thoroughly.
● Hold regular team meetings and keep a record, (or minutes) of all that is said.
● Identify individual team roles and record individuals' progress.
● Prioritise your work so that you will not hold up other team members' progress.
● Do not be afraid to ask for, or indeed offer, help to other team members.
● Do stay committed at all times to your team and the project's goals.
● Do not procrastinate.

FIGURE 6.2   *The end of a successful family fun run*

CASE STUDY *Charity Fun Run*

Throughout this Unit reference has been made to a real event that was organised by a group of Advanced Vocational A Level students. Money was raised for a local charity and local newspapers ran stories and photographs on the event. The event involved sponsorship and catering, in fact it was the students who ran the barbecue after the event. Many families took part and were keen to support their local college, parents were keen to support their children and friends were keen to participate. The most asked question was: 'Will you be doing another one next year?' You bet! Consumer led events are always the best.

Evaluating the project

You should have your evaluation methods in place before the event itself in order to allow you to answer the question: Have you met the targets and original objectives that you defined at the beginning of the planning stage?

ACTIVITY

Evaluate your team's event or project and your own performance.

As part of the requirements of this Unit you are required to evaluate the relative success of the project and your own input.

What you have done already:

You have established your team, organised your event or project, and staged it. You now need to evaluate the relative success of the event and the work that went in to planning and organising it.

So, how successful was your event? Would you do it differently next time?

You must produce an individual assignment which an external verifier or inspector can pick up and see just what your event was, how it all went, and how you evaluated your performance.

You are to collect all of the evidence that you and your event or project have generated and present it in a suitable way.

Your report should cover the following areas/tasks:

1 Show that you have followed your earlier business plan
2 Show how you tackled the health, safety and security of your event
3 Report in detail on any disruptions during the event. How did you deal with them?
4 Gather evaluation feedback from appropriate sources through a simple questionnaire.
5 Report on these results in graph form.
6 Identify key factors which affected individual, team and event performance, and explain why.
7 Present an overall evaluation, taking into consideration all team comments. Make suggestions and improvements for future events.

You should attempt to include some photographic evidence in this final task.

Factors affecting performance

There are a number of aspects of your planning, organisation and the event itself that you should consider in the evaluation of your event and these are discussed next.

Did your team meet their objectives?
A good starting point would be to look at the objectives you stated earlier on in the Unit and see whether or not you met them all? Many teams do not achieve all their stated objectives but end up covering all sorts of other, often unexpected, issues.

An example of this would be an unexpected problem that was dealt with quickly and smoothly, like a car parking field becoming boggy and cars having to be pushed out of the field. Consequently the last thing your customers will remember is your smiling faces in their rear view mirrors as you help them out of a potentially sticky position. Some may even make a donation to your cause and even write letters of thanks! Some customers may have been looking for a car wash service, would you have been entrepreneurial enough to have thought of this?

ACTIVITY

Aims and objectives checklist

Referring back to your earlier stated aims and objectives, produce a checklist and honestly assess your team's performance. Do not be afraid to make critical constructive comments for future projects.

You might like to consider asking a member of another team to chair this meeting, as it could get personal. Do offer to do the same in return.

You can check your aims and objectives and their effectiveness, by using *performance indicators (PIs)*. These are often used in reviewing and 'rounding the quality circle', and is a way of checking what you have achieved. Examples of performance indicators are given below:

QUANTITATIVE   – numbers of participants
– ratio of staff to customers
– actual tickets sold in relation to total possible
– level of participation

QUALITATIVE   – subjective comments from clients and external staff involved
– comments can be formal (questionnaire) or informal quoting clients, photos, video, etc.

EFFECTIVENESS   – how well were all targets met?
– financial accounting compared with original estimates, did you overspend?

EFFICIENCY   – best use of resources (human, physical, financial)
– budgets

ACTIVITY

Specific performance indicators

One of the most effective methods of event evaluation is through the use of performance indicators.

You are required, using the information above, to design your own event specific performance indicators. That is, decide what aspects of the planning and organisation you wish to assess. Decide what aspects of the outcome of the project you wish to assess and reflect these in a range of PIs.

PIs can be used to give you both statistical and subjective data to use as a basis for your evaluation and comparison. They also provide you with hard evidence when considering what you would have done differently and how.

Reviewing

You should consider distributing an evaluation feedback questionnaire to your customers and perhaps one to your team members. Below is an example of the questionnaire the Fun Run team designed to help them with their evaluation.

FEEDBACK QUESTIONNAIRE–EXAMPLE

DUCHY COLLEGE FUN RUN

To enable us to improve on our efforts and performance for future events we would appreciate it if you could spare five minutes to answer the following questions:

1 How did you find out about the Fun Run?
Answer

2 How far did you have to travel to take part in the Fun Run?
Answer

3 Do you agree with sponsorship raising and profits of the event going to a local charity?
Answer

4 Did you enjoy the actual run? It was in fact only 3.5 kms! Any highlights?
Answer

5 Were you and your children pleased with their competitors' medals?
Answer

6 Did you feel that the food and drink, barbecue, etc. was a good idea?
Answer

7 Can you suggest any improvements we could make for next year?
Answer

THANK YOU for supporting our event, without **you** it would never have been possible.

Please place the completed questionnaires in the box by the barbecue table. If you want details of next year's Fun Run, please write your name and address below.

Name

Address

THANKS AGAIN AND SAFE JOURNEY HOME.

What other forms of evaluation could you use to help you with your reviewing process?

You should by now:

- Have considered and designed the method by which you will evaluate your event.

As you get more confident with your planning you will realise that reviewing is the strongest way to improve. 'Looking back is the only way to move forward'. This is known as the 'do and review cycle', or the 'improvement cycle'. These cycles relate both to the work and commitment you have put into the project and the work and effort committed by your team.

Your personal review

We are all individuals and while some of your group may gauge success in one way, others may see or feel it in a different way. Personal Indicators of a successful project or event may include the following:

- Your photo appears in your local newspaper.
- Your team's photo appears in your local newspaper.
- You raise a large amount of money for charity.
- You earn respect from your peers.
- You earn respect from your teachers and tutors.
- Your parents are proud of you.
- Comments from your feedback questionnaires are all very positive.
- You are asked immediately to organise another successful event.
- You achieve the grade you were aiming for in your assignment.

Some of these criteria are more important than others and some are just about the 'feel good factor'. After all, we all like the feeling of success.

Your team's review

There are some questions that may help you in reviewing your event or project. Don't be afraid to be critical, but ensure that your comments are constructive. If you identify a problem or constraint then you should discuss this with your group and make recommendations for the future. Key indicators of a successful team project or event:

- Did we meet our objectives?
- Did we meet our key deadlines?
- Was the project successful?
- Did the team really work well together?
- Did we achieve our objectives within our budget?
- Did you work well as an individual and did being part of a team hinder you at all?
- Have you made new friends as a result of working as a team?

You should by now:

- Have considered and designed both the personal and team indicators to allow you to evaluate the contributions made by team members and complete the 'do and review' cycle.

Giving and taking criticism

A word of warning here, it is very tempting to skip much of the reviewing, especially if some things didn't go according to plan; if things did go wrong who, exactly, was to blame? Some members of your group may find it hard to take criticism in any form and you should be prepared to talk about this at length. An interesting angle is that for every negative comment you make, try to make a positive one as well. You may also consider turning identified problems into solutions. For example, if you are asked to help look after a crèche of young children why not organise games and activities and make their afternoon more than just a babysitting exercise. You may be surprised at how much you enjoy yourself and may well find yourself being complimented by parents.

Saying 'thanks'

You will, almost certainly, have had much help along the way from a variety of sources. These may include a variety of sponsors, parents, media contacts, friends, teachers and tutors.

DO

REVIEW

FIGURE 6.3 *The 'do and review' cycle. You should never stop doing this.*

 ACTIVITY

Saying 'thanks, and how about next time?'

In your team decide who should go on your thank you list. If in doubt add them! Try to send them a copy of a newspaper report which includes a photograph. If they are a sponsor try to get a photo which shows their company name.

At the end of a project you have an excellent opportunity to reflect and learn from your successes and failures. Whether you intend being involved in a similar project again, or not, it is always useful to make recommendations for the future. These findings must be included in your final report and may help future events to succeed where maybe you failed.

Do you feel good about what you have been involved in over the last few months? Do you feel proud of what you have achieved? If so, then you will probably be already planning your next event or project. 'Good luck' and who knows, you may even choose to follow a career in event management.

 ACTIVITY

The 'feel good factor'

We have mentioned this phenomenon earlier in the Unit but it really comes into its own as part of the final reviewing process. Make up a display board in the entrance foyer of your school or college

DISCUSSION

'LOST OPPORTUNITIES'

'Looking back with hindsight' provides you with a golden opportunity to make you realise how you would do things differently next time.

Make a list of the opportunities that you can identify that you feel you should have capitalised on. For example, if you ordered 150 cans of soft drinks at 20p each, and sold them at 30p, and they all sold out within the first half an hour of your event, ask yourself two questions. Firstly, could you have charged 40p and secondly, could you have sold 300 cans?

Work out just how much extra profit you would have made in this hypothetical, but very familiar type of scenario.

Be honest and think about organising your next event or project, as any observations made now will definitely help in the future!

showing a good variety of photos obtained from various sources. The best ones should be from your local newspaper, but do try to include unusual and candid shots taken by parents, friends, teachers and tutors.

ASSESSMENT EVIDENCE

In order to complete the Leisure and Recreation In Action Unit you are required to work as part of a team to plan, carry out and evaluate a real project of your choice. As part of the Unit you are required to produce a range of assessment evidence. The Unit specifications state that you need to produce the following:

- A business plan for a leisure and recreation project. The plan should be developed as a group but presented individually

It should include:

- Objectives and timescales for the project
- Description of the project
- Resource needs (human, financial and physical)
- Legal aspects of the project (health, safety and security)
- Methods to be used to evaluate the project

You will also need to show evidence of your own personal involvement in the team project. This should include:

- A record of your involvement in carrying out the team project
- Details of the task(s) you were allocated
- Details of any problems that may have arisen and how you reacted
- Details of any time deadlines you were given and whether you kept to them

Not only are you required to plan, organise and run a project, you will also have to evaluate the relative success of the project in terms of the planning stages and outcome. You will have to produce:

- An evaluation of your role in the project and the effectiveness of the team in achieving the project objectives

Key Skills

In completing the assessment for this unit, you can achieve the following key skills. These will be accredited at the discretion of your tutor on the basis of the quality of the work you submit.

COMMUNICATION, LEVEL 3
C3.1a Contribute to a group discussion about a complex subject.
C 3.1b Make a presentation about a complex subject, using at least one image to illustrate complex points.
C3.3 Write two different documents about complex subjects. One piece of writing should be an extended document and include at least one image.

Index